The Struggles of
John Brown Russwurm

JOHN B. RUSSWURM.

John Brown Russwurm, c. 1848. Courtesy of
Schomburg Center for Research in Black Culture,
New York Public Library, Astor, Lenox, and Tilden
Foundation.

The Struggles of
John Brown Russwurm

The Life and Writings of a
Pan-Africanist Pioneer, 1799–1851

Winston James

NEW YORK UNIVERSITY PRESS
New York and London

NEW YORK UNIVERSITY PRESS
New York and London
www.nyupress.org

Library of Congress Cataloging-in-Publication Data

James, Winston.
The struggles of John Brown Russwurm : the life and writings of
a pan-Africanist pioneer, 1799–1851 / Winston James.
p. cm.
Includes bibliographical references and index.
ISBN-13: 978-0-8147-4289-1 (cl : alk. paper)
ISBN-10: 0-8147-4289-0 (cl : alk. paper)
ISBN-13: 978-0-8147-4290-7 (pb : alk. paper)
ISBN-10: 0-8147-4290-4 (pb : alk. paper)
[etc.]
1. Russwurm, John Brown, 1799–1851. 2. African American intellectuals—
Biography. 3. Pan-Africanism—History—19th century. 4. African Americans—
Colonization—Liberia—History—19th century. 5. Liberia—History—To 1847.
6. Pan-Africanism—History—19th century—Sources. 7. African Americans—
Colonization—Liberia—History—19th century—Sources. 8. Liberia—History—
To 1847—Sources. I. Russwurm, John Brown, 1799–1851. II. Title.
E448.R96J36   2010
966.62'02092—dc22
[B]   2010011993

New York University Press books are printed on acid-free paper,
and their binding materials are chosen for strength and durability.
We strive to use environmentally responsible suppliers and materials
to the greatest extent possible in publishing our books.

Manufactured in the United States of America
c   10 9 8 7 6 5 4 3 2 1
p   10 9 8 7 6 5 4 3 2 1

IN MEMORIAM

Lindon Barrett (1961–2008)

Walk good.

We are considered a distinct people, in the midst of the millions around us, and in the most favoured parts of the country; and it matters not from what causes this sentence has been passed upon us; the fiat has gone forth, and should each of us live to the age of Methusalah, at the end of the thousand years, we should be exactly in our present situation: a proscribed race, however, unjustly—a degraded people, deprived of all the rights of freemen; and in the eyes of the community, a race, who had no lot nor portion with them.

We hope none of our readers, will from our remarks think that we approve in the least of the present prejudices in the way of the man of colour: far from it, we deplore them as much as any man; but they are not of our creating, and they are not in our power to remove. They at present exist against us—and from the length of their existence—from the degraded light in which we have ever been held—we are bold in saying, that it will never be in our power to remove or overcome them. So easily are these prejudices imbibed, that we have often noticed the effects on young children who could hardly speak plainly, and were we a believer in dreams, charms, &c we should believe that they imbibed them with their mother's milk.

Sensible then, as all are of the disadvantages under which we at present labour, can any consider it a mark of folly, for us to cast our eyes upon some other portion of the globe where *all* these inconveniencies are removed where the Man of Colour freed from the fetters and prejudice, and degradation, under which he labours in this land, may walk forth in all the majesty of his creation—a new born creature—a *Free Man*!

John Brown Russwurm (March 1829)

If I know my own heart, I can truly say, that I have not a selfish wish in placing myself under the patronage of the [American Colonization] Society; usefulness in my day & generation, is what I principally court.

John Brown Russwurm (February 1829)

You will not be surprised, that sometimes when difficulties & dangers surround us, we despond a little; and think, that do our best, all our efforts will be in vain. But these are only temporary; as every day's experience gives us a better knowledge of our duty, & the practicability of establishing colonies on this coast, which in process of time, may realize all the fondest anticipations of their patrons. But such is not the labor of one or five years; time must pass—difficulties are to be met and overcome; the present generation, & perhaps the next, must pass away, before we can with justice look for prosperity to crown our efforts, or the blessing of posterity our labor.

John Brown Russwurm (June 1837)

Men make their own history, but not of their own free will; not under circumstances they themselves have chosen but under the given and inherited circumstances with which they are directly confronted.

Karl Marx (1852)

Contents

Preface and Acknowledgments

I cannot now recall the first time I became aware of John Brown Russwurm. What I do vividly remember is the dearth of material there was on him as I tried to briefly map the Caribbean presence in the United States before the twentieth century in *Holding Aloft the Banner of Ethiopia: Caribbean Radicalism in Early Twentieth-Century America.*[1] In 2000, two years after the publication of that book, I gave a paper on the nature and pattern of Caribbean involvement in pan-Africanist efforts in Africa, tracing the story from Russwurm to George Padmore. In the course of doing that paper, I came to appreciate more fully the enormously important and pioneering role that Russwurm had played in the black struggle in the United States and in the infant black colony of Liberia. Despite his pioneering role, Russwurm was, relative to two other nineteenth-century figures I profiled in that paper, Edward Wilmot Blyden (1832-1912) and Robert Campbell (1829-84), the least known and, probably because of that, the most poorly understood and appreciated. Indeed, I discovered that not only was there ignorance of Russwurm and his work, but also unwarranted hostility toward him in much of the historiography that bothers to mention him.

The rationale behind the writing of this book are more fully elaborated in the Prologue, but it should be said here that with *The Struggles of John Brown Russwurm* I hope to help dispel the ignorance of Russwurm and provide the basis for a better appreciation of his exertions and contributions to the black struggle both in the United States and Africa. Through looking at Russwurm's life, the book also aspires to bring into sharp relief the constricted lives of African Americans and what that constriction meant and felt like to an extraordinarily sensitive, proud, ambitious, educated and articulate black man. Because of the richness of his archive—his letters, wide-ranging journalism and almost continuous commentary on his times—Russwurm emerges as a unique figure through which the blighted nature of black life in the "free" North may be gauged in the Early Republic in a direct and even visceral manner. Moreover, Russwurm was the first African American to publicly struggle with and resolve, in his own way, the perennial dilemma of whether to stay and fight in the United States or to leave in search of a fuller and more dignified life elsewhere. He chose Liberia, which would present new challenges. His heroic exertions there are also examined and appraised here. Such exertions compromised his health and probably shortened his life. Russwurm died in Liberia before his fifty-second birthday in 1851.

I am indebted to the following archives and their staff: the George J. Mitchell Department of Special Collections and Archives, Bowdoin College, and especially its director, Richard Lindemann, who has been extraordinarily helpful from the very earliest stages of my research on the this project right to the very end; the Maine Historical Society, especially Jamie Kingman Rice; the Maryland Historical Society, especially Christopher Becker; the Tennessee State Library and Archives; the William L. Clements Library, University of Michigan, especially Janet Bloom; the Library of Congress; the Beinecke Rare Book and Manuscript Library, Yale University; the Special Collections Research Center, Syracuse University; Columbia University libraries, especially the Inter-library Loan Office; the Wisconsin Historical Society; the New York Historical Society; and the Schomburg Center for Research in Black Culture, New York Public Library.

This project first took shape while I was the recipient of the Josephus Daniels Fellowship, supported by the National Endowment for the Humanities and the Ford Foundation, at the National Humanities Center. I am therefore very grateful for this support and shall always treasure the memory of my time at the NHC. Without the research support from the Department of History, University of California, Irvine, I would not have been able to complete the book at this point in time.

I am also grateful to Richard Blackett, Dickson D. Bruce, James Brewer, Robert Hill, Richard Newman and Ekwueme Michael Thelwell who read an early version of the manuscript and provided helpful comments and encouragement. New York University Press expressed an early interest in this project and patiently awaited its completion. I thank Deborah Gershenowitz, Gabrielle Begue and Despina Papazoglou Gimbel for steering it through to publication. Deirdre Mullane, my literary agent, also has my thanks for her work on this project.

Claudette and Sado have endured the trying final stages of this project with patience, understanding and good humor for which I am deeply grateful. My mother is no longer with me but I am sustained by her sacrifice and everlasting love. My father, thankfully, remains and remains a source of inspiration and support.

The book is dedicated to the memory of my dear friend Lindon Barrett, a brilliant scholar, a dedicated teacher, a courageous fighter and lover of life and sunshine, who was suddenly taken away from us in the prime of life. He was one of the most remarkable and wonderful human beings I've ever known.

A Note on Quotations

Quotations, unless otherwise indicated, are reproduced as they appeared in the original sources, retaining the idiosyncrasies of spelling and punctuation peculiar to their authors and the conventions of their time.

John Brown Russwurm

Prologue

The Man Out of Place

He is almost completely missing from the annals of the Pan-African movement. The two leading studies of the movement do not even mention him, let alone register or analyze his contribution.[1] A third mentions him only briefly and in passing, devoting four sentences to the pioneer in a book almost three hundred pages long.[2] The great George Padmore, in his Olympian, if polemical, historical overview of the Pan-African movement, correctly registers his name among the New World pioneers of Liberia but has him leading twenty-one African American emigrants to the settlement almost a decade before he actually left the United States—alone.[3] And despite his Jamaican roots and Caribbean allegiance, he is unknown and so unremembered in his native island and the rest of the archipelago. His name is absent from Jamaican and Caribbean history books, and he has no pedestal in the remarkable pantheon—from Blyden to Padmore to Fanon to Rodney—of Caribbean Pan-African intellectuals and activists. It is true that he left the Caribbean at an early age, but so did Blyden, and unlike Blyden he returned to the Caribbean as a young man, in the vain hope of resettling there.[4] Moreover, early in his youth he became fascinated with Haiti and the Haitian Revolution, wrote and spoke about them, and seriously considered and even planned to settle in the "Black Republic" after graduating from college. His interest in Haiti abided with him, even after his emigration to Liberia, to the very end of his days. He is better known in the United States, but not by much; there his image is distorted in much of the historical scholarship, and his true achievements are inadequately recognized and appreciated.

John Brown Russwurm, as I shall demonstrate and argue, deserves better. His pioneering efforts, achievements, and example—as educator, abolitionist, editor, government official, staunch emigrationist, and colonizationist—put him in the vanguard of the Pan-African movement. Moreover, Russwurm's own internal struggle with the perennial Pan-Africanist dilemma of whether to go to Africa or stay and fight in the United States was the first of its kind carried out and resolved in the public domain. That struggle was robust and energetic, and its path to resolution and the resolution itself tell much of the times in which he lived and the limited options available to himself and those of the African diaspora who yearned for a full and dignified life as human beings, unencumbered by the horrors of slavery, racism, and white supremacy.

What follows is a brief overview of the life and struggles of John Brown Russwurm, ending with an assessment and determination of his proper place within the Pan-Africanist tradition. This biographical portrait, an entry into the historical record, is especially necessary because Russwurm has had no scholarly biography.[5] It is accompanied by a selection of Russwurm's own writings that not only lay bare the trajectory of his political thinking and contribution but also provide an important perspective on the challenges and struggles of his time. The selection begins with his writings on Haiti while he was still a student at Bowdoin College and follows his output through his editorship of *Freedom's Journal*, ending with his work in Liberia on the *Liberia Herald* and additional material from his governorship of Maryland in Liberia. Though enormously rich and varied as well as impassioned and powerfully analytical, Russwurm's writings have never been previously anthologized. But the combined neglect and ignorance of his writings do not reflect their intrinsic and historical value. Russwurm's writings in fact provide a unique entrée into the thinking of one of Afro-America's first organic and most gifted intellectuals as he struggled with the problems of black life from the early national to the antebellum period and searched for their resolution. Russwurm was also one of the most remarkable and valuable witnesses of the age. He occupied a unique and unparalleled point of view on the American republic, the African diaspora, and the wider drama of the times. In the age of black slavery, Russwurm was not only freeborn but also among the first African Americans to receive a university education; he had lived in the Caribbean and Canada before moving to the United States; he was an unblinking observer of and commentator on the condition of African Americans as well as a courageous fighter against white supremacy and for black emancipation and uplift. In short, Russwurm's was a distinct and articulate voice, one especially worthy of our attention and respect.

John Brown Russwurm, then, has two broad objectives: to provide a biographical portrait of the man, including a critical assessment of his contribution, and to give readers an opportunity to more readily and directly peruse and engage with Russwurm's own writings, in their richness, complexity, passion, and pathos, as well as their insights and blindnesses, strengths and weaknesses.

From Boy to Man

Born in Port Antonio, capital of the eastern Jamaican parish of Portland, on October 1, 1799, John Brown Russwurm was the son of a black mother and a white American merchant on the island, John R. Russwurm. Virtually nothing is known of the mother, not even her name. Russwurm himself was surprisingly silent on the subject. A number of nineteenth-century sources referred to her as a "Creole" woman, which is hardly helpful. An 1848 report in the *Portland Transcript* (Maine) informed its readers that Russwurm's father had, as was "very common" in the West Indies, "married a colored lady, from a very respectable family, by whom he had his son John."[1] She has been variously ascribed the status of slave, free woman of color, and "housekeeper," a combination of concubine and domestic servant or domestic slave.[2] She is said to have been a "Negro," and recently one scholar has described her as a "mulatto" and Russwurm as an "octoroon," but without evidence to support either claim.[3] The brutal truth is that we know virtually nothing about her, so she is an enigma and is likely to remain unknowable. Given the Jamaican planter and merchant class's preference at the time for light-skinned black women, Russwurm's mother might well have been a "mulatto," but the evidence is elusive and probably nonexistent. Perhaps, as some have speculated, she died in childbirth or soon after the boy was born;[4] this would help to explain Russwurm's silence, since he would not have known her or would have known her only slightly. Were Russwurm the typical, so-called "Jamaican mulatto" of the early nineteenth century, one would be inclined to attribute the silence to a deliberate suppression of African antecedents stemming from the impulse that Edward Long, the eighteenth-century planter-historian, memorably dubbed the "pride of amended blood."[5] But Russwurm was by no means typical of his Jamaican caste or class, nor was he ashamed of his dark skin. On the contrary, he was proud of his blackness and his African ancestral homeland.

As was generally the case with such white-nonwhite unions in the British Caribbean at the time, much more is known about Russwurm's white father.

The senior Russwurm, the son of a German immigrant, was born in 1761 into an upper-class Virginia family and went to England as a youth to complete his education. After some considerable time in Britain, he returned to the United States but soon moved to Jamaica to seek his fortune. When he arrived on the island is uncertain, but he probably did so in his early thirties. Operating as a merchant rather than as a slave plantation owner, he apparently loved his black mistress and treated her as a wife; it was later claimed that Russwurm was officially married to her, but this is improbable, given the mores—if not the laws—of the time.[6] He became a justice of the peace and an assistant judge in Portland. By all accounts, he also loved his son, his firstborn, and was keen to protect the boy from the ravages of racism.[7] In 1807 he sent the eight-year-old to boarding school abroad. But unlike the majority of his class in the British Caribbean, he sent his son not to Britain but to Montreal to be educated. The reasoning behind the choice of Canada, let alone Montreal, remains a mystery, though Russwurm Senior's settling in Maine, near the Canadian border and relatively close to Montreal, suggests that he wanted to be closer to his son than sending the boy to England would have allowed. It is also possible that he planned to move to Maine before sending Russwurm to Montreal. Russwurm's later writings on the Caribbean suggest that he probably returned regularly to Jamaica during school holidays, as was the pattern for upper-class boys who studied abroad. Five years after sending his son to Montreal, Russwurm Senior left Portland, Jamaica, to settle in Portland, Maine, then a province of the Commonwealth of Massachusetts. Why or how he chose Maine as his new residence is also open to speculation. The family claimed that he went to Maine "for his health," which of course is not an explanation at all.[8] Why not Boston? What was wrong with Rhode Island? At best, it might help us to understand why he left Jamaica, not why he went to Maine. As already indicated, Maine might very well have appealed to him because of its relative proximity to his son's school across the border in Quebec. However, it is noteworthy that he did not return to the South, where his influential and wealthy slave-owning relatives lived, but chose instead to take up residence in a state that had outlawed slavery.[9]

Some accounts claimed that he arrived in the United States with his son, but the most reliable suggests he did not. Young John was, however, rather fortunate that after his father married an American widow, Susan Blanchard, a woman in her twenties, who already had three children, he was accepted as a full member of the new family. The senior Russwurm, who was more than twice his wife's age, must have been fearful of Susan Blanchard's reaction at discovering he had a "black" son.[10] According to Susan Blanchard Russwurm's own account, her husband spoke fondly and with great interest of the boy John in Quebec but revealed the true relationship only after he became fatally ill. He need not have worried. A remarkable woman, Mrs. Russwurm was not only educated and enlightened but also extraordinarily generous. "She decided, at once," reported the *Maryland Colonization Journal* in its tribute to Russwurm, "to adopt the boy into her family, and he was immediately sent for."[11] She also insisted that the boy be given his father's name, thus becoming John Brown Russwurm rather than John Brown, as he had previously been known. Susan Russwurm was apparently the only mother John ever had, and most certainly the only one he had after the age of eight, when he left for school in Quebec.[12] Their mutual regard, affection, and love would continue up to Russwurm's untimely death in 1851.

By all accounts John Russwurm was happy to have been reunited with his son and only child. He was unashamed and, given the tenor of the times, remarkably open in his association with and pride in the boy. Instead of disowning little John—described as "a mulatto of fine personal appearance and manners"—or hiding him away from the society of his friends, John Russwurm, as one of Maine's local historians of the nineteenth century noted, "did not conceal the relationship" between himself and the boy. On the contrary: "He was proud of his son. He introduced him into the best society in Portland, where he was honored and respected. He attended the best schools and had all the privileges that other boys of the best families enjoyed."[13]

But these sunny days, though not as bright as the local historian would have us believe, did not last for long. On April 3, 1815, a few months after John joined the family, his father died.[14] John was left entirely in Mrs. Russwurm's care with a small legacy, which was largely used up in settling the estate.[15] His wealthy relatives, the Russwurm clan in the South, provided no support to John and seldom bothered to even answer his letters of entreaty. In an angry letter to his older cousin John Sumner Russwurm, John complained of the lack of reply to his earlier correspondence. "After having waited a considerable time," Russwurm wrote in July 1819, "I concluded to address you once more, and that for the last, if you saw fit not to answer it. Concerning myself[,] nothing more shall ever escape me concerning my situation in life." He apparently heard nothing from his cousin for almost seven years. And when John Sumner Russwurm condescended to write, he was evidently interested in finding out about the legacy his uncle (John Brown's father) had left him (some two thousand dollars), being held on to by a tricky Maine lawyer. In the end, Sumner Russwurm got his cut, but at the expense of others, much to the displeasure and disappointment of his uncle's widow, who essentially regarded him as a crook. "I think if I cannot depend upon your Honour and friendship," she wrote him, "there is nothing in this world I can depend upon." There is no evidence that he ever made her whole.[16] The burden thus fell exclusively upon Mrs. Russwurm, who continued to treat the young Jamaican as her own son. Some years later, James Blanchard, a son from her first marriage, noted that Mrs. Russwurm "has done all she could have expected had he been her own son. I sometimes joke Mother," he revealed, "about her black son[,] the Gov[ernor,] and tell her that I am jealous—that she thinks more of him than she does of either of her white sons."[17] But Susan Blanchard Russwurm had far more love and decency than she did money. True, she had inherited money, the house, and the seventy-five-acre farm at Back Cove (Westbrook), which John Russwurm had bought in 1812 soon after his arrival in Maine and where she had lived after their marriage.[18] But in addition to her three children from her first marriage, she had the responsibility of caring for John and his infant half-brother, Francis Edward, who had been born only a year before Russwurm Senior died.[19]

But John encountered more difficulties than just financial ones during this period in Maine. According to Mrs. Russwurm, he lived with the family for the next two years after his father's death but attended school for only half of the time. "It was rather difficult at that time," she explained, "to get a colored boy into a good school where he would receive an equal share of attention with white boys, and this I was very particular should be the case."[20] The death of his father combined with the racism encountered in Maine more than likely pushed John to decide on returning to and trying his chances in Jamaica.

John had lived the first fifteen years of his life outside the United States and in the relatively privileged and tolerant (for one of his class and color) environments of Jamaica and Montreal.[21] It must have been difficult for him to adjust, especially given the sudden relatively diminished family circumstances after his father's death. He had never forgotten his Jamaican connections and now insisted upon returning to the island.[22] Mrs. Russwurm thought it inadvisable, but he "seemed so desirous" of going back to the island, which he regarded as "his home," that she "very reluctantly" consented. "I shall never forget," Mrs. Russwurm wrote, "the day I carried him to Portland and parted company with him—the sorrow he expressed at parting with my children, particularly his infant brother, showed how strongly he was attached to us all. I offered to bring him back, and try and get some good man for his guardian. He said 'no; that will not better my color. If I was a white boy, I would never leave your family, but I think it is best for me to go.'"[23] Russwurm was thus aware of not only the financial burden that his presence added to the straitened Blanchard-Russwurm household but also the extra load that the disability of his color imposed upon those close to him as well as himself. For contrary to popular lore, New England was by no means free of racism. Thus, in the spring of 1817 and before his eighteenth birthday, Russwurm sought to get away, back to Jamaica, not only to help himself but also to help those who had loved him and whom, in return, he loved and cared for.

Back in Jamaica, Russwurm, without resources of his own, met with disappointment. He became increasingly unhappy and dissatisfied, especially since he was unable to find any of his father's friends alive. He had reckoned on receiving their assistance.[24] One obituarist claimed that Russwurm's dissatisfaction in Jamaica stemmed from the fact that the "habits and tastes acquired by education in the United States, rendered Jamaica no longer a pleasant place of abode."[25] But this is simply asserted without evidence or corroboration. And Russwurm's early interest in emigrating to Haiti, and his subsequent decision to settle in Liberia, hardly support this argument. He wrote his stepmother a sorrowful letter telling of his Jamaican woes. She answered immediately, advising him to return to Maine at the first opportunity. But he was on his way back to the United States before it could be delivered to him. Arriving in Portland, Russwurm received news that his stepmother had remarried.[26] Not wanting to impose on the family and uncertain as to how he would be received, he remained in town rather than return to the farm where he had lived with the Blanchard-Russwurm family. But his stepmother, now Mrs. Hawes, got word of Russwurm's presence in town and his looking "cast down." What Russwurm could not have known was that Susan had not forgotten her "adopted son," as she described him, one whom she had "so much reason to love." She continued to look out for him: "Part of my marriage contract," she revealed, "was, that John should have a home when he needed one." On hearing the news of John's desperate plight, she sent a man "with strict orders not to return without John." She soon thereafter found Russwurm a guardian, Calvin Stockbridge, a small merchant and member of a prominent New England family, with American roots stretching back to 1635. Stockbridge, a remarkably decent man, described as a "mainstay of the Baptist cause in North Yarmouth," and an overlooked hero in the story of Russwurm, took in the young man and furnished the funds for another year of education.[27] As we shall see, from that moment right up to his death in 1834, Calvin Stockbridge served as a wonderful father to John. Russwurm noted that Stockbridge was his most constant and most reliable correspondent in Maine during his time in Africa. In a rather scolding letter to his younger brother, Francis, Russwurm expressed sorrow at the news of Stockbridge's death and of the manner in which he had learned of it. "Mr. Adam Wilson had the kindness to find me a paper containing a few lines on the subject. It is so long since I have heard from North Yarmouth that I know not but half the town may be dead," he lamented. "My last is from Mr. C. Stockbridge the most regular correspondent and the one who seemed to take the deepest interest in my welfare, in this distant land."[28]

With Stockbridge's financial assistance, Russwurm attended Hebron Academy, an elite New England school that was founded in 1804 and opened its doors to students the following year. Located in Hebron, Maine, approximately thirty miles north of Russwurm's home in North Yarmouth, Hebron Academy was the humble creation of the local Baptists in Hebron and surrounding towns, endeavoring to cater to the educational needs of a growing population. It began with sixty to seventy students, boys as well as girls, and two teachers and was housed in a modest wooden structure. Its religious and ideological ambitions were less humble. As its rules reveal, Hebron was a doctrinaire Christian institution as much as a broadly educational one. Morning and evening prayers were mandatory. The Holy Bible and the *Beauties of the Bible* were its main texts, though the *Columbian Orator*, arithmetic, geography, and English grammar had their place. Such Greek and Latin authors as students were usually examined in to obtain admission to universities were given their place in the curriculum. But rule 12 made Hebron's key educational mission even more explicit: "It shall be the particular duty of the preceptor to endeavor to impress upon the minds of his pupils a sense of the being and attributes of God, and of his superintending an all-wise Providence, and of their constant dependence upon and obligation to Him, and their duty at all times to love, serve and obey Him, and to pray to Him. And to inculcate the doctrine of the Christian religion regularly and at stated times at least once a week."[29]

Russwurm apparently spent less than a year at Hebron, but that was long enough for him to hate the place, even though he made good friends there and was a valued member of one of its fraternities. If he had experienced racism there, Russwurm failed or refused to mention it anywhere in his writings. His only articulated complaint was of the school's ideologically and spiritually stifling environment. In a June 1819 letter to a friend with whom he had attended Hebron, Russwurm, signaling the first indication of his iconoclastic bent, rejoiced in the news that the school had burned down earlier in the year. "I consider it as the jud[g]ement of Heaven for their treatment of the few independent souls who resided with them during this past year," he wrote. "True is the saying 'all for the best,' for we see it plainly proved in the visitations of heaven on the Hebronites." Brief though his time there was, Russwurm was remembered by the president of the board of trustees of the academy in 1891 as one of Hebron's distinguished alumni—no doubt a Hebronite attempt to bask in Russwurm's reflected glory. "Russworm" is how the president of the trustees repeatedly spelled the former student's name.[30]

In November 1819, Susan Russwurm's brother, Josiah Goold, described young John as "remarkable, steady and fitting for College."[31] But Russwurm lacked the necessary resources to go to college. He left Maine the following year to earn them himself. He worked as a teacher in black schools in Philadelphia, New York, and then Boston to save enough to continue his own education. This opened up a new world for Russwurm, for it was his first experience of sustained contact with African Americans beyond the tiny community that resided in Maine, which hovered around a thousand for the century between 1810 and 1910. Russwurm was in fact coming from one of the whitest states in the union.[32] Most of his teaching was done in Boston, where, as his stepmother explained, Russwurm was "eminently successful, and had many warm friends among the most respectable and intelligent of that city."[33] Starting in 1821, Russwurm taught advanced children in the African schools in Boston until 1824, when he left to attend college in Maine. His $300 annual teacher's salary would prove to be essential for the continuation of his own education. But Boston was even more significant in Russwurm's political and intellectual evolution, for there he developed close friendships with notable black figures—the "black leadership class," as one historian dubs them—such as Prince Saunders, Primus Hall (son of Prince Hall), Rev. Thomas Paul (who was instrumental in his appointment to a teaching position), George Middleton, Thomas Dalton, James Barbadoes, and David Walker, to name only a few.[34] These associations served him well in the years to come. It was also in Boston that Russwurm became intimately familiar, for the first time, with the collective plight, struggles, and aspirations of African Americans, especially the free people of color. But Boston's greatest and most enduring impact upon the young teacher was almost certainly Russwurm's interest in the fate, heroic history, and symbolism of Haiti and its leaders.

The first three decades after Haitian independence in 1804 witnessed a heightening interest among African Americans in the "Black Republic," only the second independent state to emerge in the Americas. Haitian emigration societies would be formed in African American communities in Boston, Philadelphia, New York, and Baltimore, among others. And despite the instability of the Haitian state, thousands of black Americans sought a new home there. One of the key promoters of Haiti as the possible home and asylum to black America was Prince Saunders. Saunders (sometimes spelt Sanders), who preceded Russwurm as teacher at the African School, became an indefatigable advocate of African American emigration to Haiti. Born around 1775 in Lebanon, Connecticut (some say Thetford, Vermont), Saunders from the age of nine grew up and was educated in Vermont. Recognized early for his brilliance and promise by influential white supporters, he attended Moor's Charity School at Dartmouth in 1807 and 1808. With the strong recommendation of President John Wheelock of Dartmouth and other prominent white supporters in Vermont and New Hampshire, Saunders moved to Boston, apparently to work with a distinguished Unitarian minister, William E. Channing, for the "elevation of the colored people."[35]

However, for his first four years in Boston, beginning in November 1808, Saunders taught at the African School. By 1811 he had become secretary of the African Masonic Lodge; also in that year he founded and administered the Belles Lettres Society, a literary group of young white men. Against opposition, Saunders in 1815 managed to successfully persuade Abiel Smith, a merchant and philanthropist, to bequeath $4,000 to the African School. While teaching at the school, Saunders came to know the Rev. Thomas Paul, the esteemed founder of the black Baptist Church in the United States. Two years before Saunders arrived in the city, Paul, a leading member of Boston's black community, had founded the African Meeting House, where the African School operated. Under the influence of Paul Cuffe, to whose daughter Saunders was for a time engaged, both men advocated the emigration of African Americans to West Africa and the Christianization of the continent. Cuffe, the pioneering African American captain, shipowner, and pious Quaker, had spent time in Sierra Leone and Britain between 1810 and 1812 and had become enamored with the idea and prospect of transporting African Americans to the colony.[36] It was thus in the role of African colonization advocates that both Saunders and Paul sailed for London in 1815, seeking British abolitionist support for the scheme.

While in London, Saunders was persuaded by the abolitionist leadership, particularly William Wilberforce and Thomas Clarkson, to become an advisor to Henri Christophe, the Haitian "emperor," with whom they had a remarkably close relationship. Christophe, who was at the time engaged in an ambitious modernization project in Haiti, sought the support of teachers and educationalists to realize his dream. Saunders met Christophe in February 1816 and for the next two years was strikingly energetic in his role as

Christophe's advocate and courier to the Court of St. James as the British pondered diplomatic recognition of Haiti. Returning from his first official mission to Britain in the fall of 1816, Saunders brought two teachers from England who were expert in the Lancastrian method of teaching and who proved to be remarkably successful in their efforts. Back in Haiti, Saunders himself organized several schools and has been credited with introducing vaccination into Haiti, personally inoculating Christophe's children.[37] He encouraged Christophe to invite African American emigration as a way of countering his "mulatto" rival, Alexandre Pétion, who controlled the southwestern half of Haiti. Such emigrants would provide loyal support for Christophe while serving to dilute the influence of Catholicism, which bolstered Pétion.[38] Such a notion dovetailed neatly with Christophe's project of Haitian nation building, since Christophe, an Anglophile who had been born in the British colony of Grenada, entertained the outlandish idea that for Haiti to develop, its people needed to become English speakers and Protestants. To Christophe, the English language had an added advantage, as he explained in a letter to Wilberforce: "The teaching of English literature in our schools will eventually, I hope, cause the English language to predominate over French; the only means of preserving our independence is to have absolutely nothing in common with a nation against which we have so many grievances and whose conduct tends only to our destruction."[39]

During his stay in London in the middle of 1816, Saunders produced *Haytian Papers*, his translation of official Haitian documents aimed at garnering support for Christophe in his struggle against Pétion, through the support of the British public, with the ultimate goal of Haiti's diplomatic recognition. The book met with some success in Britain and was also widely distributed and read in the United States, especially among the free people of color.[40]

But Saunders offended Christophe by issuing the book without his prior knowledge while claiming on the title page that it was "by authority" and carrying the words after his name, "Agent of the Haytian Government." To make matters worse, Saunders's rather flamboyant lifestyle in London at the expense of the Haitian government riled Christophe, who recalled him to Cap-Henri, Christophe's capital. Falling out of favor with Christophe, Saunders returned to the United States.[41] There, despite his personal estrangement from Christophe, he continued his energetic efforts on Haiti's behalf, ably propounding in speech and writing the virtues of black emigration to that country. He issued an American edition of *Haytian Papers* in Boston and traveled and spoke in the major northern cities, with New York, Philadelphia, and Boston being the primary places where he was heard by large audiences.[42]

Speaking before the American Convention for Promoting the Abolition of Slavery, Saunders urged his audience especially those he dubbed "practical Christians" to do whatever they could to end the civil strife in Haiti, in order to advance "the great cause of African improvement and happiness."[43] But he claimed that despite Haiti's current problems, "Among the various projects or plans which have been devised or suggested in relation to emigration, there are none which appear to many persons to wear so much the appearance of feasibility, and ultimate successful and practical operation, as the luxuriant, beautiful and extensive island of Hayti (or St. Domingo)."[44] His address was issued as a pamphlet and widely distributed in the "free states" and Britain.

Because of Saunders's tireless effort and effective advocacy, Thomas Clarkson interceded on his behalf with Christophe. Though still rather skeptical and debilitated by a stroke, Christophe received Saunders in October 1820. Saunders persuaded Christophe to grant him a ship and $25,000 for transporting interested African Americans to Haiti. But before the documents could be drawn up and the arrangement sealed, Haiti was once again in revolt, and Christophe, deserted and betrayed by his guards, was doomed. He committed suicide with a bullet to the heart. Pétion's "mulatto" successor, Jean-Pierre Boyer, reunited Haiti under his control, and in the chaos Saunders was robbed of everything, including his clothes. Saunders met with Boyer and argued the case for African American emigration to the island while also seeking relief. He was unsuccessful on both fronts but only in the short run. Saunders described Boyer as "very much prejudiced against the blacks" and lamented the chaos that had ensued on Christophe's death. By July 1821 he was back in Philadelphia. But in a striking reversal a few years later, he accepted a position in Boyer's government as attorney general and apparently retained this position until his death in 1839.[45]

Saunders may have accompanied Thomas Paul on his trip to Haiti on May 31, 1823, but the evidence is inconclusive.[46] Paul, who had agitated since 1808 for the opportunity to serve as a Baptist missionary in Haiti, was finally given his chance by the Baptist Missionary Society of Massachusetts. The society appointed him for six months in Haiti and left open the possibility of his establishing a permanent mission if there were prospects of success. Paul arrived in Haiti in July 1823 and was warmly welcomed by the Haitian authorities, including President Boyer, who met and assured Paul of his support. For several months Paul preached in the major cities of Haiti. But his lack of facility in the French language, let alone the local creole, was an insurmountable barrier to any prospect of wider success. After three months of effort he decided to return to Boston, though not before developing a warm admiration for the Haitian people and the island. (The entire island of His-paniola, including the eastern section previously held by the Spanish—now the Dominican Republic—was under Haitian rule from 1822 to 1844.) Back in Boston he maintained close contact with Haiti and helped facilitate the emigration of a group of black Bostonians to work and settle in the island. But his greatest intervention was his steadfast promotion of Haiti to all who would listen and his encouragement of black emigration there. In July 1824 he published a remarkable letter in the *Columbian Centinel* that was widely reprinted. He was induced to write the letter, he noted, "in the hopes that those free people of colour especially, who are disposed to seek an asylum for the enjoyment of liberty, and the common rights of man in a foreign clime, may be benefitted by this publication." Paul explained that, having resided in Haiti for several months, he was "fully persuaded that it is the best and most suitable place of residence which Providence has hitherto offered to emanci-pated people of colour, for the enjoyment of liberty and equality with atten-dant blessings." He lauded the people as well as the island itself, "delightfully situated, abounding with all the necessaries and even the luxuries of life." Paul concluded:

> A country, the local situation of which is favourable to trade and commer-cial enterprise, possessing a free and well regulated government, which encourages the useful and liberal arts, a country possessing an enterprising population of several hundred thousands of active and brave men, who are determined to live free or die gloriously in the defense of freedom, must possess advantages highly inviting to men who are sighing for the enjoy-ment of the common rights and liberties of mankind. The time, I trust, is not far distant, when all wise and good men will use their influence to place the Free Coloured People of the United States upon the delightful island of Hayti.[47]

Paul himself did not return to Haiti, as is sometimes claimed.[48] He contin-ued his ministry in Boston and continued to promote Haiti and its symbolic importance. A local paper reported that in 1825 "the Africans, their descen-dants, and other colored citizens celebrated the acknowledgement of the Independence of Hayti, by a public address, delivered by the Rev. Thomas Paul, in the African Meeting House in this city, by a well provided dinner, and demonstrations of joy and gratitude." Toasts were offered to "Indepen-dent Hayti," "may she be a *Nursery* of Freemen, Patriots, and Philanthropists," and to the "*Government, and Army, of Hayti.*—One has proved by *black-and-*

white that it knows how to maintain Freedom, Equality, and Independence. The other, that they can always beat their enemies *black-and-blue*."[49] Paul suffered from ill health for many years and died of consumption in April 1831 at the age of fifty-seven.

The closest relationship that Russwurm established in Boston was with the Paul family. He worked closely with Paul while teaching at the African School and probably boarded with the Pauls. Back home in North Yarmouth it was even claimed that Russwurm had married one of the Rev. Paul's daughters and had moved to Baltimore with her before they migrated to Liberia together.[50] Was there any fire to the smoke? It is certainly possible that Russwurm got engaged to either Anne Catherine or her younger sister, the abolitionist activist Susan Paul.[51] The Rev. Paul and David Walker would later serve as the Boston agents of *Freedom's Journal,* which Russwurm coedited after graduating from Bowdoin College.

Thus the political environment at the time, charged with discussions of Haiti, and Russwurm's close relationship with Thomas Paul and to a lesser extent Prince Saunders more than likely had an overdetermining effect on Russwurm. It was almost certainly in Boston that Russwurm began to cultivate his deep and abiding interest in Haiti and an early desire to emigrate to the heroic nation after graduation.

During his time in Boston, Russwurm's stepmother, the former Mrs. Russwurm, profoundly aware of the limited prospects for a talented young black man in the United States, advised Russwurm to emigrate to Liberia. Russwurm, however, "firmly declined doing so" and decided to get a college education. He entered Bowdoin College, Brunswick, Maine, in 1824 and graduated in 1826, making him one of the earliest black graduates of an American college and the first from Bowdoin.[52]

Founded in 1794 but with its first class entering in 1802, Bowdoin had been created as a local alternative to Harvard. Entering at the junior class level, Russwurm must have already possessed a good grasp of Latin and Greek, philosophy, history, arithmetic, the natural sciences, geography, and biblical knowledge, as stipulated in the college regulations. The curriculum of the junior year built upon these skills with a bias toward the classics "translations into Latin and Greek alternatively every fortnight," state the regulations. The senior year was largely given over to the sciences (chemistry, mineralogy, astronomy), mathematics (especially geometry and trigonometry), and philosophy. And across both years, significant attention was given to oratory and English composition. All in all, Bowdoin provided Russwurm with a good classical education and significant grounding in other branches of the humanities and the natural sciences.[53] Russwurm's favorite subjects were in the humanities. A close friend of his later reported that Russwurm was "mainly in his taste and acquirements, a *literary* man. . . . His reading was very extensive, yet select. His main fort[e] was history and politics, particularly of Modern Europe, in which he excelled. . . . His family and Library were to him the world."[54]

Russwurm was rather lucky with Bowdoin. By the time he matriculated, the college had on its faculty some of America's most distinguished progressive, antiracist, and abolitionist intellectuals. And the decade of the 1820s was to produce some of the college's most distinguished alumni Henry Wadsworth Longfellow, Nathaniel Hawthorne, Horatio Bridge (Hawthorne's lifelong and closest friend, and biographer), and Calvin Stowe, the abolitionist husband of Harriet Beecher Stowe, whose *Uncle Tom's Cabin* was actually written in Brunswick after her husband's return to Bowdoin as a professor. In addition to producing a remarkable number of senators and congressmen, Bowdoin could boast a president of the United States, Franklin Pierce, among its graduates of the 1820s. Russwurm also enjoyed good fortune with the student body. Nehemiah Cleaveland (1796–1877), historian of Bowdoin, on account of his family's and his own long-standing associations with the college, almost certainly knew Russwurm. His editor, Alpheus Packard (1798–1884), who completed the *History of Bowdoin College* after Cleaveland's death, would have taught Russwurm as Bowdoin's professor of classical literature (1824–42). Their remarks about Russwurm's experience at Bowdoin thus carry some weight. They were probably more accurate than not when they observed, "to the credit of his [Russwurm's] fellow-students in Brunswick, that peculiar as his position was among them, they were careful to avoid everything that might tend to make that position unpleasant." Cleaveland, in particular, was very proud of his alma mater: "Honor to the college which, disregarding a general but illiberal prejudice, admitted to its privileges this member of a proscribed caste!" he exclaimed. "Honor especially to the memory of him who turned to so good account his discipline at Brunswick!"[55]

But one swallow does not a summer make. Henry G. Russell, the college chaplain, was aware of the dangers of smug self-congratulation. In a chapel talk given on Russwurm in 1947, he concluded that the college community had a right to be proud of Bowdoin for "pioneering in collegiate racial tolerance." But, he enjoined, "If our pride is to be more than a backward-looking antiquarian sentimentalism, then I think we must ask ourselves what we are doing today, in November 1947, to increase brotherliness and good will among all men. We stand here today surrounded by a host of goodly witnesses from the past; let us just see to it that by our attitudes—and by our deeds[—]we are worthy to march with them."[56] As late as December 4, 1961, Bowdoin's registrar could boast of only three other black graduates since Russwurm's time: Samuel Dreer and Arthur Madison, both of whom graduated in 1910, and John Mitchell, who gained his degree two years later.[57]

Despite the generally hospitable reception, Russwurm must have felt out of place at Bowdoin not only because of his color but also on account of his age. On the verge of his twenty-fifth birthday, he was much older than his fellow students, virtually all of whom were in their teens. (Though it was certainly an exceptional case, Cleaveland had even entered Bowdoin at the age of thirteen and graduated at seventeen.) Color, however, trumped age in Russwurm's conspicuousness at Bowdoin. Yet instead of being ostracized on account of color, as black students on American campuses commonly were well into the twentieth century, Russwurm was in fact invited, soon after his arrival at Bowdoin, to join the prestigious and liberal-minded Athenaean Society, whose members included Hawthorne and Bridge. His elegantly handwritten reply, dated October 30, 1824, is preserved in his archive: "Gentlemen of the Athenaean Society, With alacrity I accept your kind invitation."[58]

Given the temper of the times, it is probable that Russwurm encountered some racism at Bowdoin.[59] But if he did, it appears not to have been sufficiently egregious for him to have registered it anywhere in his writings, and it does not appear in the reminiscences of those who knew him well, or perhaps he felt embarrassed to mention it. Russwurm, who was always proud and dignified, also took measures to avoid embarrassing situations. Thus, although his friends and fellow Athenaeans Hawthorne and Bridge called upon him several times at the carpenter's house, "just beyond the village limits," where Russwurm boarded, Russwurm never returned their calls. Bridge believed that this was because of the Jamaican's "sensitiveness on account of his color."[60] This observation is supported by the profile of Russwurm written by James Hall, his closest friend and colleague. A white doctor who also happened to be a Bowdoin man (Bowdoin Medical School, class of 1822), Hall first met Russwurm in 1831 in Liberia. Thereafter the two men developed a close friendship, actually living under the same roof until Russwurm got married in 1833, and worked closely together—primarily through regular correspondence after 1836—right up to Russwurm's death twenty years later. Hall has provided the most detailed and intimate, and probably also the most perceptive, description of Russwurm. He recalled that Russwurm was "rather above the ordinary size, and when in good health, straight and erect."

Reflecting the Victorian obsession with craniometry that was so common-place in his profession, Hall noted that Russwurm's head "was well formed, having a broad forehead, and a good facial angle." And noting something that is corroborated by the extant portrait of Russwurm, Hall observed that Russwurm's eyes were "his most distinguishing feature large, keen and pen-etrating, lighting up under excitement with remarkable brilliancy." In his deportment, Russwurm was "always dignified and gentlemanly, never giv-ing indication of other than strict good breeding." Hall also testified to Russ-wurm possessing a "good sound intellect; its most remarkable quality being a keen perception of the true character of men and things." He noted that Russwurm was

> exceedingly sensitive, amounting even to jealousy, and having once lost confidence in a person, he seldom, if ever, re-acquired it. He was usually very reserved and distant to strangers, never opening himself until he was satisfied he had no evil to apprehend from so doing. He was exceedingly jealous of any allusion to his position in society as a colored man, and it required the greatest delicacy in the choice of words to render even praise acceptable to him, when coming from a white man. Few, probably, have suffered so much from such causes of this nature as Mr. Russwurm.[61]

As late as January 1826, Russwurm was set on emigrating to Haiti, the heroic, newly created black republic. In a letter to his cousin in Tennessee, John Sumner Russwurm, he confessed that he could not boast of his circum-stances, "having at present but just able to keep my present standing," but claimed that "after August, brighter prospects will dawn upon efforts of many years. If not particularly invited by the Haytian Govt then, I shall study Med-icine in Boston previous to an emigration to Hayti."[62] Russwurm had devel-oped an early, deep, and lifelong fascination with Haiti, its revolution, and its brilliant leader Toussaint Louverture. While still a student at Bowdoin, he wrote a twenty-two page essay, "Toussaint L'Overture [sic], The Principal Chief in the Revolution of St. Domingo." Though Russwurm noted that Lou-verture was not "faultless," and that "beyond all doubt his character had its blemishes," the modern student of Haiti, with the benefit of two centuries of historiography on the subject, cannot help noticing that Russwurm's essay is marked by the hagiographical treatment of Louverture prevalent in aboli-tionist writings of the early nineteenth century. Russwurm, however, seemed aware of this when he wrote that "the historian, from whom these facts are drawn, had it not in his power" to record Louverture's failings. Nevertheless,

Dr. James Hall (1802–89), first governor of Maryland in Liberia, from 1834 to 1836, when he returned to the United States as general agent of the Maryland State Colonization Society. He was succeeded in that position by Russwurm. He established a close friendship and professional relationship with Russwurm from 1831, when Hall first went to Liberia, right up to Russwurm's death in 1851. Courtesy of the Maryland Historical Society.

the essay, executed with a fine narrative and mature analytical thrust, reveals Russwurm's impressive grasp of the complex twists and turns of Louverture's remarkable career and astonishing accomplishments. And Russwurm certainly builds the case in the body of his essay to conclude, "It is only the sober language of truth to say, that the talents and virtues of Toussaint L'Ouverture, entitle him to the grateful recollections of his liberated countrymen that his character exhibits many of those qualities which have distinguished the most illustrious governors and commanders and that his sufferings and death left a stain of treachery and cruelty on the government under whose merciless oppression he perished."[63] Russwurm had evidently devoted much time and effort researching the subject, a task eased by the command of French that his Montreal education had necessitated. But it is also evident that Russwurm drew heavily—indeed to the point of plagiarism in places—upon the *History of the Island of St. Domingo*, a volume anonymously published in London in 1818 that came out in the United States in 1824, just a year before Russwurm wrote his essay. An outstanding work of scholarship and fine prose, the book is arguably the most comprehensive and authoritative of the many contemporary narratives of the Haitian Revolution.[64]

Perhaps because of this fascination with Haiti and his ambition to emigrate there, Russwurm's commencement address at Bowdoin was "The Condition and Prospects of Hayti," a remarkable speech that attracted widespread attention and praise. A reporter from the Portland *Eastern Argus* covered the graduation ceremony, which took place on September 6, 1826. He registered the "peculiarly interesting" fact and "perfect novelty in the history of our Colleges" that among the "young gentlemen" receiving the honors of the college and assigned parts in the commencement exercise was "a Mr. Russworm [sic], a person of African descent." Russwurm, understandably, was a little nervous at the start but soon regained his poise. According to the *Argus*, he came on the stage "under an evident feeling of embarrassment, but finding the sympathies of his audience in his favor, he recovered his courage as he proceeded." Unlike many of the speakers, who "spoke in so low a tone of voice as not to be heard by a considerable part of the audience," Russwurm "pronounced his part in a full and manly tone of voice, accompanied with appropriate gestures."[65]

Lasting about ten minutes, as the commencement exercise required, Russwurm's was a concise and beautifully framed argument that defended a principle and its manifestation in the form of the Haitian Revolution and Haitian independence. To Russwurm, the "principle of liberty" was fundamental and incontrovertible. It was implanted in the breast of every human being,

First page of Russwurm's commencement address in his own hand. Courtesy of the George J. Mitchell Department of Special Collections & Archives, Bowdoin College Library, Brunswick, Maine.

regardless of whether the person was "placed under the torrid suns of Africa, or in the more congenial temperate zone." All efforts to stifle this principle were as fruitless as would be "the attempt to extinguish the fires of Etna." Furthermore, "It is in the irresistible course of events that all men, who have been deprived of their liberty, shall recover this previous portion of their indefeasible inheritance." The Haitian Revolution was illustrative of this principle and held "a conspicuous place" in the events of the day. After "years of sanguinary struggle for freedom and a political existence," the Haitians had declared their independence on the "auspicious day" of January 1, 1804. This dearly won freedom the Haitians were determined to keep, preferring death to a return to their former condition. The revolution had transformed the Haitian people, making them "new creatures," who now "stepped forth as men, and showed to the world, that though Slavery may benumb, it cannot entirely destroy our faculties." Its leaders, Louverture, Dessalines, and Christophe, proved this.[66] Russwurm painted a rather glowing picture of the condition of Haiti. A republican form of government, he told his audience, was "so firmly" established that "in no country are the rights and privileges of citizens and foreigners more respected, and crimes less frequent." But his oration was a celebration and defense of Haiti and its revolution, so maligned and besieged at the time.[67] Contrary to the propaganda depicting the Haitian people as savages, Russwurm saw them as "brave and generous." And he rightly observed that "if cruelties were inflicted during the Revolutionary war, it was owing to the policy pursued by the French commanders, which compelled them to use retaliatory measures." "For who," he asked, driving his point home,

> shall expostulate with men who have been hunted with bloodhounds—who have been threatened with an Auto-da-fé—whose relations and friends have been hung on gibbets before their eyes—have been sunk by hundreds in the sea—and tell them they ought to exercise kindness towards such mortal enemies? Remind me not of moral duties, of meekness and generosity. Show me the man who has exercised them under these trials, and you point to one who is more than human. . . . The cruelties inflicted by the French on the children of Hayti have exceeded the crimes of Cortez and Pizarro.

The twenty-two years of Haitian independence, "so gloriously achieved, have effected wonders," he declared. "No longer are they the same people." And he saw an equally glorious future ahead for the citizens of the black republic: "With a countenance erect and fixed upon Heaven, they can now contemplate the works of Divine munificence. Restored to the dignity of man to society, they have acquired a new existence their powers have been developed: a career of glory and happiness unfolds itself before them." Russwurm looked forward to the time when Haiti, "treading in the footsteps of her sister republicks, shall, like them, exhibit a picture of rapid and unprecedented advances in population, wealth and intelligence."

The presentation was received with "hearty applause."[68] The *Argus* described it as "one of the most interesting performances of the day." Clearly impressed by Russwurm, the reporter went on: "It is but just to add that Russworm has conducted with great propriety during the whole course of his college life, and has always had the esteem of his classmates. He intends, as we are informed, to settle in Hayti. He will carry with him the best wishes of all his acquaintances for his happiness and success in life." Alive to the historic nature of the occasion, the *Argus*, believing its readers "would feel an interest in a literary performance so novel under all its circumstances," carried a substantial extract from Russwurm's speech. This, in turn, was picked up by the *Boston Courier*, the *Boston Centinel*, the *Boston Commercial Gazette* (which boasted of Russwurm, "He belongs to this city"), the *Norwich Courier*, and the *National Philanthropist*, among others.[69] The Baltimore-based newspaper *The Genius of Universal Emancipation*, edited and published by the pioneering and bold abolitionist Benjamin Lundy, carried the extract on its front page under the title "African Eloquence." At Bowdoin, and Brunswick and environs, Russwurm's speech was such as to enter popular lore. A generation later, memory of the occasion and events surrounding it remained green. Writing in a local newspaper in 1848, an unnamed man who described himself only as one "connected with the college some few years after Mr. Russwurm graduated," shared his story: "We have often heard the following anecdote told of a good old lady of the village who was present at the Commencement Exercises. After Mr. Russwurm had spoken, and just as he was leaving the stage, she remarked loud enough to be heard by all in the vicinity, 'Well, I do declare, the negro has done the best of them all.'"[70]

Although Russwurm did not study medicine in Boston, he would have done so if he had been provided with the necessary financial resources. He sought—or more accurately, his former guardian (Calvin Stockbridge), sought on Russwurm's behalf—the help of the American Colonization Society but was refused.[71] He had in fact, in preparation for a medical education, attended lectures on anatomy and chemistry at Bowdoin College Medical School in his senior year at college.[72] But for unknown reasons he did not immediately depart for Haiti. As late as October 1826, he was still seriously thinking of emigrating to Haiti; indeed, in a letter written that same month, Stockbridge reported that Russwurm would "probably go to Hayti soon" if he did not find a job. Russwurm first moved to Boston after his graduation (not New York, as is generally claimed), where he stayed with the Rev. Thomas Paul, who had sponsored his earlier appointment as a teacher in the African School there. He had been highly praised as a teacher, and black Boston, though happy for Russwurm, had grieved his loss when he left for Bowdoin two years earlier. The School Committee would have gladly re-employed him, especially since he now possessed the rare and added equipment of a college education, but there was no opening; the teacher who had replaced him after he went to Bowdoin was giving "good satisfaction," and the committee thought it improper to dismiss the man.[73] After a wide canvassing of opinion, Russwurm turned down an offer made to him by the American Colonization Society to take up a post in Liberia.[74] By the end of the year he had moved to New York City, where he immersed himself in the embryonic abolitionist movement and black uplift work. There, largely because of the attacks on black people by some of the New York newspapers, he, Samuel Cornish, and a group of black supporters in the city met at Boston Crummell's house and decided to establish a periodical of their own, *Freedom's Journal,* America's first black newspaper.

Freedom's Journal

Pleading Our Own Cause

Two bright, young black men became editors of *Freedom's Journal*. The senior editor, Samuel Cornish (1795?–1859), who was about thirty-two years old, was born in rural Delaware of free parents. Little is known about his youth except that it was largely spent on the land, which remained in his affections to the end of his life. In 1815 he went to Philadelphia and there received training for the ministry by the pastor of the First African Church, Presbyterian. Licensed to preach in 1819, he spent the next six months as a missionary to slaves on Maryland's Eastern Shore. Living in New York by 1821, Cornish organized the New Demeter Street Presbyterian Church, where he was ordained in 1822 and where he preached until 1828.[1]

His junior partner was the twenty-seven-year-old Russwurm. The two men respected each other and got on well together but were quite different in temperament. Cornish, a child of the South, cautious, steady, some say even conservative, was a deeply religious man guided by his Christian faith. Russwurm, child of the islands, Canada, and the North, was highly sensitive and relatively impatient with ignorance and prejudice, so that he chafed under the racist indignities of American life. Underneath a quiet and dignified exterior, he was a man bursting with passion and indignation. Classically trained and well read, he was, unlike Cornish, a child of the New England enlightenment and had little time for revealed religion. His writings and the testimony of his closest friend, James Hall, suggest that he was probably a Deist, and in New York it seemed that most of his white friends were members of the Society of Friends. Writing in 1835, the philanthropist and Christian zealot Gerrit Smith (then a supporter of colonization), in lamenting that Russwurm was "the only liberally educated colored man" in Liberia, hastened to add, "and he, unhappily, is not pious." Smith was acquainted with Russwurm and his writings from the days of *Freedom's Journal*.[2] Only toward the end of Russwurm's life did he, following his wife,

Samuel Cornish (1795–1858), cofounder and senior editor of *Freedom's Journal*. He served from March to September 1827, after which Russwurm edited the paper on his own. Courtesy of the Schomburg Center for Research in Black Culture, New York Public Library, Astor, Lenox, and Tilden Foundation.

become a Christian, joining the Protestant Episcopal Church in Cape Palmas, Liberia, where he lived.[3]

Cornish and Russwurm complemented each other in personality and temperament. They shared a profound and passionate commitment, which they both regarded as a sacred responsibility, to advancing the interests of the black population in the United States and elsewhere. They both struggled against the oppression and degradation of black people while simultaneously seeking the self-improvement of African Americans through self-respect, self-reliance, and, most of all, education. In many ways, both Cornish and Russwurm were old-fashioned moralists who attempted to instill the traditional virtues and combat old and new vices that they saw afflicting the black urban population especially; *Freedom's Journal* was filled with such teachings during Cornish's time with the paper as well as after he left. But Cornish was especially keen on warring against Sin, large and small. Though Russwurm is known to have drunk alcohol while living in Africa, it is not known if he did so while in the United States. Cornish, however, was a teetotaler and was at one time active in the temperance movement.

Freedom's Journal made its intentions clear from the first issue, published on March 16, 1827: "We wish to plead our own cause. Too long have others spoken for us. Too long has the publick been deceived by misrepresentations, in things which concern us dearly, though in the estimation of some mere trifles; for though there are many in society who exercise towards us benevolent feelings; still (with sorrow we confess it) there are others who make it their business to enlarge upon the least trifle, which tends to the discredit of any person of colour; and pronounce anathemas and denounce our whole body by the misconduct of this guilty one." Addressed "To Our Patrons," this front-page editorial, which occupies two and two-thirds of its four columns, expanded upon the condition of Afro-America and how the editors perceived the paper's wider role within the struggle. The editors sought not only to make *Freedom's Journal* a "medium of intercourse" between African Americans in different states but also to have it serve as a forum opened to its constituency of readers on "subjects which concern us." Much like Lenin with his newspaper *Pravda,* Cornish and Russwurm saw *Freedom's Journal* as an organizer; they sought to meld the scattered black population in the United States into one people, with the *Journal* as its advocate and articulate voice. As Russwurm wrote a few months later: "Union is every thing; and could our brethren but be united in their efforts, we might effect almost any thing."[4] The editors urged those who had the franchise to make "independent use of the same," wishing them not to become the "tools of party." Similarly, they urged black people to support their paper regardless of religious affiliation, especially since it intended to transcend sectarian and denominational differences within the community. *Freedom's Journal* saw itself as an educator, in both the narrow and the wider sense of the term, and emphasizing this role, it promised to "urge upon our brethren the necessity and expediency of training their children, while young, to habits of industry, and thus forming them for becoming useful members of society." It aimed to awaken Afro-

America from the "lethargy of years" to make "a concentrated effort for the education of our youth." And the editors, aiming to discourage the wasting of time and effort in the "perusal of works of trivial importance," regarded it as their duty "to recommend to our young readers, such authors as will not only enlarge their stock of useful knowledge, but such as will also serve to stimulate them to higher attainments in science." They promised to impart useful knowledge on "the general principles and rules of economy" and to provide "many practical pieces" to assist in the community's self-improvement.

Freedom's Journal promised to live up to its name. It intended to "arrest the progress of prejudice" and to serve as a "shield" against its evils. "The civil rights of a people," it declared, "being of the greatest value, it shall ever be our duty to vindicate our brethren, when oppressed, and to lay the cure before the publick."[5] Though the paper would be primarily and inevitably aimed at the free people of color with the hope of also serving as a "public channel," the editors promised "not to be unmindful" of those still in the "iron fetters of bondage." "They are our kindred by all the ties of nature," declared Cornish and Russwurm. And, they continued, "though but little can be effected by us, still let our sympathies be poured forth, and our prayers in their behalf, ascend to Him who is able to succour them." Africa, they also promised, would not be ignored. Indeed, "useful knowledge of every kind, and every thing that relates to Africa, shall find a ready admission into our columns." Moreover, "as that vast continent becomes daily more known, we trust that many things will come to light, proving that the natives of it are neither so ignorant nor stupid as they have generally been supposed to be."[6] They pointed to the Republic of Haiti as disproof of the racist calumny of black inferiority.[7]

Probably the most remarkable antiracist and vindicationist item in the paper was a long, mournful essay, "The Mutability of Human Affairs," written by Russwurm and published in three parts in 1827.[8] "During a recent visit to the Egyptian Mummy," Russwurm began, "my thoughts were insensibly carried back to former times, when Egypt was in her splendor, and the only seat of chivalry, science, arts and civilization. As a descendant of Cush, I could not but mourn over her present degradation, while reflecting upon the mutability of human affairs, and upon the present condition of a people, who, for more than one thousand years, were the most civilized and enlightened."[9] During the course of this reverie, Russwurm's thoughts turned to the magnificent achievements of the Egyptians, their relations with Ethiopia, the rise and fall of powerful nations and empires, and the implications of history for Africans around the world. Drawing on biblical scholarship, history, and science, he concluded that the Egyptians were not white and that their relations with the rest of Africa were intimate and enduring. Anticipating arguments put forward by Cheikh Anta Diop, Martin Bernal, and others more than a century later, Russwurm concluded that the Egyptians were neither white nor black but "a copper coloured race."[10] "But who can convince us that the intellectual powers of man are inferior, because nature's God has tinged his complexion with a darker hue? The doctrine is contrary to all the evidences we have of the creation," Russwurm declared. Still, the argument developed and persisted in modern times that black people not only were inferior but even constituted a different species from human beings, with the craniologists describing them as "something between man and the brute creation." He prayed that another Solomon might rise "in this age of enlightened reason, and convince the world, that our people naturally, are not worse than other men."[11] He recognized that the racist argument was difficult to dislodge on the basis of countervailing evidence alone, given the material interests of those who propounded it. Nevertheless, he argued, there was hope when one looked back at the rise and fall of nations—Egypt, Greece, Rome, Spain, Napoleonic France, Britain, Russia. A "fairer day is yet to dawn upon our longing eyes," though "when this will be we cannot tell." And as he had remarked in his earlier meditations on Haiti, "human affairs are continually revolving," so "who will predict that the day may not come when our people shall be duly considered in the scale of nations, and respected accordingly. We are no enthusiasts, but it must certainly be considered uncommonly miraculous that mutability shall attend all other nations."[12] "The Mutability of Human Affairs" is a seminal work in African American thought.[13]

Cornish and Russwurm in the end promised their readers that "whatever concerns us as a people will ever find a ready admission" into the paper, "interwoven with all the principal news of the day." More a magazine than a newspaper, *Freedom's Journal* largely lived up to its editors' promises. It reported the news but focused more on history, editorials, essays, and poems directly relevant to the struggle and ambitions of black people.[14]

Congruent with its international scope and pan-African ambitions, *Freedom's Journal* established a network of foreign as well as domestic agencies. Significantly and unsurprisingly, Haiti was the first country to have a foreign agent of the *Journal*.[15] Agents for the *Journal* also operated in Canada and England, as well as across the United States. Among them was the militant black abolitionist David Walker of Boston, whose name appeared in the very first issue as an "Authorised Agent." Walker also contributed to the paper, and it was in *Freedom's Journal* that his 1828 "Address Delivered before the General Colored Association" in Boston first appeared in print.[16] A few months later he developed it into his justly famous and militant *Appeal*, published as a pamphlet in 1829.[17]

One of the primary objectives of *Freedom's Journal* was to advance the fight against the advocates of black colonization in Africa and elsewhere. The American Colonization Society (ACS), founded in 1816, was one of the primary targets. A strange amalgam of racists and humanitarians, the ACS sought the settlement of free African Americans and freed slaves in Africa. Some of its members, including slaveholders, thought that African Americans had no place in the young republic as free citizens; others, the humanitarians, thought that they would never receive full citizenship in the United States and thus sought a homeland in Africa. With federal support, a colony called Liberia ("land of the free") was established in 1821 and expanded into the interior over the decades.[18]

The northern free black population, at least in their public pronouncements, generally viewed the ACS as anathema, an organization aimed at their removal from the land of their birth. Russwurm attacked it even more ferociously than Cornish ever did. As late as January 1828, Russwurm pulled no punches in criticizing the ACS. Free people of color were interested not only in the improvement of their own condition but also in the "emancipation of [their] brethren who are in bondage." And "never shall we consent to emigrate from America," Russwurm declared, "until the prior removal from this land of their degradation and suffering." Moreover, he continued, "even then, we would not ask the aid of the American Colonization Society, to carry us to their land 'flowing with milk and honey.'"[19] As he declared on another occasion, "We are all, to a man, opposed, in every shape, to the Colonization Society."[20] Of course, not even the free people of color in the North, let alone the entire population of 2.3 million African Americans, were uniformly opposed to colonization. If that had been the case, no one would have emigrated to Liberia under the auspices of the ACS—and thousands did. From shaky premises, Russwurm, however, made a logical conclusion: "That our people do not wish to be colonized in any country whatever, should be a sufficient reason against the *scheme*, if Liberia were even a paradise."[21]

In September 1827, six months after the first appearance of *Freedom's Journal*, Russwurm became the sole editor. Because Russwurm later embraced colonization, it has been widely asserted in the literature that Cornish resigned over differences between himself and Russwurm on colonization. The assertion is absurd on its face: one would logically assume that if there were irreconcilable differences between a "senior" editor (Cornish) and his "junior" (Russwurm), the latter would be the more likely to go. Moreover, not only is there no evidence to sustain the claim, but all the evidence indicates that the two men parted on amicable terms, and certainly not in dispute over colonization. Cornish's letter of resignation is worth quoting in full to clear up some of the controversy:

> Six months of our Editorial labours having expired; by mutual consent, and good wishes for the prosperity and usefulness of each other, our connection in the *Journal*, is this day dissolved, and the right and prerogatives exclusively vested in the Junior Editor, J. B. Russwurm.
>
> The reasons for the dissolution of our connection, are as follows:— fully persuaded that it will be for my health and interest, I have resolved to remove to the country; and with the consent of the Presbytery of New York, of which I am a Member, and to whom I am responsible, as circumstances will permit, to devote myself exclusively to the work of the Ministry, as a Missionary, or otherwise, as I may be most useful in the country.
>
> I, therefore, fully convinced of the usefulness and necessity of *Freedom's Journal*, in elevating the tone of feeling, and improving the moral and domestic condition of our brethren, do recommend the same, in the hands of its present Editor, whose education and talents so amply qualify him for its duties, to the liberal patronage of our brethren and friends.

The letter is signed and dated September 14, 1827.[22] Of course, one could say that Cornish's letter is a polite ruse, covering genuine differences. But at the time of his departure both men generally saw eye to eye on colonization. Indeed, if there was a difference between them on the question, it would be that Russwurm expressed a stronger and more vociferous opposition than Cornish ever did, not the other way round. The first challenge in establishing this fact is to disentangle the writings of the two men, since the editorials are unsigned or are simply signed "The Editors." However, between August 3 and 31, 1827, a series of articles in epistolary form were sent from Connecticut and addressed "To the Senior Editor."[23] Since the senior editor was Cornish, that fact rules him out as the author. They were unsigned, but the internal evidence of the articles makes clear that they were written by Russwurm. Thankfully, because of the controversy they elicited—one that spilled over from the *Journal* into the pages of the *New York Observer*—it became even more explicit and incontrovertible that these were indeed written by the "Junior Editor."[24]

The series sheds important light on Russwurm's feelings and thinking; it is a melancholy meditation on the conditions of the sons and daughters of Africa as he found them on his way to and in Connecticut, particularly New Haven and Hartford. I shall return to these articles later on. For now, I would like to concentrate on what they and his riposte to his critics ("Wilberforce" and the Rev. Dr. Samuel Miller of Princeton) tell us about Russwurm's position on colonization at the time Cornish resigned. His third dispatch, sent from New Haven and published on August 17, explicitly addressed colonization and the ACS, thereby drawing the wrath of friends of the Society. Russwurm spoke of visiting a "Mr. W----," "whose feelings have long been warmly enlisted in our cause." But he had a problem with W----: W---- was a colonizationist. The conversation between the two turned toward colonization and was soon deadlocked: "Vain were all our efforts, to convert 'l'un au l'autre:' as I found him, so I left him; and as I entered, so I departed." Russwurm complained that the ACS appeared to have "some few friends" in New Haven. Almost everywhere he called, Russwurm noticed that "the views of the Society were immediately introduced for conversation." He continued:

The Society has been very zealous and successful in imposing upon the public, the foolish *idea* that we are all longing to emigrate to their land of "*milk and honey*," and a thousand other Munchausen stories, too trifling and inconsistent to be repeated. I deem it high time that our friends, in different parts of the Union, should know the truth of the matter that we are all, to a man, opposed, in every shape, to the Colonization Society, and its *consistent President* [Henry Clay]. Justice to some Colonizationists here, compels me to state, that they candidly acknowledged they did not believe, that the climate of Liberia was suited to the constitution of emigrants from the New England and Middle States. You well know, that such men as W---- [probably Supreme Court Justice Bushrod Washington, of Virginia, nephew of George Washington], C---- [probably Henry Clay, Kentucky senator and slave slaveholder], M---- [probably Virginia politician Charles Mercer, another of the prime movers in founding the ACS], and a long Southern list, care not whether the emigrants die the next day after their arrival in Liberia, or not; having obtained all they desired, our removal from this country for their own personal safety, and the better security of their slaves. Methinks, slave-holders must be somewhat lacking in their crania, to dream even of being able to keep in the nineteenth century, nearly *two millions* of their fellow beings enslaved! Knowledge must spread. It cannot be kept from them. Did all other methods fail, I verily believe, like heaven's fiery lightnings, it would descend upon them. Can the *justice* of God tolerate so much iniquity and *injustice*?[25]

These are hardly the words of a colonizationist, as "Wilberforce," a member of the ACS, fully recognized to his chagrin. After quoting in full the above passage, he sighed: "Now really I could not well conceive a better method of checking the progress of *African rights* in all their extent, than to attack in the *name* of these *rights* the American Colonization Society. The ignorant, coarse, bitter way in which he assails this best friend of black men, may disarm and destroy itself. But if not,—if he has any influence with his coloured brethren, or is desirous of promoting their best interest—how can he speak thus of this society?"[26]

Russwurm published a vigorous riposte to "Wilberforce" in the same issue in which he carried the letter, drawing the attention of his readers to "the communication signed '*Wilberforce*.'" It was a document worth reading by all who had been "halting between *Colonization and Anti-Colonization*," wrote Russwurm. He had published the letter at the special request of "the Rev. Dr. Samuel Miller, Professor of Ecclesiastical History and Church Government, in the Theological Seminary, at Princeton, N.J." The good Dr. Miller had "thought proper to inform us" that the enclosed letter by "Wilberforce" had not been written by him or any member of his family. But, Miller wrote, "*as I, in the main, approve its contents,* I take the liberty of transmitting it, and of requesting a place for it in Freedom's Journal." Having set up the context of the "Wilberforce" letter, Russwurm went to work, rebutting it with logic laced with sarcasm and irony—an effective and robust polemic. He again urged his readers to peruse "Wilberforce" so that they might judge for themselves "what liberal ideas our Colonization friends (according to the Rev. Dr., our best,) entertain of us generally. It is a fact, worthy of notice, that our bitterest enemies think not more contemptibly of us, than do Colonizationists generally." He challenged "Wilberforce" to come out of the shadows of anonymity and enter the arena under his own name—"stand forth on his own name"—for a fair fight. He told "Wilberforce" that he had published his letter only because Miller had sent it along, for, "though we are persons of colour, we are not ignorant of the contents of the '*African Repository*' [organ of the ACS]"—suggesting that "Wilberforce" had nothing fresh to say on the subject. While he was willing to pay every attention to those "who style themselves our friends . . . we should be wanting in our duty towards our brethren, did we not express ourselves openly and candidly upon all subjects which concern them, without fear of such men as 'W.'"[27]

The Rev. Dr. Miller was so offended—and perhaps even frightened—by Russwurm's response to "Wilberforce" that he did not bother to write to *Freedom's Journal* itself but instead sent a letter to the *New York Observer* on the matter. He was angry that his name had been mentioned in the paper in connection with "Wilberforce." Not that he wished to distance himself from the tone and content of "Wilberforce's" letter; on the contrary, he now said that he "fully" approved of it. He just thought it was simply not the done thing, bad manners—though he did not say so in so many words—that his name should have been mentioned at all; he had acted merely as the facilitator and transmitter of a message. Complaining, he wrote: "I make no complaint of the very *delicate* course which these Editors have taken with respect to the communication of which I was . . . the mere vehicle. They have undoubtedly a right to manage their own affairs in their own way." He then went on to accuse them of "persevering [in] efforts to arraign the motives, pervert the professions, vilify the characters, and defeat the success of . . . colonization," which went against the "best interests of our coloured population." He had already notified the editors at the time of sending "Wilberforce's" letter that he wanted his name taken off the subscription list. Miller explained that he had been a subscriber to the *Journal* from its commencement with the cherished hope that it would be so conducted as to "exert a favourable influence on the great cause of the improvement and final emancipation of the children of Africa throughout our country." Lest one get the impression that he was a radical abolitionist, Miller pointed out that the improvement and emancipation he sought should come "with all possible speed consistent with the happiness of the nation"—a nation, it should be added, of which a large portion was under the hegemony of a slave-owning class. But over time, Miller explained to the readers of the *Observer,* he had grown "so entirely dissatisfied with the spirit and apparent tendency" of the *Journal* that, although he had not yet paid for his year's subscription, he simply did not choose any longer to "receive it into [his] house."[28]

Russwurm wrote to the *Observer* in reply to Miller, but the editors were willing to publish only a portion of his letter, claiming that the letter was too long. Russwurm believed that had Miller's letter been twice the length of the one actually published, the *Observer* still would have carried it in its entirety. Not willing to submit to the sabotaging of his response by the *Observer,* Russwurm decided to publish in *Freedom's Journal* his own letter in full alongside that of Miller. He expressed his surprise to the editors of the *Observer* at seeing the letter from Miller, in which "many useless words" had been set forth to prejudice the public against the editors of *Freedom's Journal* through "a partial statement" concerning "Wilberforce." He wanted to correct the record. Miller, he explained, had written two letters to the *Journal*. In one, marked "private," he had asked to end his subscription. In the other, he had asked that the *Journal* should publish the enclosed item from "Wilberforce," threatening to have it published elsewhere if the *Journal* refused to carry it. Unlike the first letter, the second did not have "private" written above it. "We appeal to the judgment of the public, whether we have acted *indelicately* towards the Doctor?" Especially since Miller had so fully endorsed "Wilberforce's" letter, "without enjoining privacy," was the *Journal* not "fully warranted in connecting the two names"? Miller, he wrote, had complained about *his* response to "Wilberforce," turning a blind eye to the latter's attack upon the Junior Editor.

He had no regrets about questioning the motives of the leading members of the ACS. "We have done nothing more than we have a right to do—nothing more, than is done daily as it regards public men." If he had vilified any man's character, he called upon Miller to "specify the injured individual, and nothing shall be wanting on our part, to make all the atonement in our power." As to the withdrawal of Miller's support of the *Journal*, Russwurm was not particularly bothered, as "not one in three" of the paper's white patrons supported the ACS; and among "our active friends" throughout the country, three to one were directly opposed to it, considering it as "warring with our best interests." "That our people do not wish to be colonized in any country whatever, should be sufficient reason against the *scheme*, if Liberia were even a paradise." The utmost that would ever be effected by the ACS would be "but 'sowing the wind and reaping the whirlwind.'" While he revered "the Doctor" as a minister and honored him as a scholar, "we must be indulged in saying that he is better acquainted with Ecclesiastical History and Church Government, than with politics or *colonization*." Russwurm's high-octane rejoinder burned to the very end with the same flame of indignation: "The days, we feel thankful, are past, when ecclesiastical censure could exclude a man from the converse of his dearest friends. We are in a land of Liberty; and though prejudices are against our acting as freemen, they shall not compel us to relinquish our pens. We will arraign the motives of all pretended friends—we will strive all in our power to open the eyes of our brethren, upon all subjects which concern them—fearing no man, but appealing to the Searcher of hearts, for the purity of our motives."[29]

Miller was livid. He denounced *Freedom's Journal* from his pulpit, pronouncing upon it "a sentence of eternal condemnation," according to a local newspaper.[30] Miller's vigorous response, it turned out, was motivated not only by political differences with Russwurm over the colonization question but also by the desire to defend a dear friend under attack. For although Miller gave little away as to the true identity of "Wilberforce," and "Wilberforce" himself refused to take up Russwurm's challenge to shed the cloak of anonymity, there is more than enough evidence pointing at the Rev. Dr. Archibald Alexander under the *nom de plume*. Alexander, the first principal and professor appointed to Princeton Theological Seminary when it was founded in 1812, was not only Miller's colleague but also his closest friend and confidante. Alexander was one of the earliest colonizationists, author of the most authoritative history of the movement written in the nineteenth century and staunch defender of the ACS, for which he would serve as a vice president in later years. His contemporaries never failed to remark upon his striking resemblance to the great British abolitionist William Wilberforce, which probably explains his use of the name. One of Alexander's students, Theodore Wright, who was the first black person to study at the seminary, recalled ten years after the event that the *Journal* became a forbidden item after the exchange with Dr. Miller: "All the faculty and students gave up the paper." Wright, the sole African American student there at the time, was delighted with the arrival of so bold an organ in that "dark and gloomy period," when the indignities suffered and the attacks upon the free people of color were so widespread. The doctrine of "colonization was spreading all over the land; and it was popular to say the people of color must be removed. The press came out against us and we trembled. . . . Then we despaired." But *Freedom's Journal*, he said, "came like a clap of thunder!" Through the *Journal*, the "united views and intentions of the people of color were made known, and the nation awoke as from slumber." It announced the facts in the case, "our entire opposition" to colonization.[31] Doubtless thousands of others across the nation applauded Russwurm's courageous stand on the subject.

Now, what is remarkable about Russwurm's angry, bold, and ferocious attacks upon the ACS and its supporters in 1827 is that insofar as we can identify Cornish's own voice, that is, separate from Russwurm's, we do not hear this type of language. Cornish's is less forthright, more compromising, and conciliatory toward the ACS and the colonizationists. Only after Russwurm resigns and after Cornish starts *Rights of All* in May 1829 are we able to hear Cornish in his own right and distinctly. Fortunately, a little incident created a major opportunity for us to hear Cornish. But there is also a second opportunity even more contemporaneous with Russwurm's pronouncements to hear Cornish on the subject. In May 1837 the *Colored American*, a newspaper edited by Cornish, published an editorial entitled "Colored People Always Opposed Colonization." The article was a reprinting, almost in its entirety, of an editorial published ten years earlier (on June 8, 1827) in *Freedom's Journal*. In his prefatory note, Cornish, keen on showing how advanced for its time the *Journal* had been, proclaimed that the article's anticolonization doctrine was "neither Tappan nor Garrisonian. It is Bibleism, and we claim some instrumentality in teaching it to both of these good men (Tappan and Garrison)." Cornish explained that he was the author of that particular editorial.[32] His views, sensibilities, and writing style as expressed in other publications, such as *Rights of All*, and the historical scholarship on Cornish give no reason to doubt this claim.

So what do these articles tell us about Cornish's views on colonization? The editorial in the *Journal* was triggered by a scurrilous one published in the *Georgetown Columbian and District Advertiser*. The *Advertiser* noted the advent of the *Journal* but doubted that it was actually edited by "free negroes residing in New York" and instead expressed the "fear" that the paper was actually edited by "busy white men." The *Advertiser* was sorry to perceive that one of the first acts of the *Journal* was "an attempt to prejudice their brethren 'gainst the Colonization Society, by rendering them distrustful of its objects and suspicious of those wise and philanthropic men . . . whose sole object has been the amelioration of their condition."[33]

Cornish apologized to his readers in advance for "any warmth of feeling that may be apparent in this discharge of our duty." It had always been his object to "use the most pacific measures, studiously avoiding every thing that might tend to irritate the feelings of any." But when the editor of the *Advertiser* "loses sight of that courtesy which is justly due from man to man, we think him a subject rather to be castigated, than reasoned with." Cornish thought it pitiful that the editor, in "a badly written paragraph," should question the capacity of black people to conduct the affairs of the *Journal*: "We do not wonder that a mind trained to prejudice, and accustomed to habits of oppression and cruelty, should be so contracted in its views."[34] There the castigation ended and Cornish turned to the ACS itself.

He denied prejudicing the minds of black people against the ACS but stated, "That we are opposed to colonization in principle, object, and tendency, we unhesitatingly affirm." He explained that in soliciting support of colonizationists for the *Journal* he had never hidden his views. He opposed colonization "unless it be merely considered as a missionary establishment." He then added, "Yet, if we were wrong, our minds were open to conviction, and we wished to see the subject discussed. . . . If the [ACS] possess any merits, it cannot lose by investigation; but if the motives of its founders will not bear investigation, it ought to sink." What is remarkable about this passage is that unlike Russwurm, who had no hesitation in castigating the motives of the colonizationists, Cornish portrayed colonization as an open question, a matter worthy of further inquiry. He went on to "admit that there are many of our friends, in the purity of whose motives, we have no doubt, [who are] favourable to the views of that Society." He further "concede[d] much to the zeal of our [colonizationist] friends." Indeed, he declared that "there are many friends of colonization, whom we respect, and for no consideration, would we be guilty of treating their opinions lightly. Their objects are emancipation; the salvation of Africa; and the extermination of the slave trade. Nothing could be more worthy the philanthropist, and the Christian." His disagreement with them concerned method: "Are there not other means that would be more efficient in accomplishment of these objects?" He believed that the "natural tendency of colonization is to retard emancipation"; that the conversion of Africa could be accomplished by missionary stations; and that colonization might disrupt the slave trade but had managed only to shift the trade from one coast of Africa to another. He concluded:

> We hope that the friends of colonization will not move another step in the business, until they submit to a calm and thorough discussion of a subject, in which every man of colour is deeply interested. And as our columns are more accessible to our brethren than any others, we hope they may be the medium of the discussion. Until this is done, and our minds, which we hold open to conviction, are convinced of the expediency of the plan, we shall feel it our duty to say to our brethren, "Abide in the ship, or you cannot be SAVED."

The tone as well as the content of Cornish's pronouncements on the subject of colonization differs from Russwurm's. Russwurm did not merely question the motives of the colonizationists; he was certain that he already knew what they were—ignoble and utterly contemptible. Cornish, in contrast, did not publicly question their motives, let alone condemn them. Russwurm argued that colonization by deliberate *design* was aimed at retarding the pace of emancipation—colonizationists wanted "our removal from this country for their own personal safety, and the better security of their slaves"—whereas Cornish perceived colonization as having a *natural* tendency to retard emancipation. Cornish saw far many more good people among the colonizationists than Russwurm did in 1827, though he considered them misguided; Russwurm saw them as almost wholly evil but made allowances, grudgingly, for the few good ones he found among them.

Cornish's position on colonization became even more temporizing by June 1829. He apologized for even having to address the subject at all. He felt forced to do so, however, when on June 6 the *New York Observer* carried a seemingly innocuous two sentences about Cornish's new paper, *Rights of*

All: "The Rev. S. E. Cornish, of this city, has issued the first number of a new paper, called *The Rights of All*. The publication seems to have been occasioned by the recent change in the principles of the *Freedom's Journal,* on the subject of Colonization."[35] The speculation was incorrect, but Cornish devoted almost the entirety of his editorial page rebutting it. In "An Error Corrected," Cornish wrote that he was "sorry" to see the notice in the *Observer* claiming that the *Rights of All* had been issued "merely in consequence of the change of the *Freedom's Journal,* in respect of African Colonisation." He had "plainly stated" in the first issue what the aim of the new paper was: the "improvement of society." He went on to explain that even if he had been the only coloured man in America, if as much "corruption and sin" existed as there now were, he would still feel it his duty to issue the paper. "Such is the christian charity of the Editor," he wrote, "that he would feel as much concerned for the improvement of virtue and religion, among the white population as among the coloured." He was as keen on saving the soul of the king of Great Britain as the souls of the sable kings on the continent of Africa. He went on for several paragraphs in this vein, asserting his duty to correct "error" and "sin" in the world and his editorial role as "an afflicted watchman" on the wall. Then he returned to the issue of colonization: "That the establishment of a colony on the coasts of Africa should be considered a christian charity, and that it will be a powerful engine in spreading civilisation and religion, throughout that vast continent, I have no doubt, and that it should from the commencement have been considered a missionary colony, and wore a missionary aspect, I am equally bold asserting. But that it is ever going to meet the object many contemplate, or ameliorate the condition of the vast body of our coloured population, I never shall believe." It was "trifling" to talk of repaying Africa the debt owed her by returning her sons to the coast: "I consider that the shortest way to accomplish this grand object is, to do her sons justice where ever we find them." However successful and prosperous Liberia might be, it would "never reduce" the black population in the United States. "Send 20 thousand annually to the colony, and yet this population will increase from 40 to 50 thousand yearly." Should this vast body in the United States be forgotten in "our zeal for the interest of a small colony"? Liberia, Cornish maintained, had attracted the interest, efforts, and prayers of the "christian public" in the country to the detriment of those remaining. Cornish ended on an apologetic note: "This much in answer to the gratuitous censure of the *New York Observer*, sentiments we should not have advanced at this time, but for the necessity of the case. The subject though important, we should with confidence have confided to the hands of deity."[36]

Thus, as in the editorial he had published two years earlier in *Freedom's Journal*, Cornish refrained from questioning the motives of the colonizationists. More unequivocally than previously, he portrayed the establishment of a colony in Africa as an act of charity and "a powerful engine in spreading civilisation and religion, throughout that vast continent," even though, as before, he said he would prefer the establishment of missionary stations. What he questioned was the wisdom of the enterprise, not its object: it diverted attention from the quest for justice in the United States; it diverted resources unfairly and unwisely; and its growth would never be sufficient to accommodate the natural increase in the black population in the United States. It is noteworthy, too, that Cornish perceived the notice in the *Observer* as a censure and that he issued the editorial on the subject out of a felt necessity.

What does this all mean? First, it establishes that the legend that Cornish resigned because of Russwurm's procolonization stance is just that—a legend, at best born of ignorance, if not downright maliciousness. Russwurm was not at that point a colonizationist, and Cornish was not as boldly anticolonizationist as he would become in the 1830s. Second, and more importantly, it establishes that Russwurm, *not* Cornish, was the more uncompromising of the two on the question of colonization in 1827. Cornish's depiction of the ACS and the colonizationists was far more accurate and fair than Russwurm's had ever been. Russwurm's depiction was far more impassioned and inflammatory and gave little quarter to acknowledging the complex and contradictory constituency of the ACS. Indeed, contrary to the assertions of others, it is plausible that Cornish, in many ways a rather conservative and mild man of the cloth, may have regarded Russwurm as a hothead, far too radical for his taste, especially given the way Russwurm conducted himself in the exchanges with "Wilberforce" and Miller. Cornish may very well have been frightened to continue an association with the paper, given the backlash Russwurm's pronouncements would and did provoke. Significantly, both Miller and "Wilberforce" addressed their complaint against the "junior editor" to Cornish, presumably in the hope that the "senior" man would dismiss or at least discipline Russwurm and rein in his virulent anticolonizationist tendencies. But instead of coming to the defense of his colleague and the *Journal*, Cornish resigned without ever penning a riposte to Miller and "Wilberforce." Russwurm was thus left on his own to defend himself and the project of *Freedom's Journal*. It is probably not merely coincidental that Cornish relinquished the editorship of the *Journal* just after the appearance of Miller's letter in the *New York Observer*. Both Archibald Alexander (under the guise of "Wilberforce") and Samuel Miller were respected and influential men in the Presbyterian Church and headed its main institution of learning in the country, Princeton Theological Seminary. As an ordained Presbyterian minister, Cornish was vulnerable to the wrath of such men. His protégé and fellow Presbyterian Theodore Wright, with whom he maintained a close relationship, would have provided Cornish with advance intelligence of the uproar created by *Freedom's Journal* on the Princeton campus. A student at the seminary at the time, Wright might have acted as an emissary for his teachers, Alexander and Miller, imparting warning or threat to Cornish. It is plausible that the church might have even demanded Cornish's resignation from the paper. The ACS and the colonizationists were, as Wright noted, in the ascendant at the time and had the support of the most powerful people in the nation, including the leading churchmen.[37] Only in the 1830s did they encounter sustained challenge to their hegemony. At that point an emboldened Cornish became more outspoken, even going so far as to coauthor (with Wright) a pamphlet against the ACS.[38]

Thus in the 1820s, *Freedom's Journal* was a bold, plucky, but lonely, weak, and vulnerable crusader. Benjamin Lundy supported the ACS, and William Lloyd Garrison, who later became the archenemy of the colonizationists, was himself a colonizationist before 1831.[39] Even the wealthy African American businessman James Forten of Philadelphia refrained from signing his own name when he sent letters to the *Journal* criticizing the ACS. "A Man of Colour" was all he would reveal of his identity.[40] Not until 1837, fully a decade after he wrote, and now under the protective umbrella of the growing abolitionist movement, was the name of Forten publicly attached to the letters.[41] No doubt it was from this sense of isolation and utter exposure, especially now that he was editing the *Journal* alone, that Russwurm solicited the support of the venerable Rev. Richard Allen, bishop of the African Methodist Episcopal Church of the United States, as he signed his name, to come to his aid against the attacks of the colonizationists. The bishop acquitted himself well. His critique of the colonization project was in fact more pointed than that of Cornish and accorded more closely with that of Russwurm. "Can we not discern the project of sending the free people of colour away from this country?" Allen asked rhetorically. "Is it not for the interest of the slave holder, to select, the free people of colour out of the different states, and send them to Liberia? Will it not make their slaves uneasy to see free men of colour enjoying *liberty?*" He did not doubt that many good men supported sending the free people of color to Liberia, but, said the bishop, "they are not men of colour." "This land which we have watered with our tears and our blood, is now our mother country and we are well satisfied to stay where wisdom abounds, and the gospel is free." Russwurm was delighted with the response of "that aged and devoted Minister of the Gospel."[42]

Cornish and Russwurm, the evidence suggests, parted on good terms. Printed immediately below Cornish's 1827 letter of resignation is a notice signed by Russwurm stating that as Cornish would be traveling through the country he had agreed to accept a general agency of the *Journal* and was thereby "authorized to transact any business relating to it."[43] In all subsequent issues of the paper, right up to the last one dated March 28, 1829, the Rev. S. E. Cornish was listed as the general agent. Symbolically, having Cornish as an agent was probably important and indicated some continuity under Russwurm's editorship, but in practical terms this perhaps meant little: Cornish was busy with his ministry and his agency for the New York African Free School. Further, the increase in the number of agents for the paper cannot be so readily attributed to Cornish's efforts as is frequently suggested. At the end of 1827, one agent of the paper was "C. Stockbridge, Esq." of North Yarmouth, Maine, the man who had been young Russwurm's guardian and benefactor; the agent in Portland was his childhood friend Reuben Ruby. Those in Massachusetts included not only a friend from his Boston days, David Walker, but also the venerable Rev. Thomas Paul, who had first gotten Russwurm his job in the African Free School, and with whom he later lodged in 1826 before moving to New York.

There is no evidence that Cornish wrote anything for the *Journal* after his resignation, and insofar as he had a presence in the paper at all, it was largely through his perpetual advertisements (sometimes even occupying the front page) of "Land for Sale" (real estate in upstate New York and elsewhere provided by Gerrit Smith), reports on his work for the New York African Free School, and announcements for weddings that he had conducted.[44] Certainly Russwurm felt burdened by the responsibility of bringing out a weekly paper, not only as editor but also as de facto financier. Subscribers took the paper but seldom paid (a problem that was not unique to *Freedom's Journal*); the general practice at the time was for subscribers to receive their newspapers and pay later. Cornish learned from his experience at the *Journal*, and when he started the *Rights of All* he demanded that subscribers pay in advance. (Russwurm did the same thing in Liberia when he later founded and edited the *Liberia Herald*.) By the time *Freedom's Journal* closed in March 1829, Russwurm was owed hundreds of dollars that he stood no chance of collecting.[45]

3 —

Quitting America and Its Cost

For Russwurm, doubt and disillusionment about African Americans' prospects in the United States soon set in. Even at his most combative, he had asked difficult questions that were not merely rhetorical and to which he did not have answers: "Can the *justice* of God tolerate so much iniquity and *injustice*?" and "When will the monster, prejudice, be done away, even from among the Christians?"[1] Under his sole editorship, Russwurm's *Journal,* to the astonishment and with the objections of some subscribers, began to provide an increasing amount of space to the advocates of colonization. Although the journal had always provided space for arguments contrary to its avowed editorial position, it now carried what many subscribers regarded as an alarming number of procolonization articles, mainly reprinted from the ACS's journal, the *African Repository and Colonial Journal.* By February 1829, Russwurm publicly announced his volte-face. To the consternation of his readers, he somberly declared, "Our views are materially altered." Having always maintained that when convinced of error he should hasten to acknowledge it, he believed that that moment had arrived. He explained that his change of heart was not the "hasty conclusion of a moment": he had "pondered much" on the subject and read "every article within our reach, both for and against the [ACS]." Russwurm was fully aware of the cost of his apostasy: he knew that his new "doctrines" were in opposition to those of the majority of his readers, "to many of whom we are personally known, and for whose opinions we still entertain great respect." But he was determined to stick to his new positions: "How unpopular soever they may be, *we know,* they are conscientious ones—formed from no sordid motives; but having for their basis, the good of our brethren." There was no better option than emigration to Africa: "We have carefully examined the different plans now in operation for our benefit, and none we believe, can reach half so efficiently the mass, as the plan of colonization on the coast of Africa." Russwurm thought it "mere waste of words, to talk of ever enjoying citizenship in this country: it is utterly impossible in the nature of things: all therefore who pant for th[is], must cast their eyes elsewhere."[2]

44 |

In his search for what he called a "desirable spot," Russwurm had decided upon Africa through a process of elimination. Europe, "overburdened with a starving population," was ruled out. Asia? Even if all other circumstances were favorable, distance was "an insuperable barrier." "Where then shall we look so naturally, as to Africa?" Russwurm was careful to point out that in preferring Liberia he did not wish to deprive any of the right of choice between that country and Haiti, "as [it] is not our object to say ought against Hayti or the able ruler at its head." He had to concede, however, that it was "a fact well known to all" that African Americans had strong objections against emigrating to Haiti, "arising in many cases, from the unfavourable reports of those who have returned."[3] Mindful of this fact and perhaps drawing upon the experience of his own abortive return to Jamaica, he elsewhere declared that "those who had tried their fortunes in the West Indies" had been "disappointed and unsuccessful."[4]

What triggered this apparently sudden change of heart is not at all clear. No catalyst can be identified, and it does appear, as Russwurm himself wrote, to have been a decision arrived at after an accumulation of experience and observation, capped by careful study of the limited options available to African Americans.[5] Extremely observant and sensitive, as his travel dispatches in *Freedom's Journal* powerfully demonstrate, he, like Blyden, Robert Campbell, Claude McKay, and so many other Caribbean migrants to the United States after him, simply found the degradation unendurable.[6] A highly educated and cultivated man, Russwurm was also very proud, a quality his white critics saw as arrogance,[7] and he chafed under the daily humiliation of black life in the United States, probably with less patience than his African American counterparts did, largely because he knew of other worlds—in the Caribbean, in Quebec and probably even in Maine, where he was relatively sheltered—where the disabilities of color were not as punitive. Writing of the Jim Crow degradation he had experienced on the boat from New York to Connecticut, Russwurm asked plaintively, "As I do not possess neither the humility nor patience of Job, how can I tamely submit to be so treated?"[8] In the United States, "the mere name of colour, blocks up every avenue." If the black man has the feelings of a man, "he must be sensible of the degraded station he holds in society; and from which it is impossible to rise, unless he can change the Ethiopian hue of his complexion. He may possess wealth; he may be respected; he may be learned; still all united, will avail him little; after all, he is considered a being of inferior order; and always will be, as no opportunity will ever be afforded him to cultivate or call into action the talents with which an All-wise Creator may have endowed him."[9] After living fourteen years in the United States without seeing any discernible improvement in the condition of the black population, despite their extraordinary exertions and his, Russwurm, it appears, had simply had enough and sought to leave the place as soon as possible for Liberia; some of his letters to Ralph Gurley from this time sound desperate, like the cry of a drowning man.

But no justification or explanation could assuage the wrath of his former anticolonization comrades. The controversy began immediately after Russwurm announced his new position. In a letter written on February 24, 1829, a mere ten days after his statement appeared in *Freedom's Journal*, Russwurm reported that those "few words . . . have caused me some persecution already, from the more influential of our people, and Mr. Cornish has signified his intention of answering me in this week's *Journal*." Used to standing on his own and standing up to a fight, Russwurm seemed hurt but genuinely calm: "Like [Martin] Luther . . . when dissuaded by his friends, from attending the Diet at Worms, I am determined, that nothing shall be kept back from the fear of men's frowns."[10] He was burned in effigy. The free people of color in Philadelphia were the most vociferous in their objection to Russwurm's turnabout. He reported that two "numerously attended" meetings had been held in the City of Brotherly Love against him, ending in "useless declamation." But by the time he arrived there—and he seemed unafraid of going there—in early May, the "violent persecution" "raging" against him had "considerably subsided." Somewhat scornful of his critics, Russwurm wrote: "Now, I am present, face to face to my accusers, but little has been said as yet."[11]

Russwurm remained undaunted and expressed confidence that "though some may be suspicious of the motives, still, all who know me will do me the justice to say, that the change in my views is a real one—arising from a correction of error in my former opinions."[12] His confidence was not misplaced. And it is no accident that people in Philadelphia, the city in which Russwurm had spent the least amount of time and was thus little known personally, were the ones to persecute him most viciously.

In New York, where Russwurm was best known, Cornish did not write the threatened denunciation of his former colleague and friend in *Freedom's Journal*. Months later, Cornish was still at a loss to explain Russwurm's "sudden change" of heart. As astonished as those who made "many inquiries" to him, Cornish could only regretfully dispose of the question as to why Russwurm had changed by "classing it with the other novelties of the day."[13] Sorrow, rather than anger, characterized Cornish's reaction to his former colleague's embrace of colonizationism. Not only did he refrain from ad hominem attacks upon Russwurm, but he also sent word to the ACS, during the latter's extensive trawl for references before appointing Russwurm, that his former colleague was "worthy of all confidence" and that he was "willing to bear full testimony as to R[usswurm]'s correct habits and exemplary deportment."[14] A similar response came from the Reverend Peter Williams, black pastor of St. Phillip's Episcopal Church in New York, despite his adamant opposition to the ACS. In a powerful Fourth of July speech against the colonizationists, he declared:

We are NATIVES of this country, we ask only to be treated as well as FOREIGNERS. Not a few of our fathers suffered and bled to purchase its independence; we ask only to be treated as well as those who fought against it. We have toiled to cultivate it, and to raise it to its present prosperous condition; we ask only to share equal privileges with those who come from distant lands, to enjoy the fruits of our labour. Let these moderate requests be granted, and we need not go to Africa nor anywhere else to be improved and happy. We cannot but doubt the purity of the motives of those persons who deny us these requests, and would send us to Africa to gain what they might give us at home.[15]

Nevertheless, Williams, who had worked closely with Russwurm in the founding of *Freedom's Journal* and other racial uplift efforts in New York, especially related to education, not only refrained from criticizing Russwurm when he decided to go to Africa under the auspices of the ACS but quietly lent support to his friend.[16] Despite his opposition to the ACS, Williams, as he later maintained, saw it as his "duty" to aid, "in all [his] power, on his way," any man of color who had carefully considered and was determined to emigrate to Africa. Thus, he wrote, "I helped John B. Russwurm to go to Liberia, and as a token of gratitude for my aid in the case, he sent me his thermometer, which I have now hanging up in my house." Charles C. Andrews, the white principal of the New York African Free School, also lent support to Russwurm.[17]

Russwurm's friends in Boston did not forsake him either. When doubts were raised about the *Journal* in the spring of 1828, David Walker, chief among others, vigorously defended the editor and the paper. Even after Russwurm's apostasy, Walker remained an agent of the paper, despite his strong opposition to the ACS. He published, as we have seen, the first version of his famous "Address" in Russwurm's *Journal* in December 1828, and he also kept in the paper the little advertisement of his secondhand clothing store at 42 Battle Street, Boston, right up to the last issue of *Freedom's Journal*. Even after the storm broke over Russwurm's announcement, black Bostonians sought his return as a teacher in their school. In February 1829, Russwurm reported that "the people of colour in Boston are now making an effort to replace me in my old situation in the [African] Free School." It appeared to have been a definite option for Russwurm, "*but,*" he declared in underlined words, "*my desire is to settle in the colony* [Liberia]—and to be the means of drawing many others, there, who are now as opposed to the colony as they can be."[18] Russwurm might have been ostracized by many of the free people of color in the North, but his ostracism was never universal. Contrary to the assertions of his detractors, he did not emigrate to Liberia out of material desperation or lack of prospects, let alone venality of principles.[19] If anything, his decision sprang from the growing awareness of his spiritual desperation in the suffocatingly racist environment of the United States—a reading of the American social and political landscape that told him that the North as well as the South was incapable of supporting the growth of a strong and dignified black populace enjoying the benefits of full citizenship. The "free" states were not free, he maintained:

> It must be evident that the universal emancipation so ardently desired by us & by all our friends, can never take place, unless some door is opened whereby the emancipated may be removed as fast as they drop their galling chains, to some other land besides the free states; for it is a fact, that prejudices now in our part of the country, are so high, that it is often the remark of liberal men from the south, that their free people are treated better than we are, in the boasted free states of the north. If the free states have passed no laws as yet forbidding the emigration of free persons of colour into their limits; it is no reason that they will not, as soon as they find themselves a little more burdened.[20]

"It is not our province here," he declared in one of his most somber jeremiads, "to enquire why prejudices should be in the pathway of the man of colour, all we know is, that they are there, and are ever likely to remain." Hence "we conclude," he wrote, preempting Marcus Garvey by a century, "that all efforts here, to improve the mass of coloured persons must prove abortive; and this conclusion we adopt from the evidence of our own eyes."[21] Rightly or wrongly, this was the deduction that propelled his action. Some might call it pessimism, but he regarded it as realism—a cogent and unsentimental appraisal of the situation. Toward the end of his time at the *Journal,* Russwurm seems to have also despaired about not only the obstacles thrown up by racism but also the willingness and capacity of his people to even struggle against them:

In the bosom of the most enlightened community upon the globe, we are ignorant and degraded; under the most republican government, we are denied all the rights and privileges of citizens; & what is still worse, we see no probability, that we as a community, will ever make it our earnest endeavour to rise from our ignorance and degradation. The vain & idle things of the moment occupy our minds, and woe betide the being who has the [te]merity to denounce them, and tell us what we should aim at employing our time more profitably. He is denounced in turn.[22]

But as Russwurm pointed out repeatedly, he had enemies, and explanations were of little use. While Cornish could not account for Russwurm's change of heart, others were far less modest about their powers of divination, if not explanation, and far less generous in their conclusions. The puzzle was easily solved. All they saw were sordid motives. They showered Russwurm with abuse and denunciations, venality of principle being the primary charge. As he had planned before making public his endorsement of colonization, Russwurm resigned—he was never fired—from *Freedom's Journal* in March 1829 and, with the support of the ACS, left for Liberia later that year.

A year and a half's absence from the United States did little to temper the anger against him in certain quarters. Indeed, some grew more angry with Russwurm rather than less so with the passage of time. Thus one black Philadelphian, though further provoked by Russwurm from afar, was still fuming in April 1831. Writing to William Lloyd Garrison's staunchly anticolonization newspaper, the *Liberator*, he released his barrage against Russwurm:

This John B. Russworm *[sic]* is known, I presume, to every one of us; his ingratitude is but too deeply stamped on the minds of many, who have been requited in a manner, which neither time nor space will ever obliterate. After he subverted the pledge he made to his colored brethren, he left, to our satisfaction, his country—suffused with shame—and branded with the stigma of disgrace—to dwell in that land for which the temptor MONEY caused him to avow his preferment. He has resided there more than a year, publishing doubtless to the satisfaction of his supporters, their many glorious schemes, and eulogizing to the very skies the prosperity of his goodly LIBERIA. Not contented with lauding the retreat in which and about which he may flame with impunity, he has the audacity to reprove those with whom he played the traitor. Out of much he said, let this suffice as example:

"Before God, we know of no other home for the man of color, of republican principles, than Africa. Has he no ambition? Is he dead to everything noble? Is he contented with his condition? Let him remain in America."

To this we reply, that before God, we know of no surer burial place than Africa, for men of any color; that we will never envy John B. Russwurm his ambition; and that we will pray God, that his notions of nobleness may never enter our hearts.[23]

Another correspondent from the same city and to the same publication was equally upset with Russwurm, who, he said, when employed in the editorial department of *Freedom's Journal,* had been "paid for services which were not rendered." He continued:

> Mr. Russwurm tells us, he knows no other home for us than Africa. If he were in Philadelphia, and would make this assertion to me, I would tell him it was a palpable falsehood, and would prove it by his former editorial documents. I would ask whether Mr. R. would have gone to Africa even on a visit, had he been in flourishing circumstances? I answer, no. I am too sensible of this fact, that he would as reluctantly fall victim to the lion, the tiger, the serpent, or the climate, as any one of us: it was real necessity that drove him to seek in Africa an abiding home, as he terms it; and as his usefulness is entirely lost to the people, I sincerely pray that he may have the honor to live and also die there.[24]

Russwurm was not without his defenders. A Portland, Maine, newspaper came to the aid of one of their own:

> We perceive that the motives of this gentleman [Russwurm] in becoming a convert to the "Colonization scheme," are bitterly impeached by a correspondent of the *Liberator.* There ought to be some very prominent fact to justify the uttering of a suspicion to the prejudice of his integrity. He was educated in this neighborhood; his family connections are our neighbors; his personal acquaintances are numerous, and their confidence in his honesty unbounded. No young man, probably, has gone out from us with a fairer moral character. An unfavorable change is not, indeed, an impossible thing; but there must be very substantial evidence of apostasy from moral rectitude, to obtain any credence here. So much we feel it our duty to say, as the accused is far away, and cannot defend himself.

A reasonable enough argument, one might think. But Garrison, a late-comer to the anticolonization cause, one who was stumping for the ACS when Russwurm was opposing it, would have none of it, and simply reprinted this defense of Russwurm in order to attack it. "Mr Russwurm's character, as an intelligent and moral man, has never been impeached by us," he declared, as he immediately contradicted himself: "If his vanity had not been superior to his judgment, and his love of distinction greater than his regard for consistency, he would never have been seduced away to Liberia. Nobody supposes that he was openly bribed; but many believe that the Colonization Society held out extraordinary inducements to secure his conversion. It must be remembered that Mr. R., as Editor of *Freedom's Journal*, was bitterly opposed to the Society; but all at once, when his pecuniary affairs were desperate at home, he mysteriously altered his mind, and went to Liberia."[25] From another angle, a Washington, D.C., newspaper criticized the *Liberator* for accusing the ACS of "*bribing* Mr. Russwurm to change his opinions." The writer, who evidently had close connections to the ACS, went on to assert: "We happen to be well acquainted with the circumstances of Mr. Russwurm's conversion and emigration to Liberia. *We know*, that so far from being *bribed* a *penalty* was inflicted upon him by the Society, on account of his former hostility, and he was required to retract his errors in the same paper by which they had been published, before the Society would permit him to go to Liberia. We have seen the documents." Garrison dismissed the argument. "Our readers already understand, without further explanation, in what manner we believe Mr. Russwurm to have been influenced in his 'conversion and emigration to Liberia,'" he wrote. "A man is bought in more ways than one. As to the 'penalty which was inflicted upon him by the Society,' we dare say Benedict Arnold would have incurred a similar one after *his* conversion, to please his purchasers, had they required it."[26]

Even the gentle and gentlemanly Cornish was later to denounce Russwurm in the most intemperate tones, placing his former colleague and comrade, as Garrison had seven years earlier, in the company of Benedict Arnold (the American synonym for traitor ever since the Revolution) and southern slaveholders. Writing in January 1838, almost nine years after Russwurm had departed from the United States, he accused his former colleague of subscribing to the "dangerous doctrine" of "Take Care of Number One"—which words formed the title of his editorial. This doctrine, he declared, had "carried Mr. Russwurm to Liberia," "made Arnold sell his country, and . . . plunged the South into the guilt and shame of a cruel system of slavery." That he wrote this editorial with the intention of chiding African Americans into supporting his journalistic efforts hardly excused the attack on Russwurm.[27]

The denunciations of Russwurm tell of the strong feelings his action elicited among some African Americans, and of the remarkable fear and loathing of colonizationists and even emigrationists (those who advocated emigration independent of the ACS project) in some quarters, but nothing of the man's real motives. They also tell of the genuine feeling of betrayal: their golden boy, their "first" college graduate (as they all thought he was at the time), their brave black knight who took on and vanquished the likes of "Wilberforce" and Miller, as well as the ACS itself, had suddenly told them he was mistaken and had forsaken them for the enemy camp, the diabolical ACS. It *was* bitter stuff to swallow. If they felt betrayed and hurt, Russwurm also felt the sting of their attacks. He did not hesitate to hit back. But he was at times remarkably philosophical and detached about the whole affair. "I know that I have enemies among our people who have left no stone unturned to injure my reputation—and I assure you, that the change in my views has tended nothing to diminish their number," he wrote Gurley in July 1829. "I must not wonder at the persecution I have undergone however, as any person placed in my situation would have had nearly the like difficulties to encounter."[28]

Contrary to the claims of his detractors, all the evidence suggests that Russwurm had a genuine change of heart and that he was courageous enough to make it public and act upon it. He entertained the grand and noble idea of building a dignified home in Africa for the children of the diaspora in their ancestral homeland, a "portion of the globe" where "the Man of Colour freed from the fetters and prejudice, and degradation, under which he labours in this land, may walk forth in all the majesty of his creation—a new born creature—a *Free Man!*"[29] A fortnight before writing those words, in a letter to Gurley, Russwurm noted: "If I know my own heart, I can truly say, that I have not a selfish wish in placing myself under the patronage of the [ACS]; usefulness in my day & generation, is what I principally court."[30]

Remarkably, despite the avalanche of abuse heaped upon him and the colonization project, Russwurm not only remained convinced of the rightness of his decision but also repeatedly expressed confidence that his critics would soon see the errors of their ways. He *was* at times self-righteous. Moreover, he saw growing evidence that the colonization argument was gaining ground among the free people of color, evidence no one else had apparently discerned. In the very letter from Philadelphia in which he reported on the "violent persecution" against him there, Russwurm could still write: "The cause is gaining ground in the minds of many who are ashamed to acknowledge it; and the day I believe is not far distant, when all our people who would be an accession to the colony, will be as anxious to locate themselves there, as foreigners now are of emigrating to America."[31] That day, in fact, never came—a massive miscalculation on Russwurm's part that issued, I think, from his own enormous and blinding enthusiasm for the colonization project and his inability to comprehend how any of his peers would choose to remain in the United States, given the injustices and indignities they had to suffer. He underestimated the widespread fear among African Americans that migration to Liberia meant an early grave; that the many discouraging, if exaggerated, reports from Liberia had frightened would-be emigrants; that some even chose to remain in bondage rather than go to Liberia; that many had imbibed negative ideas about Africa abroad in American society and wished to have no association with the continent; that African Americans had grown attached to American soil, the land of their birth; and that some genuinely disbelieved that any white person, especially given the ACS's associations with slaveholders, could have their interest at heart—in some parts, rumor spread that those who went on the ships for Liberia were being sold into slavery.[32] Given these obstacles to emigration, which abolitionist opposition added to from the 1830s, what is remarkable is not that so few went but that so many chose to go to Liberia. But blinded by his own optimism about colonization and by an unwavering confidence in his own judgment, Russwurm found the reluctance of others to emigrate all the more incomprehensible and achingly disappointing.

His Philadelphia critics would have been surprised to learn that the ACS did not welcome Russwurm with open arms and that its board did not make Russwurm rich. Ralph Gurley, its secretary, had attempted to recruit Russwurm soon after his graduation and had always entertained the idea of sending Russwurm to Liberia under the auspices of the ACS.[33] But some board members of the ACS were now suspicious, especially given Russwurm's previous position and bitter attacks against them. Russwurm understood their doubts. "I cannot think harshly of [them], when I call to mind, how warm an opposition champion I have been. It caused me to smile however," he admitted to Gurley. "As I have publicly renounced my former errors, all doubts I hope will now be removed from the minds of the most doubting."[34] He was wrong. The board continued, long after his February 14 statement in *Freedom's Journal*, to solicit references from virtually everyone of standing who knew Russwurm. Seven months passed between the time Russwurm made his desire known to Gurley (January 1829) and the final approval (July 1829) by the board to employ him. The ACS's hesitation in appointing Russwurm was not matched by any reticence to make the most of his change of heart. Under the caption "Candid Acknowledgment of Error," the *African Repository* gleefully announced: "The Editor of Freedom's Journal, Mr. Russwurm, (a very respectable, and well educated coloured man in New York,) who has for several years, been decidedly and actively opposed to the Colonization Society, in his paper of 14th February, candidly and honourably confesses that his opinions in regard to our Institution, have become entirely changed." The *Repository* followed the note by reprinting Russwurm's editorial in its entirety.[35] Russwurm was finally appointed to the office of superintendent of schools in Liberia and was charged with reviving the short-lived if not stillborn *Liberia Herald*.

It is difficult to doubt Russwurm's seriousness and nobility of purpose after reading his public pronouncements as expressed in the *Journal* and his private letters to the ACS prior to leaving for Liberia. Even before he was formally offered a position, he volunteered to hone his printing skills at the Rensselaer School in upstate New York. He sought to understand the different school and pedagogic systems that might be appropriate for Liberia. C. C. Andrews of the New York African Free School kindly offered him the opportunity to learn about the "mutual instruction" methods used there. But Russwurm also wanted to learn more of the Pestalozzian method of instruction (so called after its Swiss pioneer, Johann Heinrich Pestalozzi) and planned to do so while in Boston, "where his [Pestalozzi's] system is better understood than elsewhere" in the United States. In another letter he informed the ACS that with the present limited population of the colony, the Boston Free School system, with which Russwurm was intimately acquainted, could be introduced in Liberia "to much advantage." As he told Gurley, "I should like to *export* all the knowledge I could from the [United States]" to Liberia. He also sought to export books: were Gurley to send him a letter of authorization, he would be happy to seek donations in Boston not only to establish an academy in Liberia but also to augment the colony's library. He offered to carry additional types for the printing press in Liberia and was sorry that his offer to take charge of and accompany a group of African recaptives (Africans rescued from slave ships on the high seas) back to Africa could not be accommodated.[36]

Russwurm traveled to Maine in August and visited his relatives in North Yarmouth. He apparently stayed long enough in the state to receive his master of arts degree from Bowdoin at the beginning of September.[37] But from the end of March, when he relinquished his editorship of the *Journal,* Russwurm devoted much of his time to settling his business affairs. He was in debt, but he was owed considerably more than he himself owed. He soon realized that he would never be able to collect all that was owed him. "From the general poverty of our people, I find great difficulty in collecting, and long to see an end to the business," he told Gurley. Russwurm not only understood the predicament of his debtors, most of whom were delinquent subscribers to the *Journal*, but became reconciled to the fact that he would just about be able to collect enough from the "considerable amount" owed him "in different parts of the Union" to pay off his own debts[38]—so much for the accusation that Russwurm had not rendered services that he was paid for! (His Philadelphian accuser was probably one of his numerous delinquent debtors.) Russwurm was "a loser, not a gainer by his labours," Thomas Jennings and Peter Williams, associates of the *Journal*, later pointed out.[39] Little wonder that Russwurm complained of the "thankless" and "most trying" nature of his job as editor.[40] That he was not fired was probably due to the fact that no one was there to fire him. Though some had contributed at the founding of the paper—exactly who and how much, we do not know—by the time Cornish left, Russwurm was officially the editor as well as the "proprietor" of *Freedom's Journal*.[41] Russwurm seems to have survived partly through teaching—he taught evening classes at the African Free School—rather than from income provided by the *Journal*.[42] Throughout the life of the paper, the subscription rate remained at $3 annually, payable in two half-yearly amounts in advance, or $2.50 if paid at the beginning of the subscription. But from the debts that accrued, it is clear that the editors never followed their own guidelines. As we have seen, even Professor Miller at Princeton received his copies for months on end without paying his subscription fees. Financial difficulties were exacerbated by cancellations of subscription by a substantial number of white subscribers sympathetic to the ACS in disagreement with the *Journal's* criticism of the colonization project. Russwurm's dispute with Miller, as revealed earlier, lost him the support of those at Princeton, at least, who had previously subscribed. Like the subscription rates, those for advertisement remained the same for the life of the *Journal*. The rates were, apparently, relatively moderate: for over twelve lines and not exceeding twenty-two, the first insertion was seventy-five cents, for each repetition it was reduced to thirty-eight cents; for persons advertising over the year it was reduced by 15 percent, and for those who advertised for 3 months it was reduced by 6 percent. The *Journal* seems to have done reasonably well in this area, generally carrying two pages of advertisement in every issue. But how much of the money for these it actually received is another matter, and some of the debts owed him that Russwurm complained of were probably incurred by delinquent advertisers and not just subscribers who could not or would not pay up.

Liberal-minded wealthy whites and the more well-heeled among the black population would from time to time give money to the paper, especially when it seemed on the brink of going under.[43] Welcome though this was, the paper's survival remained uncertain and precarious over the two years. Russwurm managed to put out the *Journal* by himself and with the periodic support of two young black apprentice printers, whom he referred to simply as "my two young men" and "my two boys."[44] In his final editorial, "To Our Patrons," he revealed that the *Journal* had been started with the understanding that the whole of his time would be devoted to editorial work and that none of the manual labor would fall upon him, "but how disappointed we have been, we need not mention." He admitted that the paper had often been issued with many typographical errors, "which when our inexperience in printing is taken into account, should not be matter of much surprise." He was therefore not astonished that he had been "slandered by the villainous— that our name is a byword among the more ignorant, for what less could we expect?"[45] At the end of 1828 he noted that "to suit the taste of a few is always difficult; more especially where the great body consider themselves as competent judges, and more than qualified, to issue such a publication as ours. We do not intend to complain; but we really hope, some of our learned advisers will undertake the publication of a journal; they will then find, that it is invariably easier to advise than to perform."[46]

In many ways, including financially, *Freedom's Journal* was an albatross. It probably had over eight hundred subscribers, but that tells us nothing of the income received, which was far below the amount the subscription would suggest. In the meantime, the actual number of readers of the *Journal,* by all accounts, far exceeded the actual number of subscribers, since the paper was widely shared.[47] How Russwurm managed to produce the paper alone for eighteen months under these extraordinary constraints remains a bit of a mystery. Cornish launched the *Rights of All* at the end of May 1829 and by August complained that he was more than $170 "out of pocket." He too made the initial mistake of sending out the paper to the subscribers before they paid. The subscription terms called for a dollar in advance or two dollars otherwise. He complained that from the recipients of eight hundred copies he had sent out monthly he had "only received 36 dollars and 50 cents." Despite the public appeal for support of the *Rights of All* by respected figures in the community, such as Thomas Jennings and Peter Williams, by October 1829, a mere six months after it began with such fanfare, the *Rights of All* was no more.[48] That *Freedom's Journal* was able to last as long as it did was due not so much to the "magnanimity of [its] editors," as one scholar recently suggests, as to the magnanimity of Russwurm, who, after all, was the sole editor and publisher of the journal for eighteen months of its twenty-four-month life.[49]

Russwurm's personal sacrifice was great, but what irked him most was the audacity of those "bold enough" to accuse him of "improper motives." "My character," he told Gurley, "is my all, and the man who attempts to injure me by assailing it, in reality, robs me of every thing."[50] This consideration led him to ask in one of his later editorials: "Who has made half the sacrifice we have to oppose the Colonization society? who has laboured half so much by night and by day for the same end? who has had to bear the brunt of the battle, while those who led us into action, were sitting quietly at home? who has suffered so much for conscience' sake?" Let none consider these as "vain boastings," he pleaded. "We merely insert them to refresh the memories of those, who are now loud in denouncing our change."[51]

Russwurm never "killed" the *Journal*, as one writer claimed.[52] Despite the rancorous atmosphere, he wished the paper well and anticipated and prepared for its continuation. "I expect *Freedom's Journal* will be continued under the care of Mr. Cornish," he wrote Gurley, fully a month before his final issue.[53] He had apparently already discussed the future of the *Journal* with Cornish. And in the final issue itself he announced on the editorial page: "We are authorized by Mr. Cornish (who succeeds us in the publication of the *Journal*) to state that the next No. will appear during the first week of May: in the meanwhile it is his urgent request, that exertions be used by the different agents to enlarge the subscription list."[54] (In a note on the same page he asked the paper's agents "in different places" to accept his "feeble thanks for their exertions on behalf of *Freedom's Journal*.") Presumably, the press, types, and other equipment were in place for Cornish to continue the work. But the next issue of *Freedom's Journal*, did not appear in the first week of May; it never appeared at all. Instead, on May 29, 1829, the *Rights of All*, edited by Cornish, made its debut.

In his farewell editorial, which was at once tender and bitter, Russwurm ended with the following words: "Prepared, we entered the list; and unvanquished we retire, with the hope that the talent committed to our care, may yet be exerted under more favorable auspices, and upon minds more likely to appreciate its value."[55] In late September 1829, after a brief visit to see his friends in Boston and his family in Maine, John Brown Russwurm sailed from Baltimore for Liberia.

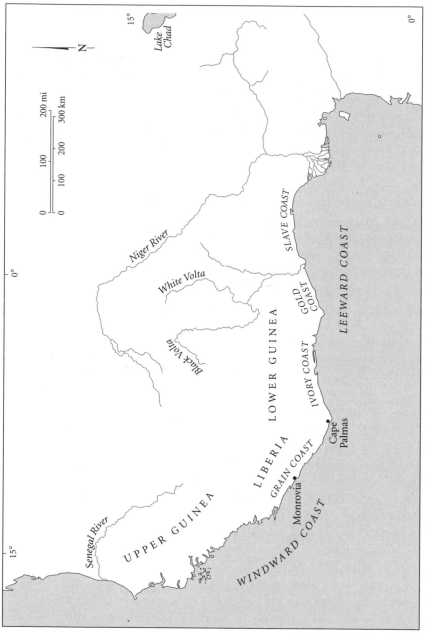

Liberia and its neighbors in the early nineteenth century

4

"We Have Found a Haven"

In the Land of His Fathers

Russwurm arrived in Monrovia on November 12, 1829, fifty-eight days after leaving Baltimore. As he wrote afterwards, it was an "uncommonly long passage," even for the age of sails. This was largely because his ship entered the doldrums twice: twelve days the first time and another ten days off the Cape Verde Islands. Still, Russwurm had no complaints, the captain treated him with the "greatest politeness," and everyone landed in good health. He rejoiced on arriving in the "land of [his] fathers." "I cannot describe what were my first sensations upon landing," he wrote to a friend less than a week after reaching Monrovia.[1] Like Edward Blyden, Alexander Crummell, and so many other New World Pan-Africanists after him, Russwurm saw his arrival as much more than an individual migration; it was to him a fulfillment of prophecy, a part of the process leading toward the redemption of Africa. But accompanying the elation of arrival was the New World arrogance of "civilizing" Africa, which afflicted virtually all of the nineteenth-century black intellectuals who sought to make a home on the continent.[2] "I am not sorry," he reported, "that my feet now rest on 'terra firma,' and in the land of my fathers, believing as I do that it is decreed by Him who reigns above, that the descendants of Africa now in America must return and assist in the great work of evangelizing and civilizing the land: the decree has gone forth, that 'Ethiopia shall stretch her hands unto God;' and were you here one Sabbath, you would believe that the commencement of prophecy was taking place." Like his postrevolutionary Haitians, the African American colonists in Liberia had been utterly transformed by the new life in Africa: "Ah! it is so pleasing to behold men who formerly groaned under oppression, walking in all the dignity of human nature, feeling and acting like men who had some great interest at stake."[3]

Alert and curious, within less than a week of his arrival, Russwurm had already developed a good preliminary assessment of the lay of the land: the religious life and institutions of the community; the material culture of the colonists, especially the condition of their houses; the health and economic activity of the colonists, especially trading; the recaptured Africans; and the Mandingoes, practitioners of Islam and formidable traders ("a settler must be uncommonly shrewd, if he gets the better of one in a bargain"). Russwurm liked and admired the Mandingoes who turned up to see him. They were keen to hear him read from one of his Greek books, and they in turned read to him and prayed in Arabic, which reminded him of his friend Prince Abdul Rahman Ibrihima. Russwurm had gathered information about King Boatswain, as the colonists and whites called Sao Boso, the leader of the most powerful African community in the region, whom he dubbed "the Napoleon of these wilds." But most of all, he had quickly developed a good idea of what was needed educationally. There was only one school in Monrovia, taught by a Mr. Shepherd, a colonist from Richmond, Virginia. "The cause of education has not yet received that attention from all which it ought," he told Plumley, agent of the ACS. Shepherd complained that he had not received the support promised. "He says he is almost discouraged," Russwurm told Plumley. "I have endeavored to encourage him, knowing from experience that of all men who labor in behalf of the public, teachers generally receive poor pay. It is an unthankful office; and did not we look beyond the present hour, our hearts would faint within us." There was need for an academy and more schools, Russwurm reported. "Shall we tell you that our children are perishing from lack of instruction? Shall the Macedonian cry come to your ears, and we be left to perish? I hope for better things." He attended an examination of Shepherd's school and was impressed with the performance of the children, who recited their grammar and geography. Shepherd needed more space—he had only thirty children in the school—and there was need for an infant school. Russwurm himself could train such teachers. Could not the people in New England, "the land of schools," lend their assistance? Russwurm inquired.[4]

Driven, passionate, and eager, Russwurm not only took on the job of superintendent of schools but also simultaneously served as colonial secretary, one of the few important positions in the administration of the colony that was open to election by the colonists. As if this were not enough, Russwurm combined these positions while effectively launching and editing the *Liberia Herald* and serving as a partner in a merchant house he established with his Afro-Virginian friend Joseph Dailey.[5] The number of hats Russwurm wore during these early years of the colony's founding reflected not only his remarkable qualities and qualifications but also the dearth of similarly educated black people in Liberia at the time, a major problem for the colonizationists that took almost a generation to overcome. As late as 1842, when he was governor of the Maryland colony in Liberia, Russwurm lamented that he could find no one to replace his recently deceased colonial secretary, John Revey, despite turning his eyes to "every quarter of Liberia." Unlike Russwurm, Revey was not a member of that very rare species, the black college graduate. He in fact had gone to Liberia two decades earlier at the age of sixteen "with an imperfect education, such as the New York free schools for colored children afforded," and had augmented it largely through studying on his own. Yet so undereducated were the Liberian population that Revey's death posed a major challenge. "The idea is painful," Russwurm noted, "that we have not an individual to fill his place."[6]

Russwurm was profoundly aware of the problem of a practically nonexistent educated personnel in Liberia but could see no way around it. Drawing up a balance sheet of the accomplishments of the *Herald* on its first anniversary, Russwurm explained that he had hoped to do more with the paper but that the "poor state" of his health and the "various duties devolved upon [him] during the greater part of the time" had prevented him from doing so. "The whole of a man's time should be devoted to the *Herald*," he continued, "and from having other duties to perform, we have considered ourselves merely as temporary until some better qualified person could be obtained."[7]

Relaunched in 1830 after an abortive attempt four years earlier, Russwurm's *Herald* was effectively West Africa's, and probably the continent's, first black newspaper.[8] With the motto "Freedom is the Brilliant Gift of Heaven," the first issue, just like *Freedom's Journal*, emphasized the progressive role of education and Russwurm's commitment to its dissemination. In one of his 1827 dispatches from Connecticut, Russwurm expressed his deep "disappointment and pity" that some of the "brethren" he had met on the boat had not read *Freedom's Journal* but had had the audacity to make "ignorant observations" concerning the paper. "Could I help grieving for their ignorance? . . . Could I help feeling deeply anxious upon the subject of African Education?" he asked rhetorically.

Let every other thing be done to improve our condition, all our labour will be in vain, if this forms not the ground work—the grand Archimedean lever. How important, then, that all our leading men should have a due sense of its inestimable value—should strive all in their power, though deprived themselves in early life, from circumstances beyond their controul, to disseminate it. Truly it is the pearl above all earthly value, one particle of which, all the mines of Golconda and Potosi cannot purchase. So entirely am I devoted to the cause of Education, that all others seem to me of minor consequence; and while in meditation upon it, all others are forgotten.[9]

The same passion and commitment abided with him in Liberia, and he seems to have perceived the paper as an organ for his superintendency of schools.

Like black nationalists before and after, Russwurm advocated self-improvement through education. In words almost identical to those of Garvey a century later, Russwurm, now residing in Liberia, wrote:

Of all employments to which a rational being can devote his leisure hours, that of self-improvement, is the most honorable, profitable and durable. There is no station, to which such an one, especially, if a young man, may not qualify himself for in the process of time, and in a free government like ours, aspire after. It is true, such an effort is the labor of days, months and years, but what then? [D]oes the distant prospect of success deter the merchant from shipping his goods to foreign countries—does the prospect of rough and stormy weather, and gales ahead, deter the adventurous mariner from the ocean?

Moreover, without education "no government can long exist in a state of freedom: it is the link which binds man to his fellowman, & teaches him his duty to his kindred, his country, and his God." Russwurm narrated the role that education had played in the advancement of Europe and America and counseled emulation. Africa, however, was no newcomer to the advancement of knowledge: "As low as Africa has descended in the scale of nations, she can with propriety claim the invention of letters, as the honor rests between the Egyptians & Ethiopians."[10] The opening of each school was a moment for rejoicing; the arrival of more teachers and books, an occasion for celebration. And Russwurm announced with pride the introduction of free public education in the colony. He repeatedly called for schools for the recaptured Africans in their settlement known as New Georgia. "Ever . . . an advocate of early education," Russwurm in 1831 again called for infant schools in the colony. He was especially keen on such a provision being made available to the children of native Africans so that they might begin at an early age the process of self-reliance and self-development: "The deaths which have occurred among Missionaries on this coast, demonstrate pretty conclusively, that if Africa is ever to be civilized, the work must be effected by her children, who have been prepared for the work. And who will prepare them?"[11] His advocacy of education was unrelenting and vociferous. To Russwurm, education was not only vital to individual growth and development but the "object which we consider of most vital importance to the future prosperity of the Colony."[12]

His pleas for help were constant. "Our friends in America," Russwurm editorialized in 1831, "can hardly conceive the great need we stand in of able instructors, and the many openings which daily offer for the labours of teachers. For centuries to come our constant cry must be, 'come over and help us.'"[13] In 1832, he was glad that free schools had now been in each of the three settlements for over a year, and he had every reason to believe that "great blessings have been conferred on the rising generation by their establishment." But he was not easily satisfied: "Our wants are great, the Recaptured Africans are unprovided for, and we stand in much need of an higher school, into which our most promising lads from the different settlements may be removed."[14] Though very progressive on the woman question, Russwurm failed to call for a high school for girls.[15] Primary education, however, was made equally available to boys and girls in the colony. Russwurm rightly perceived the much wider import of education for the development of the colony and the standing of the African in the world. It was for him an urgent matter, and he pressed it hard. "If our friends at home wish to see the experiment fairly tested, of a colony composed of such material as ours, making advances in knowledge and civilization, give us schools and competent teachers," he pleaded. "Let the strictest economy be practiced in every other department, but let teachers be amply compensated." He continued:

The African for ages has been unjustly reproached for want of genius & incapacity to acquire the more abstruse branches of education, but let the experiment be tried on Africa's soil, and we shall see whether the descendant of Africa, in the land of his forefathers, freed from the contumely, which daily looks down upon him in America, will not satisfy the most prejudiced that all are the workmanship of one God, who has allotted to his African as well as his American children, a diversity of gifts.

In the providence of God, we trust the day is not far distant, when we shall see worthy successors to those renowned men of ancient Africa, who were born and reared on its soil. Africa has been deemed the land of monsters, henceforth let it be the land of promise to all her descendants.[16]

As he had done in *Freedom's Journal*, Russwurm wrote in the *Herald* articles on self-improvement and education such as "Maxims for Parents," and "Advice to the Young." In "Every Man the Architect of His Own Fortune," which he had previously published in *Freedom's Journal* in 1828, Russwurm provided his readers with a deep and unsparing meditation on self-improvement and self-fashioning.[17] And he carried in the *Herald* a short manual, "How to Teach a Child to Read," written by his friend the Rev. T. H. Gallaudet, formerly of the American Deaf and Dumb Asylum in Hartford. Russwurm had visited the school in 1827 and had been profoundly impressed and moved by the work done there.[18]

But even going by the incomplete extant files of the *Herald*, it is evident that the paper covered a wide range of other subjects. The local developments in Liberia, especially wars in the hinterland, trade, and agriculture, attracted wide coverage. The slave trade, both locally and internationally, was a frequent topic of reportage. Russwurm himself wrote a long article in several parts entitled "The System of Slavery: Sanctioned or Condemned by Scripture?" and a small note on the origin of the modern slave trade in the Americas. He was remarkably well informed of developments in the wider world and kept his readers apprised of international affairs, especially the turbulence in Europe that would later be dubbed the "age of revolution." In 1831 he wrote a long essay, which ran over a number of issues of the *Herald*, entitled "A Sketch of the Immediate Cause of the French Revolution," focusing not on the period before 1789 but on the turmoil beginning in 1814 and extending to his day. Developments in Martinique were reported, and anything Haitian was also carried in the paper. His fascination with the black republic had not waned with time and distance. When Charles Mackenzie, a former British diplomat, published a two-volume book entitled *Notes on Haiti, Made during a Residence in That Republic*, Russwurm read it and within a year of its appearance put it to use in the *Herald*, carrying excerpts from it under the title "Toussaint, Christophe, Petion" in order to spread the glory and challenges of the Haitian Revolution to his fellow Liberians. Russwurm devoted almost three-quarters of a page to a biographical portrait of Tadeusz Kosciuszko, the hero of Polish nationalism and the American Revolution, making particular note of Kosciuszko's freeing of his serfs, but apparently ignorant of Kosciuszko's wider abolitionist impulses, which Jefferson had betrayed. "The name of KOSCIU[S]KO *[sic]* will be pronounced with veneration as long as there exists beings who know virtue and cherish liberty," concluded Russwurm. The *Herald* reported the death and funeral of Simón Bolívar—"this great and good man," Russwurm called him—and printed the full text of the inscription on his tomb at Cartagena, Colombia.[19]

The *Liberia Herald* quickly became a leading newspaper, demanded at home as well as elsewhere in West Africa and the United States, where its agents operated. Its articles, especially editorials, were frequently reprinted in American publications, such as the ACS's *African Repository and Colonial Journal*. Russwurm continued to preach the virtues of colonization, and the reprinting in the United States of one of his editorials from the *Liberia Herald* on the subject triggered the renewed denunciations of Russwurm that came chiefly out of Philadelphia in 1831. Outside Liberia itself, developments in the United States, more than anywhere else, attracted Russwurm's unwavering attention. In addition to receiving publications and news from arriving passengers in Monrovia, he kept abreast of events across the Atlantic through a large circle of correspondents, black and white. He noted with horror the developments in Ohio in 1829 when the "Black Laws" were enforced and mobs attacked unoffending black citizens in the state. Probably as many as two thousand black Ohioans, mainly from Cincinnati, the center of the anti-black riot, left the state for Canada in 1829 and 1830. Russwurm had accurately predicted the passage and implementation of such laws, but he took no joy in the fulfillment of his prediction—"God forbid, that we should undertake to justify the passing and putting such into execution"—though he could not help noting, somewhat immodestly: "As the experienced mariner foresees the approaching tornado, for hours, before it actually comes on and takes in sails and prepares for the worst, so did we foretell, and give notice of what was to be apprehended." Unlike the unfortunate people in Ohio and elsewhere, Russwurm continued, "We have found a haven, to which we invite all our race, who have the independence to think for themselves, and a courage to dare the worst, in pursuit of *Freedom*." Knowing the reputation of Liberia as a graveyard, Russwurm, ever the propagandist of the colony, attempted to assuage the fear by telling his readers that all new countries were subject to certain diseases and that Liberia was no more subject to disease than others.[20] Canada was not the solution: "Do not the Resolutions of the Legislature of U[pper] Canada, speak volumes? Are they [the black refugees] not seen as intruders?" Would not the prejudices of Ohio be "planted and matured in Canada?" Answering his own questions, he concluded, "It requires no prophetic eye to foretell that to them and their posterity, there is no abiding place on the other side of the Atlantic. Canada will hardly afford them a temporary shelter against the bleak winds of a winter."[21] The Haitian option he now dismissed even more categorically than he had earlier: "The experiment has been tried, and hundreds have returned back; with these words in their mouths, 'if we are to be slaves, let us be slaves in America.'"[22] It was in his editorial on the Ohio crisis that he expressed the words that so offended his detractors in Philadelphia: "Before God, we know of no other home for the man of color, of republican principles, than Africa. Has he no ambition? Is he dead to every thing noble? Is he contented with his condition? Let him remain in America: Let him who might here be an honor to society,—remain a sojourner in a land where it is impossible to be otherwise. His spirit is extinct, and his friends may as well bury him *now*."[23]

But neither Russwurm's cajoling nor his hectoring helped to increase the number of emigrants; his vigorous defense of Liberia probably helped to boost flagging morale in Liberia and pleased the colonizationists in America, but it seemed to have done little else. For he persuaded relatively few, and fewer than he was willing to admit. Only a small number of even those who escaped the pogrom in Cincinnati, let alone those in the rest of Ohio, chose Liberia as a haven.[24] One of the two young black printers who worked with him on *Freedom's Journal* had promised to emigrate and continue to work with Russwurm in Liberia if a printing position could be secured for him. Before leaving for Africa, Russwurm persuaded the ACS to make the would-be emigrant an offer, but within a month he had to write back to Gurley with disappointing news: "My young man upon whose faithfulness and skill I counted considerably, declines going for the *present,* having a great desire to finish his trade here [New York City]; and probably like many others, is of the opinion, that I ought to embark first, as a *pioneer* in the good cause."[25] Russwurm's young printer might have been frightened from the idea of going by those who thought that Liberia was a "pestiferous Golgotha," a graveyard for both blacks and whites.[26] You first, Mr. Russwurm! His young man never went to Liberia. Russwurm was similarly unsuccessful in attracting his close friend Edward Jones to join him in the colony, despite his flattering entreaties:

I long to see young men, who are now wasting the best of their days in the United States, flocking to this land as the last asylum to the unfortunate— I long for the time when you, my dear friend, shall land on the shores of Africa, a messenger of that Gospel which proclaims liberty to the captive, and light to those who sat in great darkness! Oh, my friend, you have a wide career of usefulness before you, and may that Being who has promised his support to his followers ever be nigh to you, and strengthen and make you a second Paul to this Gentile people! Our time is but short in this transitory world, and it therefore becomes us to labour with all our might, lest the darkness overtake us before we are aware of it.[27]

Jones, who had graduated from Amherst College two weeks before Russwurm's own graduation from Bowdoin, had become friends with Russwurm and for a time had worked with the latter on *Freedom's Journal*. The friendship was such that in 1828 Russwurm, despite his animus at the time toward the ACS, contacted them on behalf of Jones, who sought funds from the society to finance his studying medicine before emigrating to Liberia. Russwurm in fact went so far as to assure Gurley that if the same offer tendered to himself by the ACS in 1826 (and apparently repeated in 1828) were made to Jones, Jones would certainly accept "with pleasure." Jones, Russwurm pointed out, was "a young man of fine talent and liberally educated," and he expressed confidence that "one so well qualified could not be found among our colored brethren."[28] Despite Russwurm's valiant effort, Jones did not get the support of the society for medical training and in the end studied theology at Andover Theological Seminary and the African Mission School in Hartford, Connecticut, before his ordination in the Episcopal Church in 1830. But for reasons that remain unclear, and to Russwurm's chagrin, Jones did not go to Liberia. He instead chose to emigrate to the British colony of Sierra Leone, established earlier and on a similar basis to that of Liberia. The Church Missionary Society, based in Britain, exercised great influence in Sierra Leone. This fact might have influenced Jones, the Episcopalian, to choose the British colony over Liberia. There he spent the remainder of his career as a missionary, journalist, and educationalist, becoming principal of Fourah Bay College, West Africa's leading institution of higher learning.[29]

Russwurm had hoped to attract a solid cadre of educated, enterprising African Americans, especially from the urban North, committed to the cause of creating a new nation of refuge in Africa. But the overwhelming majority of those who chose Liberia were in more desperate circumstances. Many were from the South and had been recently manumitted on condition of immediate emigration to Africa; in Russwurm's view they generally had little experience of self-reliance and the enterprising spirit that the new colony required. Moreover, a disproportionately large number of emigrants to Liberia were female, and this sexual imbalance retarded the growth of the colony. At times Russwurm despaired of ever attracting sufficient emigrants of any kind to make the enterprise viable. Though he recognized that "the more inviting the situation of the colonists is made in Africa, the more will the respectable parts of the colored people in the United States be encouraged to emigrate at their own expense and take up their residence here," he was still amazed at the reluctance of African Americans to emigrate. "It is really astonishing," he wrote to a friend in 1837, "how infatuated some of the people of color are in preferring bondage in [the] U. S. to freedom in Africa." He attributed this preference to their "ignorance, & the debasing state they have been in for generations."[30] The optimism repeatedly expressed by Russwurm prior to emigration that his northern peers and near-peers would emigrate to Liberia, especially in the light of his pioneering example, thus proved to be unfounded. He was probably more self-deluding than misled when he boasted in one of the last issues of the *Journal:* "We feel proud in announcing to our distant readers, that many of our brethren in this city [New York], who have lately taken this subject into consideration, have like ourselves, come out from the examination, warm advocates of the Colony, and ready to embrace the first convenient opportunity to embark for the shores of Africa."[31] In fact, precious few of the educated free people of color followed in his wake. Indeed, he had expected not only that they would follow but that some would accompany him on his way over. "I think I could procure a dozen or more of our young men of the first standing to emigrate at the same time with me," he wrote Gurley at the beginning of 1829.[32]

The lack of response from New York especially disappointed him. He doubtless took some pleasure, however, in discovering that William Cornish, Samuel Cornish's only son, had emigrated to Monrovia in 1846. Under the title "Important Testimony from Liberia," the ACS's organ, the *African Repository and Colonial Journal,* gleefully reprinted two letters sent by William to his father. How these letters ended up in the pages of the *New York Journal of Commerce* from which the *Repository* reprinted them is something of a mystery. But that was of little moment to the ACS. What interested them was that the son of one of their long-standing opponents had opted for colonization and that William Cornish reported delightedly to his father about the colony. "When I considered," he wrote Samuel Cornish soon after his arrival in Monrovia, "that I was for the first time in my life breathing a free atmosphere, and in a country where the white man does not hold sway, and an individual, however humble, if he qualifies himself, may attain to eminence and distinction, I really felt surprised that I could have remained contented so long in America. I sincerely think, that if the colored people of the United States could only see what a fine country this is, and might be made by a little exertion, their prejudices against the Colonization Society and the Colony would be entirely removed."[33] By 1849, Cornish had moved south from Monrovia to settle at Cape Palmas, where his father's former colleague, Russwurm, was then in his thirteenth year as governor of Maryland in Liberia. He was listed among those who got married that year, his wife apparently a member of the influential McGill family. He ran a small school in the community, and in 1850 he lent his name to a memorial addressed to the "colored people of Maryland," touting the merits of emigration to Maryland in Liberia.[34]

Russwurm must have regarded William Cornish's odyssey as a vindication of sorts. But he was also wise enough to know that one New York Cornish did not an exodus make. Only 84 of the 4,472 African Americans who emigrated to Liberia between 1820 and 1843 came from New York—less than 2 percent. In Maryland in Liberia, only 7 of the 1,150 who settled there between 1834 and 1852 came from New York, a mere half a percent of the total.[35] "New York is a city," he wrote in the *Liberia Herald* in 1832, "from which we have looked for more from our brethren, than merely passing angry vetoes against the [American Colonization] Society." Russwurm demanded to know whether the free people of color in New York enjoyed any more respect or privileges than their counterparts in Charleston and New Orleans. Since the honest answer had to be no, the conclusion, Russwurm argued, was inescapable: "We are for emigration."[36] But Russwurm now recognized that despite all his pleading and hectoring, the job at hand was much more difficult than he had anticipated. And he candidly summed up the challenge in one of his darker and more reflective moments in a letter to one of his close friends:

> You will not be surprised, that sometimes when difficulties & dangers surround us, we despond a little; and think, that do our best, all our efforts will be in vain. But these are only temporary; as every day's experience gives us a better knowledge of our duty, & the practicability of establishing colonies on this coast, which in process of time, may realize all the fondest anticipations of their patrons. But such is not the labor of one or five years: time must pass—difficulties are to be met & overcome; the present generation, & perhaps the next, must pass away, before we can with justice look for prosperity to crown our efforts, or the blessing of posterity our labor.[37]

Yet despite these frequent moments of gloom Russwurm never once contemplated a return to the United States, except for a visit. In 1831 he wrote that he had heard "from some persons who have lately arrived" in Liberia that it was "currently reported" in America that he was "anxious to return to the U. S." but was not allowed to do so. "This is really laughable," Russwurm publicly declared and simply left it at that.[38] "We have chosen this land as our abiding place," he wrote John Latrobe, president of the Maryland State Colonization Society, in 1843. "In its defence, we are willing to spend & be spent."[39]

Eight years earlier, however, he was not so sure. In an 1835 letter to his half-brother, Francis Russwurm, he wrote somberly: "I suppose I shall live & die in Africa, but I hope not in Liberia; for more fanaticism, bigotry & ignorance I never saw amongst men, not excepting even the two last agents of the

A. C. S.ʺ⁴⁰ He detested the haughty attitude of the colonists toward *educated* Africans, if not Africans in general. The colonists, especially the early settlers, he said, "are unwilling to divest themselves of the idea of inferiority whenever circumstances have thrown educated native Africans in their society. 'He is native' is enough."⁴¹ This fatal and cancerous chauvinism, mixed with colorism, was there from the start. James Hall recalled being a guest at a dinner party given by Governor Mechlin, around 1832, attended by eighteen to twenty of Monrovia's nonwhite elite. "The dinner lasted some two hours or more, dining and wining, and several volunteer toasts were offered, as 'The (our) Governor;' 'The Colonization Society;' 'Liberia;' 'Commerce and Agriculture;' finally winding up with 'The *Fair* of Liberia;' which last created significant and not pleasant looks on the part of some very dark gentlemen present. The Governor very adroitly came to the rescue by suggesting to the proposer, "The Fair *Sex* of Liberia," you doubtless meant?' 'Certingly, sir; yes sir;' and all was satisfactory." In case the readers of the *African Repository* missed the significance of the story, Hall explained: "*Fair* is a specific term with Liberians, signifying the shade of color; as 'a little fair; *quite* fair; *very* fair; almost white, and so on.'"⁴² Russwurm almost certainly would have been in attendance and therefore would have witnessed the incident. Though light-skinned himself, he was consistently and fiercely opposed to all forms of racial or color prejudice.

But his primary complaints concerned the governing of Liberia under the agents of the ACS. As early as the middle of 1832, Russwurm began to express his misgivings, so much so that he secretly encouraged John Latrobe to establish a separate and autonomous colony in Liberia run by the Maryland State Colonization Society rather than the ACS itself. Not wanting to furnish ammunition to Garrison and other "enemies of colonization," Russwurm tried hard but discreetly to get the ACS to reform its practices on the coast, albeit to little avail. He wrote to the ACS's chief officer, his friend Ralph Gurley, outlining the many problems that needed addressing.

The medical care of the colonists was one of his primary complaints. Dr. George P. Todsen, the chief physician in Monrovia and the only trained doctor in the colony, was a disaster. He outrageously overcharged both missionaries and settlers. In May 1834, Russwurm was "sorry to inform" Gurley of the death of six recently arrived Presbyterian and Methodist missionaries. Todsen had attended to all of them and with one exception had pronounced them safe from the fever. Not only did they perish, "notwithstanding the boasted skill of Dr. Todsen," but the good doctor had "presented his bill for attendance" amounting to $1,000! Another missionary couple, the Rev and

Mrs. Spaulding, received a medical bill for $238, "besides one or two bills since" of unknown amount. Disgusted, the Spauldings quickly sailed back to the United States, the reverend taking a letter from Russwurm and promising to speak directly and confidentially to Gurley about affairs in the colony.[43]

The newly arrived emigrants, the most vulnerable, would be lucky to see Dr. Todsen in a month, though the ACS paid him for attending to their needs. "Should the poor of the colony come to him, he turns them over to his waiters Chase & Moore frequently with a hearty cursing, with the saying, that he is obliged to attend them gratis for 6 months only. Should a poor colonist send for him and wait for the Dr to come to *him*, the disease would have to cure itself." The complaints came not only from Russwurm but from other colonists and visitors. "If my word is doubted," Russwurm told Gurley, "I can appeal to any respectable person in the colony." After cataloguing the failings and horrors of Dr. Todsen, Russwurm hoped that Gurley and the ACS board would "now be convinced that his [Todsen's] only aim in coming to Africa is to obtain all he can by *extortion* in his charges." But Russwurm in fact had another complaint against Todsen: the man was "continually endeavoring to sow discord in the colony." He was unfairly undermining Gov. Pinney's authority, even among visitors to the colony, in an attempt to obtain the office of governor himself. Russwurm expressed admiration and sympathy for Pinney, whom he described as "indefatigable with the limited means at his command" in directing the affairs of the colony. "Let King Solomon arise from the grave and be appointed Gov[ernor] of Lib[eria], and Dr. T would be dissatisfied as he wants *the Chair of State himself*." Russwurm repeated the same charge against Todsen four days after writing to Gurley. In a letter to Latrobe he voiced an even greater danger that he perceived emanating from Todsen's ambition: "I fear some civil commotion if he remains as nothing will satisfy him but the chair of state."[44]

Not getting any joy from Gurley or the ACS board after years of complaint and despite the seriousness of his indictment, Russwurm wrote to Latrobe complaining of "what a pest & scourge the Board of Managers (excuse me as I am aware you are one of its members) have imposed on us in sending us Dr. Todsen." He pleaded with Latrobe, who was himself quickly becoming as disillusioned as Russwurm: "Can we not have Dr. Todsen recalled?" He hoped that after hearing the reports of two returning missionaries on the subject of Todsen's doings in Liberia, Latrobe would "urge the matter" on the board. But although Dr. Todsen was eventually recalled, he remained at his post for far too long, especially given the grave damage he was doing to the colonists and the reputation of the colony. For Russwurm was concerned not only about the well-being of the colonists, especially the poor, but also about the negative impact that the unnecessarily high mortality rate would have on attracting other African Americans to Liberia. Russwurm's belief in the Liberian project never wavered; what bothered him was the incompetent and ineffectual execution of the project under the auspices of the ACS. Thus he sought to protect the project, which he thought was a grand and noble one, from the ACS itself. For that reason, Russwurm never publicly voiced his criticism of the ACS, since he did not want to provide ammunition to the enemies of colonization. He therefore repeatedly stipulated the private and confidential nature of his communications on the problems he observed and encountered in Monrovia, even after he had left for Cape Palmas and worked exclusively for the Maryland State Colonization Society. From the very start of his correspondence with Latrobe on the attempt to establish a separate settlement at Cape Palmas, Russwurm underlined the confidential nature of his communications: "I beg that all my letters to you may be considered as private." Six months later he wrote Latrobe, "[K]eep my communications from the columns of the Newspapers," as if Latrobe had betrayed his confidences, which he had not. His letters to Gurley were frequently marked "Private & Confidential" and underlined. One of the reasons behind Russwurm's ending his business partnership with Joseph Dailey was that Dailey's letters criticizing the ACS and the situation in Liberia were being "quoted by those opposed to the [American Colonization] Society." In 1840, in responding to inquiries made by Judge Samuel Wilkeson, who had replaced Gurley as de facto chief executive of the ACS, seeking Russwurm's frank assessment of ACS's conduct of affairs in Liberia, Russwurm marked his letter "Private." As if that were not enough, he closed by saying, "My letter is a private one, and I shall feel hurt to see it in print."[45] This was fully four years after Russwurm had left the employ of the ACS at Monrovia.

Todsen was not the only problem. The colony lacked a proper code of laws, as Russwurm had "repeatedly" pointed out. Writing almost fourteen years after the founding of the colony, Russwurm asked Gurley: "Will you believe the fact that but one estate has been properly settled since the foundation of your colony[?] So much for Probate Courts." The vice-agent, he added, ought to be paid so that he had more time to devote to the duties of the post. "Our wants are inexpressible," Russwurm told Gurley. In another letter, marked "Private & Confidential," detailing some unhappy developments in the colony, he concluded by telling Gurley: "This is a letter of bad news but as others would probably send a garbled statement I thought it best to give you the facts as they appear to me." And the facts as they appeared to Russwurm as citizen and colonial secretary in Monrovia were grim. But the ACS, partly because it was somewhat overwhelmed by the challenge of financial problems at home and of governance in Liberia, did little and responded far too slowly.[46]

From expressing his misgivings discreetly and privately, Russwurm by 1834 became somewhat more public, at least in Liberia, in uttering them. He felt obliged to do so, even though he was constrained on account of his employment in the service of the ACS and its governing of the colony. An additional constraint was self-imposed: Russwurm had committed himself so fully to colonizationism and the Liberian project that it was hard for him to publicly admit difficulties in its implementation. The three governors under whom he served—Joseph Mechlin, John Pinney, and Ezekiel Skinner—were at best paternalistic and often contemptuous of both native Africans and colonists. The colony around Monrovia was poorly administered, without even the veneer of democratic participation of the colonists, let alone the Africans. The little democracy that existed came directly out of a revolt by the colonists over the autocratic and high-handed rule of an earlier governor, Jehudi Ashmun, whom the colonists had put to flight in 1824.[47] Although Gurley, the ACS's general agent, had dealt directly with the crisis of 1824 and thus was fully aware of the democratic desires of the colonists, he refrained from pushing for further reforms. He probably thought the board would not entertain further changes in that direction. Thus the dictatorial powers of the governors became increasingly intolerable to many of the older and more educated colonists. Three years after leaving Monrovia, Russwurm reflected on the problems of the colony in a letter to Judge Samuel Wilkeson (successor to Gurley as the general agent), who had solicited advice from Russwurm. He informed Wilkeson that if all those who called themselves colonizationists had been actuated by the right spirit, "their earnest desire would have been not only to transport the people of color across the Atlantic, but to have made their home, in the fatherland, an inviting asylum" for all who might wish to emigrate. Had they done this, the problem would be, not to find sufficient numbers to emigrate, but to deal with the rush of those who would be anxious to go to Liberia. More could be done by the colonists themselves, but they needed the ACS's "judicious encouragement, and the promotion of deserving men to office." Moreover, he told Wilkeson, in the appointment of governors, "the patrons at home, ought to know that the Colonists are becoming too enlightened to receive and respect every one, whom the partiality of friends may think qualified."[48]

Privately at least, others were less polite. James Brown, a colonist in Monrovia, told the ACS board that although he was a supporter of colonization, certain agents, in particular J. B. Pinney, and their actions were "calculated to chill my zeal."[49] In 1833, Joseph Dailey, Russwurm's business partner in Monrovia, described the position of governor as that of a "complete monarch." Seven years later, it was still the same to Dailey. A "nasty sickly 'nigger' colony," Liberia was, he wrote a friend in America, "the greatest despotism endured by any people of Christian denomination, upon the earth." Like many of the more educated colonists, he especially resented the incompetence and arrogance of Mechlin. "Is it not murderous," he wrote to a friend in Philadelphia, "that a man should come 3 thousand miles to be free & then have his liberty abridged by another whose moral & intellectual qualifications are insignificant in the extreme[?]"[50] Newly arrived colonists were ill fed and poorly housed and too frequently died of diseases because of the administration's lack of care and consideration. When an American ship's captain remonstrated with Mechlin for issuing to new immigrants "beef which was literally green and fish so rotten that it scarcely hung together," Mechlin simply replied that the bad must be used first.[51] The complaints from colonists, including Russwurm, and visitors to the colony became so uniformly alarming that Mechlin was recalled to Washington in 1834 and relieved of his governorship, though the official explanation was resignation on the grounds of illness.[52]

Though Russwurm was, according to Blyden, "the only colored man on the [West] coast [of Africa] who had received a liberal education," and though he was "commonly regarded as the most capable man in Liberia," he, as well as other qualified colonists, was overlooked by the ACS board in Washington for the governorship.[53] Instead, the ACS sent out another prejudiced white man, Pinney, a Methodist minister, who turned out to be even more tyrannical than Mechlin. Under his governorship in the early nineteenth century the most serious crisis in the governance of Liberia occurred. Pinney had violated the justice system as stipulated by the constitution without any reference to the parent body, the ACS, let alone the colonists. The people protested the measure and Pinney issued a proclamation declaring that the people were disloyal and seditious. Russwurm had been in the courthouse when the protest against the law began and had "publicly and freely" advised Pinney to adjourn and await the decision of the ACS board on the constitutionality of the new law. Pinney refused and insisted that Russwurm print the proclamation in the *Liberia Herald,* which was, after all, government owned and which served as the government's publishing organ. Russwurm was thus caught up in the middle of the crisis. The people knew that he sympathized with them, but this was not enough to prevent their attack upon the instrument of the proclamation, the presses of the *Herald.* Informed by the sheriff of the attack upon the presses, Russwurm went out into the night to plead with the mob, and, as he explained later, "persuaded them that the press etc. were mere machines which had cost a good deal of money in America, & the removal of two or three pieces would effect all the objects which they had in view. Accordingly they spared the press on my petition & merely carried away the springs which were deposited nearly opposite in the same street." Russwurm emphasized to Gurley that he had had "no hand in originating the mob" and that all his efforts had been to save the press if possible. The first he had known of the attack on the press was when he was informed by the high sheriff. He had spent the whole evening at his house entertaining visitors from the nearby settlement of Caldwell and had been at home between 9:00 and 10:00 p.m. when the sheriff called.[54] Stressed by the crisis, Pinney fell ill— he had long been regarded by the colonists as "deranged"—and resigned his governorship.[55] Pinney and the man who succeeded him, Skinner, believed that Russwurm had been far more involved with the mob than he had made out. The evidence suggests that they were wrong. Russwurm certainly sympathized with the mob ("I predicted that the people would allow no such proclamation to be printed," he told Gurley), but there is no evidence to suggest that he aided and abetted their action or that he had prior knowledge of what they were about to do. It is interesting to note, however, that Russwurm's demands of the mob were minimal: he apparently never told them to leave the press and the premises and merely advised them to remove only two or three pieces. Maybe he could not have reasonably demanded more than he did, given the "enraged" (his word) disposition of the mob.

He and his business partner Dailey were dubbed as "Nullifyers" by their detractors, including some of the colonists, such as vice-agent Colin Teague, his son Hilary Teague, and Jacob Prout, who had sided with Pinney during the crisis.[56] Soon after his arrival in June 1835, Skinner dismissed Russwurm from all governmental responsibilities. Russwurm responded by standing for one of only a handful of elective offices, the position of vice-agent. Though Skinner campaigned, even on the Sabbath, against Russwurm and bloated the roll of voters by allowing the recaptives to vote, Russwurm won, but not the overall majority of the votes cast for the three candidates. Skinner decided, capriciously and against the existing ordinances, that there would have to be a runoff. He similarly dismissed objections when it was pointed out to him that he was going against the existing regulations. Russwurm took no further part in the election charade, but this did not stop Skinner from boasting that had Russwurm stood again and won he would have simply vetoed the appointment. The fact that the governor lacked the legal power to do so never bothered Skinner.[57] From his own correspondence, Skinner appeared to have been even more mentally unhinged by the crisis in Monrovia than Pinney ever was. In one of his tinily written and dense letters he told Gurley: "I shall have no difficulty with the people, as it is known that I am determined, to exercise my Constitutional right and in future *veto* every man who illegally resists the Government; It is known that I go consistently Armed & that I am determined to be obeyed"![58] So much for being the servant of the people. At least according to George McGill, a former vice-agent, Skinner did not realize how close he came to having to use his gun: "Had it not have been fear of flying in the face of the [American Colonization] Society people would have expelled him from the Colony" after he had voided the elections.[59] "Great injustice has been exercised towards me by Mr. Pinney through the instigation of my enemies the Teagues and Prout," Russwurm wrote Gurley, "but . . . I can . . . in silence with a clear conscience" endure it. "But is there to be no end to these things? Is Mr. Pinney's successor to throw himself & all the influence of Government into the same hands? One would hardly believe it, but such is the fact, nevertheless: and the Governor of Liberia, at this moment is the nominal *head* of a party in *politics and religion*."[60]

Though the ACS board generally sided with Russwurm during his conflict with Skinner—for instance, reappointing him as colonial secretary after his removal by Skinner—it determined that Russwurm should continue as editor of the *Herald* but with an "editorial assistant" appointed by Skinner. Russwurm resigned his editorship.

The year 1835 was a tough one for Russwurm and marked his lowest point of disillusionment with Liberia. "I suppose I shall live and die in Africa, but I hope not in Liberia," he confided to his brother Francis in September.[61] In 1835 he informed the ACS board, "I have given every pledge any man can give who is a respecter of the laws of his country by investing all my earnings in real estate in the colony & placing my wife & child under the protection of its laws; but I have suffered so much persecution of late that I am almost tempted to abandon all & flee to a land where the laws cannot be altered or amended to suit party purposes."[62] He did not flee. He stayed in Monrovia, though not for long.

Russwurm, as his letter revealed, had recently become a husband and a father. According to one who knew him better than most, after his marriage Russwurm became "emphatically a domestic man. His Family and Library were to him the world."[63] And his domestic life was his refuge from the storm of Monrovia. Relatively little is known about Russwurm's immediate Liberian family. We know that he married Sarah McGill, daughter of the vice-agent

George McGill, in 1833. The following year their first child, George Stock-bridge, was born. He was followed in 1836 by James Hall, who was born in Cape Palmas but died in infancy. In 1839 Francis Edward (generally known as Frank) was born. The couple had one daughter, Angelina, followed by another son, Samuel Ford.[64]

The McGills were among the earliest, most well-known, and most influential settler families in nineteenth-century Liberia. The patriarch of the family, George McGill (1787–1844), was born a slave in Maryland but managed to purchase the freedom of himself and his father, brothers, and sisters. He was already a relatively successful teacher and small businessman in Baltimore before he volunteered to leave the United States for Liberia under the auspices of the Maryland State Colonization Society. McGill had in fact previously expressed his dissatisfaction with life in the United States when, inspired by Prince Saunders, he and his close friend Anthony Wood, a former slave from the Caribbean, led a party of Baltimoreans to Haiti in 1819. Disappointed with the Haitian government's apparent rescinding of a promise of free transportation for African Americans, McGill returned to Baltimore, but he forever maintained a place in his heart for Haiti, its revolution, and its achievement of independence. His son, Samuel McGill, who was about six when his father returned from Haiti, inherited this love for the black republic. Writing twenty-five years after the event, Samuel recalled that his father, after his return, would "talk to me about the Haytians, their revolution, its horrors and the final triumph of the blacks." Though Samuel was only six years old, his father gave him a copy of Sir James Barskett's monumental *History of the Island of St. Domingo* (the same volume that had such a profound influence on the young Russwurm). Samuel McGill, writing in 1854, could recall the opening lines of a poem in praise of Haiti that he had recited as a young boy at a concert hall in Baltimore. His father never returned to Haiti but was determined to leave the United States. George McGill left for Monrovia in 1827, having accepted a teaching appointment in the colony.[65]

Writing about the emigrants on the *Doris*, who arrived in Monrovia on April 11, 1827, the governor singled out McGill (mistakenly calling him John instead of George McGill) and mentioned the importance of his appointment. Contrary to the commonly accepted claim that his wife and children traveled with him in 1827, the governor reported McGill's "great regret, as well as my own, . . . that the discouraging and false reports relative to the state of the Colony, propagated in Baltimore . . . prevented his bringing out his family." He trusted that an arrangement would be made for "procuring them a passage" without McGill having to return to the United States to do so.[66] The absence of his wife and children did not, however, diminish McGill's enthusiasm for the colony. As well as working as a teacher, he served as a Methodist preacher in Monrovia, and by August 1827 he had been chosen to serve on a five-man committee that drafted an address to the "Free People of Colour in the United States," professing the virtues of colonization and the Liberian project.[67] Some three years later he returned to Baltimore and brought over his wife Angelina and their five children. As he bravely wrote in a letter from Monrovia dated June 18, 1830, the results were heartbreaking: "I landed here in sixty days after we weighed anchor at Baltimore, and as you may have heard, my wife having been sick nearly the whole voyage expired three days after my arrival, to my extreme distress and that of my children. I trust to recover again, by divine aid. Otherwise we are doing well; my children have recovered from the fever, and are much pleased with their situation."[68] It is hard to imagine that the children, one (Urias) as young as eight, would have been "much pleased" at the time.

McGill also started a prosperous trading business in Liberia that would grow and expand its operations rapidly over the next sixty years. He was elected vice-agent in 1833 but, as indicated earlier, became increasingly disillusioned with the governance of the colony. Working closely with Russwurm, he encouraged Latrobe, Hall, and the Maryland State Colonization Society to establish their own colony in Cape Palmas. When in 1834 James Hall recruited Monrovia settlers to help establish the new colony at Cape Palmas, McGill joined him. He and his four sons Samuel, James, Urias, and Roszelle now established business operations in Cape Palmas as well as Monrovia. Samuel would later study medicine in the United States and serve as colonial physician at Cape Palmas, James entered politics, and Urias became a ship's captain, but they would all also operate as businessmen. As early as 1842, the McGill family was depicted as a model of the rich possibilities opened by colonization. At a large colonization meeting attended by both black and white Baltimoreans that year, after Samuel McGill had given a rousing speech on the merits of Liberia, John Latrobe pointed to the trajectory of the McGill family as living proof of the benefits of African American emigration to the colony. George McGill, Latrobe reminded his audience, had been a colored citizen of Baltimore of "ordinary standing for one of the better class" before leaving for Liberia. But now, "[B]ehold the results of that one man's removal." George McGill was the second officer in the colony of Maryland in Liberia. His daughter was the "wife of John B. Russwurm, Esq., the governor of that colony—his eldest son is the gentleman who has addressed you this evening—his second son [James] is now a commission merchant in Liberia and commercial agent for the largest mission station on the coast—and his third son [Urias] has for the past two years been supercargo of a vessel out of the port of Baltimore, trading on the coast of Africa with a cargo under his sole control of $20,000. And now," continued Latrobe, "can there be found in the whole United States a coloured family of the intelligence, standing and respectability as that of George R. McGill? And to what cause is this surprising change to be attributed? To colonization! to the removal of the coloured man from the influence of the white race." The audience's response to Latrobe's speech exceeded expectations. According to the report in the *Maryland Colonization Journal*: "Mr. Latrobe's address was very short, confined mainly to the subject as illustrated by the McGill family, but it was a convincing and powerful one, and was most warmly applauded by the audience. In fact we doubt if there ever was gotten up a colonization meeting in Baltimore productive of more interest in the cause. As proof of which they came down liberally with the cash at the close of the meeting in aid of the large expedition which is now fitting out." By 1854 the brothers (James, Urias, and Roszelle, now joined by Samuel) had established McGill Brothers, with shipping and mercantile activity that extended not only along the West African coast but also to Europe as well as across the Atlantic. Writing in 1853, James Hall, who knew the family and Liberia well, described the McGills as "perhaps the most distinguished family in the Colony."[69]

Sarah McGill was the only daughter of George and Angelina McGill. Like her four male siblings, she was born in Maryland and traveled with her parents to Liberia in 1830. Since she was a child at the time, it is safe to assume that when she married Russwurm three years later she was probably in her late teens (Samuel, who was older than Sarah, was born around 1813) and he would have been thirty-three years old. The surviving archives yield little about Sarah McGill Russwurm. She was relatively well educated and apparently a businesswoman in her own right.[70] But what is clear from the available evidence is that she had a remarkably close and loving relationship with her husband. Russwurm missed her terribly and confessed to being more than a little irritable and short-tempered when she traveled on her own to the United States, leaving him alone for months on end.[71] She was his confidante and best friend. As early as February 1834, Russwurm informed Latrobe of "Mrs. R. at my elbows" as he wrote his letter. In that case she was helping her husband in answering Latrobe's inquiry of what was the most suitable architecture for housing in Cape Palmas, recommending the two-story ones that she had apparently seen at Gorée Island.[72] She would remain at his elbows for the rest of his life. Because of Russwurm's poor health, she also spent a con-

Urias Africanus McGill, Russwurm's brother-in-law, a leading member of probably the wealthiest family in nineteenth-
century Liberia. The picture was taken in Monrovia, Liberia,
1854. Courtesy of the Library of Congress.

siderable amount of time helping to nurse him. He in turn was remarkably
protective and solicitous of her well-being. In 1852, a year after her husband's
death, Sarah Russwurm and her children moved to Monrovia, where most
of the McGill family lived and had their business headquarters. It was there
in 1854 that her brother Urias Africanus McGill had his portrait taken by
the pioneering African American daguerreotypist and man of letters Augustus Washington. Housed in a double case beside Urias's portrait is that of a
hitherto unidentified woman. All the evidence now suggests that she was not
simply "a McGill family member," as Ann Shumard deduced, but almost certainly Sarah McGill Russwurm.[73]

The names of their children tell an interesting story in their own right.
George Stockbridge was named after Sarah's father and Russwurm's stead-

This unidentified woman is pictured in a double case with
Urias McGill. She is probably his sister, Sarah McGill Russwurm, Russwurm's widow. Like that of Urias McGill, the
daguerreotype was taken by Augustus Washington (1820–75),
a pioneering African American daguerreotypist who had emigrated to Liberia in 1853. Courtesy of the Library of Congress.

fast supporter and guardian, Calvin Stockbridge, who had died the same year
that George was born. The second child, who was born in Cape Palmas, carried the name of James Hall, with whom Russwurm had established his most
reliable and enduring friendship. Francis Edward (Frank) was named after
Russwurm's little brother, and Samuel Ford was named after Sarah's distinguished brother and Russwurm's deputy and the chief physician at Maryland
in Liberia. Angelina carried the name of her maternal grandmother.

Both George and Francis Russwurm were sent for at least part of their
secondary schooling to North Yarmouth Academy. During their time at the
academy (1850–53), the boys boarded with the Haweses, with direct responsi-

bility for looking after them devolving to Susan Hawes's first daughter, Ann H. Blanchard (1807–60). In 1851 their father had instructed that the boys attend Yarmouth Institute instead, but Mrs. Hawes and her family resisted as a consequence of a religious dispute with the head of the institute, George Woods, despite the institute's evident pedagogical superiority. George Russwurm, eighteen at the time, was recalled to Liberia by his mother to work in the business of one of his uncles and sailed from Baltimore in November 1853. As opposed to his younger brother, the fourteen-year-old Francis, whom James Hall described as "a very intelligent, promising lad" fitting for college, George was described as "of moderate ability & limited acquirements, but amiable & of good gentlemanly deportment." George, it should be said, was a rebel and gave Hall and Russwurm's Maine attorney, the long-suffering Jacob Loring, no end of trouble, including skipping school. And he was overindulged by the Haweses, who were described by Russwurm's widow and her brother Samuel McGill in a joint letter, as "really kind, but . . . very inconsiderate relatives." Francis remained at school in Yarmouth, but not at the academy.[74]

According to the *African Repository*, "Angelina V. Russwurm" was apparently an active member of the Ladies Literary Institute of Monrovia and spoke at its sixth anniversary celebration, where the great Edward Blyden was the main speaker. This took place in 1855, and Angelina may well have been a teenager at the time. A report from North Yarmouth implies that she may have visited Maine in connection with a real estate inheritance from her father. She reportedly sold the property to a local buyer. J. T. Hull, the indefatigable antiquarian of North Yarmouth, claims that in 1863 Angelina was living in Louisiana and had married a Barnes. But, writing in 1882, at least one member of the Hawes family demurred: "She was never in this country since she was a small child, but is married and lives in Liberia."[75] Finally there was Samuel Ford, who was with his parents when they visited in 1848. Mary Sagarin, in her pioneering biographical portrait of Russwurm, rightly mentioned a "fourth son" after registering George, James, and Francis but mistakenly lamented, "His name does not seem to have been recorded anywhere."[76] A small boy of about three at the time of Russwurm's visit, "Sam" certainly got mentioned by his doting father. "Sam. Ford and myself are both troubled with the diarrhea," Russwurm wrote Hall soon after arriving in North Yarmouth. Arriving back in Cape Palmas three months later, in November 1848, he reported to Hall: "Young ones all well, but sorry Mamma & Sam were left behind." Later in the same letter, he thought aloud: "I hope Sam has not suffered from effects of cold weather."[77] Mamma and Sam returned home in one piece, but Russwurm soon became ill again and died within a couple of years. Angelina, as we have seen, appeared in Monrovia in the 1850s and was mentioned in North Yarmouth lore in the 1880s. But I have encountered no other mention of Sam beyond the brief references quoted above, nor of his brothers George and Francis beyond 1853.

Such then, were the fundamental elements of Russwurm's domestic world in Africa, which nourished his soul and gave him joy and solace. During the darkest days of his struggles with Pinney, Skinner, and others in Monrovia, he wrote of his son George to his brother Francis: "Our George Stockbridge R is now over 13 months old & is as fine a child as you would see in any part of your happy land." Russwurm's family and his library were, indeed, to him "the World," as James Hall observed.[78]

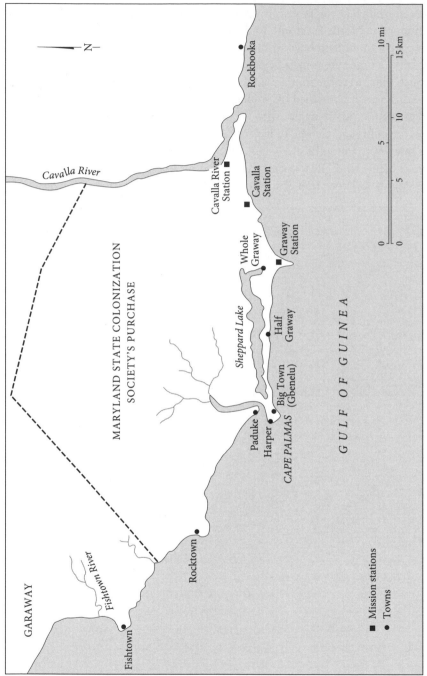

Maryland in Liberia, ca. 1840s

GARAWAY

Fishtown River

Fishtown •

Rocktown •

CAPE PALMAS
Harper •
Paduke •

Big Town
(Gbenelu) •

Half
Graway •

Sheppard Lake

Whole
Graway •

Graway
Station ■

Cavalla
Station ■

Cavalla River
Station ■

Cavalla River

Rockbooka •

MARYLAND STATE COLONIZATION
SOCIETY'S PURCHASE

GULF OF GUINEA

—N—

■ Mission stations
• Towns

10 mi
15 km

5

Governor Russwurm

The Cape Palmas Years

While the crisis was brewing in Monrovia, John Latrobe and the board of the Maryland State Colonization Society (MSCS), having gathered disturbing and damning information about the problems of governance in Liberia, were busily but quietly taking steps to establish a colony under their own auspices that would be quite separate from the ACS and its colony at Monrovia. The colony, known as Maryland in Liberia, was established in 1834 at Cape Palmas, about three hundred miles south and a week's sail away from Monrovia.

This was the culmination of significant and growing differences between the MSCS and the ACS. Unlike the ACS (whose object was "the removal of the *free* people of color, with their own consent, to Africa"), the MSCS, from as early as 1832, made explicit and public that its "avowed object was the extirpation of slavery in Maryland." Writing in 1885, Latrobe explained the relatively bold and progressive position taken by the MSCS:

> With the views entertained, nowadays, of slavery, it perhaps seem strange that there should have been any question as to the propriety of adopting [such a resolution]. But, half a century ago, slavery was regarded in the States where it existed as an institution upon whose permanence the wealth and prosperity of so many were dependent, that anything which, by possibility, might interfere with it, was looked upon with jealousy and distrust. So fixed, indeed, did it seem to be, that even those who deplored its existence, seeing no way to get rid of it, and never dreaming of the civil war which closed with its destruction, were disposed to consider it as a necessary evil, and to leave it with the future to be dealt with. . . . The action of the State Society, therefore, which frankly declared that the extirpation of slavery in Maryland was its ultimate object, was far in advance of anything that had been done in this connection in the slave-holding States, and the discussion of the resolutions was naturally careful and deliberate.

John H. B. Latrobe (1803–91), the driving force behind the Maryland State Colonization Society during Russwurm's governorship of Maryland in Liberia. Courtesy of the Maryland Historical Society.

Moreover, he continued, not only was the principle involved to be considered, "but the effect of the resolutions upon the public, and especially their effect on the Legislature," upon whose disbursements the MSCS was "practically dependent for the means of accomplishing its purposes." The state of Maryland had in fact passed legislation at the end of 1831 (in the wake of Nat Turner's uprising in neighboring Virginia) granting the MSCS $200,000, $10,000 per year over a period of twenty years. This unparalleled state largesse (the Virginia legislature rejected a similar proposed appropriation) undergirded the efforts of the MSCS and enabled even greater independence from the ACS, which envied the resources of the Marylanders. There was another important difference between the MSCS and the ACS that has been all but ignored in the extant literature: namely, the seriousness and professionalism with which the MSCS conducted its affairs. Latrobe himself only mentioned this in passing when he revealed that the MSCS had made a deliberate decision with regard to selecting members for the board of managers: "[I]n place of filling the Board with clergymen, the directors chosen were business men of intelligence and character—a good business arrangement, but one that prejudiced the Society then and ever afterwards with the clergy."[1] This arrangement was to prove remarkably successful: the MSCS was by all accounts the most ambitious and effectively run of the state colonization societies and far exceeded the ACS in its prudent management and allocation of resources.

Learning from the missteps of the ACS in Monrovia, the MSCS quickly put into place a far more democratic constitution, based largely upon the U.S. Constitution, than the one that existed in Monrovia, and the rights of both colonists and native Africans were expanded over time.[2] The government of Maryland in Liberia consisted of the agent (governor) and his assistant, who were appointed by the MSCS on two-year terms, and a secretary, who was appointed by the governor annually. All the remaining officers—vice-agent, two counselors, a "register" [sic], a sheriff, a treasurer, "selectmen" (three in 1838), and a committee on new emigrants (also three in 1838)—were annually elected by male franchise. There was a judiciary whose authority was accepted by the people and trial by jury, with the stipulation that "no one can sit on a jury who does not know how to read and write." All of these relatively democratic provisions were well in advance of the authoritarian paternalism of Monrovia, not to mention the prevailing despotism in the early European enclaves in West Africa, including British-ruled Sierra Leone. Partly because of their advanced nature and the MSCS's early commitment to self-governance, Blyden, writing two generations after the founding of the colony, averred that the state of Maryland "is forever identified with the only popular government on the Continent of Africa."[3]

Although the science of vaccination had been introduced in the United States in 1800 and Baltimore had established the first vaccination institution in the country in 1802, the ACS, located down the street in Washington, had never bothered to vaccinate emigrants to Liberia. The MSCS, in the very year that it established Maryland in Liberia, saw to it that each emigrant was vaccinated and received a general health certificate by a qualified physician before departure. Emigrants to Maryland in Liberia in the first years of the settlement also had the benefit of an imaginative and enterprising doctor as the MSCS's agent and governor, James Hall. Dr. Hall had lived in Monrovia for two years prior to his appointment and had, as he put it, "imbibed a deep interest in the colony." Moreover, he had attended "scarcely less than one thousand cases of the African fever." Hall treated the fever with Peruvian barks and their extract, quinine, which proved far more effective and less dangerous than the remedies commonly used in Monrovia, which included the use of mercury, opium, and bloodletting. This superior set of arrangements contributed significantly to the relatively low mortality rate at Cape Palmas compared to Monrovia, a difference that puzzled contemporaries.[4]

Maryland in Liberia also instituted something that few, if any, so-called "civilized" countries had at the time and that none of the other colonies on the west coast of Africa practiced: it imprisoned colonists found guilty of beating their wives. Introduced by Hall from the start of the settlement, the practice met with the approbation of the MSCS board and became a part of the legal strictures in the colony under Russwurm. To help lay the foundations for their future prosperity, each newly arrived emigrant was granted five acres of fertile land and allowed to purchase as much more as he or she wanted for the purpose of improving it, at one dollar per acre. Under the direction of the governor and at the initial expense of the MSCS, houses were erected and sold at a fixed price to newcomers. The money from this sale would then be used to erect new houses in preparation for future emigrants. To ease their settlement, the newly arrived were entitled to provision for six months. As Penelope Campbell noted: "Although the variety, quantity, and quality of goods varied with circumstances, the standard weekly allowance per person was about three pounds of meat, some fish, six quarts of bread, tea, and a half pint of molasses. Rice and palm oil were also distributed in small quantities when they could be purchased from the Africans."[5]

In keeping with its imaginative and adventurous measures, the MSCS, unlike the ACS, took the bold step in June 1836 of appointing a black governor, John Brown Russwurm. He was the first black person to be appointed governor to such a colony.[6] Russwurm's appointment was not universally welcomed by the colonizationists. As the *African Repository* diplomatically reported, "A difference of opinion is known to exist among the friends of African Colonization" on the appointment of a black governor. The ACS itself recognized Russwurm's qualities: "So far as the success of the experiment depends on the personal merit of the party in whose instance it is tried, the choice of Mr. Russwurm must be considered highly judicious." But that was not enough for the ACS: "The Parent Society is not satisfied from information carefully sought after, and, it is believed, faithfully given, that the time has yet arrived when a similar experiment could be prudently attempted on its part."[7] Black Monrovia would have to continue to wait for the end of white governorship.

Captain Joseph Nicholson of the *U.S. Potomac* toured the coast in 1836 and reported on the state of the Liberian colony. Of all the settlements that he visited and observed—Monrovia, New Georgia, Caldwell, Millsburg, Bassa Cove, Edina—Maryland in Liberia impressed him the most: its administration, its location, its houses, the health and contentment of its inhabitants, and the colonists' relations with the native Africans. Unlike the other settlements, which were almost exclusively preoccupied with trade to the neglect of agriculture, Maryland in Liberia's wise attention to agriculture was most impressive, reported Nicholson. The settlers around Cape Palmas, he observed, "appear to have profited by the errors of the older colonies, in avoiding as yet all trade with the natives of the interior, and devoting their whole energies to agriculture." He remarked upon the "good terms" with which the settlers lived with "all the Kings and [native] people of the neighborhood," setting Cape Palmas apart from the other settlements. Once again singling out Cape Palmas in his report to the secretary of the navy, he wrote: "I cannot refrain from expressing my agreeable surprise, at the evidence of industry and foresight that were exhibited through the settlement—so much have they advanced in solid prosperity in the short space of three years."[8] In a similar vein, Nicholson had nothing but praise in his letter on Cape Palmas to Latrobe. To Russwurm he wrote on December 17, 1836, expressing to the governor how pleased he was at the "very prosperous state of the colonists," which he had noted during his visit the previous day. He imparted friendly military advice to Russwurm about the building of a fort to defend the settlement just in case the "good disposition" of the native Africans toward the settlers should change and become belligerent. Nicholson even took pride in the fact that the colony was the creation of his and Latrobe's native state of Maryland. (Latrobe had actually been born in Pennsylvania but had grown up in Maryland.) "Our little colony," he told Latrobe, "has advanced surprisingly in solid prosperity in the short space of three years, and with the judicious control and assistance of its friends, must continue its career, to the honor of its friends and the happiness of the coloured man."[9]

But Nicholson was a hypocrite and a racist. For despite the notable achievements of Maryland in Liberia under Russwurm's stewardship, Nicholson, in his report to the secretary of the navy, went out of his way, as he himself recognized, "to express an opinion" on what the color of agents in Liberia should be: "I would say that it is of the greatest importance to have white agents at the respective settlements, gentlemen of general information and firmness of character. Not only do they command more respect from the Kings and natives of the country, but the colonists themselves more readily submit to their government."[10] Nicholson, interestingly enough, never reported any misgivings to Latrobe, let alone this fundamental one. The ACS pounced upon this reactionary and unfounded notion to bolster their claim that Monrovia was unready for black rule.[11] Such was the type of ideological climate within which the MSCS board made its audacious decision to appoint Russwurm to the governorship of Maryland in Liberia.

Though the board was unanimous in appointing him to the governorship, they saw their unprecedented decision of appointing a black man to such an esteemed position as a gamble and had no qualms about letting Russwurm know this. Writing on behalf of the MSCS, Latrobe told Russwurm that the unanimous vote was made "not hastily—not on the spur of the moment,—not without diligent and thorough inquiry and it may be gratifying to you, sir to know, that in departing from the Custom which has prescribed that Agents and Governors in Africa should be white men, the Board do it with a belief that your talents, ability and fidelity will fully justify them before the public in the step which they have taken." He continued:

> The Board cannot believe that their authority in force or in duration, will be less in Africa because it is wielded by other than a white man, they cannot think that the Colonists and natives will pay less respect to the representative of the law and the head of the Civil and Military government because he is of the same race with themselves. The[y] act under the conviction that the Colored race is capable of the same mental improvement with the white one, and they are glad to illustrate their principles, in this respect by the Appointment of one to the highest office in their gift, who, in his own person, bears witness to the truth of their doctrine.

Latrobe then revealed the pressure under which the board now labored, having taken its decision. The board felt, he told Russwurm, that "in the opinion of many around them in this country they have assumed a heavy responsibility. They rely on you to assist them in bearing it." However, this was an historic opportunity for Russwurm himself: "The first Colored Governor by direct appointment, in the history of Colonization, high reputation, honorable fame, are within your reach. The Board fully believe that you will aim at and obtain them." But not taking any chances, Latrobe—in addition to directing Russwurm to the previous ordinances and instructions in the archives at Cape Palmas, sending along with his letter of appointment the resolutions of the board and his commission as agent and governor—provided a detailed list of instructions, extending over twelve handwritten pages. It turns out that this long list of instructions was no implicit commentary on or expression of misgivings about Russwurm's capacity: Latrobe did the same thing when Hall was appointed. A distinguished lawyer and polymath, Latrobe was an extraordinarily imaginative, systematic, and energetic thinker and administrator and left little to chance. He somehow managed to combine these qualities with an optimistic spirit, a sense of humor, modesty, and generosity. He carried out his work with the utmost charm and courtesy, qualities that Russwurm would come to appreciate after the madness of Monrovia and the blunders of the ACS.[12]

The board had no need to tell Russwurm of the peculiar nature of his burden; Russwurm was fully aware that in a racist world there were more than individual responsibilities for a black man to bear. "I cannot express my high sense of their [the board of managers'] liberality, and the flattering manner in which they have conferred the appointment," he wrote Latrobe.

This is certainly a new era in the history of the man of color; and our community though astonished, still applaud to the skies this monument of the Board.

I accept their appointment with pleasure, and shall endeavor, by a conscientious discharge of duty to convince them and the world, "that their authority in force as in duration will not be less in Africa because it is wielded by other than a white man." . . . They have departed from the old & beaten paths, by their resolutions in my favour, and may my right hand forget "its cunning," ere I abuse their confidence. I shall enter on my duty with my whole mind engaged in it, and failure shall not arise from neglect.[13]

Russwurm remained true to his word and served with commitment and distinction for almost sixteen years up to his death in June 1851 at Cape Palmas.

The nervousness—its nature, depth, and intensity—with which the board embarked upon the experiment in 1836 was more fully revealed three years later when it uttered an audible sigh of relief:

The Board are much gratified in being able to announce that the difficulties which it was apprehended would grow out of the appointment of a coloured governor, J. B. Russwurm, Esq. have either not been realized, or have been satisfactorily overcome. The colonists, are now, generally, satisfied with the measure, and hold it to be, what in truth it is, an admission of their ability to fill all the offices of the colony, the highest as well as the lowest. Soon after his appointment, it is understood that certain of the colonists took it into their heads that law was inoperative, when not administered by a white man, and they experimented upon the efficiency of the laws in the hands of a coloured executive, very much to their cost and dissatisfaction, as it turned out. After a few such experiments they satisfied themselves, that the law was independent of the colour of its ministers, and the result of their measures was, in the end, beneficial and salutary. At this time the respect that is paid to the governor by the colonists, differs in no wise from that which Doct. Hall and Mr. Holmes [who acted as governor for a few months before Russwurm took up his appointment] received from them. As respects the natives, no difference has been observed in their treatment of the coloured governor, which at all creates a doubt as to the propriety of appointing one. . . . The situation of Mr. Russwurm has, on more than one occasion, been one of great delicacy: and he has been called upon to act in cases which required prudence, firmness, and dignity. He has acquitted himself well: and his conduct has met with the sanction of the Board. Should he persevere in his present course, his name will rank very high as a friend to Africa, and as one who has illustrated in his own person the capacity of her children.[14]

James Hall, Russwurm's friend and predecessor as governor who became the MSCS's general agent in 1836, had played a crucial role in advocating Russwurm's appointment. He reminded the board that it had "felt much anxiety . . . [in] the appointment of a coloured agent." Never a man known for his modesty, Hall now had a wonderful opportunity to gloat, which his nature forbade foregoing. "In addition to the satisfaction of having my own prediction fulfilled in the so far able administration of Mr. Russwurm," he told the board, "I have been gratified to find the measure approved of, by the leading men in every settlement which I have visited on the coast, and by all masters of vessels with whom I have had any intercourse; but more particularly by the merchants at Cape Coast [Gold Coast, today's Ghana], to whom Mr. Russwurm had been known as a man of business and a gentleman."[15]

Not only the board but also historians and contemporaries alike acknowledge and testify to Russwurm's remarkable success and quite astonishing achievements. Moreover, partly through the embarrassing example of his success as governor of Maryland in Liberia, the ACS hastened the process of self-rule and independence in Liberia proper. Russwurm developed and expanded the colony's educational system, catering not only to the American colonists but also to the African communities around Cape Palmas, and rationalized its bookkeeping and financial arrangements, tasks that his predecessors had failed at. He successfully experimented with new crops (including the introduction of breadfruit trees, which he knew from Jamaica, into Liberia) and agricultural techniques. "I am sorry to say," he reported in an 1839 dispatch, "that the sugar cane at Mount Tubman is looking rather poorly. Some look passable, but nothing like the West India cane. Some of our colonists say the land is too low; I shall, therefore, experiment again in February next on different soil." Russwurm is even owed some credit for the very presence of coconut trees at Cape Palmas. Traveling along the Liberian coast in 1841, British explorers William Allen and Thomas Thomson noted that, compared to elsewhere, Cape Palmas had only a few and recently planted coconut trees ("cocoa palms," they called them), which must have been planted a few years earlier by the American colonists. They then discovered that there was a local African taboo, or, as they put it, "a strong and very prejudicial superstition relative to the planting of that most valuable tree." The locals believed that "whoever plants one will surely die before it bears fruit, that is to say in about seven years." But their leader, King Freeman (Bede Sia Pah Niemah), "yielded at last to the exhortations of the American Governor [Russwurm] though not convinced of his arguments of the folly of the superstition, and the real evil that such a belief entails." Freeman, however, was "fully sensible of the great uses of the tree, and desirous of possessing some." To avoid the curse, he came up with an "ingenious method of providing a subterfuge. Having placed some nuts at the brink of holes previously drilled, he caused cattle to be driven about over the ground thus prepared, until all the nuts were thrown into the spaces and covered over by the hoofs of the beasts."[16]

Russwurm shifted the colony from barter to modern currency (including paper money); expanded the democratic institutions of the colony and increased their transparency; and overhauled the justice system, making it also more transparent and evenhanded. He was no power-monger and offered to resign on several occasions, and he voluntarily and eagerly diminished the amount of power he had in his own hands by stepping down as chief justice in 1846 ("I . . . earnestly beg the Board to release me," he wrote Latrobe).

His earlier experience as a merchant in Monrovia he now put to good use in making Maryland in Liberia more self-reliant and less dependent upon its patrons in Baltimore.[17] As early as April 1838, he floated the idea of a "savings Bank or a Benefit Society for mutual Relief in cases of sickness."[18] "The Governor displays the true yankee enterprise," Russwurm's assistant agent and the colony's chief physician, Dr. Samuel McGill, wrote Latrobe. "When an idea is formed it becomes with him a hobby—his last one was 'Pah Country and Ivory Trade,' now it is 'Sheppard Lake and River Cavally Canal,' so it was also with the 'Camwood trade,' until his perseverance overcame the obstacles opposed to its reception."[19]

Cape Palmas developed into what one historian called a "vivacious community" under Russwurm's leadership.[20] Writing at the end of 1845, Russwurm himself described the community as one in which the "'go ahead' principle is evidently at work." Moreover, he guarded and promoted that principle by "scout[ing] at all who are willing to 'rest on their oars,' because of past labors or honors, and suffer their families to be raised in ignorance," denouncing them as "the great stumbling blocks in the pathway of the young and rising generation."[21] Such actions did not diminish Russwurm's enormous popularity. Upon visiting Cape Palmas in 1844, Rev. John Seys, superintendent in the Methodist Episcopal Mission in Africa, wrote: "I made it a point to inquire for my own satisfaction, and was happy to find that the present administration is decidedly popular, and I hope nothing may occur to induce Gov. Russwurm to resign his office." In November of the following year, J. W. Lugenbeel, an agent of the ACS, visited the colony and was similarly impressed with the progress of Maryland in Liberia and the superintendence of Russwurm, whom he described in his private journal as the "accomplished and enterprising executive of the government." Governor Russwurm, he noted, "is a gentleman of dignified deportment, affability of manners, sociable, intelligent, and unassuming; as well qualified, perhaps, for the station he now fills, as any other individual who could be selected, whether white or colored. As far as I could ascertain, he is universally popular among the people over whom he presides. He seems to exhibit a deep interest in the welfare of the colonists, and the prosperity of the infant colony." Lugenbeel found the colonists "sober, industrious, and contented." He observed that there were "a few 'loafers and loungers,' as in other settlements in Liberia," but was quick to add, "such as may be found in almost every city or town in the United States." On the whole, Lugenbeel found "the little Colony of Maryland in Liberia . . . a very interesting place; and a very desirable residence for all colored persons who wish to enjoy the privileges of freedom and equality, and who are capable of appreciating the blessings of liberty."[22]

By the 1840s, the community boasted a remarkable number of mutual aid associations (including a Female Benevolent Society), agricultural societies, and choral societies. An 1850 survey of the settlement reported that there was a "singing school some years ago, very ably conducted. Its good effects may be seen in the improvement of vocal music in the Colony."[23] There were public lectures, many probably given by the governor himself; there was a lively debating society, which met twice a month; there was the Russwurm Literary Association, the Cape Palmas Lyceum (which in 1850 needed "a little reviving"), and a public library to sustain the educational life and development of the community.[24] "A spirit to become more enlightened is seemingly at work in the minds of many persons here," wrote William Prout, corresponding secretary of the Cape Palmas Lyceum, thanking a group of Baltimoreans who had shipped a collection of books to the library.[25] A brilliant protégé of Russwurm's, Prout expressed his appreciation for their benefactors' helping the community to enter the "Republic of Letters."[26] Summing up the educational developments in the colony during Russwurm's time, an early historian of the community noted: "Beginning with several mission schools, the educational movement grew, having two schools for the colonists' children when the population was still under 300, and in 1845 having three colony schools with an attendance of 70. Five day schools were reported by 1849–50 with students estimated at from 120 to 175. . . . In addition, there were . . . references in the '40s and '50s to various other associations and organizations of an educational nature."[27] As he had done prior to leaving Monrovia, Russwurm for many years struggled to establish a high school. It was finally opened the same year he died, a posthumous victory. Partly because of these educational and cultural exertions on Russwurm's part and the support of the MSCS, the state of Maryland and its colony in Africa had produced by the 1880s, according to Blyden's reckoning, a disproportionately high number of distinguished figures in Liberian history, including "two of her ablest Presidents," as well as a vice president.[28] In his letter to Latrobe praising Russwurm's "true yankee enterprise," Samuel McGill concluded: "The fact is, we can discover that our advancement is commensurate with the amount of labor and energy exerted by the principal men in the community."[29]

The period from the late 1840s to Russwurm's death in 1851 was the happiest and most prosperous in the history of Maryland in Liberia. The community was at peace with its neighbors, agriculture was good, and trade with the interior was excellent. Writing on behalf of the board of managers of the MSCS in the presentation of its fifteenth annual report, President Latrobe could not contain his ebullience, despite his wish to do so:

> The advices from the Colony up to the time of the sailing of the Packet [December 3, 1846] were of the most gratifying character, as had been, indeed, all those received during the current year; and in January, the date of the last advices, the emigrants were contented and thriving—the business of the place was on the increase—employment was readily obtained by all who were willing to work, and extended journeys had been made into the interior, opening new avenues for trade in the one direction, and for the extension, in the other, of the light and blessings of Christianity and civilization. Cases of discontent were rare, and affairs generally seemed to be as prosperous, and as likely to continue so, as the best and warmest friends of Colonization could reasonably desire. The Board are well aware how easy it is to round periods on one side of an ocean, in regard to affairs on the other, and how often the wish is the father to the thought in reports like the present; and they are, therefore, guarded in the statements that they make, saying nothing which they do not believe to be fully borne out by the testimony, not of their agent [Russwurm] only, but by the evidence of impartial visitors, who look at the Colony without any of the bias that may be imputed to avowed Colonizationists. The Board do not pretend to say that Cape Palmas is "the happy valley"—but they do say, that its condition and prospects fully equal the most sanguine anticipations of its friends and are such as to excite the liveliest satisfaction among all who feel an interest in the development of the talents and energies of that large portion of the human family, which, it has been the fashion among many, to look upon as incapable of political self-government, or high intellectual accomplishments.[30]

Russwurm had the rare combination of an acute eye for the minutiae of everyday administration and strategic thinking. He was attentive to the prosaic administrative duties of his office, and he took time, as he felt it was "[his] duty to visit all" the colonists, to "encourage the desponding (as we have many such the first year [of settlement]); to cheer the sick; & to assist the man who is laboring with all his main to put his family in comfortable quarters." But he also moved briskly in the purchasing of Fish Town, noting that although it was of little value in itself or for its trade, it had "the finest harbor on this part of the Coast, and we should dislike much to see it occupied by another nation—particularly the French. At present the natives are against the French, but what proof they will be against their rum & Dashes [gifts], it would be hard for any one to say." Observing that the French had already established a foothold eighteen miles away from Cape Palmas, Russwurm went ahead, before receiving explicit authorization from the MSCS board, and purchased Fish Town for about three hundred dollars, presenting the bill later to Maryland as an effective fait accompli.[31]

Perhaps most importantly, he handled the difficult and delicate problem of relations with indigenous Africans with skill and diplomacy, not with the brutality and rough justice of Mechlin, for instance, in Monrovia.[32] Russwurm was probably the first and one of the few leaders of the Liberian ruling class of the nineteenth century who would consciously make the effort to learn several of the languages of the surrounding African communities. He became so proficient that when Commodore Matthew Perry visited Cape Palmas in the early 1840s, Russwurm acted as his interpreter. Indeed, unlike many of the Americo-Liberian ruling elite of the nineteenth century, Russwurm was often accused by the colonists of favoring the Africans over themselves. This charge against Russwurm became particularly shrill in 1838 after he banished from Maryland in Liberia one of the leading colonists, Charles Snetter, for leading a posse of settlers intent on avenging the murder of a colonist by Africans, mistakenly attacking a group of innocent Africans, killing one, and wounding several more. Russwurm's decision to banish Snetter caused such uproar among the colonists that for the first (and not the last time) he threatened to resign his governorship. He received the full backing of the board in Maryland and decided to stay on.[33] James Hall recalled in his obituary of the man that Russwurm, "from our earliest acquaintance with him, when a single man in Monrovia, . . . was considered the peculiar friend and patron of the native African."[34] *Friend* was exactly the term used by a leading member of the Cape Palmas Africans in describing Russwurm in an 1844 conversation with Samuel McGill. "Ever since the arrival of Americans," he told Dr. McGill, "I have taken Gov. R[usswurm] for my friend. . . .There are many rash and inconsiderate men among the Americans," he continued, "who possessing neither authority nor influence, are loud in their denunciations of us Africans, but Gov. Russwurm and other influential persons, actuated by feelings of justice, condemn such proceedings as improper."[35] Joseph Roberts, who became the first black governor of Liberia, reported the same sentiments expressed by King Freeman, one of the most powerful rulers around Cape Palmas. Governor Russwurm, Freeman explained, had "always treated them kindly; and if it was not for the bad influence of certain colonists in his [Russwurm's] confidence they could get along without any difficulty."[36] Thirty years after Russwurm's death, Blyden encountered other Gleboes who remembered Russwurm with equal respect and reverence. Blyden reported that a wise parable (about the benefits of unity) that Russwurm had once used in one of his negotiations with them was "recited among [the Gleboes] to this day. So Charles Hodge, an intelligent Grebo, informed us."[37] Russwurm apparently adopted, or at least raised, a number of local African children. In relating an interesting tale of African religious conversion, his brother-in-law, Samuel McGill, mentioned in passing "the native boys of Gov. Russwurm's family, who have been for two years creditable members of the Methodist Episcopal Church."[38]

Russwurm was a shrewd governor but a compassionate one, and his compassion extended to all in need. Hall, who gained a reputation for ruthlessness among colonists and Africans alike in his conduct of affairs as the first governor of Maryland in Liberia, noted that if Russwurm's governorship—"an arduous, difficult and eminently successful administration of sixteen years"—could be said to have a fault, it would be that Russwurm was "too prone to indulgence and liberality to the poor of the Colony, and too much disposed to yield to the, often exorbitant, exactions of the native tribes."[39] This was no doubt true in Hall's eyes but not in Russwurm's. Russwurm in fact always strove to be fair in his dealings with indigenous Africans, especially in the purchasing of land for the colony. During the negotiations for the acquisition of Fish Town, he was appalled when he reviewed the earlier "purchases" made and at the way the Africans were swindled by the deals with colonial agents and settlers—including James Hall himself (who had laughed down his sleeve as he passed over bad tobacco to the Africans in acquiring Cape Palmas in 1834) and the supposed children of Christ, the missionaries.[40]

It is nonetheless an unavoidable fact that Russwurm was a member of the colonial, settler ruling class in Africa, and like all settler ruling classes on the continent in the nineteenth century, he was not above calling on the might of metropolitan armed forces to intimidate the indigenous population. Russwurm called on Commodore Perry and his big ships and big guns of the U.S. African Squadron on several occasions for this very purpose, albeit more for deterrence than actual fighting. And the governor repeatedly and frequently called on his patrons in Baltimore to provide a greater quantity of weapons and more sophisticated ones to defend the colonists. It is true that when he requested military backup and armaments he did so for defensive purposes, but he did request them. Peaceful vigilance, a known and restrained capacity for self-defense, and diplomacy were integral to Russwurm's statecraft in Liberia.[41] But remarkably in the almost sixteen years of his governorship he never waged war against any of the African groups in the settlement or the surrounding areas: for instance, even though there were repeated and clearly documented cases of looting of the settlement's warehouse, sometimes with the direct involvement of African kings and headmen, Russwurm would get better locks and night watchmen to secure it while gaining restitution through negotiation—"palaver," as both natives and colonists called it— rather than war. At times Russwurm seemed almost reconciled and resigned to loss through theft, as when he reported to Latrobe: "I am happy to say, that our relations with the natives, are of the most amicable nature—not that they have left off pilfering & stealing as much as they can."[42] Russwurm's lack of belligerence partly stemmed from sensible, enlightened self-interest: in the early years he recognized that the small colony could easily be overrun by its more numerous African neighbors. Arriving soon after the Snetter crisis of 1838, a shrewd visitor, Dr. R. McDowell, wrote of being "kindly received" by Russwurm, describing the governor as "apparently well qualified for his situation." Mentioning the "recent troubles with the natives, wherein some lives were lost," McDowell noted that Russwurm's "prudence and caution saved the colony from actual hostility and war. Indeed," he concluded, "the state of the colony, and disposition of the surrounding natives are such as to render such qualities eminently necessary."[43]

But Russwurm's relations with and policies toward native Africans also issued from a genuine desire to live in harmony and cooperation with the Africans in and around Cape Palmas. He deplored the generally "strong prejudice & hatred" he detected among the colonists, especially the illiterate and "most ignorant," toward the Africans. "If indulged in, the end must inevitably be a war of extermination of one party." Russwurm did not say so but clearly implied that victory would not inevitably be on the side of the colonists—as indeed they discovered a few years after Russwurm died. Some of the colonists—"lawless men," he called them—after committing a crime against the natives tried to insist on the Africans not having a part, even in palaver, in their trial. Russwurm sought unity, as one of the Gleboes informed Blyden many years later.[44] (The ill treatment of and contempt for Africans were among the reasons behind his leaving Monrovia in the first place.) The absence of war with his African neighbors, despite massive provocation, was one of Russwurm's proudest achievements, a pride that was shared by the board of the MSCS in Baltimore.[45] But despite his sympathy and respect for the indigenous Africans, Russwurm did not fully shed many of his New World prejudices, and as late as 1843 he still saw a key component of his job on the coast as the spreading of "civilization" in "a land of savages."[46]

Although Russwurm maintained good relations with the board in Baltimore, he was by no means a yes-man for the MSCS; he was never afraid of voicing his criticism of board policies and actions he thought inimical to the well-being of the colony. One historian went so far as to charge Russwurm with "upbraid[ing]" the board on occasions.[47] When the board proposed a significant increase in taxation for the colony's residents and their trade, Russwurm resisted, and the board eventually accepted a significantly lower tax—1 percent instead of the 10 percent originally proposed—which he and the colonists found more agreeable.[48] When the board ordered Russwurm to refund the fines legitimately imposed on and collected from Episcopalian and Congregational missions for the absence of some of their charges from drill duty with the militia, Russwurm flatly refused. Such an act, Russwurm informed the board, would undermine the justice system and discredit and embarrass the legitimate authority in the colony. Russwurm told Latrobe that the home office could go ahead and refund the fines if it felt it must, but he would not do so as governor of Maryland in Liberia. Russwurm's refusal here partly issued from a long-running battle with a racist, the South Carolinian missionary John Wilson, who was never reconciled to the legitimacy of a black man governing the colony. A Presbyterian working under the auspices of the American Board of Commissioners for Foreign Missions (ABCFM), Wilson later declared that Africans could never rise to a "full equality in all respects with white races." Russwurm was determined not to give the likes of Wilson the satisfaction of the reversal of policy the board requested. Vanquished, Wilson left Maryland in Liberia, moving his mission to the banks of the Gabon River.[49]

From the start, Russwurm's interests coincided with those of the colonizationists, but his were not identical to theirs. And Russwurm remained faithful to his primary agenda of helping to establish an asylum in Africa for those in the diaspora. If Russwurm had questions or doubts about the motives of the colonizationists, he never expressed them openly.[50] He was not one to look the Liberian gift horse in the mouth. He was simply happy to have it to ride—the alternative was traveling on foot—to help him on his journey. Russwurm's attitude was the same as that adopted and articulated by Blyden. "The coloured people of the United States," Blyden advised, "should consider it of little matter, whether the motives of African Colonization were good or evil. . . . Let coloured men . . . of every rank and station, in every clime and country, in view of the glorious achievements of African Colonization, lend it their aid and influence. Let them look at the cause and not the instruments: let them behold and contemplate *results,* and not form conjectures concerning *motives* and *intentions.*"[51] Russwurm, however, maintained far more public distance between himself and the colonizationists than Blyden ever did. And where the interests of his larger project diverged from those of the MSCS, Russwurm was never afraid to resist and almost invariably prevailed.

He exerted himself to enhance the autonomy of the colony vis-à-vis the Maryland board as well as European colonial encroachment (British and French, in particular), especially in the 1840s, and contributed to the later amalgamation of Maryland in Liberia with Liberia proper, a union that he regarded as inevitable. What needed to be worked out, Russwurm suggested, were the terms.[52] But he died before he could begin this task in earnest. Others would undertake it, and the colony united with the sister Republic of Liberia in 1857. The terms of incorporation into the republic were less favorable than Russwurm and the majority of the colonists would have liked. However, the policies and actions of corrupt, unwise, and incompetent successors to Russwurm at Cape Palmas led to a reckless, unnecessary, and unjust war with native Africans that nearly resulted in the total annihilation of the settlement by avenging Africans. With fortuitous financial support from the MSCS—James Hall just happened to be in Monrovia when the crisis broke—the Liberian government, which was broke at the time, having been paid ten thousand dollars by the MSCS, intervened on the Marylanders' behalf, making the latter indebted to Monrovia for its very survival. Maryland in Liberia thus became Maryland County, the fourth county in the republic.[53] The union had the effect of considerably expanding the territorial area of the Republic of Liberia, which had become independent in 1847, as well as strengthening the latter's political institutions.[54]

Russwurm's achievements are all the more remarkable when one considers that virtually from the start of his residence in Liberia he suffered from severe health problems, problems that only worsened over the years. Despite his touting Liberia as no less healthy than any other new settlement, its tropical diseases ravaged his body. Part of the argument that Hall made in recommending Russwurm for the governorship at Cape Palmas was that, as a black man, Russwurm could withstand the tropical environment and its perils better than a white man ever could. Russwurm in fact fared little better than his white counterparts on the coast, and certainly not much better than Hall himself, who in fact resided for about five years in Liberia, despite being virtually crippled, before returning to the United States in 1836. The pressure of work hardly contributed to his well-being: he frequently worked eighteen hours a day, sometimes finishing his correspondence at 4:00 a.m. only to rise again at 6:00. "None in your employ eat the bread of idleness in Africa," he told Latrobe, largely referring to himself. "I pledge my words."[55]

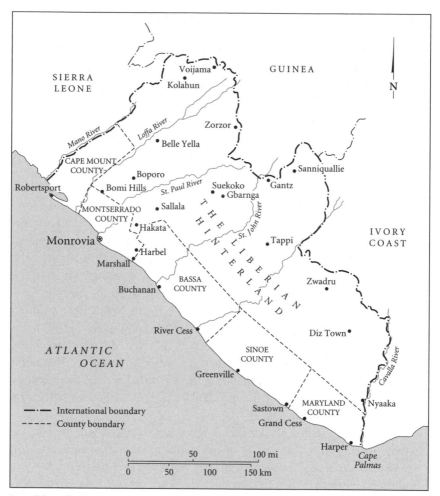

Republic of Liberia, counties on the coastal strip (after much of its territory was annexed by both the British and the French), ca. 1915

Russwurm was often incapacitated by agonizing pain, by what he called "rheumatism," which, from time to time, he mentioned in passing in his letters, but evidently understated its impact and the general state of his health. "Please to excuse this writing," Russwurm asked Latrobe as early as 1834, given that he was "troubled with the rheumatism in [his] right arm and leg."[56] It was also around this time that Simeon Jocelyn, one of Russwurm's erstwhile abolitionist friends in New York, learned that Russwurm was "so emaciated" that Jocelyn "should scarcely" be able to recognize him.[57] William Prout, his protégé and secretary, revealed, only after Russwurm's death, that four years earlier, in 1847, he had not been expected to survive, given that he had been severely ill, losing much blood through a terrible "hemorrhage of the nose."[58] Unless completely incapacitated, he continued to work during these afflictions; he had worked on documents while lying fatally ill in bed on the very day that he died. As Latrobe put it in a moving tribute to the man, Russwurm died "with harness on his back."[59] The author of the most detailed history of the Maryland colony understandably described Russwurm as a "veteran of illness."[60]

Partly because of his illness and need for medical attention, Russwurm, accompanied by his wife, Sarah McGill Russwurm, and one of their four children, made the one and only trip he ever took back to the United States. Arriving on August 10, 1848, at a record speed of only twenty-eight days' sailing between Cape Palmas and Baltimore, he received medical treatment and visited the board of the MSCS, whose members warmly welcomed and toasted their governor.[61] The board held a dinner in Russwurm's honor at Baltimore's finest hotel. There were no absentees. And John Latrobe, who had corresponded and worked so closely with Russwurm for almost twenty years, met the governor for the first time. In fact, James Hall was the only board member who had previously met Russwurm in person. By then president of the MSCS, Latrobe proudly took the chair at the dinner. Writing almost forty years later, Latrobe vividly recalled that "there was not one present who was not impressed by the grave, courteous and dignified bearing of the agent whose wise and prudent conduct of the society's affairs in Africa had given such satisfaction."[62] Almost certainly written by James Hall, its editor, the *Maryland Colonization Journal* report noted that "toasts and sentiments and brief remarks were made by everyone present. All were called upon and all responded. It would much exceed our limits to record every thing that was said, though we would be glad to have it in our power to do so." The *Journal* did print the remarks of Governor Russwurm, "who when his health was drunk, on the removal of the cloth," rose and said: "Mr. President and gentlemen—unaccustomed to public speaking and not anticipating the honor that has been done me, I find it difficult to express the feelings which your kindness has inspired. But I can most truly say, that I shall carry back to my home in Africa double motives from this day forth, to do my best to merit the confidence that has been reposed in me. Gentlemen I thank you."[63]

The idea of a dinner in honor of a "colored man" caused a "sensation" in Baltimore. "It was ludicrous," Latrobe remembered, "to see the astonishment of the Irish waiters who surrounded the table at 'Page's Hotel,' when they were called upon to render the same service to a colored man that they were in the habit of rendering to the many socially prominent citizens who were his hosts."⁶⁴ It should not go unremarked that it is to John Latrobe's credit and the relatively advanced nature of his ideas that writing in Baltimore in 1885, he thought such behavior and attitude backward—"ludicrous," as he put it.

But one of the first things Russwurm did after his arrival, even before the dinner in his honor and his medical treatment, was to make the long trip up to Maine to see Susan Hawes, his stepmother, and other relatives and friends with whom he had remained in contact over the years. Russwurm actually stayed at the Haweses'—"my old home," he called it—where everyone was glad to see him and to meet his wife and son. To the end of her days, Susan Hawes delighted in the achievements of her adopted son, "the governor."⁶⁵ Russwurm was saddened by the fact that Mrs. Hawes's eldest daughter was ill and had been for some time. But most of all he worried about the condition of his adopted mother: "It grieves me much to see the old lady have so much to do in her old age, and living without one of her boys, after having raised so many. They are all away in the Western country," he wrote Hall. His only blood brother, Francis Edward Russwurm, was living in California, working as a teacher. He worried about Francis, who had poor health, being inclined to consumption.⁶⁶ The brothers were never to see each other again. Francis died in Campo, California, at the age of forty-eight in 1862.⁶⁷

Some urged Russwurm to stay in the United States. William Fessenden, Bowdoin alumnus and abolitionist, tried to persuade him to remain and join the antislavery cause, and in Boston his old friends, black and white, apparently offered him the presidency of a projected black college.⁶⁸ But neither enticements nor any sense of obligation could bring Russwurm to abandon Africa and return to the United States—not even Susan Hawes's plight, by which he was deeply moved. Russwurm had intended to visit his alma mater during the commencement exercise but changed his mind, so homesick was he for Africa. As early as August 21, two days after his arrival in Maine, he wrote Hall, telling him that he and his wife "both long to see Africa; and having seen our friends in Maine, we are now ready to return to Africa, as soon as we receive a few lines from you, informing us *positively* of the sailing" of the Liberia packet from Baltimore to Liberia. The Maine weather did not encourage him to tarry. Now accustomed to the Liberian climate, he found that in August the weather in North Yarmouth was "so cold" that he and his wife had to sleep under two or three blankets.⁶⁹

Russwurm's home was in Africa, to which he had dedicated his life. He returned, leaving Baltimore on September 6, the same day on which Bowdoin held its commencement exercise, and twenty-two years earlier to the day on which he had taken part in another exercise and given that historic speech in Brunswick.[70] He now referred to himself as an "African"—and back home he went. From Cape Palmas, Russwurm wrote to Latrobe reporting his safe arrival on November 17 in his "free home" in Liberia. "The colonists and natives all appear glad to see me," he told Latrobe, "and are much pleased with the kind reception I met with from our honorable Board of Managers." The medical treatment he received, he reported, "has been successful, and added 12 or 15 years to my life, from my feelings."[71] His "feelings" deceived him. Russwurm became gravely ill again and was confined to bed during the early months of 1851, stoically performing as many duties as he was able to from his bed. But on the night of June 9, 1851, Russwurm died. "He had been a great sufferer from disease for two years or more," Dr. Samuel McGill reported to Latrobe, "but two weeks previous to his death he was perfectly free from pain, yet greatly prostrated; his mind until the very last remained unclouded: on the day of his death he attended to a portion of his official duties." Russwurm himself, apparently, had not expected death to strike him so suddenly: a meticulous and methodical man, he, according to McGill, "expressed no wishes in his last moments either in relation to public, or his own private affairs."[72] He was four months short of his fifty-second birthday.

Although the governor had been ill for some months, his death came as a shock to Cape Palmas. As Joshua Stewart, writing to the board of managers in Baltimore on behalf of a meeting of "citizens of Cape Palmas," noted, despite Russwurm's "long & painful sickness . . . his death was at last very sudden to us." He went on: "Sirs, as a body of citizens or subjects, Pen cannot ascribe our fealing, no sir, our lips cannot till our fealing on hearing the Report [of Russwurm's death]."[73] Both colonists and Africans went into "anxiety-laden mourning."[74] "Even the heathens in these parts ex claims [sic]—We have lost a friend and father!" Boston Drayton, a colonist, wrote to Latrobe. "His character since my acquaintance with him stands unimpeached. Persecution and trials he had, but the worth of a man is never appreciated by some while he is [alive]. So with the majority in Cape Palmas."[75] It was true not only of Cape Palmas. With more than his fair share of detractors while living, in death Russwurm was, at least in certain quarters, highly praised. His burden had been heavy in more ways than one. Sir Harry Johnston described him as "a most energetic, capable man" but also suggested that Russwurm died of "overwork and worry."[76] The white ruling class in America had watched his every move to see if a Negro could carry the burden of state. Like other black men in positions of esteem, he was not afforded the luxury of the individual to stumble as an individual; on his shoulders was the burden of the prestige of the African, "the Negro"—the fate of an entire "race." Thus Commodore Perry (who a few years later would disturb the Japanese nation with his gunboats) on his visit to Liberia reported to Washington that "we have, in the example" of Governor Russwurm of Maryland in Liberia and Governor Joseph Roberts of Liberia, "irrefragable proof of the capability of colored people to govern themselves."[77] It was meant as a compliment and was generally received as such. The same note with the same professed good intentions was struck in an "Address to the People of Maryland in Liberia" by the MSCS board of managers on Russwurm's death. "If white men have ceased to hold office or exercise authority among you, it is because he [Russwurm] illustrated the capacity of your race to fill the highest political office with an ability that could not be surpassed." It continued: "Had he failed in this, had he fallen short of what was expected of him, you would have been the losers in the opinion of the world; and the slander which has so often charged you with political incapacity, would, for a season, have been looked upon as sustained." Of course, the board was right in adjudging this the general attitude of the time. But one wonders if the board itself, despite its relatively progressive outlook, would have regarded the charge of racial incapacity sustained had Russwurm failed. Happily, Russwurm succeeded. "In the long career of happiness and prosperity which is already opening in Liberia," the board concluded, "its highest offices will doubtless be often filled by men of worth and talent. But great and distinguished as these may be, their possessors may always resort with profit to your earliest history to gather from the records of Governor Russwurm's life the most admirable examples of prudence, wisdom and integrity."[78]

Ralph Gurley, then senior editor of the *Christian Statesman*, eulogized Russwurm in notably more human terms. He had first made contact with Russwurm in a letter sent to the young black graduate on Christmas Day, 1826. And it was with Gurley that Russwurm had corresponded and made arrangements to emigrate to Liberia. Less than two years before Russwurm's death Gurley had stayed with the governor at Cape Palmas as a U.S. government commissioner on a fact-finding mission to West Africa.[79] Russwurm, he now wrote, "combined with great good sense a quiet and unostentatious manner, a gentle, modest, and amiable temper, well adapted to allay excitement, to conciliate confidence and regard, to satisfy all sober expectations, and all honest and reasonable demands. Free from ostentation and arrogance, little disposed to the highest exhibition of vanity, he fulfilled the trust committed to his hands with uniform fidelity, and in all seasons of peril and difficulty, in hours of ill health and depression, with amiable fortitude and invincible resolution."[80]

Russwurm did live long enough to witness the new spurt of African American emigration to Liberia after the passage of the Fugitive Slave Law in 1850.[81] Since the law further jeopardized the already fragile liberty of the free people of color, many of those who had previously pilloried Russwurm now turned their eyes to Liberia.[82] In the aftermath of and largely because of this law, two of the diaspora's greatest intellectuals in the nineteenth century decided to settle in Liberia. Alexander Crummell, after graduating from Cambridge, was so disillusioned with prospects in the United States, especially after the act, that he headed for Monrovia. The brilliant young Blyden came to the United States in the same year the act was passed. Not only could he not find an educational institution that would overlook his color and admit him, but he lived in constant fear of being kidnapped and sold into slavery. Arriving in the United States in May 1850, by December of the same year he had left for Liberia.[83]

Epilogue

Russwurm in His Rightful Place

In many ways, Russwurm's long absence from the Pan-African pantheon stems from three sources: ignorance of, and misunderstanding and distortions about, his life and achievements; misunderstandings about the colonization project; and controversy over the status of Liberia in the Pan-Africanist enterprise.

In a pioneering biographical portrait of the editors of *Freedom's Journal*, the distinguished Afro–Puerto Rican scholar and bibliophile Arturo Schomburg averred that "John B. Russwurm was a very brilliant journalist and teacher." But, he continued, "the question that is pertinent to ask now is, did he sell his birthright for a mess of pottage?" Schomburg answered his own question: "We believe so."[1] Unfortunately, this perception of Russwurm as a black Benedict Arnold until very recently remained unchallenged and in some quarters is still current. In a book published only in 2002, one historian went out of her way to claim that promises from the ACS "worked a transformation in [Russwurm's] attitude with regard to colonization."[2] It is a hoary and hackneyed charge that emerged immediately after Russwurm announced his change of views and intention to emigrate to Liberia. It publicly gathered steam in William Lloyd Garrison's *Liberator* and was helped along its way by Garrison himself. For Garrison not only served as the ringmaster for the one-sided assault on Russwurm but also joined in and landed a few cowardly punches below the belt himself. Though a relative newcomer to the anticolonization cause, he and not Cornish was the first to evoke the name of Benedict Arnold in speaking of Russwurm.[3] Hardly known himself for his modesty, Garrison accused Russwurm (as he later did Frederick Douglass) of "vanity," a "love of distinction greater than his regard for consistency." Russwurm, claimed Garrison, allowed himself to be "seduced away to Liberia" by "extraordinary inducements" dangled before him by the ACS.[4] As demonstrated earlier, there is not a shred of evidence to support the claim of corrupted morals on Russwurm's part. And neither Garrison nor those who parroted him have substantiated the charge; the evidence is against them. Such calumny could only tarnish Russwurm's reputation for posterity.

But undoubtedly the item that has done more injury to Russwurm's standing in the historiographical literature than any other is Bella Gross's influential 1932 essay, "*Freedom's Journal* and the *Rights of All*."[5] Extending over some forty-five pages, it is one of the longest articles ever published in Carter G. Woodson's prestigious and unrivaled *Journal of Negro History*. Though ponderous and repetitious, its many footnotes would mislead the uninitiated into thinking that this was serious scholarship on its purported subject. Indeed, many scholars have cited it approvingly and apparently unwittingly, genuflecting to its authority on the subject.[6] But in the end it is little more than a hagiography of Cornish and a scathing, ad hominem and egregious attack on Russwurm, her bête noire—literally. It would require another chapter to fully document her errors, but her arguments may be fairly summarized as follows. Whatever is good and praiseworthy in *Freedom's Journal* is Cornish's work; whatever meets with her disapproval belongs to Russwurm, who "lacked originality," "compromised a great deal, and seldom spoke clearly" (p. 248). She adduces no evidence to support these claims. Unsigned editorial material she attributes to Cornish only, when the evidence clearly suggests that they were as much Russwurm's work as Cornish's, if not more. Some articles that are clearly attributable to Russwurm she makes Cornish's. Indeed, even articles published *after* Cornish had resigned she tries to attribute to him. She claims that Russwurm, who was "indifferent to the people's wishes and needs" and whose "interests were narrow" (pp. 278–79), was "forced to resign" (pp. 246, 279).

One of Gross's primary problems with Russwurm, apparently, is that he was among "the few who sold themselves to the [American Colonization] Society for special favors and good posts in Liberia" (p. 266), especially when, according to her, "as a body, the colored people opposed the [ACS]" (p. 264). Although her essay carries an impressive number of footnotes (145), these latter, all too often, do her argument no good whatsoever. Perhaps most scandalous and damaging to Russwurm's reputation is Gross's statement that Russwurm "had the audacity to defend the policies and expulsion laws of Ohio, because, he said, 'our rightful place is in Africa'" (p. 280). It is a damning indictment of Russwurm, but is it true? In the footnote to the statement, she gives as her source *Freedom's Journal*, March 7, 1829, page 386. But that issue shows absolutely nothing to substantiate the claim: no reference to Cincinnati (the primary site of the exodus in 1829) or Ohio, let alone the statement "Our rightful place is in Africa." The page in question is largely taken up by an editorial on Liberia, "Our Vindication," with nothing along the lines claimed by Gross. But how many people have realized this? How many readers—especially in 1932, when Gross wrote those words—would have had the opportunity to consult a page referred to in a relatively inaccessible newspaper published in 1829? The chances were and still are against Russwurm. The reasonable reader would assume that a verdict handed down with such verve and certitude—"he had the audacity to . . ."—did not come out of thin air and that the *Journal of Negro History*, in whose pages it is carried, would have reviewed the essay with the requisite scholarly thoroughness. As we have seen, Russwurm did mention in the *Liberia Herald* the crisis in Ohio (which came to a head in July 1829, that is, *after* the *Freedom's Journal* had ceased to be) but said nothing along the lines asserted by Bella Gross.[7] There are many other footnotes of this kind in her essay. How many issued from sheer sloppiness in research is difficult to tell; she probably never expected anyone to ever check them.

Gross makes the patently false and easily falsifiable claim that Cornish's "favorite motto, 'Righteousness Exalteth a Nation,'" which was carried on the masthead during his time at the paper, was "conspicuously missing in numbers of the *Freedom's Journal* after Cornish resigned" (p. 248). The truth of the matter is that Cornish resigned with the issue of September 14, 1827, and the motto remained inviolate for the next twenty-seven issues—almost seven months—until April 4, 1828, when Russwurm in its stead substituted the subtitle "Devoted to the Improvement of the Coloured Population." The author of the 1993 book *The Afro-American in New York City, 1827–1860*, takes Gross's assertion on trust and repeats her legend about the *Journal's* motto.[8]

I do not know who Bella Gross was or is, nor do I know or wish to divine her motives. But she may have been driven by an opposition to black nationalism, commonplace on the American left during the 1930s when she wrote. From her perspective, Russwurm lacked what she calls "Americanism," which, she tells us, was "a passion with Cornish; in that he would never compromise, even to win immediate ends." This assertion is, incidentally, undermined by the actual evidence of Cornish's life and practice.[9] It is almost incredible to think that she is talking about the same man who abruptly left Russwurm to weather the storm at a time when *Freedom's Journal* and Russwurm (explicitly and by name) his ostensibly "junior" partner was under the most withering attacks by the colonizationists, especially in the persons of "Wilberforce" (Dr. Archibald Alexander, principal of Princeton Theological Seminary) and his esteemed colleague, Dr. Samuel Miller. When Russwurm angrily responded to his black critics who questioned his motives and integrity in deciding to leave for Liberia, he drew attention to the price he paid for boldly opposing the ACS. And when he asked rhetorically, "[W]ho has made half the sacrifice we have to oppose the Colonization society? who has laboured half so much by night and by day for the same end? who has had to bear the brunt of the battle, while those who led us into action, were sitting quietly at home?" he was no doubt thinking of the sudden and stunning withdrawal from the field of battle by his "senior" editor, the "uncompromising" Rev. Samuel Cornish.[10] Cornish, Gross declares, "wanted his people to be recognized as Americans, at least Colored Americans, if race had to be emphasized" (p. 281), implying that Russwurm did not. Her attack on Russwurm knows no bounds. She even goes so far as to suggest that Russwurm "sold" Cape Palmas African American settlers into slavery (p. 280)! Not even the *Liberator*, which she invokes to support her assertion, ever made such a claim: despite the nastiness of the attacks on Russwurm in the 1830s, it was never even alleged, let alone proven.[11] In any case, Gross's influential essay must have damaged the reputation of Russwurm in the eyes of most if not all of those who read it. That Schomburg's attack on Russwurm came after Gross's essay was published is probably not coincidental. He was extremely well read in African American history and indeed was himself a contributor to the *Journal of Negro History*. Schomburg was, therefore, more than likely influenced in his views of Russwurm by the essay. The essay's wider influence probably also helps to explain the absence of a scholarly biography of the man, since few would wish to devote such extensive attention to so unsympathetic a character.

Another argument mobilized by Russwurm's detractors, including Gross, since the early nineteenth century, explicitly as well as implicitly, suggests that it would have been far more noble to stay and fight oppression in the United States than to seek relief through emigration. Schomburg articulated this position more clearly than most when he declared his preference for the ostensible position of Cornish over that of Russwurm: "Men like Cornish, who battled in and out of season for the American colored people to remain here in the land of their birth rather than to run across the sea chasing rainbows, served posterity best, and now merit our everlasting thanksgiving."[12] The suggestion, of course, is that Russwurm went to Liberia quixotically chasing chimeras while Cornish remained at home, feet firmly planted on the ground, fighting a righteous war in the trenches against American oppression. Russwurm, of course, argued that the rainbow chasers were those who believed that American society could be so transformed that black people would receive citizenship rights on equal terms with their white counter-parts. The evidence suggests that Russwurm's going to Liberia was far less chimerical than the project his detractors had undertaken for themselves. To this day, despite the genuine advances that would have astonished Russ-wurm, the goal of basic equality and human decency across the color line remains unachieved in the United States. In any case, there is no reason to regard emigration as less noble than remaining in bondage and encouraging others to so remain in the mere hope that, primarily through moral suasion, sometime in the indefinite future—the most optimistic, including Garrison, spoke in terms of generations—freedom and equality would be attained. As the Rev. A. F. Russell, a Cape Palmas colonist, wrote pointedly in 1852:

> How can it be thought by a colored man, a poor ninety-ninth rate being in America, that he is disgracing himself or blighting his honor, to leave America before all his brethren are free? Where is the honor of hopeless oppression? Where is the honor arising from holding a few self-torturing, feeble, worse than time-wasting anti-slavery meetings in a free State? Tell-ing over to each other what they have experienced a thousand times, and will experience a thousand more, without altering their condition. Why sing to each other, we are degraded, oppressed? . . . Refuse the boon of liberty because it would please the Colonizationists for me to be free in Africa! And suppose it pleased the devil, would it alter the fact, or thing? . . . America is the place of our nativity, says the free colored man. It was ours too. What have I to do with a native land, that never saw one of my race a free man, but to leave it, for the black man's own home. . . . In the United States you are only men in shape—and when slave labor is no longer needed, years hence, you will remain in the United States if you will—holding a position somewhat analogous to the ourang-outang, "an animal," they will say, "something like a man, that used to work with our oxen, plough with our horses, hunt with our dogs," etc. What is the hope of the American black?[13]

Moreover, the belief in the achievement of freedom in the United States was largely based on religious dogma—God in his wisdom would set the cap-tives free and wipe away their tears. "Our mind is entirely at rest, in respect to the ultimate result of abolition efforts," Cornish confidently editorialized. "The cause is God's, and it is entirely under his control."[14] This, of course, was based on the at best nonrational notion—"the evidence of things unseen"—that there was a God, compounded by the equally nonrational belief (flying in the face of the black experience over at least the last five centuries) that he was merciful and good and had the interest of the oppressed children of Africa at heart. This was not only the position of Cornish, a deeply religious man, but also that of Garrison and even David Walker, the latter set apart from the others by his great desire to give God a helping hand in the struggle, rejecting the Garrisonian precepts of nonresistance and nonviolence. This did not mean that men like Samuel Cornish did not struggle against the institution; they did, but given the vastly superior strength of their adversaries, their efforts were largely ineffectual and operated at the level of propaganda. Relatively few of the free people of color risked their lives and liberty in the way that Harriet Tubman did in venturing into the slave states and leading enslaved Africans to "freedom" in the North. There was only one John Brown. And Frederick Douglass, the most outspoken black anticolonizationist of the nineteenth century, adamantly refused to join him in that noble but risky adventure to Harper's Ferry. In one of his most outspoken attacks on his erstwhile comrades among the black abolitionists, Russwurm drew attention to the ineffectual strategy they propounded and what he perceived as their lack of real effort, compounded by their costly obstruction of the Liberian project:

> The truth is, men may disclaim as much as they please against Africa, they may circulate inflammatory papers among persons too ignorant to see through their *disinterested* motives, but we challenge them to bring facts to prove any of their assertions. To the uneducated children of Africa, their daily language is, this is your country, &c. &c. all of which is true enough; but will [any] of these men who labor from such *pure* motives, do any thing more than spout, and, run from city to city, dissuading those, whose wishes are for bettering their condition, from making the *attempt*. They ought surely to be the pioneers in this march of equality, which is shortly to cover the Union, as the waters do the sea—they ought to make their dearly beloved colored brethren and sisters, not so *only* in *name* but in *fact*, and then we on this side of the Atlantic—in this land of true equality, will begin to think that there is one spark of pure disinterested benevolence in this selfseeking world.[15]

Many of those who turned to and advocated colonization, especially those in the MSCS, far from being the racist devils they are often made out to have been, were in fact abolitionists who saw no practicable and realistic means of relieving the oppression of black people in the United States except through aiding their escape through manumission and migration from the country. Rev. Russell agreed with them, seeing emigration as "the only practicable hope."[16] The case of the Quakers in North Carolina is instructive. The driving force behind the colonization movement in the state, abolitionist Quakers adamantly and courageously opposed the institution of slavery. They petitioned the North Carolina legislature to be permitted to manumit their slaves, and their petition was refused. When in 1776 a group of Quakers manumitted forty slaves, the authorities apprehended the former slaves and sold them back into slavery. The Quakers' appeal to have them released was once again turned down by the legislature. In 1816 the Quakers formed the Manumission Society of North Carolina. Because of internal divisions and pressure from the slave-owning interests and authorities they changed the name by a narrow majority the following year to the Manumission and Colonization Society of North Carolina, though the word "Colonization" was subsequently dropped from the name in 1824.[17] Writing in 1834 to a Friend in England, Jeremiah Hubbard, a Quaker from Guildford County and clerk of the Yearly Meeting of Friends of North Carolina, complained that they could never get a law to manumit slaves within the state, despite persistent effort over a span of fifty years. He expanded on the added difficulty they had encountered in freeing the enslaved:

> We have sent some to the State of Ohio, and since then, hundreds of blacks have been in a manner compelled by the laws of that State, or the prejudice of some of its citizens, to leave it and go to Canada. We have sent some to Indiana, but that State has passed laws, we hear, to forbid any more coming. We have sent some to Pennsylvania, but about two years ago, we shipped near one hundred from Newbern and Beaufort [North Carolina], to Chester [Pennsylvania]; they were not suffered to land, neither there, nor in Philadelphia, nor yet on the Jersey shore, opposite; but had to float on the Delaware river until the Colonization Society took them into possession; then they were landed in Jersey, ten miles below Philadelphia, and re-shipped for Africa.[18]

Far from ridding the United States of the free people of color, as some racists in the colonization movement had hoped, the result of the effort of the colonizationists was that the majority of those who emigrated to Liberia, especially those who went to Maryland in Liberia, were slaves manumitted by their owners on condition that they leave the country. Some slave owners went so far as to stipulate in their will that if their former slaves refused to go to Liberia they would once again be sold into slavery. This meant that for most who went to Liberia their emigration was literally an escape from the horrors of slavery, an exit from the house of bondage. The anticolonization abolitionists, such as William Garrison, had nothing in the short term to offer compared to this tangible benefit presented by the colonizationists. And as John Maynard Keynes wisely noted, "In the long run we are all dead." Some 1,200 Marylanders left for Liberia under MSCS auspices between 1831 and 1857.[19] "He who saves a life, saves the world entire," says the Talmud.

Certainly many, probably even the majority, of those members of Congress and of the southern state legislatures, such as Maryland, who advocated colonization and appropriated and disbursed funds for its execution were slaveholders and racists. But the same could not be said of many of those who actually ran the ACS and the numerous state auxiliaries, especially in the North (where the vast majority were located) and in a state such as Maryland.[20] From the start, the ACS constituted an unlikely collaboration of those who sought to defend the institution of slavery and those who were adamantly opposed to it. This strange bringing together of opposites, so apparent to observers at the time, was fully acknowledged and even applauded by the ACS itself. As early as 1819 it noted in its second annual report that, "like every effort to enlarge the stock of human happiness, it enlists in its favour the selfish, as well as the disinterested, affections of the heart." It perceived its disparate attraction as a boon. "The success of the wise and charitable purpose of the Society," it proudly declared, "is assured by the irresistible appeal which it makes to all the powerful sentiments of the heart—the most sordid and degrading, as well as the most benevolent and exalted."[21] Colonization was a compromise solution that could be and was subscribed to by both abolitionists (who sought the liberation of the enslaved and the establishment of a homeland in which the freedmen and women could live as free men and women) and the defenders of slavery (who saw the free people of color as a threat to the slavery system). Colonization, declared the ACS, should appeal to the "interest of the South, to the humanity of the North, and to the religion of the whole country."[22] Indeed, it was not until the 1830s that abolitionists began to systematically attack the project of the colonizationists; during the first decade, despite the objections of some free people of color in the North, such as James Forten in Philadelphia and Russwurm and Cornish in *Freedom's Journal,* cooperation and collaboration, not antagonism, marked the relationship. Among those who lent a sympathetic ear to colonization were figures such as William Garrison himself and Benjamin Lundy, whose paper, the *Genius of Universal Emancipation,* carried a remarkably large number of procolonization articles, written mainly by Gurley, in the 1820s. Predating the formation of the ACS, Lundy's own Union Humane Society, founded in Ohio in 1815, called for the "removal of the Negroes beyond the pale of the white man."[23] Indeed, along with distinguished abolitionists such as Theodore Weld, Arthur Tappan, Gerrit Smith, and James Birney, Lundy himself was directly associated with the ACS. And Garrison, who would later become the nemesis of the ACS, concluded as late as July 4, 1829, in an address delivered at the Park Street Church in Boston, "I call upon our citizens to assist in establishing auxiliary colonization societies in every State, county and town. I implore their direct and liberal patronage to the parent society [the ACS]."[24] What is more, he was explicitly invited by the Congregational societies of Boston to make the address "in the interests of the Colonization Society." And as his sons wrote in the biography of their father: "At the conclusion of Mr. Garrison's address Mr Pluml[e]y, an agent of the American Colonization Society, briefly urged its claims to support, and a collection in aid of it was taken up." They hastened to add that "beyond what is quoted above," Garrison had "said nothing in favor of the Society, except to commend the infant colony of Liberia."[25] But who could have asked for more?

The anticolonization charge was therefore led, not by Garrison, as the standard accounts of American abolitionism claim, but, ironically enough, by Russwurm, first and foremost, and Cornish in *Freedom's Journal* in 1827, four years before Garrison picked it up in the *Liberator,* a paper first published on January 1, 1831. Not surprisingly, even the gentle Samuel Cornish was more than a little peeved with Garrison and his fanatical band of followers and their exorbitant claims in the anticolonization fight. Writing in 1837, Cornish pointed out that Garrison and his followers were latecomers to the anticolonization cause, and he claimed "some instrumentality in teaching" anticolonizationism to both Tappan and Garrison. He supported the point by reprinting an anticolonization editorial published ten years earlier in *Freedom's Journal.*[26] Garrison's paper was inspired and sustained primarily by free people of color in the North—Boston, New York, Philadelphia—the Americans who found colonization most objectionable.[27]

In short, the caricature of the ACS as simply the evil instrument of slaveholders (when Garrison himself supported it up to at least 1830 and Gerrit Smith resigned from it only in 1834) is simply that—a caricature, which bears little resemblance to the actual organization under whose auspices Russwurm left for Liberia in 1829. Certainly, leading figures in the ACS, such as Gurley, and in the MSCS, such as Latrobe and James Hall, were generally nonracist and antislavery in their sentiments; they simply thought that the most practicable thing that could be accomplished in the early nineteenth century was to advocate and aid the colonization project. Many of their backers had a different agenda; but that was theirs. Gurley hinted at these differences in 1832 when he informed Garrison that his polemic against the ACS, *Thoughts on African Colonization,* was not only distorted but also misdirected when he used items carried by the *African Repository* rather than the official statements of the board of managers of the ACS as his primary source for pronouncements that Garrison found objectionable.[28] The problem for Gurley was that the *Repository* was, though the least authoritative publication of the ACS, an official publication; the ACS had a varied membership, was a broad church, and allowed the most discordant voices within the organization to be heard simultaneously in order to gain the widest support for the project and keep it alive. As Frederic Bancroft noted, "[I]ts immediate aim was to attract as many persons and win as much support as possible, and to antagonize no one." Accurately, if caustically, he observed: "Gentle reasonableness, pleading sophistry, and all possible avoidance of causing or receiving irritations were conspicuous features of the society's propaganda. It daily illustrated the virtue of a soft answer, self-control, and patient appeals. It was rather indifferent to logic and consistency, if it could win support to avoid disputes." It collected money from both "philanthropists and Negro-haters." The more liberal-minded members of the ACS saw Henry Clay, a slaveholding Kentuckian politician, the man among the colonizationists most hated by their opponents, as an opportunist, but a useful one. "Clay I see has been helping himself to ride on our shoulders—but as he has no doubt been of service to us, I will not scrutinize too closely into his motives," Latrobe noted shrewdly and cynically in January 1827. The presidency of the ACS, a position that Clay occupied for many years (1836–52), as well as the many vice presidencies (numbering over seventy in the 1840s), were wholly honorific and not at all executive. Thus Clay, with his odiously racist statements, no more represented the views of the ACS than did the progressive Quakers of North Carolina. The ACS, as Bancroft observed almost a century ago,

> displayed great cleverness in advertising itself by using famous men and playing with the vanity of those eager to appear great. Justice Bushrod Washington, Charles Carroll of Carrollton, Henry Clay, William C. Crawford, John Randolph, General Robert G. Harper, Andrew Jackson, John Taylor of Caroline, and many others, objects of popular admiration or curiosity, were early made high officers of the society. Lafayette was a permanent vice president and Daniel Webster, one of the founders, was after

1823, among the numerous vice presidents. . . . By reporting the presence, the speeches, and the contributions of distinguished persons at the society's anniversaries, it soon gained great notoriety and prestige at state capitals and county seats, where members of the legislatures or of the courts readily confessed their resemblances to the great by taking a conspicuous part in forming an auxillary society. Numerous men of wealth, of political or social ambition hastened to join the society in the same spirit that they would have sought conspicuous mention in an account of a patriotic celebration or a vanity fair.[29]

It is difficult for anyone who has gone through the archives and studied the history of Maryland in Liberia not to be moved and impressed by the extraordinary care and generosity with which the MSCS looked after the interests of colonists in Maryland in Liberia—even *after* independence— avoiding many of the mistakes and harshness of the ACS in Monrovia. As Penelope Campbell noted, cynics may claim that MSCS officials "abhorred unfavorable reports from Africa merely because these deterred prospective emigrants," but there is no evidence to support this claim.[30] The MSCS's leading officials, Moses Sheppard (a Quaker), James Hall, and John Latrobe, had no slaves or interests in the institution of slavery. Deeply religious in outlook—with the exception of Hall, who was a man of science and probably a Deist, if not an agnostic—they deplored slavery in every form and believed in the capacity of black people to achieve as much, given the opportunity, as any other people. There was, Campbell noted, "a singular absence of racism in Latrobe's public statements and correspondence"; like most of his colleagues, he was "genuinely humanitarian and liberal." Latrobe in fact authored the first serious biographical portrait and estimate of the great African American mathematician and astronomer Benjamin Banneker. And he did so for explicitly antiracist purposes.[31]

Hall, the most influential figure in the MSCS after Latrobe, was remarkably progressive for the times. An unsentimental man of science, he abhorred the silly and dangerous notions of racial hierarchy and behaved accordingly. He was genuinely moved by the plight of African Americans and other members of the African diaspora. A New Hampshire man, he traveled to Cuba and Haiti soon after the untimely death of his wife and while suffering from ill health, and the time he spent in the Caribbean provoked an antiracist epiphany that set him on his work. Virtually a cripple (he hobbled around with the aid of crutches) and despite his fragile health—"I am not well, or rather unwell as usual," he wrote in 1853—Hall exerted himself in doing what he could to advance black emancipation. Almost apologizing for assuming the "liberty" of addressing the free people of color in Maryland, Hall, writing in 1859, explained that he had spent almost his entire professional life interacting with or working on behalf of people of African descent. Introducing himself in the third person, Hall noted, "During this long period, he has not only been intimate with people of color, the slave, the nominally and actually free, but his business, his correspondence and almost all the acts of his life have been, more or less, intimately connected with them; and 'tis no affectation of humanity to say, mainly devoted to their interests." This devotion, he explained, did not issue from "settled principles of action, or from any philanthropic motives, but from feelings engendered by long and agreeable intercourse, from repeated acts of kindness and hospitality he has ever experienced at their hands." Having introduced himself to his audience, Hall then dropped the third person and "for plainness and convenience" addressed his audience personally. He then went on to "affirm" at the outset that "the result of my long intercourse with the race to which you belong, the native African, the slave, and the free, in this and other lands, is a firm conviction, that, as a race—or a variety of the human species—you are capable of attaining the full stature of Manhood: not equaling some other varieties in intellectual power and ability, but surpassing others, and inferior to none in moral endowments and the capabilities for the rational enjoyment of human life." I have encountered nothing in the archives to undermine the sincerity of Hall's statement. He was, or rather *made* (at least allowed) himself to be astonishingly free of the pervasive cancer of American racism. Apart from the remarkably close friendship that he maintained with Russwurm, there is more than ample evidence of his uncommon open-mindedness on the matter of "race." A striking example is the 1836 description he volunteered of the relationship he established with the African Peroh Neh, dubbed "Yellow Will," and his respectful appraisal of the man:

It would hardly be just for me to close this brief statement, respecting the relation these people [native Africans] bear to the colony, without mentioning the instance of superior energy and sagacity in a native named Yellow Will. I found him an ordinary head-man or boy, such as usually go up and down the coast, in vessels. He had formerly been a head-workman, among the natives employed by the English at Fernand[o] Po. From the time of my first arrival at Cape Palmas, he has ever been at my service in any undertaking whatever. At times when it was expected that hostilities would commence with his tribe, he still continued his services unless forbidden by the king. But in the time of greatest excitement, I never was able in any manner whatever to shake his fidelity to his people, nor would he ever give the most distant hint of their disposition or designs. His answer to all interrogatories in this respect, was, "I am this country-man, not an American. I work for you to get money, not to betray my own people; when I join the Americans I shall leave my own people, I can't have a heart for both sides." This man became more and more attached to us, until finally he concluded to leave his tribe and move to our town, where he now resides, and is regarded by both natives and colonists, as a man of enterprise and sagacity, and the most sterling integrity. I have never seen a man whose natural powers of mind I should judge transcended his; and few uneducated men in civilized life, who could reason more correctly on subjects of moment. It has been mainly through his influence and counsel that the recent purchases of territory from the inhabitants have been so successfully effected; and I doubt not but he will ever prove an able, effi-cient, and patriotic counsellor to the authorities of the colony.[32]

As Latrobe explained, Hall's relation to the colonization project was largely accidental: he played no part in the founding of the ACS, "never at any time participating in the sanguine views of its friends—more interested in the Negro race than in the removal of any part of it to Africa," yet "circum-stances nevertheless resulted in placing Dr. Hall in a field where his great usefulness gave him the reputation that now attaches to his memory." He was an astonishingly hard worker, especially given his ailments and disability. (Latrobe marveled at his "surprising power of endurance.") A serious thinker and graceful writer, Hall, apart from editing the *Maryland Colonization Journal,* authored *An Address to the Free People of Color of the State of Maryland,* which must rank as one of the most unsentimental, antiracist, and power-ful arguments for African American emigration to Liberia. We have already seen the esteem in which Hall was held by Russwurm. But it is interesting to note that Sarah Russwurm (who frequently stayed with the Halls on her vis-its to the United States) and the McGills shared Russwurm's appreciation of the man, describing Hall to a third party as "a worthy, long tried, and faithful friend of our family and of Africa." Edward Blyden, the most distinguished and influential Pan-Africanist intellectual of the late nineteenth century, once wrote to Hall: "I have always looked upon you as one of the true, outspoken friends of the Negro and Africa—really desirous of seeing him elevated, and his country opened, civilized and regenerated."[33]

Certainly Russwurm suffered none of the appalling condescension, if not downright racism, from either Latrobe or Hall, that Frederick Douglass suffered at the hands of Garrison and his followers when the former slave had the audacity to start his own newspaper and to depart from some of Garrison's positions. Garrison himself accused Douglass of "apostasy," spread the most malicious gossip against him, and never tired of leveling the loaded charge of "ingratitude" against Douglass. One of Garrison's allies, George Bradburn, went so far as to accuse Douglass of conduct he called "monkeyism." In short, Garrison and the Garrisonians engaged in a relentless and decades-long campaign of character assassination against Douglass freighted with an astonishing mass of racism.[34] This contrasting treatment of Russwurm and Douglass may appear ironic, but it is only so if one harbors the erroneous notion that all colonizationists were racists and all abolitionists were antiracists.

The condemnation of Russwurm for supping with the devil is simply unfounded; there were devils in the background all right, but those were not the ones with whom Russwurm dealt. In any case, he probably would have accepted help from the devil himself—as Rev. Russell would also have done, and as Blyden implied of himself—if it would have contributed to the escape of black people from what many regarded as the hell of the United States of America.

One of the other ironies of the criticism of the ACS is that its publication, the *African Repository and Colonial Journal,* was unrivaled, qualitatively and quantitatively, in publishing extraordinary articles on African civilizations, cultures, and history, explicitly aimed at undermining racist notions of black inferiority and also, apparently, attracting would-be emigrants to the Liberia project. George Fredrickson, one of the few historians to have carefully read (as opposed to pretending to) the publications of the ACS, was genuinely taken aback (as I was) by the remarkably modern, scientific, and antiracist thrust of much of its output. "One of the most surprising and unexpected features of the more sophisticated and philosophical kind of colonizationist propaganda," Fredrickson observed, "was its respectful, even complimentary, way of describing Negroes when it was a question of their innate racial character and capacity rather than their 'degraded' condition in America." The *African Repository,* he continued, presented "the case for a proud Negro past, which would be used over and over again by ethnological defenders of the Negro—white and black—throughout the century."[35] It was a priceless service that even the black opponents of colonization took advantage of (some rather shamefacedly and silently), cherished, and applauded. *Freedom's Journal,* particularly after Russwurm became the sole editor, republished in part or full many articles from the *Repository,* especially those pertaining to ancient

Egypt, Ethiopia, and other African civilizations. The *African Repository* was in fact used as an antiracist arsenal. As Peter Hinks has convincingly argued, these articles had a profound impact on David Walker, and their influence is evident in his *Appeal,* especially in relation to Walker's discussion of the glorious antecedents of Afro-America and the Negro generally.[36] Walker himself revealed an even more direct knowledge of the offerings of the *African Repository,* implying that he had read every issue up to when he wrote his pamphlet.[37] Thus although he railed against the ACS and referred to colonization as a "trick" and a "cunningly devised plot of Satan," Walker was a direct and indirect beneficiary of the ACS through its remarkable organ, the *African Repository and Colonial Journal.*[38] Further, though the commentary on him seldom mentions it, Walker recognized and acknowledged that there were good, if misguided, people among the colonizationists. Part of the task he set himself in the *Appeal* was to put right such misguided souls:

> It will be well for me to notice at once, that I do not mean indiscriminately to condemn all the members and advocates of this scheme, for I believe that there are some friends to the sons of Africa, who are laboring for our salvation, not in words only but in truth and deed, who have been drawn into this plan—Some, more by persuasion than any thing else; while others, with humane feelings and lively zeal for our good, seeing how much we suffer from the afflictions poured upon us by unmerciful tyrants, are willing to enroll their names in any thing which they think has for its ultimate end our redemption from wretchedness and miseries; such men, with a heart truly overflowing with gratitude for their past services and zeal in our cause, I humbly beg to examine this plot minutely, and see if the end which they have in view will be completely consummated by such a course of procedure.[39]

Indeed, in his "Address Delivered before the General Colored Association at Boston" the previous year and published by Russwurm in *Freedom's Journal,* Walker singled out Jehudi Ashmun, the ACS's first governor of Liberia, for special praise among "our white brethren and friends" who had made and were making "mighty efforts for the amelioration of our condition." That many of them, Walker declared, "have gone, and will go, all lengths for our good, is evident, from the very works of the great, the good, and the godlike Granville Sharpe, Wilberforce, Lundy, and the truly patriotic and lamented Mr. Ashmun, late Colonial Agent of Liberia, who, with a zeal which was only equaled by the goodness of his heart, has lost his life in our cause."[40] There was genuine tension, then, in Walker's attitude toward colonization. He correctly recognized the self-serving motives behind the advocacy of colonization by men such as Henry Clay, whom he rightly excoriated in the *Appeal*. But unlike Forten and Garrison, he also recognized that good, if misguided, people mingled among the colonizationists. In short, Walker condemned colonization but not all colonizationists. He separated, as he saw them with rather Blakean religious eyes, the devils from the angels, those with "the most sordid and degrading" motives from those with "the most benevolent and exalted," both of which groups inhabited the same organization, the ACS.[41] Such complexity the Garrisonians in their noble and righteous zeal chose to ignore. Even their good friends at times could not fail to point out the distortions in their depiction of the ACS. Dr. Thomas Hodgkin, the distinguished British abolitionist, wrote to the American delegates attending the 1840 Anti-Slavery Convention in London: "I admit that you have completely succeeded in drawing a repulsive picture of the [American Colonization] Society, but I do not admit that it gives a fair idea of the reality."[42]

The truth is that the colonization movement was far more heterogeneous than the dominant Garrisonian depiction has led many to believe. It contained within its membership at least three discernible though somewhat overlapping factions. First, it contained those we may describe as *pessimistic abolitionists,* people who were genuinely abolitionist in outlook and action but who also believed and thought, and not without good reasons, that—given the hegemony of the slaveholders within the American polity and the pervasiveness of racism within the nation as a whole—the prospect of overthrowing the institution of slavery was at best remote. This faction would include many of the Quaker colonizationists and black emigrationists, such as Russwurm, Crummell, Blyden, and many others who went to Liberia, Haiti, Sierra Leone, and elsewhere. The second discernible group, which may be described as *pacifist abolitionists,* included those who felt and thought that the overthrow of the institution of slavery, abhorrent though it was, could be achieved only at the expense of an unacceptable level of bloodshed; Haiti and Nat Turner haunted them. Colonization was thus resorted to in order to obviate such an eventuality. Many of those were Christians who had a conspicuous and inordinate level of concern for the well-being of the slaveholders. Thus theirs was an advocacy of abolition through colonization. (Interestingly enough, the Garrisonians shared this group's dread of violence and bloodshed but differed with them on the right of African Americans to remain within the United States after abolition.) Finally, there were the *racist colonizationists,* epitomized by the figure of Henry Clay, who simply felt that the United States was a white man's country, in which the place of those of African descent, insofar as they lived in the country at all, was in bondage; all free people of color should simply be removed from the country ("with their consent," of course), and Liberia would serve as a convenient dumping ground. The problem in much of the antislavery historiography since Garrison is that the Clay position is depicted as representative of colonizationists *tout court,* when in fact it was almost certainly a minority position within the ACS and the colonization movement more generally.

Russwurm was obviously hyperbolic in his 1827 claim that African Americans were all opposed to the ACS; if nothing else, his later action disproved his own claim. The legend was spread even further by Garrison in the *Liberator* and in his influential 1832 pamphlet, *Thoughts on African Colonization.* And his compilation of anticolonization resolutions by free people of color, "Sentiments of the Free People of Color," would have been more accurately entitled "Sentiments of *Some* Free People of Color." For people knew then, and modern scholarship has also shown, that opposition to the ACS was not "universal" among the free people of color, let alone the remainder of the black population. Free people of color, especially in the period prior to 1830, supported the ACS and took the opportunity to emigrate to Liberia.[43] The manumitted in even greater numbers also grasped the opportunity to escape bondage. Russwurm's apostasy might have outraged the most influential among the free people of color, but it is doubtful if the majority of the free people of color, especially those in the South, let alone the enslaved, even knew of the controversy that surrounded him, much less condemned his action.

It is scarcely possible not to be moved by how emigrants to Liberia rejoiced in their newfound freedom. "What is the matter with the Poor black man, in your Place," Henry Hannon exclaimed to the board of managers of the MSCS in 1844. Seven years after leaving Maryland, he now asked the board to tell Afro-Marylanders that "I am as *free* as a man can be. . . . I enjoy the life of a freeman, in africa, we can set in our own court house, we can have our jurymen of coloured men, we have our Council to make our buy laws for us." He asked after his friends in Baltimore and invited them all to join him in Cape Palmas, "For we can Praise *god* in this Place and no man interferes with us, neither can any man make affread or molest us, while we live under our fig tree." Thomas Gross reveled in the beauty of the place, surpassed only by that of the liberty that he now enjoyed: "When I rise in the morning before the sun is up, and view the country, east west north and south, for miles around the forest lookes beautiful and green. . . . We are all free men here, and have the privinledge of making our laws, and our children will be free citizens let them go where ever they may go." He predicted that African Americans would soon "flock to the Shores of Africa, where they can enjoy their freedom, and become an independent people."[44] All of this was made possible, in large measure, by the extraordinary exertions and sacrifice of Russwurm.

What, then, has been Russwurm's legacy? His contribution to Liberian development was immense. That the tensions between Africans and Americo-Liberians remains unresolved to this day cannot be attributed to Russwurm. He sought an asylum for the oppressed "children of Africa" abroad in the ancestral homeland. But more than any other leading figure of his time—and certainly before Blyden and Crummell—he sought unity between those from abroad and their continental brothers and sisters, despite their acknowledged cultural differences. Like Garvey after him, he sought a home free from the indignity and abuse of white supremacy. Moreover, he helped inspire those who followed—Blyden, Crummell, Garvey, Nnamdi Azikiwe, and, perhaps most of all, George Padmore—who sought the liberation of the continent from white domination. His aspirations and practices were directly connected to the anticolonial movement on the continent in the twentieth century. Liberia is and was flawed, but it was an astonishing source of inspiration and symbolic power, especially in the late nineteenth and early twentieth centuries.[45]

Ironically, Russwurm also left behind an anti–black nationalist legacy. His powerful and persuasive attacks on the very colonizationists he later joined galvanized the free black population in many parts of the northern and midwestern United States. With his appeal for a powerful and united black political force in the United States to combat the injustices meted out against the African American population, he helped inspire the Negro Convention Movement and gave urgency and substance to the modern abolitionist cause.[46] This in turn contributed to the "Americanism" that advocated focusing on transformation and liberty in the United States rather than looking abroad, in Africa or elsewhere; its corollary was hostility toward colonizationism and emigrationism. In this way, Russwurm reared the eagle of anticolonizationism, which attempted to pluck out his own eyes once he reversed his position; as one of his Philadelphia critics pointed out in 1831, Russwurm's own editorials in *Freedom's Journal* formed an effective arsenal to be used against his new position.[47] In addition, Russwurm and Cornish pioneered the black press in the United States, bringing attention, through their example, to its utility and force in the struggle for a people's rights. Many others, including Douglass, Du Bois, and Garvey, would follow in their footsteps.

Russwurm's legacy is rich and varied and places him among the pioneers of the black struggle in the modern period. Not only does Russwurm belong to the pantheon of Pan-Africanists; he was the first modern one. He was also the trailblazer for a long line of Caribbean intellectuals who went to Africa (many settling there for life) and contributed to the Pan-African struggle—Blyden, Robert Campbell, William Draper, Benito Sylvain, Theophilus Scholes, Henry Sylvester Williams, Ras Makonnen, George Padmore, Dudley Thompson, and a host of others, including Frantz Fanon and Walter Rodney.[48] For his exertions, sacrifice, ambition, and, most of all, his wide-ranging achievements in the United States as well as on the continent of Africa, far many more than realize it are deeply indebted to John Brown Russwurm. He deserves his place alongside the most selfless and courageous fighters for an emancipated humanity and in particular among those who most earnestly sought the liberation of that branch of humanity Russwurm affectionately called the "children of Africa," among whom he was proud to include himself.

— II —

Selected Writings of
John Brown Russwurm

Editorial Note

The following selection has been guided by a desire to provide the reader with a broad sampling of Russwurm's own writings, reflecting his preoccupations, mode of thinking, and style of expression over the course of a lifetime. The larger objective, however, is to make available to the interested reader the relatively sustained expression of the richness and complexity of Russwurm's thoughts and emotions over time.

Starting with his earliest known writings, which, significantly, revolved around the subject of the Haitian Revolution and its meaning, the anthology follows Russwurm as he thinks and writes in the pages of *Freedom's Journal* and subsequently during his period in Liberia. Between 1830 and 1834 he founded and edited the *Liberia Herald,* which, like *Freedom's Journal* before it, provided Russwurm with an instrument for expression. In 1836 Russwurm was appointed agent and governor of Maryland in Liberia, the colony established south of Monrovia by the Maryland State Colonization Society. Originally founded in 1834, Maryland in Liberia would be governed by Russwurm up to his death in 1851. A staunch advocate of African American emigration to Liberia, Russwurm now took on the responsibility of realizing some of his ideas of creating an asylum for the diaspora on the African continent. His dispatches, generally produced once every six months, provide a good indication of some of the challenges he faced and how he approached and coped with them.

In addition to the published writings, included here are letters, generally private and very personal but instructive, written by Russwurm at different stages of his life. Although he was remarkably open about his feelings in his public pronouncements, these letters nevertheless provide invaluable and much greater insights into Russwurm's interior life. In his letters one discerns his profound sense of loneliness and isolation over most of his life; here he expresses his doubts, fears, apprehensions, and misgivings about the Liberian project, as he seldom did in public.

Beyond the selection of the documents themselves, I have generally refrained from much intervention. Apart from the introductory note to each subsection and explanatory notes here and there as deemed necessary, the documents are essentially reproduced as they appeared in the original sources, retaining the idiosyncrasies of spelling and punctuation peculiar to their author and the conventions of his time. The intention is to minimize the editorial mediation between Russwurm and the reader. Let Russwurm be Russwurm, no more, no less. Asterisked footnotes are Russwurm's; numbered endnotes are my own. Titles of published articles are more often than not those of Russwurm; where they are not, they are my own insertion and are in brackets. I have attempted to minimize the use of *sic;* if something appears amiss, awkward, or strange, that is how it appears in the original.

1

Early Writings

---

*On September 6, 1826, Russwurm, the first black graduate of the col-
lege, delivered the following address as his contribution to the commencement
exercise at Bowdoin College. The subject matter revealed Russwurm's profound
and abiding interest in the history, symbolism, and fate of the Haitian Revolution. The speech was extensively covered and praised in the local and national
press. It was his first public pronouncement, on this or any other subject. But
Russwurm had in fact being thinking, reading, and writing about Haiti for
years before his commencement and at least up to the years he lived and taught
school in Boston (1821–24). He had also seriously considered and planned on
settling in Haiti. Nine months before his graduation he revealed in a letter to
a cousin: "I can not boast of circumstances, having at present but just able to
keep my present standing; but after August, brighter prospects will dawn upon
efforts of many years. If not particularly invited by the Haytian Govt then, I
shall study Medicine in Boston previous to an emigration to Hayti."[1]*

*An essay written in Russwurm's hand has survived from his Bowdoin days.
The twenty-two-page "Toussaint L'Overture [sic], the Principal Chief in the
Revolution of St. Domingo" is a remarkable document. Though Russwurm notes
that Louverture was not "faultless" and that "beyond all doubt his character
had its blemishes," the modern student of Haiti, with the benefit of two centuries
of historiography on the subject, cannot help noticing that Russwurm's essay is
marked by the hagiographical treatment of Louverture prevalent in abolitionist
writings of the early nineteenth century. Russwurm, however, seems aware of
this when he writes that "the historian, from whom these facts are drawn, had it
not in his power" to record Louverture's failings. Nevertheless, the essay, executed
with a fine narrative and mature analytical thrust, reveals Russwurm's impressive grasp of the complex twists and turns of Louverture's remarkable career and
astonishing accomplishments. And Russwurm certainly builds the case in the
body of his essay to conclude that "it is only the sober language of truth to say,
that the talents and virtues of Toussaint L'Ouverture, entitle him to the grateful recollections of his liberated countrymen—that his character exhibits many*

| 131

of those qualities which have distinguished the most illustrious governors and commanders—and that his sufferings and death left a stain of treachery and cruelty on the government under whose merciless oppression he perished."[2]

The narrative of "Toussaint L'Overture" and the research conducted by Russwurm in creating it provided the platform for his later, more analytical argument so forcefully presented in "The Condition and Prospects of Hayti."

The Condition and Prospects of Hayti

The changes which take place in the affairs of this world show the instability of sublunary things. Empires rise, and fall, flourish, and decay. Knowledge follows revolutions and travels over the globe. Man alone, remains the same being, whether placed under the torrid suns of Africa, or in the more congenial temperate zone. A principle of liberty is implanted in his breast, and all efforts to stifle it are as fruitless as would be the attempt to extinguish the fires of Etna.

It is in the irresistible course of events that all men, who have been deprived of their liberty, shall recover this previous portion of their indefeasible inheritance. It is in vain to stem the current; degraded man will rise in his native majesty, and claim his rights. They may be withheld from him now, but the day will arrive, when they must be surrendered.

Among the many interesting events of the present day, and illustrative of this, the Revolution in Hayti holds a conspicuous place. The former political condition of Hayti we all doubtless know. After years of sanguinary struggle for freedom and a political existence, the Haytiens on the auspicious day of January first 1804 declared themselves a free and independent nation. Nothing can ever induce them to recede from this declaration. They know too well by their past misfortunes; by their wounds which are yet bleeding, that security can be expected only from within themselves. Rather would they devote themselves to death than return to their former condition.

Can we conceive of anything which can cheer the desponding spirit, can reanimate and stimulate it to put every thing to the hazard? Liberty can do this. Such were its effects upon the Haytiens—men who in slavery showed neither spirit nor genius: but when Liberty, when once Freedom struck their astonished ears, they became new creatures: stepped forth as men, and showed to the world, that though Slavery may benumb, it cannot entirely destroy our faculties. Such were Toussaint L'Ouverture, Desalines and Christophe![3]

Source: John Brown Russwurm Collection, George J. Mitchell Department of Special Collections & Archives, Bowdoin College Library, Brunswick, Maine.

The Haytiens have adopted the republican form of government: and so firmly is it established, that in no country are the rights and privileges of citizens and foreigners more respected, and crimes less frequent. They are a brave and generous people. If cruelties were inflicted during the Revolutionary war, it was owing to the policy pursued by the French commanders, which compelled them to use retaliatory measures.

For who shall expostulate with men who have been hunted with Bloodhounds,—who have been threatened with an Auto-da-fé—whose relations and friends have been hung on gibbets before their eyes—have been sunk by hundreds in the sea—and tell them they ought to exercise kindness towards such mortal enemies? Remind me not of moral duties, of meekness and generosity. Show me the man who has exercised them under these trials, and you point to one who is more than human. It is an undisputed fact, that more than sixteen thousand Haytiens perished in the modes above specified. The cruelties inflicted by the French on the children of Hayti have exceeded the crimes of Cortes and Pizarros.[4]

Twenty two years of their Independence so gloriously achieved, have effected wonders. No longer are they the same people. They had faculties, yet were these faculties oppressed under the load of servitude and ignorance. With a countenance erect and fixed upon Heaven, they can now contemplate the works of Divine munificence. Restored to the dignity of man to society, they have acquired a new existence—their powers have been developed: a career of glory and happiness unfolds itself before them.

The Haytien Government has arisen in the neighbourhood of European settlements. Do the public proceedings and details of its Government bespeak any inferiority? Their state papers are distinguished from those of many European Courts, only by their superior Energy, and more exalted sentiments; and while the manners and politics of Boyer emulate those of his Republican neighbours: the Court of Christophe had almost as much foppery; almost as many lords and ladies of the bed-chamber; and almost as great a proportion of stars, and ribbons, and gilded chariots, as those of his brother potentates in any part of the world.[5]

(Placed by Divine Providence amid circumstances more favourable, than were their ancestors, the Haytiens can more easily than they, make rapid strides in the career of civilization—they can demonstrate that although the God of nature may have given them a darker complexion; still they are men alike sensible to all the miseries of slavery, and to all the blessings of freedom.)

May we not indulge in the pleasing hope, that the Independence of Hayti has laid the foundation of an Empire that will take a rank with the nations of the earth—that a country, the local situation of which is favourable to trade and commercial enterprise—possessing a free and well regulated government, which encourages the useful and liberal arts: a country containing an enterprising and growing population, which is determined to live free, or die gloriously: will advance rapidly in all the arts of civilization.

We look forward with peculiar satisfaction to the period when like Tyre of old, her vessels shall extend the fame of her riches and glory, to the remotest borders of the globe;—to the time when Hayti treading in the footsteps of her sister republicks, shall, like them, exhibit a picture of rapid and unprecedented advances in population, wealth and intelligence.

2

Writings from *Freedom's Journal*

Part A. *Uplift, Abolitionism, and Opposition to Colonization*

Freedom's Journal, *the first black-run and -owned newspaper in the United States, commenced publication on Friday, March 16, 1827. In the first three items below, the editors, Samuel E. Cornish and John B. Russwurm, outlined their rationale and hopes for the paper. Unless otherwise indicated, the other articles in this section are attributed to Russwurm.*

To Our Patrons

In presenting our first number to our Patrons, we feel all the diffidence of persons entering upon a new and untried line of business. But a moment's reflection upon the noble objects, which we have in view by the publication of this Journal; the expediency of its appearance at this time, when so many schemes are in action concerning our people—encourage us to come boldly before an enlightened publick. For we believe, that a paper devoted to the dissemination of useful knowledge among our brethren, and to their moral and religious improvement, must meet with the cordial approbation of every friend to humanity.

The peculiarities of this Journal, render it important that we should advertise to the world the motives by which we are actuated, and the objects which we contemplate.

We wish to plead our own cause. Too long have others spoken for us. Too long has the publick been deceived by misrepresentations, in things which concern us dearly, though in the estimation of some mere trifles; for though there are many in society who exercise towards us benevolent feelings; still (with sorrow we confess it) there are others who make it their business to enlarge upon the least trifle, which tends to the discredit of any person of colour; and pronounce anathemas and denounce our whole body for the misconduct of this guilty one. We are aware that there [are] many instances

Source: *Freedom's Journal*, March 16, 1827.

of vice among us, but we avow that it is because no one has taught its subjects to be virtuous: many instances of poverty, because no sufficient efforts accommodated to minds contracted by slavery, and deprived of early education have been made, to teach them how to husband their hard earnings, and to secure to themselves comforts.

Education being an object of the highest importance to the welfare of society, we shall endeavour to present just and adequate views of it, and to urge upon our brethren the necessity and expediency of training their children, while young, to habits of industry, and thus forming them for becoming useful members of society. It is surely time that we should awake from this lethargy of years, and make a concentrated effort for the education of our youth. We form a spoke in the human wheel, and it is necessary that we should understand our pendence on the different parts, and theirs on us, in order to perform our part with propriety.

Though not desirous of dictating, we shall feel it our incumbent duty to dwell occasionally upon the general principles and rules of economy. The world has grown too enlightened, to estimate any man's character by his personal appearance. Though all men acknowledge the excellency of Franklin's maxims, yet comparatively few practise upon them. We may deplore when it is too late, the neglect of these self evident truths, but it avails little to mourn. Ours will be the task of admonishing our brethren on these points.

The civil rights of a people being of the greatest value, it shall ever be our duty to vindicate our brethren, when oppressed, and to lay the case before the publick. We shall also urge upon our brethren, (who are qualified by the laws of the different states), the expediency of using their elective franchise; and of making an independent use of the same. We wish them not to become the tools of party.

And as much time is frequently lost, and wrong principles instilled, by the perusal of works of trivial importance, we shall consider it a part of our duty to recommend to our young readers, such authors as will not only enlarge their stock of useful knowledge, but such as will also serve to stimulate them to higher attainments in science.

We trust also, that through the columns of the FREEDOM'S JOURNAL, many practical pieces, having for their bases, the improvement of our brethren, will be presented to them, from the pens of many of our respected friends, who have kindly promised their assistance.

It is our earnest wish to make our Journal a medium of intercourse between our brethren in the different states of this great confederacy: that through its columns an expression of our sentiments, on many interesting subjects which concern us, may be offered to the publick: that plans which apparently are beneficial may be candidly discussed and properly weighed; if worthy, receive our cordial approbation; if not, our marked disapprobation.

Useful knowledge of every kind, and every thing that relates to Africa, shall find a ready admission into our columns; and as that vast continent becomes daily more known, we trust that many things will come to light, proving that the natives of it are neither so ignorant nor stupid as they have generally been supposed to be.

And while these important subjects shall occupy the columns of the FREEDOM'S JOURNAL, we would not be unmindful of our brethren who are still in the iron fetters of bondage. They are our kindred by all the ties of nature; and though but little can be effected by us, still let our sympathies be poured forth, and our prayers in their behalf, ascend to Him who is able to succour them.

From the press and the pulpit we have suffered much by being incorrectly represented. Men, whom we equally love and admire have not hesitated to represent us disadvantageously, without becoming personally acquainted with the true state of things, nor discerning between virtue and vice among us. The virtuous part of our people feel themselves sorely aggrieved under the existing state of things—they are not appreciated.

Our vices and our degradation are ever arrayed against us, but our virtues are passed by unnoticed. And what is still more lamentable, our friends, to whom we concede all the principles of humanity and religion, from these very causes seem to have fallen into the current of popular feeling and are imperceptibly floating on the stream—actually living in the practice of prejudice, while they abjure it in theory, and feel it not in their hearts. Is it not very desirable that such should know more of our actual condition, and of our efforts and feelings, that in forming or advocating plans for our amelioration, they may do it more understandingly? In the spirit of candor and humility we intend by a simple representation of facts to lay our case before the publick, with a view to arrest the progress of prejudice, and to shield ourselves against the consequent evils. We wish to conciliate all and to irritate none, yet we must be firm and unwavering in our principles, and persevering in our efforts.

If ignorance, poverty and degradation have hitherto been our unhappy lot; has the Eternal decree gone forth, that our race alone, are to remain in this state, while knowledge and civilization are shedding their enlivening rays over the rest of the human family? The recent travels of Denham and Clapperton in the interior of Africa, and the interesting narrative which they

have published;[1] the establishment of the republic of Hayti after years of sanguinary warfare; its subsequent progress in all the arts of civilization; and the
advancement of liberal ideas in South America, where despotism has given
place to free governments, and where many of our brethren now fill important civil and military stations, prove the contrary.

The interesting fact that there are FIVE HUNDRED THOUSAND free
persons of colour, one half of whom might peruse, and the whole be ben-
efited by the publication of the Journal; that no publication, as yet, has
been devoted exclusively to their improvement—that many selections from
approved standard authors, which are within the reach of few, may occasionally be made—and more important still, that this large body of our citizens
have no public channel—all serve to prove the real necessity, at present, for
the appearance of the FREEDOM'S JOURNAL.

It shall ever be our desire to conduct the editorial department of our paper
as to give offence to none of our patrons; as nothing is farther from us than
to make it the advocate of any partial views, either in politics or religion.
What few days we can number, have been devoted to the improvement of
our brethren; and it is our earnest wish that the remainder may be spent in
the same delightful service.

In conclusion, whatever concerns us as a people, will ever find a ready
admission into the FREEDOM'S JOURNAL, interwoven with all the principal news of the day.

And while every thing in our power shall be performed to support the
character of our Journal, we would respectfully invite our numerous friends
to assist by their communications, and our coloured brethren to strengthen
our hands by their subscriptions, as our labour is one of common cause,
and worthy of their consideration and support. And we do most earnestly
solicit the latter, that if at any time we should seem to be zealous, or too
pointed in the inculcation of any important lesson, they will remember, that
they are equally interested in the cause in which we are engaged, and attribute our zeal to the peculiarities of our situation, and our earnest engaged-
ness in their well being.

THE EDITORS

Proposals for Publishing the Freedom's Journal: *Prospectus*

As education is what renders civilized man superior to the savage: as the dissemination of knowledge is continually progressing among all other classes in the community: we deem it expedient to establish a paper, and bring into operation all the means with which our benevolent CREATOR has endowed us, for the moral, religious, civil and literary improvement of our injured race. Experience teaches us that the Press is the most economical and convenient method by which this object is to be obtained.

Daily slandered, we think that there ought to be some channel of communication between us at the public: through which a single voice may be heard, in defence of *five hundred thousand free people of colour*. For often has injustice been heaped upon us, when our only defence was an appeal to the ALMIGHTY: but we believe that the time has now arrived, when the calumnies of our enemies should be refuted by forcible arguments.

Believing that all men are equal by nature, we indulge the pleasing anticipation, that as the means of knowledge are more extensively diffused among our people, their condition will become improved, not only in their daily walk and conversation, but in their domestic economy. Our columns shall ever be open to a temperate discussion of interesting subjects. But in respect to matters of religion, while we concede to them their full importance, and shall occasionally introduce articles of this general character, we would not be the advocates of any particular sect or party.

In the discussion of political subjects, we shall ever regard the constitution of the United States as our polar star. Pledged to no party, we shall endeavour to urge our brethren to use their right to the elective franchise as free citizens. It shall never be our object to court controversy, though we must at all times consider *ourselves* as champions in defence of oppressed humanity. As the diffusion of knowledge, and raising our community into respectability, are the principal motives which influence us in our present undertaking, we hope our hands will be upheld by all our brethren and friends.

SAMUEL E. CORNISH,
JOHN B. RUSSWURM.
Editors and Proprietors.

Source: *Freedom's Journal,* March 16, 1827.

[Raising Us in the Scale of Being]

Anxiously solicitous for the well-being of our brethren, we cannot put this number of our Journal into their hands, without offering some important thoughts for their consideration and practice.

Born in this Republican country, constituting one of its constituent parts; attached to its climate and soil; we feel interested in the improvements of all its parts; more especially that to which we immediately belong.

Our situation is one of equal responsibility and interest: the further decrease of prejudice, and the amelioration of the condition of thousands of our brethren who are yet in bondage, greatly depend on our conduct. It is for us to convince the world by uniform propriety of conduct, industry and economy, that we are worthy of esteem and patronage. But to obtain which, we must use all diligence to form to ourselves a virtuous and intelligent character. This will disarm prejudice of the weapon it has, too successfully used against us; and it will also strengthen the hands of our friends in their efforts in our behalf.

It is our duty and privilege, by the faithful improvement of all the advantages which we possess, to convince a Religious and Republican nation, of the importance and policy of raising us in the scale of being. It becomes us, therefore, never to neglect any of the means of education within the reach of ourselves or children.

As to industry, and its handmaid economy, they carry their own reward, and are honourable in every capacity of life. And if ever any people had reason to adhere to all these particulars we are *that people*; for none have been kept so long in the rear; none have suffered so much from the hands of a people professing the christian name. The injuries done us have been unprovoked, and numerous. Humanity sickens at the mere recital of them.

Yet these considerations, instead of discouraging, should rather excite us to vigorous efforts in all the departments of life. From the present aspect of things, we may reasonably cherish the pleasing hope, that as the means of education and comforts are increased, our conditions will become more improved in all particulars.

There are many grievances which we have to encounter, and which the publick can remove without any sacrifice on their part; while at the same time the removal of them, would to us, be of the highest importance. And as the publick become acquainted with these circumstances, we are encouraged in believing that they will take pleasure in removing them and granting us

Source: *Freedom's Journal*, March 23, 1827.

new facilities. It will be our constant endeavour to expose our disadvantages, and appeal to their better judgment and feelings.

Meanwhile, we deem it important that the conduct and efforts of our brethren should correspond with the dictates of wisdom and duty. Let all our mechanics be punctual in their business and engagements; following the example of some among us, who have distinguished themselves; and whose conduct, and character have ever conduced to the honour and praise of their brethren.

Such as fill domestic capacities, should endeavour to emulate the character and attain to the honour and confidence of Eliezer the servant of Abraham.

To conclude, we should rejoice to see all our brethren, whether engaged in sacred or secular employments, exercising more than ordinary prudence and industry.

[Samuel E. Cornish

John B. Russwurm]

Haytien Revolution

Although the following article appeared as an unsigned editorial, it was almost certainly written by Russwurm. It concisely reprises the key arguments put forward in his commencement address, delivered only a few months earlier, and executes them with the same excitement, celebration, analytical prowess, and élan. It is noteworthy, too, that this article served as a concrete illustration of "mutability in human affairs" (see the essay with that title below), a subject about which Russwurm was writing at the time. Indeed, the essay on the Haitian Revolution appeared in the same issue of the journal that carried the first installment of Russwurm's essay on mutability.

The last half century will ever be regarded as a period in which changes the most interesting, and occurrences the most remarkable in the history of man have happened.—And the revolution of St. Domingo, which developed the resources and aroused the energies of a people deemed but a step above the brute creation, is not the least remarkable and interesting.

Fifty years ago, when the flame of civil and religious liberty was first kindled in this country, and spread *too soon* across the Atlantic,—who, of all the gifted souls that genius marshalled under its standard, would have predicted such an event? Did the mighty spirit of Burke, when he beheld in his "mind's eye" all the horrors that afterwards befell poor France, or could the "prophetic ken" of

Source: *Freedom's Journal*, April 6, 1827.

Fox foretell this anomaly of nature? The man who could think it possible that the degraded African slave would take up arms in defence of his birthright and spend his heart's blood for its possession, would have been regarded as a madman, and his reflections branded as the dreams of a visionary.

But times have changed. We have seen the establishment of an independent nation by men of our own colour; the world has seen it; and its success and durability are now placed beyond doubt. There is something in the firm establishment of a free government by those who but lately were in the bonds of slavery that strikes us as manifesting in a peculiar degree the interposition of Divine Providence.

The commencement of the revolution of St. Domingo was looked upon with horror by men in all parts of the world. It was thought so unnatural a crime, that slaves should rise against their masters, that their downfall was earnestly desired and frequently prayed for by every one. Other revolutions have happened; other governments have been formed, but under far different auspices. The American revolution which first led the way in asserting the great principles of liberty, was hailed with enthusiasm by the wise and the good. It found advocates even in England, against whose oppression they were contending. The French revolution too, ere it acted those deeds of terror and madness which will not soon be forgotten, had supporters and well-wishers in every heart, except those whose feelings were blunted in the service of a cold and chilling despotism. But the revolution of St. Domingo, which taught the world that the African, though trodden down in the dust by the foot of the oppressor, yet had not entirely lost the finer sensibilities of his nature, and still possessed the proper spirit and feelings of a man—no one wished it well—no fervent prayer was put up for its success—none bid it "God speed." In their glorious career, alone and unaided, save by the arm of HIM who is ever ready to protect the oppressed, the Haytiens withstood the power of the greatest monarch that ever sat upon a throne. So true is it, that "the race is not always to the swift, nor the battle to the strong."

When we reflect upon the condition of those men who bade defiance to the chosen troops of Napoleon, commanded by one of his bravest generals, we are struck with astonishment and admiration. Most of their leaders were of little education—of still less experience in military affairs, and more expert in the use of the hoe and the spade, than in wielding a sword or levelling a musket. But the *occasion* called forth their hidden powers. The cause for which they fought developed talents unknown before to the possessor.—And soon as the standard was raised and the blow that was to unrivet their chains forever, was struck, thousands arose of young and old—bond and free, eager to expose their lives and property in defence of what to every man should be dearer than life itself. The struggle of liberty against slavery; of light against darkness, cannot last long. And tho' our brethren of St. Domingo had to contend against "fearful odds," (being opposed by the flower of the French army,) yet such success attended their noble efforts, that in a short time there was scarcely a Frenchman left on the island. Of the fifteen thousand troops which Napoleon had deemed sufficient to rivet new fetters for *"the slaves,"* very few returned to France to tell him the news of their disaster. Disease, famine, and the sword destroyed one after another, till finally Leclerc himself, fell in the land over which in the proud exultation of his heart he had fondly hoped to rule. Thus perished the French army, and so perish every attempt against the liberties of a people.

Mutability of Human Affairs

I.

During a recent visit to the Egyptian Mummy, my thoughts were insensibly carried back to former times, when Egypt was in her splendor, and the only seat of chivalry, science, arts and civilization. As a descendant of Cush, I could not but mourn over her present degradation, while reflecting upon the mutability of human affairs, and upon the present condition of a people, who, for more than one thousand years, were the most civilized and enlightened.

My heart sickened as I pondered upon the picture which my imagination had drawn.—Like Marius surveying the ruins of Carthage, I wept over the fallen state of my people.—Wherefore is it, that a gloom pervades the mind, while reflecting upon the ages which have passed; and which, like the "baseless fabrick of a vision," have scarcely left a wreck behind them? But such applies not to Egypt: for her obelisks and pyramids, which attest her greatness still remain, amid the grandeur of the desert, full of magnificence and death, at once a trophy and a tomb. But her kings, to preserve whose bodies from sacrilegious hands, they were erected, where are they? Have they not been torn from their "vaulted sepulchres," and exhibited to a gazing world? *Have not they too been bought and sold?* Methinks, the lesson to be derived from this, should warn other potentates, who are lavishing the hard earnings of their industrious subjects upon their costly mausoleums, of the vanity of their labours. The admirable command of our Lord to one of his disciples, who was desirous of going to bury his father, "let the dead bury their dead," should convince us that it matters little, where this corruptible body

Source: *Freedom's Journal,* April 6, 13, and 20, 1827.

is laid, after the immortal spirit has once left it; and that nothing which we can do, can reach its ear in the dull mansions of the tomb.

In reflecting on these interesting but mournful truths; the changes which had taken place within the last fifty years, were also presented to my view. On an ideal map of the Western continent, I beheld in many parts, villages, towns and cities, arisen and arising, where thirty years ago, nought but the footsteps of the savage had ever disturbed the "deep solitude of the forest," or chased the "wild deer from his covert." In the old world, the changes which have taken place, are awfully instructive. In many parts we behold the lenient policy which swayed the government of Napoleon compelled to give place to the misrule of former days. In France, the house of Bourbon, after having been exiles for twenty years, are restored to the throne of their ancestors. But the mighty Ruler, whose word was law over the greater part of Europe; "who was gentle in the manner, but vigorous in the deed," where lies he? On the rocky shores of sea-girt St. Helena!

History informs us that Cush and Menes (the Misriam of scripture) were the sons of Ham. The former is supposed to have settled in the Arabic Nome, near the Red Sea, in Lower Egypt; whence his descendants spread over the southern regions of Asia, along the Persian Gulph, and the easterly parts of Africa, on the western borders of the Red Sea; and the latter, the Northerly parts of Africa, including Upper and Lower Egypt and Barbary.

Mankind generally allow that all nations are indebted to the Egyptians for the introduction of the arts and sciences; but they are not willing to acknowledge that the Egyptians bore any resemblance to the present race of Africans; though Horodotus, "the father of history," expressly declares that the "Egyptians had black skins and frizzled hair." All we know of Ethiopia, strengthens us in the belief, that it was early inhabited by a people, whose manners and customs nearly resembled those of the Egyptians. Many of their divinities were the same: they had the same orders of priesthood and religious ceremonies: they made use of the same characters in writing: their dress was alike: and the regal sceptre in both countries was in the form of a plough. Of their philosophy little is known, their wise men, like those of the Indians, were called Gymnosophists: they discharged the sacred functions like Egyptian priests; had their distinct colleges and classes of disciples; taught their dogmas in obscure and mythological language; and were remarkable for their contempt of death. Other writers of a later date than Herodotus, have asserted that the resemblance between the two nations, as it regarded their features, was as striking, as their doctrines were similar. The celebrated Mr. Salt, in his travels in Abyssinia, discovered several monumental remains, the hieroglyphics on which bore a strong resemblance to those engraved on the sarcophagi of Egyptian mummies.

II.

Descended from the same great progenitor; settled on the borders of the Red Sea, and having constant intercourse both by land and water with their brethren, the Egyptians; the Ethiopians must have been inferior to the most extravagant opinions entertained by the warmest advocates for the intellectual inferiority of the African race, to have degenerated so soon from their original state.

There *must have been considerable intercourse between the two nations,* not only from the favourable position of the two kingdoms, but also from the historical fact, that in the year 3277, A.M. Bocchoris, king of Egypt, was overthrown and succeeded by Sabaccon, an Ethiopian prince, who is supposed to have been the So of the Scriptures. We are further informed, that Tharaca, who succeeded and reigned during eighteen years, and upon whose decease, the throne reverted to the ancient Egyptian line of kings, was also an Ethiopian. The more we investigate, the more are we inclined to believe, that there could not possibly have been any great difference as to the state of the arts and sciences in the two kingdoms; and as to the difference of features, who has the presumption to say that it was greater than that existing between us and the present race of Arabs, who are also generally allowed to be descended from Cush, our great progenitor.

It is, I conceive, generally known that the first great monarchy of Assyria was founded, as were likewise the Republics of Sidon, Tyre and Carthage, by the descendants of Ham; and also that the chief nations of Africa, with whom the Romans had any intercourse, besides the Egyptians, were the Numidians, Mauritanians, and the Gaetuli. Between them and the Ethiopians, there never existed but little intercourse; for the latter always preserved their liberty and independence. In confirmation of which, we find their queen Candace spoken of in the days of the Apostles, when the Roman power was at its greatest height, and the nations above alluded to, had become provinces of the empire. From this it must be evident; that but a small part of Africa could have been known to the ancient Greeks and Romans; for that spirit of conquest which led Alexander to weep because he had not other worlds to conquer, and Julius Caesar to contest with the barbarous tribes of Britain, (from whom he could expect nothing but the mere honour,) would have prompted the former to have crossed the burning sands of Zahara [Sahara], even to the far-famed city of Timbuctoo; and the latter, instead of the voluptuous arms of Cleopatra, to have marched his victorious legions (or by the Red Sea to have coasted) into Ethiopia, and added to his present list, the names of a few more cities plundered and burnt, a few more thousands slain, and left to whiten nature's face.

But of what complexion were the original settlers of Egypt and Ethiopia? Was it white or black? I humbly conceive neither, but rather the copper-colour of our Aborigines. To prove which, we have only to observe the effects of climate upon the present races of men. We have before stated that the two races were black, while the present race of Arabs, who must be descendants of Cush or Menes, remain to this day, a copper coloured race. How is this to be explained? are we to suppose that the present race of Arabs have degenerated, while the original black colour has remained good? From the circumstance that black is confined exclusively to hot climates; while the copper colour is seen in different quarters of the globe, even in the more temperate parts of the hot; from the fact that a colony of Portuguese who settled on the coast of Africa, after a little over a century were hardly to be distinguished from the surrounding natives, we conceive that the advocates of a superior and an inferior race, must bring forward more proofs in support of their Utopian theory. Pliny ascribes the colour of the Africans to the ardor of the sun in that climate. For he says lib. 2. cap. 78. "Ethiopas vicini sideris vapore torreri, adustisque similes gigni, barba et capillo vibrato, non est dubium."[2]

But who can convince us that the intellectual powers of man are inferior, because nature's God has tinged his complexion with a darker hue? The doctrine is contrary to all the evidences we have of the creation. But what are the *strong arguments* adduced by the advocates of this system? The people of colour are ignorant and degraded—nothing can ever be made of them—God formed them to serve their fairer brethren—endowed them with faculties little superior to the tribe of Ourang Outangs. They want all the finer feelings of men—are an insensible and ungrateful race—and to render these prejudices still stronger, the craniologist exclaims, their retreating foreheads evidently denote them another race, something between man and the brute creation!

Oh, that another Solomon might arise in this age of enlightened reason, and convince the world, *that our people naturally, are not worse than other men—that we are ignorant and degraded, because none have extended towards us a faint glimmering of that light which is daily shed over the rest of the community—that we want the finer feelings, because like the precious ore in nature's bosom, they have never been called into action—that we are evidently insensible and ungrateful, because prejudice and custom have never placed us in situations to manifest these virtues, and to exhibit to the world, that the Parent of All never intended that the original nature of one man should differ from that of another.*

But what is the colour of a man's skin in comparison to his moral and intellectual worth in society? Were the question asked of many who look down upon a man because his complexion happens to be darker than their own, how few could give a satisfactory reason for their prejudice. When we reflect that the seat of colour, which is called the *rete mucosum* is in a thin mucous stratum, interposed between the cuticle or dead surface of the body and the true skin, is *what contains throughout its substance a black pigment which gives a colour to the skin, while the cuticle and cutis deviate but little in all men*, where is the intelligent and reasonable man who will boast of his superior intellectual natural powers, because we have never been *placed in situations for intellectual improvement?*

III.

The ancient Ethiopians were considered as a blameless race, worshipping the Gods, doing no evil, exercising fortitude, and despising death:—

> "The sire of gods and all the ethereal train
> On the warm limits of the farthest main,
> Now mix with mortals, nor disdain to grace
> The feasts of Ethiopia's blameless race;
> Twelve days the powers indulge the genial rite
> Returning with the twelfth revolving light."[3]

Believing that we have sufficiently proved to the satisfaction of every unprejudiced mind, that the Egyptians and Ethiopians were of one colour, and possessed a striking similarity of features; were equally civilized and had the same rites of religious worship, we now turn our immediate attention not only to the mutability which has attended the fortune of their descendants, but other nations also.

If we except 130 years under the Persian yoke and 204 under the Macedonian, the kingdom of Egypt continued an independent government until the time of the second Triumvirs, when the disastrous battle of Actitum, (in which Anthony lost all the laurels acquired during a whole life,) reduced it from its former splendor to a province of the Roman Empire, under Augustus. Since that period, Egypt has continually decreased in population, wealth and civilization; and had not her stately monuments stood unshaken amid the convulsions which have since rent the world; as little perhaps would have been known concerning her; as little sympathy would have been felt for her oppressed and degraded children, as for poor Ethiopia's.—For the present descendants of the ancient Egyptians are an ill-looking and slovenly people immersed in ignorance and sloth, and presenting to the eye of the observer a very striking contrast of features from any of the specimens which have reached us of their ancestors.

But Egypt and Ethiopia are not the only kingdoms where we behold the effects of the mutability of human affairs. The extensive Empire of Macedon's proud king, has passed into other hands and even Greece, herself, bows before the proud sceptre of the Moslem.

Oh, that another Leonidas might arise in this her time of need, and drive the flag of the Crescent from the second land of freedom, arts and refinement. Awake, ye Greeks, think on the spirit of your "ancient sires;" like them, let your breasts be opposed as ramparts in defence of your country's soil; like them, die all freemen, and live not to witness the despotism of your oppressors!

Time has not spared even imperial Rome, but she and her conquests, which comprehended the greater part of the civilized world at that period have changed masters. All that remains of her and them can give but a faint idea of the one, or hardly convince us of the truth of the other. Popish writers would feign convince us that the sceptre of the Caesars had passed into their hands—that Italy, the native country of all that is stupendous, great or beautiful, either in ancient or modern times is theirs' but O, how unlike is Rome in the nineteenth century, to the Rome of the Scipios and the Caesars! But while she remains, like her coliseum, after having passed successively into the hands of the Heruli, the Ostrogoths and the Lombards, until the final dissolution of the Western Empire, in 774, by Charlemagne; Constantinople, her sister, for whose prosperity the most christian Emperor Constantine was so solicitous, has had her share of adversity; her holy temples erected to the worship of God, have been profaned with Mohamedan rites, and the haughty Turk reigns over her provinces.—And while the ancient mistress of the world has sunk comparatively into mere insignificance, a new rival has arisen, whose name at the period to which we refer, was scarcely known; and her natives considered as a fierce and unconquerable body of barbarians. Her fleets now cover every sea, and her bold and adventurous sons every clime.

If we reflect upon the present condition of Russia, which before the time of Peter the Great was hardly considered as a civilized power; who then would have believed that in the 19th century she would have held the preponderating balance which she now does, in the politics of Europe. Spain in the loss of her South American possessions has taken a retrograde step—her cruel policy in their government—the despotism which has ruled her court, and the neglect of her own fruitful soil, have met their merited reward, and we rejoice at it.

And though our people, as a body, more particularly, have to lament the changes which have brought us into contempt and degradation; yet we are not so selfish as to mourn at the improvement of other nations; and the great progress which man has made in the knowledge of his natural rights and privileges; with which the despotic will of the monarch has no right to interfere, and for which after having this due estimate of their importance, he has been (and we trust ever will be) willing to devote his life to maintain them untrammelled and free.

As it regards the condition of our people, how painful soever the subject may be to our feelings, we feel it our duty to touch upon it. To us the subject is ever an unpleasant one to think upon; but without feelings of animosity, desirous of doing all the possible good we can, in our day and generation, and relying firmly upon the justice of a righteous God, we believe that a fairer day is yet to dawn upon our longing eyes. When this will be we cannot tell: but we believe that a few of the disadvantages which we are now under may be avoided by a more discreet line of conduct; by practising prudence and economy in our expenditures and by showing to the world, that it is our fixed determination to put to shame the unguarded and hostile expressions of our enemies.

That as a body, we are as degraded in many parts of this happy land as we can possibly be, the casual observation of the passing traveller has often recorded. What though the proud Turk lords it over ancient Greece, and would exercise a conquerors' power over her fair sons and daughters, yet have *they been treated like our brethren*? What though Mr. E. may assert, that our brethren in the South who are still in bondage, are better provided for, and more comfortable than the peasantry in some parts of Europe, do not daily facts evidence the contrary? Do they not show that many good men through a desire to please party, assert things which their cooler judgment disapproves. Look at Russia, or Poland in their former dark state, or at the feudal times of other kingdoms: can they be compared to the *happy and enviable lot* of many of our brethren? And as human affairs are continually revolving, who will predict that the day may not come when our people shall be duly considered in the scale of nations, and respected accordingly. We are no enthusiasts, but it must certainly be considered uncommonly miraculous that mutability should attend all other nations.

We are informed that the gospel was first received in the burning sands of Africa with great eagerness. "African Christians soon formed one of the principal members of the primitive Church. During the course of the 3d century, they were animated by the zeal of Tertullian, directed by the abilities of Cyprian and Origen, and adorned by the eloquence of Lacta[n]tius. But where are their descendants to be found? Is it not time to enquire after the descendants of men who have hazarded their lives to preserve the faith of the Gospel pure and unadulterated?"

People of Colour

The following was published in two parts as an editorial. It was unsigned, but from its content, argumentation, and style—including the explicit echo of Russwurm's other essay, "Mutability of Human Affairs"—I adjudged it written by Russwurm and have accordingly attributed it to him.

I.

Every attempt at a thorough discussion of this subject has always been met with a cry of *danger*. "You will excite the slaves to insurrection," say they. But I ask if there is now no danger? If every slave owner feels as safe when he goes to bed as if he were surrounded by a free peasantry? If not, what means those pistols under his pillow, and that loaded rifle over it? And is there even now no small degree of danger, what will be the case, when the slaves in the West Indies and the Spanish States, become all free citizens? On the subject of danger, I am happy again to avail myself of the language of Mr. Buxton.[4] "I do not mean to say, that there are not very great perils connected with the present state of the West Indies. On the contrary, I am quite sure—as sure as it is possible for any man in the house [House of Commons] or in the country to be—that there is imminent peril at the present moment; and that that peril will increase, unless our system be altered. For I know wherever there is oppression, there is danger—wherever there is slavery there is great danger—danger, in proportion to the degree of suffering. But the question is, how that danger is to be avoided. I answer, that it is to be avoided by that spirit of humanity which has avoided it in other places—by doing justice to those whom we now oppress—by giving liberty for slavery, happiness for misery. But even supposing the danger of giving to be as great as the danger of withholding; there may be danger in moving, and danger in standing still—danger in proceeding, and danger in doing nothing: then, I ask the house, and I ask it seriously—whether it is not better to incur peril for justice and humanity, for freedom, and for the sake of giving happiness to millions hitherto oppressed; or, whether it be better to incur peril for slavery, cru-

Source: *Freedom's Journal,* April 6, and 13, 1827.

elty, and injustice, for the sake of destroying the happiness of those wretched beings, upon whom we have already showered every species of calamity? I know there is danger. Danger! why? because the few inflict, and the multitude suffer gross injustice. But I confess it does appear to me to be the most extraordinary of all arguments, to contend that the danger arises not from slavery itself, but from the discussion of slavery in this house. What, then, does the slave require any hint from us that he is a slave, and that slavery is of all conditions the most miserable? Why, sir, he hears this; he sees it; he feels it too, in all around him. He sees his harsh uncompensated labour: he hears the crack of the whip; he feels, he writhes under the lash. Does not this betray the secret? This is no flattery; these are counsellors which feelingly persuade him what he is. He sees the mother of his children stripped naked before the gang of male negroes, and flogged unmercifully; he sees his children sent to market to be sold at the best price they will fetch; he sees in himself, not a man, but a *thing;* by West Indian law, a *chattel,* an implement of husbandry, a machine to produce sugar, a beast of burden. And will any man tell me, that the black, with all this staring him in the face, and flashing in his eyes, whether he rises in the morning or goes to bed at night, never dreams that there is injustice in such treatment, till he sits down to the perusal of an English newspaper, and there learns, to his astonishment, that there are enthusiasts in England, who from the bottom of their hearts deplore, and even more than they deplore, abhor all *black* slavery! There are such enthusiasts; I am one of them; and while we breathe, we will never abandon the cause, till that *thing,* that *chattel,* is reinstated in all the privileges of man."

It is of no use now, for any of *us* to declaim about the danger of the discussion. We cannot help it if we would. It is begun out of our reach in the British Parliament, by men who spurn all control but that of Christian principle, and who will continue it, until the enormity of the evil is fully searched out and made known, until the evil itself is fully and forever destroyed. The thing will be done. It *certainly* will. Look at it a moment. The fact that nothing effectual has hitherto been done *by law* for the mitigation of its evils, warrants us in the supposition that nothing will be done, if those concerned are left to themselves. There seems to be a sort of futility about it. Slavery, as it actually exists, and as it will probably always continue while human passions remain the same, is "twice cursed," in him who suffers and him who inflicts it. We had many exhibitions of its character, during the late ardour in behalf of the Greeks. It would be instructive to take any of the addresses, speeches, or resolutions made on that occasion, and to see how many of the most odious features of Turkish slavery may be fairly matched in this free and enlightened country. Some of them may be rendered stronger in degree, by the ferocity of the Turkish character. And there is some difference in the detail. For instance, there is not the same "uncertainty" to the black as to the Greek slave, "whether he shall enjoy the earnings of his own industry["]; for the black must labour continually, with the full knowledge that he *shall not* enjoy them. He has not even the poor hope of the wretched Greek to animate him in his toils. There are not wanting instances, where masters have held out to their blacks the hope of freedom as an incitement to industry; and then, when the poor slave, by the labour of his nights and holidays, had saved the sum required to buy him free, he has found that "all the earnings of a slave belong to his master," and he is still as far from freedom as ever.—The law is so. He has no redress. It may not be so frequent an occurrence as in Turkey, but it is not owing to any *law* that it is not. There is another difference. Says Mr. Webster[5] in his speech, "In the whole world no such oppression is felt as that which has crushed down the wretched Greeks. In India, to be sure, it is bad enough in principle; but in the actual feeling of oppression, it is not to be compared. There the oppressed natives are themselves as barbarous as their oppressors; but here have been seven millions of civilized, enlightened, Christian men, trampled into the very earth, century after century by a barbarous, pillaging, relentless soldiery[. . . .] The world has no such misery to show." True, we have only two millions, not "civilized, enlightened, nor Christian." Though living a hundred years in the midst of a "civilized, enlightened, and Christian" land, they are still a barbarous, ignorant, and heathen race, and without any fair prospect of ever being otherwise. How ever gratifying to our *feelings* it may be to see "a people of intelligence, ingenuity, refinement, spirit, and enterprise" thus oppressed, I ask if it is not equally abhorrent to our moral *principles,* that a people claiming this character for themselves, should for so many ages act the part of *oppressors*? And that they should purposely and of design, keep two millions of their fellow men in the very lowest state of degradation? Who that knows the pleasures of intellectual improvement and refined society, and the delights of domestic happiness, would consent to give them up, even if enjoyed in Turkish bondage? What generous mind would not rather be the Greek than the black? And so far as the laws have effect, the black is as absolutely subjected to the caprice of his master, whether actuated by passion or by lust, as the Greek. Public opinion may indeed operate to some extent in the more populous and refined districts, but there is abundant evidence to show, that in many parts of the slave territories, the despotism is exercised as absolutely as in Turkey. Lord Althorpe,[6] in the debate before referred to, said, "The honorable member for Sandwich has stated broadly and has quoted various documents to prove it that the slave is perfectly contented and happy. If we look only to the clothing and food allowed to these unfortunate beings, it is enough to convince any reasonable man, without further investigation, of the necessity of an alteration in the present system; and it is idle to the last degree, to talk of the happiness and comfort enjoyed by them. But it is said that some of these happy slaves are so conscious of their bliss, that they have even refused to take advantage of an offer of liberty, and have preferred to live and die in slavery. If the object were to prove the low state to which as moral creatures, these beings have been reduced, nothing could be stronger than this single statement. Good God! can it be imagined for a moment, that a man, possessing the least particle of the sympathies and affections of his species, should prefer to doom himself without remorse, to slavery for life; that he should doom his children after him, from generation to generation, to be born, to live, and die, in the bonds of slavery; that he should doom for ever his sons to the lash of the slave driver, and expose his daughters to the will and power of a cruel task-master? If any thing, I say, can raise feelings of indignation and horror in the breast, it would be the knowledge of such a fact as this."

Said Mr. Brougham,[7] on the same occasion, "In Jamaica too, I am told all is perfect; and that the black, who must be allowed to be the best judge of his own happiness, is perfectly contented with his lot—so well contented that he would not change it. But unfortunately for this assertion, it appears from consulting a single page of the Jamaica gazettes, that it cannot be supported. It is curious to observe the broad and most unequivocal contradiction given by these gazettes to this grave statement of the Jamaica assembly—for it thence appears that many of the blacks have shown a most pointed desire to change their happy situation. In a single page of these gazettes, there are no less than fifty "Runaways," persons quitting this enviable situation, not only with a certainty of many privations, but at the risk of all the severe penalties which attach to their crime."

Such are the views and feelings of some of the most enlightened philanthropists in the world. And something will certainly be done in the case. The thought is not to be endured for a moment, that the present state of things should last always. It would seem almost like an imputation upon Divine Providence to believe that he had suffered two millions of his creatures to become so involved in calamity that there was no possibility of a rescue. If God is just, something will be done. It will be done with our consent or against it; by our efforts, or in spite of them. The decree is past, and it hastens to its accomplishment.

It cannot be believed that while all the rest of mankind are advancing in the march of improvement, two millions of the race in free America, shall be left in irretrievable degradation. The foundations of rights and duties are becoming known. And have the blacks neither duties nor rights? The Christian sees with delight the efforts that are made to diffuse the gospel of life among the heathen. And shall the blacks be the only heathen?—The philanthropist fondly believes that the character of man is rising, swelling, bursting its ancient limits and the bonds with which despotism had sought to confine it. Shall the divine principles remain stationary only among American slaves? Despotic power is gradually yielding to the influence of public opinion. The old monarchies and aristocracies, where the many labor for the few, and government is administered for the benefit of rulers and not of subjects, are trembling and tottering to their fall. Witness the anxiety of the Holy Alliance to repress every thing like revolutionary principles, and every thing that goes to promote general improvement and elevation of character. But they will not be successful. Every friend of freedom feels that they cannot succeed. There is a law of nature against them. An impulse has been given to the minds of men which is irresistible. And shall the laws of nature be suspended only in the freest country on the globe? Can we believe that God regards slavery here with so favorable an eye, that he will repeal that law by which he has made provision for the renovation of this miserable world?

II.

Such then is the importance of our enquiries respecting the extirpation of slavery.—Philanthropy has been put off for many years with fair speeches, and pathetic lamentations over the evils of slavery, and the difficulty of applying a remedy. It is time to do something; neither can the urgency of the case be satisfied with any half-way measures. We may as well look the subject fairly in the face, and make up our minds that the point to be aimed at is the entire and speedy *abolition* of slavery. For whether we choose it or not, the thing will be done. And we must adapt our measures to meet the exigency, which is a pressing one. We cannot go about and about the point. We have no time to try palliatives. We *must* adopt some measures for the very speedy accomplishment of the object. The Colonization Society, excellent as is its plan, is altogether too slow in its operations and too feeble in its powers. The seeds of revolution, as the despots of Europe would say, or in American language, the principles of freedom, are too rapid in their growth, and too much cherished by the circumstances of the present day, and too quick and irresistible in their operations, to wait for the drizzling process of transporting two millions of people across the Atlantic. *Emancipation must take place on the spot where slavery exists.* Nothing short of this will meet the exigency; and we shall only be throwing dust in each other's eyes, if we talk of any thing short of this. We may inquire and debate, and exercise all the wisdom we have, about the details of the mode in which it is to be done, but the thing to be done is incapable of alteration or debate. It can neither be divided nor shunned. It is just one simple thing, and is to be taken so, as much as a declaration of war.—We need all the wisdom, and the concentrated energy of the whole nation, to overcome the difficulties in the case. But where the case is so desperate, difficulties should only stimulate to more extraordinary efforts.

I gladly leave it to wiser heads than mine to mature a plan for this purpose. I will only with modesty show my opinion in regard to a few particulars, which I deem important to be kept in view.

1. It must be made a *national* business.—The whole nation share in the disgrace of slavery, in the guilt of introducing and perpetuating it, and in the danger which threatens our free institutions, our national union, and our friendly intercourses with other nations. Every politician sees that the only point of danger to our union is in the existence of slavery. Wise men are exceedingly apprehensive that a permanent division of views and interests will arise between the slave-holding & the non-slave-holding states! And this source of ill feeling will be continually growing worse, as the effect of slavery upon our foreign relations, and our national prosperity becomes more apparent. It will be increased too by the intemperate madness of those who uphold the slave system. The nation cannot bear every thing, and if the indignation of the people should compel our government to withdraw her protection, and give notice that the slave states are to be left to themselves, I tremble for the consequences. The abolition of slavery ought to be a national business too, from its bearing upon our foreign relations. We are not yet through with the conflicting claims arising out of the late war. The business of detaining British citizens under the slave laws, is not settled. The points of contact will be vastly more numerous, and the relations vastly more complicated, when all the blacks in the West Indies become free citizens. Complaint is already made, that runaway slaves had means of joining the emigrants to Hayti, and Congress is called upon to interpose the national arm for the preservation of this species of property. I regret, that while the interests of a hundred thousand Indians, already in a train of prosperity, compared with their state a few years ago, should receive, not more indeed that their due, but a very marked attention in the inaugural discourse of our new President, there should not have been some slight allusion to the interests of *two millions* of our fellow-subjects, more wronged, more degraded, and more hopeless of relief from any quarter but the national government. The President under whose administration effective measures shall

be taken for the abolition of slavery, will deserve the name of having accomplished a work of the greatest difficulty, and having delivered his country from the greatest calamity, and secured the highest claim upon the gratitude of posterity. The attention of President Adams might well be directed to it, as the noblest object of ambition that he can set before him at the commencement of his official term. If any thing can be done under the constitution as it now is, let it be done; and if not let the constitution be amended.

2. The idea of emancipating all the slaves in the United States by purchase, must be wholly scouted. There is no reason in this world why the slave-holders should be hired to be just. I have before attempted to show that the relation of master and slave is wholly a creature of the laws. The law authorized it upon the supposition that it was for the public good, that is, for the good of both master and slave. This Mr. Clarkson has fully shown in regard to the introduction of slavery into the colonies of England and France. In his "Thoughts," before referred to, p. 16, 17, he proves that both Elizabeth and Louis XIII were made to believe that it was for the *interest of the Africans* to be brought to America, "that they might be converted to Christianity."[8] If now it can be made to appear, as it can most manifestly, that it is not for the public good that the relation should be continued, but that the interests of the whole community, masters and slaves, whites and blacks, require its abolition, the sovereign power of the nation has a right to say that it shall cease. If it be said that the nation has no right to interfere in the private concerns of individuals, I answer, that Congress did, by the restrictive system assume the right of legislating for the interests of the merchants, against their wishes; and I believe that all parties, however they may differ on the question of expediency, are now satisfied of the *right* of Congress to do as they did on that case. They have an equal right to legislate within *constitutional* limits for the benefit of the planters, against their wishes. I shall here be told of *vested rights*, which the planter has, as he says, to property which he acquired under existing laws, and which cannot be justly taken from him by a new legislative enactment. But does not every change of public policy alter the value of property, and often destroy it? Did our merchants ever ask pay for their vessels which rotted at their wharves under the restrictive system? or our manufacturers for their establishments which became worse than worthless to them at the return of peace? And is slavery such a righteous and precious species of property, that it is to be regarded as more sacred than ships and houses? I discard the idea of a vested right which cannot be controlled by the public interest. If the slaveholder claims any right excepting one which the laws have given, and which they therefore may rescind I put him to the proof. And I trace his title back,

either to its original fraud and violence in Africa, or to the birth of his slave in America. The former is given up. And as to the latter, I ask if there is any principle of natural right which says that this child should be subjected, he and his posterity for ever, to the arbitrary will and tyranny of another, and moreover to the condition of a brute, because by mere accident and by no fault or will of his own, he was born of a person who had been previously in the condition of a slave? Clarkson, p. 14. And if the nation is not bound in *justice* to buy these negroes from their masters in order to make them free, most certainly there is no principle of political expediency which would authorize the expenditure of five hundred or a thousand millions for this object. It would indeed be the dictate of sound policy to consult the present interests of the planters and to conciliate their feelings as much as possible. But neither present interests nor warm feelings will authorize a continuance of this great national evil. Provision must be made by law for emancipating our slaves where they are. If they can be removed out of the country it is well. But the first thing to be considered is, that they must and will be free.

[A Trip through New England]

During the summer of 1827, Russwurm took an extensive trip through Connecticut and Massachusetts. He dispatched six reports in the form of letters to Cornish, capturing his impressions, encounters, thoughts, and feelings. Together they constitute a remarkable document and must figure among the very first African American travelogues.

I.

NEW HAVEN, July

Dear Sir,

As want of time, and the imperious calls of duty, have never permitted you to visit New England; a few hasty lines, perhaps, principally devoted to an inquiry into the present condition of our race in that highly favoured part of the Union, may excite a moment's interest, and be worthy of a moment's perusal. However imperfect the sketch may be, all I hope, will be forgotten, from the motives which prompt me to the undertaking.

About 7 A.M. the steam-boat Hudson left ----- Slip, for New Haven, Conn. crowded with passengers. The fog, which was considerable at the time of our

Source: *Freedom's Journal*, August 3, 10, 17, and 31, and November 2 and 9, 1827.

departure, grew more dense as we receded from the city; until I almost began to fear, that we should be compelled to put into some port, before reaching our destined haven. About 11 A.M. however, it cleared away beautifully, leaving all above sunshine, and all beneath waters; and reminding me very forcibly of human life, which, often at its commencement, appears surrounded by almost insurmountable difficulties; arising from want of friends, poverty, and many other evils to which human nature is subject; and which, to us weak and erring mortals, is always a cause of complaint and despair; but which, after overcoming, through prudence and economy, we behold serene and beautiful, gliding peacefully, like many a sweet rivulet, among the cliffs through various meanderings until it reaches its termination. Such appeared the day, the remainder of which was delightful.

I will say nothing of the delightful views which every where meet the eye, in passing through the Sound; as my local knowledge is not sufficient to enable me to particularize. Of the passengers as little can I say. Two or three fine countenances appeared among the crowd. The subject of the late African celebration in this city, occupied the attention of not a few, and many an inquisitive glance was cast at me; which, certainly, you know, could not arise from any thing remarkable about me; but from the perusal of a certain sheet, sold by a rascally set of villains, to defame and lower us as much as possible in public estimation. One would suppose, we were already low enough, but it seems these fellows think we may be lowered still a little more; and I believe they are right. For none will question the remark of a certain Editor, who truly observes "that the advance the free blacks had made of late years is really incalculable."

I felt sorry, that so many apparently respectable gentlemen should countenance such libels, by purchasing, and freely circulating them among their friends: it certainly indicated but a small portion of sound sense: for how various are the interesting subjects which might always be profitably discussed on such passages. Nothing, however, displeased me more, than the ignorant observations of our brethren on board the boat, concerning the JOURNAL; thinking that the aforesaid trash and it were one. "They had frequently seen the JOURNAL on board; heard the remarks of the passengers; and if I looked around I might see one in the hands of the passengers:" How great my disappointment and pity were, that any of our race could be so ignorant concerning the purposes for which the JOURNAL was published, I need not write. Could I help grieving for their ignorance? Could I be ignorant of the causes of our degradation? Could I help feeling deeply anxious upon the subject of African Education? Let every other thing be done to improve our condition, all our labour will be in vain, if this forms not the ground work—the grand Archimedean lever. How important, then, that all our leading men should have a due sense of its inestimable value—

should strive all in their power, though deprived themselves in early life, from circumstances beyond their controul, to disseminate it. Truly it is the pearl above all earthly value, one particle of which, all the mines of Golconda and Potosi cannot purchase. So entirely am I devoted to the cause of Education, that all others seem to me of minor consequence; and while in meditation upon it, all others are forgotten.

You may be sure that but little was said during the passage. For how could conversation be maintained, where it was perceptible that great prejudice existed on the one side, and considerable independence and hauteur of mind on the other. In all such cases a man's own thoughts are his best resources—with them he can revolve plans, which may have the happiness of thousands of his fellows at stake: for vitiated must be his mind, who cannot, on such occasion, flee to its innermost recesses for shelter from the injustice of the oppressor, or the contumely of the proud. To me the idea is always consoling, that this is only our probationary state—that in the next, no man will be valued or despised on account of the complexion which an European or African sun may have imprinted.

> "Life is a frost of cold felicity,
> And Death the thaw of all our vanity."

As yet I have said nothing concerning my accommodations on board the boat; not through forgetfulness, but because the recollection of such occurrences is always painful. No accommodations were there for coloured passengers, and it was altogether owing to the friendliness of my brethren, that I received what I did. The labours of the previous week had nearly exhausted my wearied frame, and when I enquired after breakfast, for a b[e]rth, none could be had, though nearly all were unoccupied; it being contrary to all the rules of *humanity*, and *justice*, and *equality*, that a person of colour, however respectable, should sleep in the cabin of the Hudson. O! tempora, O! mores! How honourable are such things to this enlightened age! how honourable to the enlightened and humane proprietors of the Hudson! Ought not such trifles to be published to the world, that all may feel grateful to such noble and consistent defenders for *liberty* and *equality*!—Such things, we know, are mere trifles, and are unworthy of a moment's thought; but as I do not possess neither the humility nor patience of Job, how can I tamely submit to be so treated? Much has been said upon the pleasure of visiting strange parts; but to a man of colour, what are these? Many who profess themselves friendly, and with whom we are acquainted, dare hardly recognize us, assisting by their unmanly conduct to strengthen and encourage existing prejudices.

I had almost forgotten to mention, that among the passengers were four sons of Erin, who after wandering through various parts of the Union with indifferent success, were about to try their luck in the "land of steady habits." We should think, their chance for success would be but small, from the many whom we daily see traveling from one part of the Union to another; but who ever saw one of them discouraged?

Before 5 P.M. I was safely landed in New Haven, at some distance from the city—over a mile I should think.

Yours, &c.

II.

NEW HAVEN, *July*

Dear Sir,

As the object of my visit was principally among our brethren, I had determined previously to leaving New York, to procure lodgings among them, if I tarried one day only in a place. After some inquiry, I found myself comfortably settled in the family of Mr. S----. The remainder of the day was spent in enquiries, and in making a few calls upon the most respectable of our brethren, who all appeared rejoiced to see me in N.H., and promised to use all their influence, in forwarding the object of my visit. They immediately saw the great advantages likely to arise from the JOURNAL; and the necessity and expediency that we should possess such an engine, under our own control. After much consultation of what was most expedient to be done, it was determined to call a public meeting, to take the subject into consideration; and see what our N.H. brethren were willing to do towards upholding our hands, in our labours for the common good of our race.

Early the next morning, accompanied by Mr. S----, I waited upon Mr. J----, who preaches to our brethren here. Mr. J----, was at his rooms, where I had the pleasure of seeing several fine engravings. The firm, you well know, have acquired no small degree of celebrity, from the various beautiful specimens of their skill, which are daily before the public. Their name was familiar; but little did I think to find Mr. S.S.J. so great a philanthropist, and so warm a friend to the improvement of our brethren. He is a practical and active philanthropist; not one, who wishes well to us, and would be willing to do his part, if others would aid; but one, who feeling the importance of that admirable precept of our LORD, "do unto others, as ye would that others should do unto you," strives all in his power to walk in the footsteps of his Lord and Master; feeling assured, that though his labours are among the despised of the earth, at the final day; they will not be less acceptable to HIM, who knows no difference between the prince and the beggar.

> "A black man's heart may be as white and fair
> As polar snows, or cherub's garments are;
> While thine as black as hell, and stain'd within,
> Belies the lily whiteness of thy skin."

Are not such men more to be esteemed, than those who have slain their tens of thousands, and desolated cities? Are they not the "salt of the earth?" How blind then is human judgment, which awards more honour to the warrior, than to the "Man of Roses!"

At Mr. J----'s rooms, I had the honour of an introduction to the Rev. Dr. D. of Yale College. From his exalted station, you naturally expect something more than common in his countenance, nor are you disappointed; the most casual observer would immediately select him from a hundred others, as a man of superior intellect: and according to my notions of craniology, (not Dr. Spurzheim's) would perceive that the individual was one who could think deeply, and reason profoundly, upon almost any subject upon which he thought proper to fix his attention: in fact, it would recur to him, that he was (what the Dr. is in reality,) a deep mathematician; being one of the greatest which the country has produced.

As the subject of conversation previously to his entrance was Colonization, Mr. J---- briefly repeated the principal objections which our brethren had to the Society, and the leading members thereof. Mathematicians, are men who say but little; such was the case of Dr. D. I believe he is one of the Vice Presidents of the Society. A few more common place remarks, and a polite invitation from the Dr. concluded the interview.

New Haven possesses many distinguished individuals, upon nearly all of whom I waited, and was politely treated by all, except one. But what of that? My little knowledge of human nature had taught me enough to know that great men, like *little men*, have their *likes* and *dislikes*. I had not lived so long without profit. I hope the word politeness will be properly defined in Mr. W's forth-coming Dictionary. But the individual whom I had the greatest desire to see here, was Aristides. He is the author, you well know of three essays, I believe, (as I could not procure them,) published last spring in the New Haven Chronicle, against the views and designs of the African Improvement Society of New Haven. But who is Aristides? A man of considerable respectability—a man of considerable property, acquired by his own individual exertions. More than all this, Aristides is a man of sound sense—a shrewd man; and one of whom, I should suppose, his equals would stand in some awe. Better than all still, and the redeeming part of his antipathy against us, is, that Aristides is willing to hear what we have to say in our defence against his views; and to convince our readers of the truth of this, we are proud to assure them that Aristides is a subscriber to the FREEDOM'S JOURNAL. With Aristides I had but little conversation, as time on neither side permitted it. His pieces would be very acceptable to us, as some champion among our brethren might be found, who would be willing to enter the arena against him. But I have said so much concerning others, that you begin to think that the all-important subject of the present condition of our people, has been forgotten. No such thing. Can a mother forget her infant? Can a man of colour the present degraded state of his brethren? Can he exist, and not be anxious, to use all the means in his power to better it? From what I could learn, I should think the present number of persons of colour in N.H. amounted to nearly eight hundred. Among them are some respectable characters, who, by the exercise of prudence and economy, have acquired handsome little properties. I rejoice whenever I see such, as a double incentive is placed before every one who owns only *one foot of ground*, to conduct with prudence and economy, in order to acquire more. Such, my dear Sir, have been your views on this subject; and such, it becomes you to urge upon our brethren through the columns of the JOURNAL. But while we rejoice at the respectability, which some of our New Haven brethren have acquired; we cannot help mourning, that so many should remain as vagabonds and outcasts—a nuisance to society, and a disgrace to us all. Hence I view the objects which the African Improvement Society of New Haven are anxious of accomplishing, as one of the noblest in which men of enlightened minds can engage. What can be more enobling to the dignity of man, than to enlighten his fellow—to convince him that education and good conduct are all which ought to distinguish one man from another. Surely, their labour is one of love, which should meet the cordial support of every Christian. The Society numbers among its members nearly all the most distinguished citizens of New Haven. As yet little has been done; nor ought we to look for much, as the Society has been but lately established.

Our brethren here, have a wooden building, built, I suppose, for a church. It is in a very unfinished state, and is a rough looking thing. It answers pretty well, however, as it matters not, from whence our prayers ascend, whether from the broad waters of the Atlantic, or the burning sands of Zahara, provided our hearts be humble and truly penitent. The city supports two schools during three months in the year, for the instruction of colored children, which must appear to every one too short a time. As the African Improvement Society have got into operation, we trust something more will be done for their instruction. For in vain do men talk of sending us, nearly as ignorant as the beasts that perish, to Liberia, to be governors, judges, and generals, &c. &c. Let us behold their efforts here to enlighten us, and fit us for colonists; let their professions and principles agree, before we have any thing to do with their scheme.

—*Yours, &c.*

III.

NEW HAVEN, July

Dear Sir,

As stated in my last, a meeting was held in the evening, in the African Meeting-House, according to previous appointment. Sorry am I to say, that the number assembled was very few. Females, be it written to their credit, composed a large majority; in fact, the spirit of enquiry among them, whether derived from their mother Eve or not, is always greater than among an equal number of males. Hence we find so many more of them engaged in the active duties of Societies, which have not only the moral improvement of man in view, but whose aim is also, to disseminate the charities and necessaries of life among the poor and sick. After a fervent prayer by Mr. J----, and the object of the meeting having been briefly stated; extemporaneous addresses, well suited to the occasion, were delivered by Messrs. O----, A----, and B, recommendatory of the JOURNAL. The speakers all endeavoured to present the object in a fair light, and in my humble opinion, acquitted themselves very creditably. The meeting adjourned, after having accomplished but comparatively little. While I feel thankful for the zealous endeavours of our friends here, to forward the extension of the JOURNAL; I cannot help regretting that so many of our brethren should absent themselves from the meeting; for how could it appear in any other light, than a dislike and an opposition to any effort which had a tendency to raise us in the scale of beings. These are lamentable facts, but true.

Next morning I waited upon Mr. W----, whose feelings have long been warmly enlisted in our cause. He stands ready, I may say, upon the authority of friends, to engage in any cause which shall have a tendency to promote African Education: and, in prosecution of this important subject, he is willing to go East and West, North and South. As usual, the conversation immediately turned on African Colonization; but vain were all our efforts, to convert "l'un au l'autre:" as I found him, so I left him; and as I entered, so I departed. The Colonization Society appears to have some few friends in New Haven. Almost every where I called, the views of the Society were immediately introduced for conversation.

The Society has been very zealous and successful in imposing upon the public, the foolish *idea* that we are all longing to emigrate to their land of "*milk and honey*," and a thousand other Munchausen stories, too trifling and inconsistent to be repeated. I deem it high time that our friends, in different parts of the Union, should know the truth of the matter—that we are all, to a man, opposed, in every shape, to the Colonization Society, and its *consistent President*. Justice to some Colonizationists here, compels me to state, that they candidly acknowledged they did not believe, that the climate of Liberia was suited to the constitution of emigrants from the New England and Middle States. You well know, that such men as W----, C----, M----, and a long Southern list, care not whether the emigrants die the next day after their arrival in Liberia, or not; having obtained all they desired, our removal from this country—for their own personal safety, and the better security of their slaves. Methinks, slave-holders must be somewhat lacking in their crania, to dream even of being able to keep in the nineteenth century, nearly *two millions* of their fellow beings enslaved! Knowledge must spread. It cannot be kept from them. Did all other methods fail, I verily believe, like heaven's fiery lightnings, it would descend upon them. Can the *justice* of God tolerate so much iniquity and *injustice*?

You may well suppose, I could not omit, though much hurried, visiting the cabinet or minerals, gallery of paintings, library, &c. &c. appertaining to the College. Yale College, one of the first institutions of the kind, in the country, was founded in 1700, and located in New Haven; but the next year it was removed to Saybrook, and in 1716 again to New Haven. The buildings are the three Colleges, each four stories high; 100 feet in front, and 40 feet deep, built of brick; an elegant chapel of the same materials; and in the rear, a fine building, the lower part of which, serves the students for a refectory; and the upper for a cabinet of minerals, and a lecture room for the professor of chemistry. The library contains about ,000 [sic] volumes. Theological works occupy a considerable number of the shelves. Among them are many rare and valuable works. The Cabinet of Minerals belonging to Yale College, is the most extensive and valuable in the Union: besides its intrinsic value, it possesses many advantages from its admirable arrangement. The specimens of Basalt, from the Giant's Causeway, Ireland, and Aerolite from Weston, Conn. are really *noble*. The specimens of Agate, Marble and Organic* remains, were various and particularly fine. But from the hurried manner in which my visit was performed, I cannot particularize one-tenth part of what is really worthy of notice. In the same Hall, stands the collection belonging to the American Geological Society, which also contains many articles wor-

---

* Animal.

thy of notice. I was much pleased with beholding several cases in the Cabinet, inscribed "Citizens of N.H." They speak volumes in favour of the public spirit and liberality of her citizens.

New Haven is one of the pleasantest towns in the Union. It is handsomely laid out, and shaded with trees; the streets crossing each other at right angles. To city travellers, it has more the appearance of a country town, than many petty country villages. Having previously heard much concerning its Burying Ground, I could not depart without paying it a visit. It is really deserving of the celebrity it has acquired. It is the finest I ever saw. The ground is divided into certain square lots, which have been sold to different individuals, and by them surrounded with a low railing, in many instances, with the initials of the family inscribed. The monumental slabs are in a finer order than we generally see them. Some are really elegant. I was particularly struck with those erected on the College lots, and General Humphrey's. It would be well for other towns to follow the praise-worthy example of New Haven, in laying out their future burying places.

About 11 P.M. I repaired to the stage-house, where I had a small *specimen* of Yankee politeness, in the bar-keeper inviting me to go to bed for one hour, for which he had the *condescension* to charge only twenty-five cents. The stage was not ready till some time after twelve, when four others and myself took our seats within, where we found one weary passenger. Nocturnal traveling, you know, is scarcely ever pleasant, at best; more especially when we happen to find ourselves in the company of strangers. A few common place remarks therefore, were pretty much all that was said on the occasion. But when day-light appeared, and displayed to us Sol, rising from his ocean-bed, the exclamation was general on the grand and imposing spectacle before us. For who can behold the Sun rising in all his splendour, and not reflect on its great Architect?

About 6 A.M. we arrived in Middletown, the present location of Capt. Patridge's Academy. The town has a pleasing appearance; at least in passing through the principal street. In M. many persons of colour reside. Merely passing through, I had not the means of making any enquiries concerning their numbers, standing, &c.

I am happy to be able to state, from information that their improvement of late has been considerable. Means are about to be taken to erect a house of worship for their sole use. This augurs well, as we may always expect something more, when we find them so spirited. Union is every thing; and could our brethren but be united in their efforts, we might effect almost any thing. As light, however, is disseminating daily, we may confidently look for more of it among them. A few miles from M. we took in a young man from Cincinnati, Ohio; apparently not more than thirty, his gray hairs would almost persuade one that he was between fifty and sixty. He stated one fact concerning a celebrated mercantile house in M. which is worthy of being repeated. It was this: that the "Post Notes" of E. Bank, often circulated in Cincinnati, the day after they were dated in Connecticut! How the Bank maintained its credit so long is mysterious. It has, however, since failed, and sorry am I to say, that in its train, it has brought nearly loss of fortunes to many worthy individuals. The ride from M. to Hartford was very agreeable, as the morning was fine, and the passengers though nothing willing, to converse, troubled me not with impudent insinuations.

About eight, A.M. we arrived safely at Hartford, with fine appetites for breakfast. Having a letter of introduction to a respectable man of Colour, I was unwilling to try the politeness of Hartford landlords, for notwithstanding the fame which Connecticut has acquired in distant lands, for intelligence and liberal feelings, in no part of the Union are the people more prejudiced against persons of colour. In travelling in the stage, I have ever considered myself, so far as money would go, as good as the best; and holding this opinion, have ever been unwilling to accept any other treatment than the best.

Yours, &c. &c.

IV.

HARTFORD, July

Dear Sir,

Having delivered my introductory letter to Mr. G----, I was kindly received and entertained by him during my stay here. As my time was to be short, I delayed not, in publishing the object of my journey, among our brethren; but though I found many wellwishers to the undertaking, few were willing to aid us by their subscriptions. But I must not omit to mention, as some excuse, in a measure, for their backwardness, the expense they have lately incurred in the erection of a pretty little brick church, and the shortness of my stay. From our ignorance generally, you are aware, that it requires some time, before our people can be made to comprehend the usefulness of any new enterprize; more especially, one, of the nature in which we are engaged. After walking about the *city* considerably, and seeing all pretty much that was worthy of observation, and being stared at by every petty shop-keeper, and his dandy-clerk, and every half-bred countryman, as *some strange animal*, I returned to Mr. G----'s, with my head "pretty full of notions," concerning Hartford politeness.

New England, you know, is generally considered as Yankee land, by the Middle and Southern States; but Connecticut and Vermont are the states, where you behold the original Yankee, with all his notions, restlessness and inquisitiveness. "Where are you from, *if I may be so bold?*" "Where are you going, *if I may be so bold?*" are common questions from these polite folk. Hartford is a pleasant town, but will bear no comparison with New Haven, its great rival. The state-house, which is now undergoing some repairs, has a fine appearance; but, I suppose, it will not compare with the one, about to be erected in N. Haven; for I must inform you, that the rivalry between these *two large cities* is so great, that each must have a state-house for the legislature to meet in, every other year—colleges, that the polite citizens of each, may enjoy equal literary advantages—and as the one is about to have a canal, the other of necessity must dig one also, in order that its good citizens may enjoy the pleasures of canal navigation. It is really silly, to see the spirit of opposition carry things so far: why will not the good citizens of Connecticut, invest the thousands about to be expended in the erection of another state-house, for the use of Yale College, or some other institution?

I am aware, that my remarks are beneath the notice of the enlightened citizens of Connecticut; but I care not; as they are not written for their edification, but merely to employ an idle hour. In no part of the Union is prejudice carried to a greater extent than it is here: the house of God even, is not exempted from it; as I am credibly informed, that until very recently, one church did not admit persons of colour within its consecrated walls! I mention the fact, not as affecting myself more particularly, as no organ-loft or third story shall ever contain me, but as a small specimen of Hartford liberality. If it be our duty ever to lay aside pride and prejudice, in any place, and on any occasion, it must be in the house dedicated to the worship of God, and on that day, which he has consecrated to his service.

Having an introductory letter to J.P----, Esq. of the American Asylum for the Deaf and Dumb, was the greatest pleasure. I embraced the opportunity which it offered, of visiting the various departments of that celebrated and benevolent institution. By Mr. P----, I was introduced to the different officers; and I embrace with pleasure, this method of rendering my thanks for their polite treatment, and the gratification I enjoyed from my visit. The first thing, which immediately strikes the eye of the visitor, is the order and regularity which reign throughout; and the smiling countenances, and apparent happiness of these unfortunate beings, towards whom, until very recently, the means of education have never been extended. Though we are naturally led to suppose, that there must have been Deaf and Dumb persons in all ages of the world, we read nothing concerning any attempt having been made to instruct them, till the time of Pedro de Ponce, who lived in the sixteenth century; and of whom, it is recorded to his honour, that he instructed the Deaf and Dumb, and *taught them to speak*. Since then, among the many who have distinguished themselves, the names of De L'Epee, Dr. Watson, Sicard and Braidwood stand pre-eminent. The latter commenced an Academy, in Edinburgh, in 1786, with only six pupils, which he continued to his death in 1806. Dr. Johnson, *whose partiality* for the Scotch is well known, speaks very favourably of it in his Journey to the Western Isles; and it appears to have been a subject of considerable curiosity and wonder to his enlightened mind: for, says he, "after having seen the Deaf and Dumb taught arithmetic, who would be afraid to cultivate the Hebrides?"

Every thing is done by signs, even to teaching the letters of the alphabet. The quickness of these signs, which to us seem as incomprehensible as the hieroglyphics of the ancient Egyptians, are perfectly understood by them; as the most casual observer may notice, from the intelligence which, at such moments, beams through their countenances. Of all the acts of the legislature of Connecticut, none reflects more honour upon the state, than the Asylum at Hartford. To do good is ever pleasant; but to be the first in leading the way, and pointing us to objects who have hitherto been regarded as useless members of society, not from any misconduct on their part, but from the decrees of an All-wise Creator, *is still more pleasant*. Connected with the Institution are mechanic shops, where such of the pupils as choose it, may be instructed. I challenge any one, who has the least spark of humanity about his heart, to visit one of these shops, and behold the skill, industry, and activity, of these silent workmen, and not feel thankful that the hand of philanthropy has been extended to create for them *almost* a new existence. It would have delighted you, to have seen the look of recognition which lighted up the faces of many, at beholding Mr. S----, who accompanied me. He is, you know, a citizen of H----. I examined several specimens of their work, and, according to my poor judgment, must pronounce them equal to any I ever saw.

The mode heretofore practised in Europe has been to instruct them in *Writing, Manual Speech*, or *Dactyolology, Vocal Speech*, and the *explanation of the meaning of words*: whether it is the same at the Asylum I cannot say, as I only witnessed the examination of the pupils in the two first. Their present number amounts to about one hundred and fifty: and no one who beholds their apparent comfort, contentment and lively countenances, and reflects on the inanimate countenances of others of their brethren, unto whom the advantages of education have never been extended, can hesitate one moment concerning the propriety of patronising the Asylum. The building is pleasantly situated on the rising eminence, nearly two miles, perhaps, from the state-house.

Washington College, a new foundation, principally, if not wholly, under the control of Episcopalians, is also located at Hartford. Want of time prevented a visit to it. I learn, however, that it has gone into operation under very favorable auspices. The number of students amount to about sixty.

From what is set forth in the commencement of these letters, you naturally expect me to say something concerning the situation of our brethren here: but I can only state a few facts concerning them. Their number has, I believe, been computed at five hundred: but whether there has ever been a regularly formed society among them, I cannot say positively; but at present, it strikes me, that one was formed some years ago. If not, measures are about to be taken to form one; as they have now a house of their own to worship in. No school has yet been instituted by the generosity of the citizens of Hartford, for the education of their children: it may be, that they are tolerated and permitted to occupy some little corner in the different free schools, and when the teacher finds time, he devotes a few *heavy* minutes to their instruction; reminding me of an anecdote recently related by a traveller from the South, of certain zealous missionaries there, "who, when their hearers within the building, (whites,) became inattentive and sleepy, would address a few words to those without, (coloured,) exhorting them to bear their lot, with patience, and to bless God, for having bestowed on them *such christian masters and mistresses.*" When will the monster, prejudice, be done away, even from among Christians? Until near the breaking up of the Cornwall school, established and supported by the benevolence of the religious public, no admission was allowed, nor provision made for youths of colour; (Africans,) though it was evident that some of the youths, there assembled, from the different parts of the globe, had more of *colour* in their skins, than many, against whom the doors of the seminary were closed. The friends who were so zealous in removing "this barrier," merit our thanks; though the almost immediate breaking up of the school, allowed us not to profit by their wise and honourable interference.

Between eight and nine next morning, I left Hartford in the mail stage, in company with a young Bostonian, for B. We had travelled but a few miles, before we took in three other passengers; a lawyer, bankrupt and farmer, all young men. The former, profession-like, was all talk and somewhat witty; while the farmer, who have never hardly been out of the boundaries of his native town, listened with all possible attention to hear the 'squire talk, "half confiding, half doubting." After safely dropping his squireship, the farmer, following the example set him, began to relate anecdotes concerning his townfolk; and few young ladies in the town of -----, escaped his notice. He displeased me much, in speaking disrespectfully of an agricultural life; but as my sheet is already well filled, I must leave my notice of the bankrupt, &c. for the next.

Yours, &c. &c.

TO REV. SAMUEL E. CORNISH,[9]
BOSTON, AUGUST

Dear Sir:

As you are aware of the reasons which have delayed the remaining letters of this series, I shall proceed without making any unnecessary apologies. My travelling companion the bankrupt, whom I shall style *Mercator*, though, according to his own story, hardly twenty-two, and brought up and educated principally in the country, was a young man who had seen high life upstairs and downstairs. Like the prodigal son, he was on his return home, after having ruined his health, and spent his patrimony. His history is but short. At the age of sixteen, his parents wishing to make him somewhat smarter than common, prevailed upon a Kilby-street merchant here to take him into his counting-room. With him, Mercator remained two years, until his failure; when unwilling again to return to a country life, he departed for our great commercial emporium. Having a prepossessing face and fine figure, with good recommendations from his late employer, young Mercator found but little difficulty in procuring employment in a house of considerable celebrity. With his last employer, Mercator continued the remaining years of his minority: when having arrived at the age of sweet twenty-one, and feeling like all young men who think they are wiser than older heads, he determined to set up shop for himself, and accordingly hired one in Pear street; which he soon stocked with the most fashionable goods. Young men are apt to form a wrong opinion of the world; with them all is sunshine; every one who professes friendship, is of a truth their friend. Many years, however, do not pass over their heads, before they grow wiser, though at the expense of their purses. Such was the case with Mercator. He found friends and customers enough who were willing to run in debt, considering it as a favour; but a demand of payment created them his enemies. But this was a mere trifle, in comparison to other evils to which Mercator had subjected himself: and as he concealed not the truth from us, who were strangers, neither shall I. Poor Mercator had become dissipated, and having once joined the throng of the votaries of Pleasure, he knew not where to stop; but was insensibly carried with the stream, until he found himself a ruined man in purse and reputation. Shunned by those who had zealously courted his company when in prosperity—harassed by creditors, our city became no delightful residence to the poor bankrupt; and accordingly, having packed up the few remaining articles of his once abundant wardrobe, and seen all his fond anticipations of making at some future day, a figure in Wall-street, dashed to the ground, with heavy steps and a still heavier heart he embarked on board the celebrated boat "Fulton," for "the land of steady habits." Before dinner time, the Bostonian and myself again found ourselves in full possession of the stage, the lawyer, farmer and Mercator, having left us some miles behind; the latter cheating the driver of his fare, and calling upon his good and ready friend, the farmer, to testify to the truth of the fact. To what meanness will not pride and poverty prompt a man!

About 6 P.M. we arrived safely at Worcester, after having travelled over a road none of the most comfortable. Worcester is a town of some note in this state; being the largest inland town in New England, and I should suppose, there were few superior to it in the Union. Located about forty miles from one of our first seaports—in the heart of one of our most agricultural counties, it possesses signal advantages over many other towns not so favourably situated. The Agricultural Society of Worcester county have there erected a fine brick building for their use. The town has a pleasant appearance; its citizens cannot be considered as city or country-folk merely, but partaking in a large degree of the advantages of both, without any of their disadvantages. But few persons of colour reside in the town.—From Worcester to Boston the road is one of the best in the country, but though I have travelled it several times, I can say but little concerning the different towns, having always been my lot to travel by night. About midnight we arrived in Boston, over the Western Avenue.

Boston, you know, has been called "the Edinburgh of America," and never was a title more properly bestowed; if we take into view the high literary standing of her citizens; the number & excellency of her public schools; the various literary publications issued annually from her presses; and though last, not least, the publication of the North American Review. This publication has made Boston the focus of literature; every distinguished literati has been eager to enrol his name among the contributors to its pages, and hence the judgment of the reviewer has been seldom called in question. To a man of wealth and education, Boston is certainly the first city in the Union for a residence. The city is pleasantly situated on a peninsula, and though the streets have not that width and regularity with ours, the buildings generally are better and have a finer appearance. In no part of the country, are more substantial and elegant buildings than the granite ones in different parts of the city. Boston has been so often described by abler pens, that I feel like trespassing on your time, in saying much concerning it. Some few lines however I must write. Had Boston nothing else to recommend her to our notice, her public schools would be enough to fix the attention of every enlightened man. These are subdivided into Primary, Grammar, Male and Female English High Schools and a Latin School. The whole system throughout is more thorough and comprehensive than in any other public schools, in the

Union, having already gained for her an honourable distinction in Europe and America. The school houses are spacious and airy, and as public buildings are honorable to the city. The new market house recently erected, of granite, is the most elegant structure of the kind in the Union; and travellers have asserted, that it was not excelled by any in Europe. Of a truth, Bostonians owe much to the determined perseverance and enlightened views of their chief magistrate, John Quincy, Esq.

About two thousand persons of colour reside here. Their advantages for education, though small compared to other citizens, is in my humble opinion superior to any other city in the Union. The city authorities, aided by the generous donation of Abiel Smith, Esq. support two primary and one grammar school, for children of colour. Were the committee for the grammar school to pay equal attention with the committee for the primary—were equal inducements held out to boys of colour by the distribution of prizes annually, and an advancement to a higher school—we might hope, before many years, to behold some well-educated young men who would be a credit to us, and to the city in which they were educated. But we fear, many years will elapse before we behold this great desire of our heart. The same principle, recognized in different parts of the land, "that a little reading and writing are enough for our children," is also abroad here in the minds of many who are warm-hearted friends to our race. From this want of education has arisen the idea of "*African inferiority*," among many, who will not take the trouble to enquire into the cause.

Boston is the place where that sweet poetess of nature, *Phillis Wheatley*, first tuned her lyre under the inspiration of the Muses, putting to shame the illiberal expressions of the advocates of slavery in all parts of the globe. So incredible were the public concerning the genuineness of her poems, that they are ushered into the world with the signature of the Governor, Lieutenant-Governor, and other distinguished men of Massachusetts affixed to them. O Liberality, thou art not certainly a being of this lower sphere! for why should the natural powers of man be rated by the fairness of his complexion?

> "Colours may be white or dark,
> For the body is a clod;
> 'Tis the intellectual spark,
> Shows the lineaments of God."

This is not the time nor place to enter into more particulars concerning her. She has left behind her a small volume of poems, as a rich legacy to our race; and in the language of Horace, "monumentum aere perennius, regalique situ pyramidura aitius."[10] To our shame I write it, *"our Poetess"* lies buried in the Northern-Burying-Ground, without a stone to mark the spot, where repose African genius and worth. This, I hope, will not be long the case: if our brethren here, do not feel able or willing to erect a monument, let a general contribution be made by us through the Union—let us evince to the world that we are not insensible to the fame and renown which her writings have conferred upon us—*that we are proud of them.*

We are naturally led to suppose that the farther north we travel, the less prejudice we have to encounter. Mistaken idea! Travel north and east, west and south and prejudice block up your way. What is the reason? Why this is not their country—let them go back to their native Africa—they have become too free (in a republican country,) exclaim some of our good friends. Does a man of colour evince the least intelligence? "I guess you were not brought up in these parts," is the first remark. What do our "tried and consistent friends" labor to inculcate? The man of colour while here can be nothing—but send him to the Elysian fields of Africa, and he returns to America, in two or three years a man of first rate intelligence; worth thousands; Captain of a company of a dozen men, including first and second Lieutenant and Ensign; Justice of the Peace; and Collector of the Customs for the *city of Monrovia, in the Territory of Liberia, on the continent of Africa!!*

Yours, &c.

VI.
TO REV. SAMUEL E. CORNISH
BOSTON, *August*

Comparatively speaking, Boston is the richest and most aristocratic city in the Union. Here reside many individuals with princely fortunes. The objects most worthy of a stranger's notice, are the State-House, State-street, with its numerous Banks, the new Market-House, Faneuil-Hall, (the cradle of American liberty,) the Athenaeum, Central Wharf, the Western Avenue or Mill-Dam, the Common, and Beacon-street, with its Macadamized pavement. The State-House is a massive, brick building, on Beacon-street, somewhat more elevated than any other, and affording from its cupola fine views of the city, harbour and islands, and the surrounding country. The Common, with its Mall, is the public place of promenade for the citizens: it contains between forty and fifty acres, and was the generous donation of a citizen. The Mall is handsomely ornamented with trees. The Common contains a basin of water, which has been known from time immemorial by the name of the Frog-pond; and a few trees, among which is the far-famed Elm "of great renown."

Central Wharf, with its fine and uniform block of brick stores, is said to be the handsomest wharf in the world, and certainly no city in the Union can show any thing equal. The stores are built near its middle, affording sufficient room on each side, for vessels to unload, for a passage way for carts, and a handsome footpath for passengers. Beacon-street, paved on the principle of the celebrated McAdams, is a fine street, inhabited wholly by men of the first standing in society. From what I have seen of it, I prefer it to the old mode of paving. Roads made on this principle, require some considerable time before we ought to consider them as finished; but when they are so, they can be made as even as the floor of a house. I should think the success which has attended Mr. McAdams' plan in Great-Britain, would induce other of our cities to make a trial of his system.

Our coloured brethren here have a Grand Masonic Lodge, which is entitled the African Grand Lodge of Boston, Massachusetts. It is the first institution of the kind among us, and I believe, derives its charter from Great-Britain. At any rate, it holds but little fellowship with the different lodges in the city, from what cause I know not. As there is a mystery about every thing connected with masonry still, *notwithstanding the great light thrown upon the subject by the publications of Capt. Morgan,* I can enter into no particulars concerning the fraternity, the number of its members, or its standing. They have a fine lodge room in Cambridge-street, and from appearances I should think the Society to be in highly flourishing condition.

Our brethren here have also three Religious Societies, viz. one Baptist, and two Methodist; one or two Mutual Relief Societies, and a Debating Club. Of the Mutual Relief Societies I can say but little; never having learned their number of members, or seen their constitutions. The objects contemplated by them are noble; and I hope they will proceed in their laudable endeavours of assisting the sick and needy. Our views on this subject we have already expressed in the early numbers of the JOURNAL. The Debating Club consists of about eighteen or twenty members, who meet once every two weeks, for the discussion of extemporaneous subjects. Whether any written compositions are read, I know not. Debating Clubs, when properly conducted, have been found highly useful, from the debates which often come before them, a spirit of energy is engendered, which leads to profitable reading and reflection on many subjects, which otherwise would have escaped our notice. It would be well if we were to follow the laudable example set us by our Boston friends. Care should be taken, that one long-winded speaker does not occupy too much of the time of such societies; nor that any member speak more than twice on any subject, occupying but eight or ten minutes each time. These, I am aware, are things of minor importance, but nevertheless they are highly important to the well being of every debating society.

I have already stated the number of the coloured population of this city, and sorry am I to add, that very few are mechanics; and they who are, almost universally relinquish their trades for other employments. This, I suppose, is principally owing to the want of patronage on the part of the public; and to an irregularity too common among us, on their part. But few of our brethren have improved their opportunities of acquiring *fast property*; for I am informed by wiser and older heads, that their opportunity in years gone by for acquiring property were tenfold what they are at present; a new spirit, however, is abroad among some of the younger members, which we trust, will be the means of effecting great good. We are an oppressed and degraded race, but we trust that the contempt and opposition we meet with, instead of damping will tend to make us more zealous in the pursuit of whatever is honest, and just, and of good report. Upon the whole, I should judge, that the condition of our brethren here at large, had improved considerably of late years in point of comforts, morals and intelligence. Of course there will always remain some unworthy members here, as well as elsewhere—a disgrace to us and to society at large: but the whole ought not to bear the stigma for the misconduct of a few; as there is enough of vice and its concomitant evils among the most favoured classes of society.

Boston is emphatically a place of steeples; for no city in the States can equal her in the number of her houses of worship according to her population, and in no city is the sabbath kept with more due reverence. The police regulations here are excellent, closing all groceries, liquor stands, (porter houses here unknown) and shops of every description by 10 o'clock at night: the good effects resulting from which are, that the streets are more retired and quiet by that hour, than ours generally are by twelve o'clock.

Business calling me, I paid a short visit to Salem, about fourteen miles from Boston, a town much celebrated in the annals of the East India Trade. Salem is a pleasant town, with some streets with fine and princely buildings; with others with buildings bearing all the marks of having been put together immediately after its first settlement. The persons of colour residing in the town amount to about four hundred. Their opportunities for the acquisition of property, are I believe better than commonly falls to our lot in the different cities. Many of them are owners of a comfortable house and lot, certain testimonials (which we should be glad to see many more of our brethren) of their economy and industry. Salem is the residence of our friend R. who, by uniform propriety of conduct, and an undeviating attention to business has gained the respect of all classes of the citizens. I found him just recovering from a long fit of sickness; so weak as to be unable to accompany us on our promenade through the town. The Marine Society of Salem have here erected a fine building for the uses of the society, which

I believe consists wholly of masters and supercargoes who have been round the Cape of Good Hope. Their collection of East India and Chinese curiosities is the richest in the country. There are but few museums equally valuable: I can say but very little concerning it, owing to the shortness of my visit, which had to be regulated by the time which the gentleman who had charge of the museum had to spare; for you are to be informed, that it was an act of great condescension in allowing us persons of colour to peep at it, as no money is ever taken as the price of admission. The road from Boston to Salem is superlative in every sense of the word, being the *dearest* and *finest* in the country.

Boston has ever been celebrated for the correct and enlightened views of her citizens on the subject of the African Slave Trade. It was owing to this, that one of her representatives who a few years since voted in favour of its extension into a certain portion of the country was burnt in effigy and lost his seat in the National Legislature. We have always had warm and zealous friends here; for who has not heard of the philanthropy of the Smiths, Hancocks, Winthrops, and Phillips of former days? or of the zealous and unwearied efforts of the departed Woodman, "who had a hand open as day for melting charity?" But while we revere the memory of departed worth, let us not be unmindful of their followers who still remain. Where so many deserve to be mentioned, it is always invidious to particularize, nevertheless I must be excused for naming Messrs. N----, and G----. The descendants of Africa, will, I trust, ever hold both in high estimation; the one for his unwearied labours in the sabbath school, and for the improvement of the people of colour at large; the other, for his untiring exertions in the establishment and organization of the African Primary Schools. May their good counsels have a lasting effect upon our rising youth; and may the recollection of their labours of love, in behalf of our race, cheer them in their latter days; and when "this mortal shall have put on immortality," may they be as a sweet offering before the throne of the Almighty!

It is true, my dear sir, we are a people surrounded with obstacles on all sides, but notwithstanding how few of us have improved our small privileges! Were each to ask himself the question: how few could conscientiously answer it affirmatively. Like the rest of mankind, we are too apt to repine at the comforts and advantages of others, our superiors in life, without comparing our situations with those not so comfortably off, or making strenuous efforts to improve it. I know not why it is, our people are so fond of flocking to large towns and cities, unless the old proverb, "that misery loves company" is too true to be made a jest of. It is an acknowledged fact that the situation of thousands of them would be improved by a removal into the country—that the number of coloured criminals who are daily sent to jails and penitentiaries would be lessened by their removal from the scene of temptation, and yet nothing is done to lessen the evil. I do not mention these facts here as pertaining to Boston, or any part of New England more particularly; they apply with equal, if not greater force to all our larger cities. The fact is, the coloured population of Boston has increased but little of late years. We confess we feel sorry that so many petty thefts are committed by persons of colour, but what besides enlightening the minds of the rising generation, can we do? A society on the principles of the one lately established in New Haven might be the means of effecting much good. But where is the zealous and enlightened man of colour, who is willing to devote his time to the formation of such?

Yours, &c.

Betrayed by Our Own Brethren: On Fugitive Slaves, Kidnapping, Man-Stealing, and Action

The danger of being kidnapped and sold into slavery had been a constant concern of the free people of color and a reminder of the fragility of their condition even in the so-called "free states" of the North. But Russwurm became more and more alarmed by a growing trend of black people betraying other black people to slave catchers. He found such acts of betrayal difficult to even imagine, but by 1828 he could no longer deny the evidence. Beyond the strong denunciation of the "snakes in the grass," Russwurm used the platform of Freedom's Journal *to warn his readers of the dangers and prescribed individual as well as collective action and organization against kidnapping and "man-stealing" in cities such as New York, Philadelphia, and Boston—places that many newly arrived fugitives assumed to be safe. Following the example of a small group of antislavery activists in Philadelphia, who established in 1827 a Protecting Society for the preventing of kidnapping and man-stealing, Russwurm suggested the creation of one for New York City. Russwurm, however, emigrated to Liberia the following year. The New York Committee of Vigilance was not established until 1835, by a former Russwurm and* Freedom's Journal *associate, David Ruggles.*

Self Interest: [Betrayed by Coloured Persons]

In our last, we gave notice that several persons of colour, residents of this city, had been lately arrested as runaways:[11] since then, we have learned from creditable sources, at home and abroad, that most of those who have been

Source: *Freedom's Journal*, Nov. 7, 1828.

carried back into bondage, have generally been betrayed by coloured persons—brethren of the same flesh and kindred, for the sake of paltry lucre. It is no longer than Friday last, that a female who was arrested as a runaway, had her doom to a life of servitude, confirmed by the oath of a coloured person, who came forward voluntarily on behalf of her master, and testified to her being his slave! It is no longer than last week, since we received a letter from a respectable & intelligent correspondent, who has lately visited the State of Maryland on business, and there saw a man who had been carried back into bondage, who told him in the presence of others, that a certain coloured man, (we believe still in this city,) *did betray him by writing to his Master*. His name can be known by enquiry at this office.

We have often heard, that most of those who are taken up as runaways, were betrayed by our own brethren; but we cannot say that we ever placed implicit reliance in these reports until recently; at present the facts are too strong— we must believe; all doubt is removed. But what is to be done? Are these traitors to liberty—to their kindred—to be suffered to proceed peaceably in their nefarious traffic? It is not our wish to excite the feelings of our readers—as true chroniclers of whatever concerns their present and future welfare, we place all events in which they are deeply interested before them—we would not excite their anger, and move them to the commission of acts contrary to the laws— but we again enquire, what is to be done? What has been done to those who have been traitors to their country—what can we do conformably to the laws against these monsters—who are dead to all that ennobles man?

It is an indisputed fact, that such vile traitors should not be suffered to associate with us: and as much faith as we believe we can confidently put in the world, it would be wisdom in all our brethren who have escaped from Southern bondage, not to trust even their most intimate friends on a subject in which they are so deeply interested.

To a man of feeling, nothing can be compared to Liberty—without it, blessed with all the comforts and elegancies of this world, life is a blank—he is a mere automaton, moved by the hand and rod of his master—but with Liberty for his portion, with a crust of bread and cup of water, he can gaze abroad upon the earth with thankfulness, and hope for better days.

Again we repeat, it seems a pity that brethren who have escaped from bondage should be so inconsiderate as to settle themselves in large cities like New York, Philadelphia, and Boston—places which are visited every year by hundreds from the South. Would it not be real wisdom to choose some sequestered country village, where they would be out of danger of losing that liberty which is their inherent right by Nature.

Man was created by his Maker a free agent. Why then should he become subjected to his fellow man? Why should his freedom of action be restrained by so abhorrent a thraldom as slavery?

> "O execrable son, so to aspire
> Above his brother! to himself assuming
> Authority usurped, from God not given.
> He gave us over beasts, flesh, fowl,
> Dominion absolute. That right we hold
> By his donation; but man over men
> He made not lord; such title to himself
> Reserving, human left from human free."[12]

Self-Interest: [Shaming and Naming Names]

We are sorry to inform our readers that the business of arresting persons of colour as runaways from the South, is daily taking place in this city, and appears to be followed so systematically that we know not when an end will be put to it. Since our last, we have learned that the villain who testified against the young woman, was her own cousin! where is the man of colour, whose feelings do not burn with indignation while perusing these few hasty lines; for our part, we cannot describe ours while penning them, and inscribing the name of *Moses Smith*, formerly of Baltimore, Md. as the informer referred to. We would proclaim his name with that of one *Nathan Gooms*, of this city, (formerly from the South) from Maine to Georgia, that our brethren may be on the alert against their base and infamous practices. We have other names in our possession, but though some men would be led to draw conclusions against them, still we have charity enough for the present to hope better things;—at least, we shall delay publishing their names for a while.

In our humble opinion something ought to be done to arrest this infamous business. We leave it to older and wiser heads what course to pursue. We are sorry to see our brethren so unconcerned on the subject; and we are also sorry, that through the haste and rashness of one, the informer first mentioned, escaped from those who were in pursuit of him. We would have our brethren abroad, keep a lookout for these villains, as we are confident they will find these villains, as we are confident they will find but little peace if they remain in this city. It is certainly common cause, and how divided

Source: *Freedom's Journal*, November 14, 1828.

soever we may be on other subjects, we should unite in this for the protection of ourselves and families. We believe any man of colour who will betray one who is a runaway, would not hesitate one moment towards assisting to kidnap those who are free.

Land of Liberty

The business of arresting our brethren as runaways is still daily occurring in this city. For the last week, our Police court, has been constantly crowded by brethren, interested in the cause of some dear relative or friend, whose trial was going on, or would perhaps occur during the day. Again we warn our brethren who have cause to fear apprehension to be on the lookout as we have heard, that a Slave holder, has hinted the determination of himself and others to have *five hundred* at least, out of this city, during the *winter*.

The members of our Manumission Society, have been unwearied in their labours of love—but the duty has been so constant and pressing, that we think something should be done by us to lessen their burdens. Perhaps the formation of such a society as the *Protecting Society*, of Philadelphia for the preventing of kidnapping and man-stealing; might be of incalculable benefit; we ought and must do something, besides spending hours and of late days, as lookers on and interested, though idle spectators.

We are happy to announce that the case of Eliza Garnett, for whom so general a sympathy was felt, has terminated favourably, and we wish it were in our power to say the same generally of cases of this nature. Their success of late, has rendered slave holders, quite forgetful, that they are in a free State, and this remark we are induced to make, from the fact that in two, if not three cases, they have been bold enough during the evening to enter the dwellings of our brethren without any authority or civil process whatever, but mere physical, force having four or five men in company, and carry them off without a hearing or trial. While upon this painful subject, we cannot refrain from execrating the conduct of those traitors who make it a business to betray their brethren; and from the proceeds of their accursed gains dress genteelly, and are received into society. *Beware of such, they are snakes in the grass, charming unwary birds.* The oldest residents hardly ever knew of times of more excitement; but amidst all these trying scenes, it is cheering to have it in our power to record an instance of benevolent feeling from a citizen, *in behalf* of one of our brethren, whose cause had terminated unfavourably. His offer, was to give fifty Dollars, towards rescuing him from bondage, if there

Source: *Freedom's Journal*, December 5, 1828.

were any likelihood of a sum being raised for that purpose. If we take into consideration, that this man was a *poor man*; that his offer was to rescue a man of colour, we shall then estimate it as highly as we should.

To us he is a stranger and probably ever will be, but our constant prayers shall be, that he may be rewarded an hundred fold for his benevolent offer in the cause of suffering humanity.

Engaging the Colonizationists

The following exchanges bring into sharp relief the offense that the anticolonization editorial position of Freedom's Journal *caused, even among those who professed to be the paper's and the "black man's friend." And colonization was indeed the hegemonic and orthodox solution, not only to the problem of slavery, but also to the free colored "problem" in the United States. Thus, in the view of "Wilberforce," to be opposed to colonization was to be against the best interest of African Americans. No irony was meant or implied in the letter writer's adoption of the abolitionist nomenclature. Russwurm, in his bold retort, would have none of it, and insisted on placing the name in quotation marks and italics lettering, separating his correspondent as sharply as possible from William Wilberforce. For Russwurm, "Wilberforce" was no friend of the slave or the Negro but an impostor and at best an unwitting apologist of the status quo. It was an uncompromising and extraordinarily courageous position for which both Russwurm and the Journal would pay dearly. Despite encouragement and goading from Russwurm, "Wilberforce" never revealed his true identity. All we know is that the letter was sent to the Journal on behalf of "Wilberforce" by his friend Dr. Samuel Miller of Princeton Theological Seminary. (But as discussed in the main text above, there is good and ample evidence to suggest that the true identity of "Wilberforce" was none other than the principal of Princeton Theological Seminary, Dr. Archibald Alexander, a staunch colonizationist and Miller's closest friend and colleague.) Miller in turn objected to the linking of his name with the letter and took the opportunity to express his own strong objection to the anticolonization position of the paper. Russwurm was not shy about expressing his strong demurral.*

[An Exchange with "Wilberforce"]

Messrs. Editors,

I have looked with lively interest at the progress of your labours, as displayed on the pages of Freedom's Journal. It is a great and difficult work to cast light on the delicate subjects, which principally engage your attention, in such a way as, at once, to be faithful and prudent. I am persuaded that you feel deeply, and mean well, and that you would not, willingly, be instrumental in retarding the progress of a cause which is worthy of your best affections and labours. Yet I own that in reading the third letter of the Junior Editor of your paper, written from New Haven, and published in the Journal of the 17th inst., I was forcibly reminded of an old proverb—"Save me from my *friends*, and I will take care of my enemies." I allude especially to the paragraph relating to the American Colonization Society. It is as follows—"As usual the conversation immediately turned on African Colonization; but vain were all our efforts to convert, 'l'an au l'autre:' as I found him, so I left him; and as I entered, so I departed.

"The Colonization Society appears to have some few friends in New Haven. Almost every where I called, the views of the Society were immediately introduced for conversation. The Society, has been very zealous and successful in imposing upon the public, the foolish idea, that we are all longing to emigrate to their land of "milk and honey," and a thousand other Munchausen stories too trifling and inconsistent to be repeated, I deem it high time that our friends, in different parts of the Union, should know the truth of the matter—that we are all to a man, opposed, in every shape, to the Colonization Society, and its *consistent President*. Justice to some Colonizationists here, compels me to state, that they candidly acknowledged they did not believe, that the climate of Liberia was suited to the constitution of emigrants from the New England and Middle States. You well know that such men as W.L.M. and a long Southern list, care not whether the emigrants die the next day after their arrival in Liberia, or not; having obtained all they desired, our removal from this country—or their own personal safety, and the better security of their slaves. Methinks slave-holders must be somewhat lacking in their crania, to dream even, of being able to keep in the nineteenth century, nearly two millions of their fellow beings enslaved! Knowledge must spread. It cannot be kept from them. Did all other methods fail, I verily believe, like heaven's fiery lightnings, it would descend upon them. Can the justice of God tolerate so much iniquity and injustice?"

Source: *Freedom's Journal,* September 7, 1827.

Now really I could not well conceive a better method of checking the progress of *African rights* in all their extent, than to attack in the *name* of these *rights* the American Colonization Society. The ignorant, coarse, bitter way in which he assails this best friend of black men, may disarm and destroy itself. But if not,—if he has any influence with his coloured brethren, or is desirous of promoting their best interest—how can he speak thus of this society? Consider the objects of the society—They are no less than to erect a republic on a healthful coast—where free men *in name*, may be free men *in fact*,—and enjoy rights, which they do not, and cannot, enjoy in this country; to spread the blessings of the gospel of Christ over a whole continent, which is peopled by his fellow-men, who are perishing without it; to put a stop to the nefarious traffic in human blood which is still carried on upon the whole coast of Southern Africa, by teaching the natives the guilt of the traffic, and by furnishing an asylum for the recaptured slaves—and to afford the occasion of instant freedom to numbers of poor slaves, whose masters will let them emigrate (however wicked this may seem, yet it is true) to Africa, but will not let them be free at home. These are some of the objects of this Society, which has no earthly interest in the success of its plans but the love of doing good, and which has demonstrated the wisdom of its plans, by their success.

In all these there is no coercion. The free coloured people need not go, if they do not choose to go. The poor slaves will, no doubt, prefer Liberia to a slave-ship—or a slave plantation. And if, as your unfortunate traveller says, the climate of Liberia, is unhealthy for northern Negroes, (as to the middle states, facts are entirely against him,) yet how few are there in New York and New England of this people, compared with the great body of them, living and yet to live, farther South, to whom it will be healthy. If you are not acquainted, with the reports and the periodical journal of the society, appearing from month to month at Washington, I would advise you forthwith to get them. If you, or rather if your Junior Editor, is acquainted with them, I will not say that he is unfit for his work, but I will say the cause of Slavery, has not, in this land, so strong an advocate. How sad, how shameful, thus obstinately, to pull down what the wise and good are so laboriously, and alas so slowly building up; and that too in the name and imaginary services of a friend.

While attempting the work of a friendly censor, I will indulge in one other train of thinking dictated by a sincere regard for the cause of injured Africans, and derived from a careful observation of several years. It refers to the distinctions which are made in this country, between white men and free black men. These seem greatly to molest your associate and your correspondent Mordecai. See as follows.

"The ride from M. to Hartford was very agreeable, as the morning was fine, and the passengers, though nothing willing to converse, troubled me not with impudent insinuations. About eight A.M. we arrived safely, at Hartford, with fine appetites for breakfast. Having a letter of introduction to a respectable man of colour, I was unwilling to try the politeness of Hartford landlords, for notwithstanding the fame which Connecticut has acquired in distant lands, for intelligence and liberal feelings, in no part of the Union are the people more prejudiced against persons of colour. In travelling in the stage, I have ever considered myself, so far as money would go, as good as the best; and holding this opinion, have ever been unwilling to accept of any other treatment than the best."

And again, "I am not covetous of sitting at the table of Mr. N----, to hold him by his arm in the streets,—to marry his daughter, should he ever have one,—nor to sleep in his bed—neither should I think myself honoured in the possession of all these favours." Now every well informed and observing man knows that these matters depend upon taste and upon relative circumstances entirely. The distinction is derived from the relation of the parties to each other—and from the effects of these relations, not from any original disparity.

Thus it was that a white traveller in the heart of Africa, was, not many years ago, in an offer of marriage to a black woman, rejected with expressions of horror, at his colour, and of indignation at his impudence. On the contrary, in the expedition of Lewis and Clark—the man most admired of the whole party, and the only one, to whom the hand of *divers Indian princesses* was offered in marriage, was "*Big Nat*," (this was I think, his name,) a servant and a coloured man. The history of the Jews, to whom allusion is made by "Mordecai," will strongly illustrate the same statement. Their colour varies from the fair European to the sooty Asiatic, and yet *their condition (consequent character)* it is, which effects toward them so unfavourably the nations and the men of the earth, from Haman down to your misnamed correspondent Mordecai. There is no reasoning against these feelings. Ladies are perverse things, and cannot be forced even to *love* against their will, and on such matters, public opinion like the ladies must be humoured a little. And allow me to ask, if the way you adopt, is the best way, to plead the cause of your injured countrymen? Will it not rather produce reaction, and operate against it? We are not arguing the question, whether the slave-holders, public opinion, and the ladies ought to feel so; but seeing it is so, how ought you to write and act so as to enlighten the public mind on the rights of free, and enslaved coloured men in the United States? Think you that if this number of your paper were to penetrate to one of those large farms in the South, where, by the laborious and long continued efforts of Christians, the poor slave is beginning to read the Bible, by permission of his hard master, he would not at once tear the blessed treasure from his trembling hands, for fear that *such matter* would next be put into their hands? How think you it would effect [sic] a

Southern Legislature? How the slaves themselves of the south and west? Would it not do unmingled injury? Will it do any good to prove to them that they *deserve white wives*, and are "as good as the best, when they pay their money," or, I will add, when they do not?

Is not your work to throw light on the subject of slavery in general, and on the horrors of the slave trade, both external and internal, to elevate the character of the free coloured people of this country? and by all means that are wise and righteous, to help on the cause of final, universal emancipation?

If these are your subjects, (and they are of great and precious consideration,) then I am persuaded, that to persist in the course remarked on above, will help to perpetuate the evils you propose to remedy.

WILBERFORCE.

Wilberforce

We beg leave to refer our readers, to the communication signed "*Wilberforce*," as a document worthy of perusal, by all who have been halting between *Colonization and Anti-Colonization*. We insert it, at the particular request of the Rev. Dr. Samuel Miller, Professor of Ecclesiastical History and Church Government, in the Theological Seminary, at Princeton, N.J.; who has thought proper to inform us, "that the enclosed paper, signed 'Wilberforce,' is not written by me, nor by any member of my family; *but as I, in the main, approve of its contents*, I take the liberty of transmitting it, and of requesting a place for it in Freedom's Journal."

We place "*Wilberforce*," before our readers, in order, that they may judge for themselves, what liberal ideas our Colonization friends (according to the Rev. Dr., our best,) entertain of us generally. It is a fact, worthy of notice, that our bitterest enemies think not more contemptibly of us, than do Colonizationists generally—that nothing serves more, to keep us in our present degraded state, than the revolting pictures which are drawn by Colonization Orators on the fourth of July, and other public occasions.

As "*Wilberforce*," has taken great umbrage at certain sentences in Letter No. 3, addressed to the Senior Editor, we challenge him to disprove any thing therein stated. We think it becomes him, after having given vent to so much personal abuse against the Junior Editor, to stand forth on his own name, and convince him and others of their errors. We can assure him, that no notice would have been taken of his communication, had not his good friend, the

Source: *Freedom's Journal*, September 7, 1827.

Rev. Dr. inclosed it under his signature to us; for though we are persons of colour, we are not ignorant of the contents of the "*African Repository*," nor of what appertains to us of right, as Editors of the "Freedoms Journal." While we feel willing to pay every attention to the counsels of those, who style themselves our friends—while we concede all we can, to their mis-directed efforts, we should be wanting in our duty towards our brethren, did we not express ourselves openly and candidly upon all subjects which concern them, without fear of such men as "W." As mischievous as our paper may be considered in his opinion, and the Rev. Dr's, we candidly believe, it has already, during its short existence, effected more towards bettering our condition, and enlightening the minds of our people generally, than the Colonization Society, during its "ten years" existence.

"W.," unable to refute the statement concerning "northern Negroes," as he is pleased to style them, says, "as to the Middle States, facts are entirely against him," but without citing one solitary instance to prove this assertion, goes on to state the great objects of the Colonization Society, for which, no doubt, he will receive a vote of thanks, at their next annual meeting. Great stress is laid by "W." upon what the Society is likely to effect from the foundation of a colony in Africa, towards the Abolition of the Slave Trade, &c.; but why would he traverse the Atlantic to accomplish an object, for the attainment of which, he has only to travel to Maryland or Virginia, (if not already a resident of the latter,) and there use all his *benevolent endeavours*?

We can assure him, that with open eyes he has put a wrong construction, on the meaning of our respected correspondent "*Mordecai*." "M." has no desire for a white wife, as he has long since formed a union with one of his own colour. Having greater objects in view, we wish not to enter into a discussion concerning "ladies" taste, and other matters of a like frivolous nature.

For the objects contemplated by the publication of this Journal, we refer, "W." to our first number. There, we conceive, he will find them stated *pretty fully*, though according to his ideas, *coarsely*.

Junior Editor.
[John B. Russwurm]

[An Exchange with Dr. Samuel Miller]

The following remarks were intended for the columns of the *"New York Observer,"* but as the Editors were willing to insert but a part, we transfer the whole to our columns; believing, that had the Doctor's communication been twice its present length, the whole would have been inserted.

Messrs. Editors

We were much surprised with the perusal, in your last *"Observer,"* of a communication from the Rev. Dr. Miller, of Princeton, N.J., in which many useless words are set forth to prejudice the public against the Editors of *Freedom's Journal,* by a partial statement concerning our late correspondent "Wilberforce." We are aware, that controversies are not profitable to the generality of readers; but as your columns have been occupied by the Doctor against us, it is but justice, that our vindication should appear through the same channel.

As the Doctor has taken some considerable exceptions to our connecting his name with the communication, under the signature of "Wilberforce;" we deem it our duty to state, that we received two letters from him at the same time; one containing a request, that we should discontinue forwarding the JOURNAL; the other, (in which the Doctor fully adopted his sentiments,) enclosing "Wilberforce," and requesting for it a place in *"Freedom's Journal:"* mean while informing us, that in case of refusal, he should take measures to have it published in some other paper. Over the first letter was written *"private:"* but over the second, nothing.

We appeal to the judgment of the public, whether we have acted *indelicately* towards the Doctor? Whether after having adopted [the] remarks of "Wilberforce,["] and expressing so much interest in them, without enjoining privacy, we were not fully warranted in connecting the two names?

The Doctor complains of the manner in which we noticed "Wilberforce." We beg him to compare our remarks with the following *indelicate* and severe sentence of "Wilberforce," referring personally to the junior Editor. "The *ignorant, coarse* and *bitter* way, in which he assails this best friend of black men, may disarm and destroy itself," &c. That propriety of expression does not always predominate over human nature, is strikingly illustrated in the communication of "Wilberforce;" and that every thing which concerns our brethren, is received with a prejudiced eye, is also manifest from the Doctor's last communication.

If we have arraigned the motives of the leading members of the Colonization Society, we have done nothing more than we have a right to do—nothing more,

Source: *Freedom's Journal,* September 21, 1827.

than is done daily as it regards public men. If we have vilified any man's character, we call upon the Doctor to specify the injured individual, and nothing shall be wanting on our part, to make all the atonement in our power.

As it respects the Doctor's liberal views in reference to the support of the JOURNAL, we can inform him, that while we embrace among our white patrons, some of the first men in church and state, there is not one in three, who is friendly to colonization: and among our active friends throughout the country, three to one, are directly opposed to it, considering it, as warring with our best interests. That our people do not wish to be colonized in any country whatever, should be a sufficient reason against the *scheme*, if Liberia were even a paradise. The utmost that ever will be effected by the Society, will be but "sowing the wind, and reaping the whirlwind." While we revere the Doctor as a Minister, and honour him as a scholar, we must be indulged in saying that he is better acquainted with Ecclesiastical History and Church Government, than with politics or *colonization*.

The days, we feel thankful, are past, when ecclesiastical censure could exclude a man from the converse of his dearest friends. We are in a land of Liberty; and though prejudices are against our acting as freemen, they shall not compel us to relinquish our pens. We will arraign the motives of all pretended friends—we will strive all in our power to open the eyes of our brethren, upon all subjects which concern them—fearing no man, but appealing to the Searcher of hearts, for the purity of our motives.

From the N.Y. Observer.

Messrs. Editors.—

The unexpected introduction of my name into an editorial article in the last number of the "Freedom's Journal," published by Messrs. *Cornish & Russwurm,* of your city, seems to call for some explanation of my agency in reference to a paper complained of in that article. I have been a subscriber to their Journal from its commencement; and did cherish a hope that it would be so conducted as to exert a favourable influence on the great cause of the improvement and final emancipation of the children of Africa throughout our country.—A cause to which I am not only a warm friend, but to the progress and triumph of which, with all possible speed consistent with the happiness of the nation, I look forward with the deepest solicitude.

For some time past, however, I have been so entirely dissatisfied with the spirit and apparent tendency of that paper, that I could no longer reconcile it with my sense of duty to be found among its patrons. Accordingly, a few days since, I addressed a letter to the editors, requesting them to erase my name from the list of subscribers, and to cease sending their paper to me. For, although I had not paid for it to the end of the year, I did not choose any longer to receive it into my house. While I was preparing to transmit this request, a highly respected gentleman of my acquaintance, who is, at the same time, as cordial a friend to African rights and improvements as any man in the land, and as much dissatisfied with "Freedom's Journal" as myself, happening to step into my study, and learning my purpose, informed me that he had prepared a communication under the signature of "Wilberforce," which on account of peculiar circumstances, he could not conveniently transmit to the Editor himself, and which he requested me to inclose with the letter which I had prepared. Fully approving the substance of the piece, and not dreaming that there could be the smallest temptation to connect my name, before the public, with its contents, I did not hesitate to comply with his request.

I make no complaint of the very *delicate* course which these Editors have taken with respect to the communication of which I was thus the mere vehicle. They have undoubtedly a right to manage their own affairs in their own way. But if the good sense of this community shall be found to approve and support their "Journal" on its present plan,—if their persevering efforts to arraign the motives, pervert the professions, vilify the characters, and defeat the success of the friends of the colonization system in the United States, shall be countenanced by the enlightened friends of Africans;—if, in short, the mass of the wise and good among us, shall bear them out in their present policy, as adapted to promote the best interests of our coloured population;—then I, for one, shall be ready to acknowledge myself to have been egregiously deceived.

> *I am, gentlemen, respectfully, &c.*
> *Samuel Miller.*
> *Princeton, (N.J,) Sept. 11, 1827.*

Travelling Scraps: To Philadelphia, Delaware, Baltimore, and Washington

In the summer of 1828, Russwurm embarked on a trip from New York to Washington, D.C. He stopped in Philadelphia, apparently for several days, traveled on through Delaware to Baltimore, and ended his journey in the nation's capital. As with his trip through New England the summer before, Russwurm shared his experiences and candid thoughts and feelings with his readers. Back in New York by June 23, he began four days later to publish his remarkable journal, which he presented in five installments.

I.

Narratives of travels over a region of territory so well known as the route between our city and Washington, are scarcely ever interesting; having however taken a few scraps in those leisure moments which every traveller finds at his command, I can perceive no possible advantage in withholding them from your friendly notice, as did Tarquin of old the Sibylline verses.[13] The time of our departure from the city, I need not mention. On board the Steam Boat, I found a large number of passengers—many of them our good and indefatigable benefactors, of the Society of Friends. Little of interest occurred. I was treated as well as the prejudices and feelings of our enlightened community would allow. At the place of our landing many difficulties arose from the unusual number of passengers and negligence about carrying the few coloured passengers on board. For them no stage had been prepared; consequently we had to be conveyed four in number in an open waggon, exposed to all the inclemencies of the weather, and what was more grating to my feelings, compelled to listen to the sage remarks of the good company in which it was my happy lot to find myself placed. Why is it, that even in the estimation of men, who are really our friends, we are all classed and considered alike? It is high time that a true knowledge of our situation should become known to them: but we do not see any possibility of their arriving at this, but by a more intimate acquaintance with our enlightened brethren. Prejudices at present are so great, that if we consulted convenience and comfort alone, it would always be best to travel under the assumed name of Governor Troup's or Gen. Woolfolk's body servant, than as a free man on your own private affairs.[14] But where is the man who would assume even for a few days, the name of a great man's valet-de-chambre for the

Source: *Freedom's Journal*, June 27, July 11, 25, August 15, and 29, 1828.

sake of convenience or comfort? He must surely be wanting in all the finer feelings of our nature—in all that should adorn a man. Let me rather be tortured and gibbeted by piecemeals, travelling as a free man. I arrived safely in Philadelphia about six o'clock, P.M.

Philadelphia differs much from our business city. The uniformity of her buildings, the regularity of her streets which cross each other at right angles, and the comparative dulness which pervade them are the first things which strike the eyes of a traveller accustomed to the busy hum of New York. All that he sees reminds him of the great founder of Pennsylvania—of the man who was the first to appear covered in the presence of majesty, and who considered no sufferings too great, for conscience sake.

Though the difference between Philadelphia and New York is great; in what may be considered the public comfort and convenience of her citizens—in good order and economy which pervade every thing, public or private—in the excellency and cheapness of her markets, Philadelphia will yield to no other city in the Union.

There are numerous public buildings scattered over the city; the most celebrated of which is the Bank of the United States in Chesnut-street, fronting which stands the United States Hotel, a noble building, with nothing remarkable about its exterior to distinguish it from others. Public as well as private buildings possess a certain neatness which we look in vain for in our city. Her public councils have ever had in view the comfort of the citizens in every thing which came before them; a praiseworthy example, which, if followed by other city councils would render their fellow citizens, more comfortable in every respect.

I need not mention the happy location of the city between the Delaware and Schuylkill rivers, as possessing superior advantages; abler have done it before me.

The gradual and increasing prosperity of the city, are certain testimonials of the healthiness and prosperity of her citizens. The means of Education are extensively diffused, even among our children, who are commonly the last objects for the exercise of public charity. The male and female free schools in Sixth street, are conveniently located, and average daily at present 220 scholars each, a degree of attention which we hope our brethren in this city, who are similarly favoured, will be emulous of following.

Besides these, there are several other schools both public and private, devoted to the sole instruction of our children; a more particular description of which we must defer till our next.

II.

Besides the City Public Schools in Sixth street, there are no less than five others supported by Societies & individual charity: two in Willings Alley, Male and Female, containing each thirty-five scholars; peculiarly interesting from the fact of having been the *first schools* ever instituted for the education of coloured children, by that great friend of man, Anthony Benezet.[15] These two are wholly supported by the bequests of Mr. Benezet and other benevolent individuals.

The Clarkson School in Cherry-street, is divided into Male and Female also, each containing about 90 scholars, principally supported by the Manumission Society of the City of Philadelphia. But the school which delighted me the most, and in whose future welfare I feel the deepest solicitude, is the Infant School for Coloured children, instituted about two months since by the Infant School Society. According to my weak judgment, the Society have taken the right steps towards making a fair experiment of the beneficial and lasting effects of education upon the human mind. It is a notorious fact that the minds of many of our children are so corrupted previous to entering school from the bad example daily set before them, both at home and abroad, that the year or two which they spend so irregularly within the walls of a school House profit them but little. The Infant School Society, aware of this, have resolved to receive children at two years, and I believe yet younger into their school. So far the Society have been eminently successful not only in procuring a well qualified Instructress and Assistant, but also, in having as many pupils as they could conveniently seat and instruct. I am sure nothing would give you more pleasure than to learn, that Infant Schools for Coloured children were instituted in every city of note in the Union. In this day of general illumination, the *"Schoolmaster with his Primer"* should be an object of the first importance in every well regulated community. The schools above mentioned are all under pretty good discipline, more especially two in Sixth street, and the Female department of the Clarkson.

Should a stranger desire to see the *elite* of our people, he must visit Philadelphia, which contains a larger number of them than any other city. I know not why it is thus, unless we give our Philadelphia brethren credit for being more industrious and economical than we are; it is a fact beyond contradiction, that they are generally better off, are more respectable, and are more of them owners of real estate. The Coloured population of Philadelphia must, I should think, exceed 20,000. They are proprietors of no less than six brick churches and one frame one in different parts of the city. This is a free country for enquiry and electioneering, and our Philadelphia brethren have been nothing backward in enjoying to the full extent their rights in this respect as regards ecclesiastical matters—in truth, this mauvais spirit has been carried too far, and been the cause of much hard feeling between persons who ought to join hand in hand in every thing which tends to the advancement of religion, and the respectability of our people. I am not an advocate for fettering in the least, liberty of speech, or of the press—no—let them remain untrammeled and free while the sea ebbs and flows—while "the rivers run, and the grass grows:"—but the good order of Society requires that there should be certain bounds, even for these, which we claim as the innate rights of man.

It is the general opinion of our citizens who visit Philadelphia, that our brethren there enjoy greater advantages for acquiring property than we, but I think not so; our chances are nearly alike, and what gives our Philadelphia brethren the superiority, is a daily practice of the rules of *industry* and *economy*, while we use the former without the latter. This opinion may be considered as partial, but the future evidence of your own eyes will bear me out in it. For while the Philadelphians dress full as much as they ought, and in a manner highly becoming, we on the other hand, *think* no fashion too foolish or extravagant to imitate—it must be followed cost what it will. The difference of dress which marks the two cities may be ascribed to the different tone of feeling which pervades the citizens—with us all is bustle, hurry and dress—with them all is order, regularity and neatness.

Notwithstanding the liberal feelings of the community of Philadelphia, there are two or three presses whose Editors have descended from their "high estate" and condescended to notice us with feelings none of the friendliest. I refer more particularly to the Pennsylvania Gazette, Ariel, and that highly literary Journal the Philadelphia Monthly Magazine. That hard things should be said of us in a daily or weekly Journal, is what we may expect, but I confess my astonishment was great when I read a notice of the African Fancy Ball so styled in the Magazine. For such a publication, it was rather descending *too low*—and placing a bad precedent for others. Upon the same subject we were also lucky enough to read the *pithy* lucubrations of the wise heads of the Penn. Gazette, containing about as much truth as Gulliver's Travels. I hope all our brethren who are subscribers to these two publications feeling the remarks as they ought, will give these saucy writers, a token of their approbation by withdrawing their patronage, and bestowing it on others who are more deserving. A future number shall contain some notice of the Ariel.

III.

As stated in my last, it was my intention in this number to have said a *few* words by way of advice to our *candid* brother of the quill, the sapient editor of the Ariel, but as our Philadelphia brethren have fairly taken the business out of our hands by the appointment of a committee to answer it formally, we can but refer our readers to their report, which is contained in this and our preceding number.[16]

I am glad our Philadelphia brethren feel so sensibly this vile attempt to injure our body at large, but I question whether they have taken the wisest steps to answer it, whether coming from so contemptible a source, it deserved to be so highly honoured. For my part I believe it generally to be best to suffer all such vile publications to descend to obscurity unanswered whenever they emanate from such *obscure* sources. But I have said enough of Philadelphia for the present: at 5 A.M. one of the most rainy mornings ever experienced, I took passage in the Steam-Boat on my route for Baltimore.

The effort would be vain were I to attempt to describe my feelings when I landed at New Castle, Delaware: and yet I know not why every thing should have assumed a different appearance—even nature's face and nature's children, seemed different—I felt as though I were in a foreign country—and the U.S. troops whom I saw, strengthened the delusion considerably. It may be asked by some what could have made men and tidings appear in the light they did? I answer/slavery with its blasting influence—Slavery which causes the fairest portions of country to wither and be neglected, and man, the image of his Maker, to be but a mere tool when tet[h]ered with its iron chains. Oh, for the eloquence of a Burke to pourtray its evils—the strength of a Sampson * * * * * * * * and another * * * * * * *[sic] freedom. Who can tell what patriot spirits may be held in slavery among the countless hundreds of the South to live and die unnoticed? After such specimens as the world has had of African genius and worth, let all the advocates for African inferiority and slavery be silent.

At Newcastle we took the stage for Frenchtown, where we arrived in safety after a fatiguing ride through the rain. Some muster must have been held near, as we passed and met half-uniformed militia almost every ten minutes on horseback, waggons and carts all journeying to the parade ground. The soldiers were dressed in what appeared to be homespun green, edged with yellow, and upon the whole made but sorry figures. Had there been more taste displayed about their uniforms I should have thought them the second handed ones of some of the Philadelphia companies. In safety we arrived in Frenchtown and embarked on board the Steam-boat United States, for Baltimore, where we arrived about 6 P.M. Baltimore makes but a mean appearance from the water compared to our city with her floating palaces, or Boston with her State House, lofty spires and Central Wharf. In vain do you look around for the bustle and stir of our city—every thing seems at a stand—and what is still worse, seems likely to remain so—until the Rail Road upon which the Baltimoreans count so much is finished. That it will be of great advantage to the city I cannot doubt, but I am quite incredulous about its raising the value of property so much as many think. To a liberal minded man of Colour, Baltimore is a place of considerable interest, for two reasons quite different; the place of publication of the Genius of U.[niversal] Emancipation, and consequently the residence of that champion of our cause BENJAMIN LUNDY: 2. the residence of Woolfolk, the notorious Slave Trader, who has realized an independent fortune by his inhuman traffic. Concerning the G.U. Emancipation, I need not say one word—it is a publication older than the [Freedom's] Journal, and it would be but repetition to recount the untiring labours and self-denial, even at this day of its worthy editor. I wish we had but another LUNDY to stand forth in the "lion's den" and proclaim the iniquity of a system which carries upon its face the evils of it.

While in Baltimore a subject of considerable interest took place. The return of a man of Colour who had been sent some years before by Woolfolk to New Orleans, to be sold as a slave, as a free man worth about $13,000 to purchase his wife and astonish his former master by his wealth, was the subject of general surprise. With the evils of slavery always before the people of the South, it cannot help being a subject of daily discussion in stages & public houses, and a discerning man is not at a loss to know from what portion of the Union his fellow passengers come. There is a feeling in the minds of many on the iniquity of the system, which shewed itself on a young man, apparently a midshipman in our stage, who was of opinion that Woolfolk ought to have dangled from the yard arm long ago: to all which, you may be sure, I mentally ejaculated, amen.

IV.

My stay in Baltimore was so short that I can state but little concerning the situation of our brethren. Those of them (but a few) with whom I formed an acquaintance, appeared to advantage; but Baltimore was never designed to be the abode of your humble servant. A man of colour, educated at the north, can never feel himself at home in Baltimore: he may be respected in his business; he may be encouraged; but when we come to talk of liberty—of the rights of citizenship—of his evidence in a court of justice against his fairer brethren, we cannot but perceive that there is little justice doled out to him by the *republican* laws of the state of Maryland. In vain to them does he appeal against the iniquity of his fairer brethren: to his evidence the law lends no listening ear, and his only appeal is to his Almighty Father, unto whom the oppressed never cry in vain.

There are in Baltimore several private coloured schools well attended; but when we take into consideration the number of persons we find the subject of education, sadly neglected; and as for a public free school that is entirely out of the question in such a slave state as Maryland.

Slavery is fast expiring in some parts of the state, through the exertion of the Abolition Societies, and we hope to see the day of its final extinction; and to have the pleasure of announcing the joyful event to our readers. I was much pleased to learn that a few slaveholders had adopted the benevolent plan of educating their young domestics, under a teacher in whose principles they could place implicit confidence;—and it is the current report, that one of the coloured churches is under their entire control in every respect, consequently no doctrine must there be preached, which has the least tendency to impeach the unnatural laws of Slavery.

We are astonished when we look into the system of slavery, and see how untiring its advocates are to support its tottering fabric. I was credibly informed, both in Baltimore and Washington, that they have authorized agents, with a list of runaway slaves, who make it their sole business to visit our different northern cities for the purpose of apprehending them. And sorry am I to say, that they are frequently successful, through the treachery of our own brethren, and the imprudence of the runaways, in invariably taken care to settle in our largest and most commercial cities. After such daily instances as we are compelled to witness of their apprehension, one would think, after escaping, they would be very careful in choosing their places of abode. From Baltimore to Washington, the distance is so short, that I could not defer my visit to it; not knowing when I should again visit Baltimore, liable, as a free man of colour is, to be stopped on his route by any vagabond, who has the impudence to do so, and demand his papers. Notwithstanding all the precaution taken by slave-holders, there are hundreds of slaves who escape. And I could tell many an interesting anecdote of the dangers they had to encounter—of their plan of escape, &c.—did not the glorious cause of Freedom, dearer to me than life itself, require me to be silent.

On our route, a few rods from Bladensburg, I had the pleasure of seeing the celebrated Duelling Tree, near which, all the duels which have taken place among the great men at Washington, have been fought. There fell Decatur, the pride of the American navy: and there will fall many a brave man, so long as the barbarous system of duelling is countenanced by our leading public characters. If we except the Capitol, and the President's house, there is nothing which would strike the eyes of a stranger—for the buildings generally, though of brick, have rather a mean appearance. I was much pleased with the great care which has been taken in laying out the city, destined, no doubt, in process of time, to become a large one. But at present there is more in its name than in any thing else. The Tiber, which runs through the city, is hardly deserving of the name of a river: with us it would be considered a mere brook. Pennsylvania avenue is a fine street—not on account of its buildings, but for its width, and running as it does from the Capitol to the President's house. The Capitol is a noble building, planned and built in a style corresponding to the honourable purpose for which it was designed. I found some difficulty in visiting the different chambers, but every obstacle was removed through the intercession of a friend.

The hall of Representatives is an elegant room, said to be I believe, the largest in the world. It is supported by several columns of beautiful Potomac marble, and ornamented with a portrait of Lafayette. Every thing in it appears very appropriate and elegant. And vanity or not vanity, I could not help taking the speaker's chair for a minute, and surveying the whole with perhaps as much satisfaction as many who have sat there session after session. The Rotunda was the next room we visited, the keeper of which positively denied us admission; but seeing him permit some of the lower classes to enter, we made bold to push in also: for, be assured, under certain circumstances there is nothing like a man's pushing himself forward in the world. From Randolph's speech last winter, I expected to see but a few imperfect paintings, and my surprise consequently, was really agreeable upon beholding such finely finished historical pieces, four of which were from the pencil of Trumbull, and one from that of a lady in Philadelphia. The library, after having so many appropriations made for its gradual increase, was not as large as I expected. There were about six visiters in the room. The Senate chamber I could not enter, as the keeper had left it a few minutes previously for dinner. The Patent Office was the next place we visited. Figuratively speaking, a visiter there may find a patent for every thing under the sun. Our state appeared to have her full proportion. The Post Office Department, which, under the able management of the present Post Master General, has become quite a source of revenue to the nation, is also kept in the same building.

V.

My next object of inspection was the President's house; but in this I could enjoy but a mere outward view, as the family were at home; for although my curiosity might have been gratified by means of friends who were acquainted with some inmates of the house, I felt unwilling to take that step, and preferred denying myself of that gratification. The house, or rather palace, though a fine building, did not answer my expectations in many respects. Like many people in the world, my expectations had been raised too high, and were I to ask myself what they were, I am afraid, again like many people, I could hardly tell. As I am writing a few words about the house, the following anecdote of the present incumbent [John Quincy Adams] may be worthy of a passing notice. It appears that one of the sons of the old gentleman was on the eve of marriage with a young lady who was mistress of one female slave: after every preparation had been made for the wedding, the old gentleman stated that there was one thing yet wanting, which he declared must be done before his consent would be given—and that was the manumission of the female slave; consequently a magistrate was sent for, and freedom papers given her on the spot. Is not this trait in the old gentleman worthy of all praise—that he, surrounded as he is by the business of the nation, should think of the poor female in bondage—should insist upon her liberation, that she, too, might in truth, enjoy the heaven's choicest, dearest blessings upon man here below—GLORIOUS LIBERTY. To the last moment of my life, my visit to Washington will ever be remembered with pleasure. I went there a stranger, but departed from thence with regret: for the continued politeness of our brethren during my short stay, had rendered my visit quite agreeable. I found upon comparing past and present opinions, that I had formed quite erroneous ones of their situation in many respects. Washington was to the *South* of us, and that you know was enough to alarm my fears—to make me believe that our brethren there were as oppressed as they are in many other places. I am peculiarly happy therefore to inform our readers that the circumstances of many are quite respectable, and that some enjoy places of trust which we in vain look for at the North. It is true that the Corporation now and then take it into their noddles to pass ordinances which scare all the women and children in the city, but there are others who care not a straw for many of them, which are as contrary to the constitution as light to darkness.

There are many slaves in Washington, and dealers in human flesh resort to it from all parts of the Union. I know not if there is a greater slave mart in the States. It is certainly disgraceful that in the Capital of a Republic which boasts of the enjoyment of more liberty than other states or kingdoms, we should behold human beings in the face of open day, under the sanction of a constitution which proclaims, that *"we hold these truths to be self-evident, that all men are created equal, and endowed by their Creator with certain inalienable rights; that among these are life, LIBERTY, and the pursuit of happiness,"* exposed to view:

> "Chained foot to foot and hand to hand,
> Goaded along by scourge and brand."

But my object is not to excite the feelings of our readers: the subject is a painful one: let us leave it and the poor unhappy objects of our compassion in the hands of Him who is able to succour them. The carriage of the Southern planter, with a female slave on the spot which with us *[sic]* invariably appropriated to the trunks, is a curious sight to a stranger from the North. Such scenes are, however, common in Washington, upon the arrival and departure of these Nabobs. I had almost forgotten to mention my visit to the Secretary of the Colonization Society [Rev. Ralph R. Gurley]. The office of the Society is located in one of the brick buildings on P[ennsylvania] avenue, and contains many articles of African ingenuity from Liberia and the surrounding country, worthy of inspection. There I saw various specimens of cloth manufactured by the untutored natives; various implements of war, some of iron, and the skin of the tiger, a description of which was given in one of the numbers of the Repository. Things appeared at a stand pretty much—there were applicants for colonization, but I doubt very much whether the funds of the society will enable them to do much this season. We have been much censured for our sentiments on the subject of colonization—we are ignorant for what: that we are not in favour of colonization is no fault of ours, our private judgment is our own; we have always been candid on the subject, and wherever we have found open ears have always been ready to state our reasons for dissenting from our learned dictators. For the agent of the Society we have always entertained the highest sentiments; considering him, in every respect, a man of superior intellect without whose assistance the society would shortly descend to the "tomb of the Capulets."

At Washington it was my good fortune to become acquainted with the African prince, Abduhl Rahahman,[17] who has of late engaged so much of the public sympathy. His case is peculiarly hard, and plainly shows the vicissitudes to which all men are liable in this life of probation. Born, bred, and educated a Prince—but for forty long years a slave in a foreign land. Brought up in luxury and Eastern splendour—but for forty long years compelled to taste the bitter cup of poverty, and slavery: and yet he survives, and with God's blessing will again return to the land of his nativity.

It must be evident to every one that the Prince is a man superior to the generality of Africans whom we behold in this country. His education is also superior; and when we take into consideration his Alma Mater, our astonishment becomes greater. He is a fine Arabic scholar, and even now, at his advanced life, 66, writes an elegant hand. He appears to be well versed with the Geography of the interior of Africa, and states many facts concerning the different tribes, and the source and discharge of the Niger, of which we were ignorant. It has ever been the current belief that Timbuctoo was the only city of size in the interior; but the Prince assures us that there are two others nearly as large near the banks of the Niger. It is his opinion also that this river, celebrated from time immemorial, loses itself in the sands.

From some fairy stories in circulation among the Foulahs, Mandinges and other tribes, he believes its source has never been examined any nearer than within twenty-five miles. At W[ashington] the Prince had the pleasure of becoming acquainted with Mr. English, the celebrated Eastern traveller. The Prince is now to the North, and in due time all our readers will have an opportunity of seeing him, and testifying their respect for him by contributing their mite towards the emancipation of his family.

Part B. Our Views Are Materially Altered: Looking toward Liberia

In February 1829, after much careful consideration, Russwurm publicly announced his changed position on colonization. To the shock of his readers, he somberly declared, "Our views are materially altered." Having always maintained that when convinced of error he should hasten to acknowledge it, he believed that that moment had arrived. He explained that his change of heart was not the "hasty conclusion of a moment" but the result of "pondering much" on the subject and having read "every article within our reach, both for and against the [ACS]." Russwurm was fully aware of the cost of his apostasy, aware that his new "doctrines" were in opposition to those of the majority of his readers, "to many of whom we are personally known, and for whose opinions we still entertain great respect." But he was determined to stick to his guns, his emigrationist positions: "How unpopular soever they may be, we know, they are conscientious ones formed from no sordid motives; but having for their basis, the good of our brethren." Russwurm saw no better option than emigration to Africa, and he patiently laid out his case in a series of articles before his departure for Liberia later in the year.

Liberia: [Casting His Eyes Elsewhere]

Our readers will perceive by the statement below, received by the way of England, that a dreadful accident has lately happened to the Colony at Liberia.[18] Whatever may have been our opinions hitherto, concerning the plan of colonizing the free people of Colour on the coast of Africa, all must sympathise with the friends of the cause, that so great a misfortune should befall the Colony. In the death of Mr. Carey, the Colonists have to deplore one whose loss will not easily be supplied; and the Society, and able and persevering auxiliary, who was devoted heart and soul to the enterprise.

As our former sentiments have always been in direct opposition to the plan of colonizing us on the coast of Africa: perhaps, so favourable an opportunity may not occur, for us to inform our readers, in an open and candid manner, that our views are materially altered. We have always said, that when convinced of our error, we should hasten to acknowledge it—*that period has now arrived.* The change which has taken place, has not been the hasty conclusion of a moment: we have pondered much on this interesting subject, and read every article within our reach, both for and against the society, and we come on from the examination, a decided supporter of the American Colonization Society.

We know, that in making this avowal, we advance doctrines in opposition to the majority of our readers, to many of whom we are personally known, and for whose opinions we still entertain great respect: but how unpopular soever they may be, *we know,* they are conscientious ones—formed from no sordid motives; but having for their basis, the good of our brethren.

We have carefully examined the different plans now in operation for our benefit, and none we believe, can reach half so efficiently the mass, as the plan of colonization on the coast of Africa; for if we take a second look into any or all of them, we find them limited to a single city or state. We consider it mere waste of words to talk of ever enjoying citizenship in this country: it is utterly impossible in the nature of things: all therefore who pant for th[is], must cast their eyes elsewhere.

The interesting query now arises, where shall we find this desirable spot? If we look to Europe, we find that quarter already overburdened with a starving population; if to Asia, its distance is an insuperable barrier, were all other circumstances favourable. Where then shall we look so naturally, as to Africa? In preferring Liberia, we wish not to deprive any of the right

Source: *Freedom's Journal,* February 14, 1829.

of choice between it and Hayti; as [it] is not our object to say ought against Hayti or the able ruler at its head; but it is a fact well known to all, that our people have strong objections against emigrating to that country, arising in many cases, from the unfavourable reports of those who have returned. Sensible of this fact then, of the unwillingness of our people to emigrate to Hayti; we feel it our duty, to offer to their consideration, our present sentiments concerning African Colonization; and perhaps, what we may be able to offer hereafter, may be the means of enlightening some, whom it was our misfortune to have misled by our former opinions.

Liberia: [Unanswerable Argument]

Of late, we have thought, that the principal objections, which the mass of our brethren, have against colonization, arise from ignorance of the designs and progress of the Society. We confess, as a man of colour, that we have hitherto viewed the members of the society with jealousy—to all their labors, we have imputed wrong motives—but are we, the only one, who have formed our opinions after this manner? Is it not the imperious duty of every man of Colour, to ask himself candidly, have *I* not passed a like judgment—has not prejudice been the only organ through which *I* have viewed the labours of these disinterested men, who have toiled in our behalf for years? We know, that there are many in the world, who having once formed an opinion, no matter how erroneous, for consistency or argument's sake, adhere to it, though mountains of proof [to] the contrary should be placed before them; but we would not give a fig for the man, whose mind did not daily expand, and who, like the bee, did not gather honey, (or in other words grew wiser) in his intercourse with the world.

The American Colonization Society have met with much opposition from us, but the mist which completely darkened our vision, having been dispelled, we now stand before the community a feeble advocate of the society. We have generally wrong ideas of the society, and the members thereof. It cannot be denied that our brethren mostly, believe that Southern interest completely guide the plans of the society—that all their movements tend to fetter more closely the chains of the enslaved—and that the removal of the free from among their slaves, is *the* ultimatum of their wishes. And further, so ignorant are many of our people, that they are even afraid to trust themselves under the protection of the society, from fear of being carried into foreign lands, and sold into bondage. We have also wrong ideas upon what the

Source: *Freedom's Journal*, February 21, 1829.

society have effected & what they are now doing in our behalf. Every one who will give these objections the least examination, will perceive, that to answer them, the society need but point to the flourishing colony of Liberia, as an *unanswerable* argument in its favour, against all that can be brought forward.

We have wrong conceptions of the plans of the society; than which nothing can be more simple, namely, the removal of those among the free coloured population of the United States, who are anxious to emigrate to Africa. We ask every man of colour can any thing be more simple; here, is a land in which we cannot enjoy the privileges of citizen[s], for certain reasons known and felt daily; but there, is one where we may enjoy all the rights of freemen; where every thing will tend to call forth our best and most generous feelings—in a word, where we may not only feel as men, but where we may also act as such. Can any man of sound judgment hesitate about choice of the two? We do not expect that all will embrace the society's offer, as there are thousands whose course of life is a complete barrier against acceptance; and there are also thousands the extent of whose wishes, have never dreamed of a state, where the man of colour may not only act and feel as other responsible beings, but where all the energies of his mind impelled by the most powerful motives, will put forth their best, and astonish the most prejudiced.

The society have done much in favor of emancipation; for it is a fact, that there are many in the colony, who are indebted for that liberty which they now enjoy to the door which the establishment offers to liberal and humane slave holders to emancipate their slaves—nor is this all, as we well know, there are four or five hundred slaves now waiting (from want of funds) to be landed on the shores of Liberia, to become freemen. As the work of emancipation has thus commenced under the immediate auspices of the society, we cannot consider it out of the natural course of things to conclude, that as the means and patronage of the society extend, this great and glorious work will also advance in the same ratio, until the blessed period come, so ardently desired by the Friends when the soil of this happy land shall not be watered by the tears of poor Afric's sons and daughters.

Our Vindication

The change in our views on colonization, seems to be a "seven days won-der" to many of our readers. But why, we do not perceive: like others, we are mortal: like them, we are liable to changes: & like them, we should be allowed the privilege of expressing our sentiments; a boon which is not denied to the most abject being in this country. We are sorry, there are those who are unwilling to grant us this liberty; but as Freedom's Journal has ever been an independent paper, we shall continue to express ourselves on colo-nization, and on all other subjects which we may deem proper. It is not our object to injure the feelings of any—we feel towards them that charity, which it becomes every man to exercise to his fellow. Our columns have ever been open to a free discussion of this important subject, and they are still open; but is it reasonable to suppose, that we should grant freedom of enquiry to others, and deprive ourselves of it? We live in a day of general illumination, and it is our happiness to be among those, who believe in the feasibility of establishing a flourishing colony in Africa, which in progress of time, may be the means of disseminating civilization & christianity throughout the whole of that vast continent.

It is our happiness to be among those, who believe it to be far preferable, for the man of colour, aspiring after wealth and respectability, to emigrate to Liberia, where every incentive to virtuous action, is before him continu-ally, than to remain here, where the mere name of colour, blocks up every avenue—where if he have the feelings of a man, he must be sensible of the degraded station he holds in society; and from which it is impossible to rise, unless he can change the Ethiopian hue of his complexion. He may possess wealth; he may be respected; he may be learned; still all united, will avail him little; after all, he is considered a being of inferior order; and always will be, as no opportunity will ever be afforded him to cultivate or call into action the talents with which an All-wise Creator may have endowed him.

It is our happiness to be among those, who believe that the settlement at Liberia, offers every inducement, which any reasonable man can expect in a new country, the resources of which are but partly known, and the country but partly explored. Its climate is healthy, its soil fertile, producing in great abundance all the necessaries of life. "The vegetable productions are cof-fee, cotton, indigo, sugar cane, rice, Guinea corn, millet, & every variety of fruits & legumes. Coffee grows wild and is sold by the natives for five cents

Source: *Freedom's Journal,* March 7, 1829.

a pound. Cattle, swine, fowls, ducks, goats & sheep thrive finely requiring no further care than to keep them from straying. Fine cattle may be bought from three to six dollars a head; rice for less than a dollar a bushel; & palm oil answering all the purposes of butter & lard for 20 cents per gallon, equal in cooking to six pounds of butter."

The unhealthiness of Sierra Leone is held up as a *scarecrow*, to frighten the ignorant and timid; but it is well known to all who are the least conversant with our early history, that the Colonists at Liberia have not had, & those who shall follow, will not have, to encounter one hundredth part of the hardships which the first settlers in Virginia and Plymouth had to undergo, as the following extract from the N.Y. Spectator will show.

"The first attempt of Sir Walter Raleigh to plant a colony in Virginia, was made in 1585. One hundred and eight persons were brought thither; but they were soon embroiled with the natives, and after enduring incredible hardships, were taken off by Sir Francis Drake, in the following year, and carried back to England. A much greater number of colonists, with a more abundant supply of provisions, was sent over, by Sir Walter, in 1587. But when three years afterwards three ships were sent to their relief, not a vestige of them was to be found. And Sir Walter, having expended forty thousand pounds, was obliged to abandon the project in despair. In 1606, another expedition was fitted out by an association, formed for establishing [?] colonies in America; and in May 1607, one hundred and fifty people were settled at Jamestown. They endured every species of disaster, and before the month of September, fifty were buried. On the return of Captain Smith, from a few weeks captivity, during which time he was preserved from death by the romantic generosity of Pocahontas, he found the colony reduced to thirtyeight persons, most of whom seemed determined to abandon a country so unfavourable to human life. This resolution was prevented by the judicious conduct of Capt. Smith and the colony was augmented by reinforcements, so that in 1609, there were nearly five hundred people. But many fell sick— they were attacked by the Indians—they wasted their provisions—and the united evils of war, famine and disease soon reduced their numbers to sixty persons. It was thought they would not have existed ten days longer, had it not been for the timely arrival of Lord Delaware. For many years after this period, the colonists in Virginia were subject to incessant labor and incredible distress; and in 1624, after the expenditure of £150,000, and the arrival of 9000 persons, no more than 1800, remained. So also in the first attempts to colonize New England. The first emigrants, one hundred in number, arrived in the fall of 1607, and built a fort near the river Sagadahoc. Many of the principal men died during the following winter, and the sufferings of the survivors were so great, that they returned to England in the spring. The next attempt was made by the "Pilgrims," to the number of one hundred and twenty men, who landed on the bleak shore of Plymouth, in November, 1620. Before spring, wasted by sickness and famine, and every hardship, one half of them were dead. The survivors persevered, however, with a fortitude and resolution which nothing but the continued excitement of strong religious feeling could have inspired. But at the end of ten years, their population only amounted to three hundred souls—only one fourth of the number of colonists, now, in the eighth year of its age, enjoying health, liberty and plenty; and commanding the respect and confidence of its neighbors in the Colony of Liberia."

That Sierra Leone is unhealthy is no argument that Liberia must be too: nor because New Orleans is unhealthy, that Philadelphia or Baltimore must be so likewise. Every person discerns the weakness of such reasoning; and it will still be more evident when we take into consideration, that the lands about Cape Messurado, (on which the settlement is located,) are high and elevated, while those around Sierra Leone are low and marshy, that the town is almost placed in a marsh, & that there are a hundred causes arising from this situation to create sickness; which from the more happy location of the American Settlement, the colonists run no risk of encountering.

Finally, we would observe, that it is not our aim to deceive our brethren as to the true state of affairs at Liberia; our desire is, that they generally, may have some faint idea of the present state of this most flourishing, but infant colony. Have we any young men, whose constant prayer is to be useful in their day, and who are in want of a station: "we point to Liberia." Have we any middle aged men with families, who are anxious that their children should enjoy all the rights of freemen and who are in search of the long desired spot—we point to Liberia as our promised Land; from whose borders shall issue in progress of time thousands who shall go forth, as pioneers of civilization and Heralds of the Cross, into the vast regions of that hitherto unexplored quarter of our globe.

Colonization

We feel proud in announcing to our distant readers, that many of our brethren in this city, who have lately taken this subject into consideration, have like ourselves, come out from the examination, warm advocates of the Colony, and ready to embrace the first convenient opportunity to embark for the shores of Africa. This we may say looks like coming to the point—as if they had examined for themselves and satisfied of the practicability of the plan, are not afraid the world should know it.

The subject of Colonization is certainly important, as having a great bearing on that of slavery: for it must be evident that the universal emancipation so ardently desired by us & by all our friends, can never take place, unless some door is opened whereby the emancipated may be removed as fast as they drop their galling chains, to some other land besides the free states; for it is a fact, that prejudices now in our part of the country, are so high, that it is often the remark of liberal men from the south, that their free people are treated better than we are, in the boasted free states of the north. If the free states have passed no laws as yet forbidding the emigration of free persons of colour into their limits; it is no reason that they will not, as soon as they find themselves a little more burdened. We will suppose that a general law of emancipation should be promulgated in the state of Virginia, under the existing statutes which require every emancipated slave to leave the state, would not the other states, in order to shield themselves from the evils of having so many thousands of ignorant beings thrown upon them, be obliged in self-defence to pass prohibitory laws? Much as we may deplore the evils of slavery—much as we may desire the freedom of the enslaved; who could reproach the free states for enacting such laws? so that if no good whatever arose from the establishment of colonies, the fact that they remove all obstacles in the way of emancipation should gain for them support and good wishes of every friend of humanity, & of every enlightened man of colour. It is true, that no such laws at present are in force to our knowledge, but who can foretell how soon before they may, without waiting for the period of a general emancipation in any of the slave holding states.

Our wiseacres may talk as much as they please, upon amalgamation, and our future standing in society, but it does not alter the case in the least; it does not improve our situation in the least: but it is calculated rather to stay the exertions of those who are really willing to make some efforts to improve their

Source: *Freedom's Journal*, March 14, 1829.

own present condition. We are considered a distinct people, in the midst of the millions around us, and in the most favoured parts of the country; and it matters not from what causes this sentence has been passed upon us; the fiat has gone forth, and should each of us live to the age of Methusalah, at the end of the thousand years, we should be exactly in our present situation: a proscribed race, however, unjustly—a degraded people, deprived of all the rights of freemen; and in the eyes of the community, a race, who had no lot nor portion with them.

We hope none of our readers, will from our remarks think that we approve in the least of the present prejudices in the way of the man of colour: far from it, we deplore them as much as any man; but they are not of our creating, and they are not in our power to remove. They at present exist against us— and from the length of their existence—from the degraded light in which we have ever been held—we are bold in saying, that it will never be in our power to remove or overcome them. So easily are these prejudices imbibed, that we have often noticed the effects on young children who could hardly speak plainly, and were we a believer in dreams, charms, &c we should believe that they imbibed them with their mother's milk.

Sensible then, as all are of the disadvantages under which we at present labour, can any consider it a mark of folly, for us to cast our eyes upon some other portion of the globe where *all* these inconveniencies are removed where the Man of Colour freed from the fetters and prejudice, and degradation, under which he labours in this land, may walk forth in all the majesty of his creation—a new born creature—a *Free Man!* It was, we believe, the remark of Sir James Yeo, while on the African coast, that the natives whom he saw were a fine *athletic race, walking fearlessly*, as if sensible of their important station as men, and quite different from the thousands of their brethren whom he had seen in the West Indies and the United States: and never was a truer remark made, if we are to credit all other travellers on that Continent, who have likewise borne testimony to the same fact.

While some of our friends have wondered at our change, others have been bold enough to call them in question, and to accuse us of improper motives; of such, we ask, who has made half the sacrifice we have to oppose the Colonization society? who has laboured half so much by night and by day for the same end? who has had to bear the brunt of the battle, while those who led us into action, were sitting quietly at home? who has suffered so much for conscience' sake? Let none consider these as vain boastings, we merely insert them to refresh the memories of those, who are now loud in denouncing our change.

We have said so much lately on the subject of colonization, that we expect some will begin to think it high time that some other subject should occupy our attention; but we entreat them to bear with us a while only, our time is but short; and the more we investigate the subject, the more important it appears, & consequently the more anxious are we to throw light on the subject by holding up the present state of the colony at Liberia, and also by contrasting our present condition, with the far happier one of our Liberian brethren who are at present enjoying all the privileges and advantages to which their more active enterprise entitle them.

We are confident that the subject of Colonization needs but a candid investigation from all who are at present opposed to it to gain their support; for of all plans for the benefit of our race this stands preeminent: whilst all the opposition which can be raised, must waste itself in idle declamation. In saying this much we are not unmindful of the labours of our long tried friends the Abolitionists: gratitude forbids—justice forbids—and did we harbour such a thought our very feelings would rise in judgment and condemn us. But we are confident, that even many of them have not given the subject a fair discussion, but have left it to fight its way into the good opinion of society. All we ask, is an impartial consideration of all that can be brought in favor of the society; and after that, we are pretty confident if we cannot number them among the active friends of the society, they will be unwilling to be considered its opposers.

To Our Patrons

The time having arrived, when our connexion with the Journal is about to be dissolved, we feel it our duty to offer, for the last time, a few words to the candid consideration of those friends who have been kind enough to patronise our feeble attempt, to dispel the clouds of ignorance & folly, which surround us as a community. If we cast our eyes at home, in our own land, or abroad, in foreign lands, we find no people exactly situated as we are—we find none so low and degraded—so dead to all the noble feelings which actuate intelligent and immortal beings. In the bosom of the most enlightened community upon the globe, we are ignorant and degraded; under the most republican government, we are denied all the rights and privileges of citizens; & what is still worse, we see no probability, that we as a community, will ever make it our earnest endeavour to rise from our ignorance and degradation. The vain & idle things of the moment occupy our minds, and woe betide the

Source: *Freedom's Journal*, March 28, 1829.

being who has the [te]merity to denounce them, and tell us that we should aim at employing our time more profitably. He is denounced in turn; and certain of our females even forgetful of that modesty so becoming to their sex, assume all the [illegible] of the [illegible] race of Amazons, and run from [illegible] blessing the unlucky [illegible.]

The principal objects which we have ever had in view, have been the dissemination of useful knowledge; the defence of our community; the necessity and advantages of education; and lately the expediency of emigration to Liberia. It is admitted, that for a community to become eminently virtuous, it is highly essential, that there should be a general dissemination of knowledge; and for the attainment of this, the press is a powerful auxiliary in the hands of enlightened and virtuous men. But we are apt when taking a view of the objects which are made subservient to human happiness to forget this, as if society could exist in its present happy state, without its aid. We would then inculcate upon our readers, the necessity of extending a patronising hand to the support of whatever is calculated to promote their happiness, and to improve their minds. It is admitted, that the standard of education is deplorably low, and that some general movement should be made towards raising it—but what avail all these admissions, without an effort to do something: for it is a fact, that while the rest of the community, are daily making higher attainments in knowledge, we remain almost stationary, with prejudices increasing daily. It is not our province here to enquire why prejudices should be in the pathway of the man of colour, all we know is, that they are there, and are ever likely to remain, until the theories of our African Symmes shall take place, and produce a general amalgamation. In many things, it is our duty to experiment until we arrive at the truth; but unless we have reasonable hopes for a favourable issue they are all useless; hence then, we conclude, that all efforts here, to improve the mass of coloured persons must prove abortive; and this conclusion we adopt from the evidence of our own eyes.

In our efforts to improve our condition; we have endeavoured to place before our readers every thing which had the least tendency to improve them morally, by pourtraying virtue in the most alluring colours, & depicting vice and folly unadorned with any of those flimsy veils, with which their votaries are ever desirous of arraying them. We have kept nothing back through fear; when time and occasion called for a defence against the attacks of vile men whose aim, was principally to hold us up as beings devoid of all principle, we have boldly come forward in defence of our brethren from a principle of duty; when our vices or follies deserved censure, we have not been backward in giving it; discarding all motives of self-interest, relying wholly upon the justness of our remarks, and the necessity and sense of duty which prompted us to offer them.

Education being the principal mover to every other improvement, we have laboured constantly to place its advantages in the most striking light, by citing the blessings which have flowed from it in other portions of our country, where it is more generally enjoyed and appreciated—we have endeavoured by holding up ignorance to view, and the evils which befall society from such a state, to render our readers more sensible than ever, of the imperious necessity that more general efforts should be made for the education of our rising youth, for it is upon them only, that all our hopes for the future respectability of our people are fixed: they are [the] last stay of the departed glory of ancient Africa—if we neglect them *now*, we must never expect to see them qualified to act their part in life, any better than we have. Ten times our present number of schools would be of little benefit unless we endeavour to second those benevolent individuals who have been kind enough to establish those now in operation, by sending *our* children regularly; by placing *daily* before them examples which would tend to excite them to virtuous actions; by upholding the hands of the different teachers, by precept & example. The times at present are those of action; the community sensible of the blessings to be derived from peace, seem anxious to improve present opportunities; and shall we remain idle spectators—while others are marching onward to the temple of science, shall we not fall into the ranks also, and turn our faces toward her lofty portals, which are open to all? Truly, education "is the pearl of great price." It makes us better acquainted with our duty to our Creator & to our fellow-men; it elevates the soul and teaches us to look down with contempt upon the idle and frivolous things of the moment.

According to our ability, it has been our aim to be as practical as possible, in the few remarks which we have made at different times; and now we have arrived at the close our labours, we must say that frequently, we should rather have wa[i]ved offering any thing; knowing that we had no sufficient leisure at command to do justice to the different subjects of discussion. We commenced the Journal under the impression that the whole of our time would be devoted to the editorial department—that none of the manual labor of the office would fall upon us; but how disappointed we have been, we need not mention. We are sensible that our columns have often been issued with many typographical errors; which when our inexperience in printing is taken into account, should not be matter of much surprise. Generally speaking, an editor's office is a thankless one; and if so among an enlightened people: what could we expect? We are therefore not in the least astonished, that we have been slandered by the villainous—that our name is byword among the more ignorant, for what less could we expect? Prepared, we entered the lists; and unvanquished we retire, with the hope that the talent committed to our care, may yet be exerted under more favorable auspices, and upon minds more likely to appreciate its value.

3

Writings from Liberia

Part A. First Impressions: Two Early Letters from Liberia

Extract of Letter to Rev. A. R. Plumley, Agent of the ACS, November 18, 1829

My Dear Sir,

I embrace this opportunity by the departure of the Susan for the Leeward trade, to address you and a few other friends in the U.S. We arrived here on the 12th inst[ant], after the uncommonly long passage of 58 days, all in good health. In the high latitudes we were becalmed during 12 days and off the Cape De Verds, 10 days more; but I feel thankful to our Maker that we suffered for nothing. By Capt. Woodbury and his officers and crew I have been treated with the greatest politeness. Should you pass through Beverly, I beg you to call on him, as he has often been on the coast and can give you much information. At the invitation of Dr. Mechlin,[1] I am staying at the Agency's House. I am not sorry that my feet now rest on "terra firma," and in the land of my fathers, believing as I do that it is decreed by Him who reigns above, that the descendants of Africa now in America must return and assist in the great work of evangelizing and civilizing the land: the decree has gone forth, that "Ethiopia shall stretch her hands unto God;" and were you here one Sabbath, you would believe that the commencement of the prophecy was taking place. Ah! It is so pleasing to behold men who formerly groaned under oppression, walking in all the dignity of human nature, feeling and acting like men who had some great interest at stake; but still more pleasant to behold them assembled in the house of worship, rendering thanksgiving and prayer to Him who ruleth the nations in this land of heathen gods, surrounded by millions of immoral beings who are immersed in the grossest superstition "with eyes that see not; and ears that hear not."

I cannot describe what were my first sensations upon landing. The town contains double the number of houses one would expect, and I am informed of

Source: *Boston Recorder and Religious Telegraph*, April 28, 1830.

Caldwell and Millsbury, that each contains nearly as many. The Colonists here at Monrovia appear to be getting ahead fast; their principal dependance is trade with the natives, either in stores or at factories established in the interior. The health of the Colony has been quite good; deaths but two, the last six months. The death of Dr. Randall[2] has put a stop to all public works. Dr. Mechlin is waiting for advice: it is his intention to put the press into operation, as he is now building an office. Of the five German missionaries only two remain on the coast; one is dead, two have returned to Europe, from whence they are expected daily with their wives and families. We have two religious societies which own meeting houses, Methodists and Baptists; the German missionary sometimes preaches in the Methodist church as they have none of their own: they both keep school; one here, the other at Caldwell; and are much esteemed by the settlers. The cause of education has not yet received the attention from all which it ought. In a new settlement have we the right to expect much, my dear Sir? The majority of the settlers, being emigrants from the south of Maryland, have faint ideas of free schools. The Board of Managers have pledged their word that they would recommend the introduction of the free school system into the Colony. But I believe they must do something more, as the Colonists are hardly able to support a teacher. Mr. Shepherd from Richmond, who keeps the school here, complains very much that he has not received that support which was first promised him. He says he is almost discouraged. I have endeavored to encourage him, knowing from experience that of all men who labor in behalf of the public, teachers generally receive poor pay. It is at best an unthankful office; and did not we look beyond the present hour, our hearts would faint within us. We want means to build an academy and to establish more schools. Shall the appeal be made in vain to New England,—the land of schools? Shall we tell you that our children are perishing for lack of instruction? Shall the Macedonian cry come to your ears, and we be left to perish? I hope for better things. I hope some second Benezet[3] will arise and go through the Union, pleading our cause: from the public feeling on the subject, I know he will not plead in vain: ah Sir, when I commence on this subject I know not where to stop.

Yesterday I attended an examination of Mr. S.'s school; there were about 30 pupils present, they appeared, I assure you very well; his first class recited in grammar and geography, and acquitted themselves creditably; the under classes did the same. After an examination of three hours I came away much pleased. Mr. S. is 30 years old, formerly taught in Richmond, Va. He complained much for the want of room. He ought to be encouraged, he is a [line illegible] preached in R. He is quite intelligent in conversation. I believe an Infant school might easily be put into operation, had we the necessary apparatus, and teachers. But I think

I could qualify teachers, by observation and reading Mr. Bacon's publications which I have on the subject. Could not a Ladies' Society be formed in Boston for this purpose? Three hundred dollars would handsomely support two females. Tobacco, rum, pipes, cloth, iron pots, powder and shot are considered the currency of the country; so that if I owe a man $50 I can pay him, if a settler or foreigner, in Camwood at $60 per ton, or in ivory at 50cts [cents] for small teeth, or 8octs. for large per pound. Unless there was at the time of bargain an express agreement to the contrary. Nothing can be done without rum in trade with the natives; of all the rum which is brought to the Colony not one-tenth is consumed by the settlers. If they hold a palava [sic] or council with the natives, they must have rum to treat them. If they establish a new factory, they must have rum or nothing can be done. The present number of settlers amounts to 1500, and the farming establishments on the St. Paul's are said to be in fine order.

Provisions are brought into the Cape by the recaptured Africans, who are settled a few miles from here on lands which they call New Georgia. They amount to about 400, and are easily known from the surrounding natives by their dress and their copying as much as they can after the settlers. The great change which has taken place in their condition every way, would be enough to convince the most sceptical; it seems that transplantation has improved their natures much, for while the natives who have the same chance still adhere to their old customs, these are advancing daily in the arts of civilization. Some of them are even mechanics, and work in the settlement as such. By natives I mean those who have never been from the coast of Africa. The nearest inland trade is that of king Boatswain's people, about 150 miles distant. He is the Napoleon of these wilds, and formerly wrought as a common Krooman, though not in vessels on the coast. He has always been favorable to the Colony, and looks with contempt upon the neighboring petty chiefs and kings, all of whom I suppose pay him tribute. He holds a market every day in his chief town; settles all disputes among his people with costs of suit, after the manner of his more civilized brother; and examines into quality and quantity of such articles as are brought in for trade. His people are more civilized than their neighbors; when they appear among us, they wear pantaloons with a large piece of cloth tastefully thrown over their bodies. A Colonist at present trades in his chief town. Yesterday I was visited by two Mandingoes who wrote Arabic with great care. They are a shrewd people. They came for the purpose of bartering some native cloth. Our Capt. who was present was equally astonished with myself. I showed them a Greek book, which they desired me to read and they would read Arabic. One prayed for some minutes, to give us some idea of their pronunciation; which sounded like that of your friend Prince Abdhul Rahhahman. They subsist principally by practicing upon the superstitious nations of the other natives. They sell their charms, which consist chiefly of a few Arabic characters, as things of great value. They are called the god people; and their priests, gods. A settler must be uncommonly shrewd, if he gets the better of one in a bargain. They always inquire for new comers, as being less acquainted with their ways. They have even been known to prize things and afterwards to go in search of some Colonist to go and purchase them for them. They know the wholesale prices of things as well as the residents; and that gold and silver are worth a premium over the currency of the Colony. My health has been quite good as yet.

Extract of Letter to Edward Jones, March 20, 1830

Although the publishers of the letter did not reveal the recipient's name, the context and content make evident that Edward Jones (ca. 1808–64) was the person to whom Russwurm wrote. Jones had graduated from Amherst College two weeks before Russwurm graduated from Bowdoin College. The two men became close friends; Russwurm wrote to the ACS on Jones's behalf seeking support for Jones's pursuit of a medical education before going to Liberia, and Jones worked with Russwurm for a time at the offices of Freedom's Journal. *Jones later studied theology and was ordained a minister in the Episcopal Church. Despite Russwurm's entreaties, Jones settled in the British colony of Sierra Leone rather than Liberia and had a distinguished if controversial career in education and the church in West Africa.*

What my sensations were upon landing I can hardly describe. . . . You here behold coloured men exercising all the duties of offices of which you can scarcely believe, many fulfill the important duties with much dignity. We have here a republic in miniature. . . .

There is a great field for usefulness here; and, when I look around and behold the Pagan darkness of the land, an aspiration rises to Heaven that my friend may become a second Brainerd or Elliot[4]. . . .

I long to see young men, who are now wasting the best of their days in the United States, flocking to this land as the last asylum to the unfortunate—I long for the time when you, my dear friend, shall land on the shores of Africa, a messenger of that Gospel which proclaims liberty to the captive, and light to those who sat in great darkness! Oh, my friend, you have a wide career of usefulness

Source: *African Repository and Colonial Journal* 6 (April 1830): 61.

before you, and may that Being who has promised his support to his followers ever be nigh to you, and strengthen and make you a second Paul to this Gentile people! Our time is but short in this transitory world, and it therefore becomes us to labour with all our might, lest the darkness overtake us before we are aware of it.

It is the general opinion that the slave trade has nearly expired; but I am informed that nothing is more erroneous, as the trade was never carried on with more vessels nor with greater vigour than it has been for the last two years. Even now, while I am writing, slavers are within forty-four miles of the Colony, at Cape Mount.

Many innocent persons are sent to slavery under the pretext of crime, but in reality with a view to sordid gain; the captains of the slave ships instigating the people of a neighbourhood to bring "palavers," that is, criminal accusations against each other, and having sentence pronounced, that they may thus make up their cargo. The slave-trade is not suffered to exist within the limits of the Colony, nor is it to be found within a space of from 45 to 50 miles on each side of Cape Montserado. The whole distance from Cape Mount to Little Bassa enjoys this favoured exemption. Any person attempting to engage in this traffic within the Colony, is seized and imprisoned. Mr. Devany left several natives in prison who had been charged with this offence.[5] The crime is made piracy by their law, and none of the Colonists have ever been concerned in it. Whispers did prevail with respect to one individual, but no proof has been adduced. Mr. Devany being asked, in conclusion, whether, if the Colony should be recognized as independent by the United States and the European Governments, they had any fears as to being able to defend themselves from the natives and all others? He replied, with great promptitude, that the Colony is not in a state of complete defence; the United States' guns need remounting, and the battery repairing: if this was done, they would not have the least apprehension on that subject; and that to be thus acknowledged, was the general desire of the Colonists.

Part B. Writings from the Liberia Herald

To Our Readers: [Inaugural Editorial]

In every undertaking, similar to the one, upon which we are entering, the public generally look for something, explanatory of the writer's views: nor do we conceive they demand more than they have a right to expect. Man is an inquisitive being, and whenever any new project, of any kind whatever, is presented to his view, he considers it as his prerogative, to inquire into the project's motives. Be they good, he patronises them: be they bad, he discountenances them. The objects which we have in view, we shall set forth in a few words.

A more general dissemination of knowledge, is certainly a subject deserving the serious consideration of every man of reflection. The road, to the temple of science, is an old and beaten path: but it is a good one, nevertheless. Man may invent machinery to diminish human labor—he may propel vessels, at an almost incredible rate, by the agency of steam—but no man has ever discovered a new road up the steep hill, upon whose eminence Science has erected her proud temple. Emperors and kings, emulous of ascending her heights, have been compelled, like others, to descend to the simple A, B, C, and having gained a footing, they have crawled gradually, until they reached their various summits: and are we willing to do so as they have done. Of all employments to which a rational being can devote his leisure hours, that of *self-improvement,* is the most honorable, profitable and durable. There is no station, to which such an one, especially, if a young man, may not qualify himself for in the process of time, and in a free government like ours, aspire after. It is true, such an effort is the labor of days, months and years, but what then? [D]oes the distant prospect of success deter the merchant from shipping his goods to foreign countries—does the prospect of rough and stormy weather, and gales *ahead*, deter the adventurous mariner from the ocean?

We shall ever feel a deep interest on the subject of education; as from it flows every comfort & blessing which society enjoys. Without it, no government can long exist in a state of freedom: it is the link which binds man to his fellowman, & teaches him his duty to his kindred, his country, and his God. The perfection to which the different systems of education have advanced in Europe and America, invites the friends of the cause, in this Colony, to make one united effort at least in its favor. We rejoice at what has been done; our

Source: *Liberia Herald*, March 6, 1830.

desire is to see something further; for it is our candid belief that no subject so very interesting, in all its bearings, can come before any community. We are pilgrims in search of Liberty, and it is our duty to profit by the wisdom of those who have gone before us. I refer particularly to the pilgrim fathers of New England. Education was ever in their thoughts. No sooner had they erected their lowly dwellings than the school-house was the next object of consideration: and their thoughts were united with action. From the first settlement of the Colony, schools were put into operation, and every encouragement was held out to literary men, to emigrate from the mother country. The schools which they established have been continued to the present day, and their descendants are now distinguished for their intelligence and learning. It follows then, if we wish for like results: if we wish for the blessing of posterity: if we wish for our names in after ages to be pronounced with reverence: *we must take like step; we must make like exertions.* From the interest felt in our behalf in the United States, we know that our efforts, how feeble soever they may be, will be seconded with zeal, by our friends in that quarter.

As low as Africa has descended in the scale of nations, she can with propriety claim the invention of letters, as the honor rests between the Egyptians & Ethiopians. Ethiopia, which in former times comprehended Ethiopia, Abyssinia, and Nubia was early inhabited by a people whose manners and customs nearly resembled those of the Egyptians: they worshipped nearly the same Gods: they made use of the same characters in writing: their dress was alike; & the regal scepter of both countries was in the form of a plough. They were considered as a people, favored of the Gods, doing no evil, exercising fortitude, and despising death. It is the belief of many authors, ancient and modern, that Abyssinia was first peopled by the early descendants of Cush, the eldest son of Ham; and that the Abyssinians spoke the Original language, and were the inventors of writing. Be the case as it may, the Abyssinian dynasty is very ancient, as her princes claim descent from Menelek, the son of Solomon, by the Queen of Sheba, who died B.C. 986. There can be little doubt, that certain parts of the continent, now in a state of barbarism, were once, comparatively speaking, in a high state of civilization. We are informed that the "Gospel was first received on the burning sands of Africa with great eagerness; African christians soon formed one of the principal members of the church primitive; and that during the third century, they were animated by the zeal of Tertullian, directed by the abilities of Cyprian and Origen, and adorned by the eloquence of Lactantius." We rejoice, that, though the tribes, in the vicinity of the sea coast, have become completely demoralized from the baneful influence of the slave trade; some nations, in the interior, though not exempt from it, still possess a remnant of civilization, and present to the traveler, a faint representation of former times.

********** [asterisks in the original]

We are in hopes, through our columns to bring to light many facts relative to the Slave trade. It is the general opinion in the United States and Europe, that it has nearly ceased: but could an American or European reside on Cape Messurado, and witness the daily passage of slavers up & down the coast; & see what many of our citizens have, hundreds of their fellowmen, actually in chains, on board; he would then begin to think that the traffic was far from being discontinued. To such a pitch of audacity have many of these slavers arrived, that no merchant vessel, unless strongly armed, is secured against their piratical attacks. They have even been known to leave the Havannas and other ports, for this coast, with not more than two weeks provisions on board, depending altogether with falling in with vessels, and supplying themselves. Some governments have made the trade piracy, but of what avail, are laws, which are enacted at the distance of 5000 miles, without the means of inflicting punishment. Desperadoes, like those engaged in the Slave trade, must be deterred by the certainty of the punishment, or they never will desist. Colonies have been planted by the British, Portuguese, French, and Danish, but with the exception of the first, is either strong enough to prohibit the traffic in slaves from being carried on in its neighborhood. The average number of slaves imported [annually] into the port of Rio de Janeiro alone, for the five years preceding the treaty with Great Britain, amounted to 23,395: since then the importations in 1825, were 29,254; in 1826, 33,939; in 1827, 29,789; in 1828, 43,536; in 1829, to the 26th of March[,] 13,459!

We console ourselves under the hope, that the time has arrived, when all civilized nations have mutually agreed that the traffic shall cease; and by article 1st. of the treaty before named, it was agreed, "that four years after the exchange of ratifications, it would not be lawful for the subjects of the Emperor of Brazil, to carry on trade in slaves on the Coast of Africa, under any pretext, or in any manner whatever."

Economy is a subject, upon which we shall occasionally dwell. [I]n a young government, perhaps, nothing conduces more to its prosperity than economy, in every sense of the word; and no subject calls more imperiously upon the leading members of our society, for their daily practice, as man with all the other peculiarities ascribed to him, is also an imitative animal.

On religious topicks, no subjects of a controversial nature will be admitted into our columns; but well written essays, on the fundamental principles of the Christian religion, will be received with pleasure.

Our columns will ever be open to enlightened and liberal views on political subjects; but they shall never be made the channel of party prejudices, or personal abuse. As Editor of the Herald, we belong to no party, whatever our private opinions may be, as the citizen of a free Government.

While these subjects shall occupy our attention, we wish not to forget, that there are others in which the community feel interested. We consider our undertaking public property, and ourselves bound to do whatever may tend to enlighten the community. Should we fail, at any time, our readers must impute it to mistaken zeal, than otherwise.

The Editor.

Union

From our boyhood, we have often reflected upon the fable of the old man, who had several sons, and the bundle of sticks. It is in our humble opinion, a fine illustration of Union in a family, church, or State. How beautiful is Union in a family, where the members are all united, and each is sensible of his dependence upon the other: how beautiful in a church: how beneficial, in a State or Kingdom, where the people living under equitable and mild laws, feel it their indispensible duty, to support their due administration. The novel spectacle of a whole nation, rising *en masse*, was presented to the admiring world, in the Russian people, when attacked by Napoleon. They came forth at their country's call, to defend their altars and domestic hearths from the spoiler's hands, and heaven, approving the deed, crowned their efforts, with complete success.

Without referring to ancient times, we can present our readers with modern data sufficient for our object. Next to Russia, the Swiss Cantons present as fine an illustration as any one can desire. Amidst all the wars, which have desolated Europe for the last two centuries, they have remained just so:—a free and independent people, though but comparatively few in numbers. Few can tell, but those who have had the trial, how much can be effected by a small but united band, when fighting as these Cantons have often done, for their Liberty and Independence.

The United States of America, would this day have been colonies of Great Britain, had not the interests of the different slates, bound them in an union, which neither the gold, nor the armies of the mother country, could break.

Source: *Liberia Herald*, June 5, 1830.

But while we view the bright side of the painting, it may not perhaps be uninteresting to look on the little blemishes which here and there occupy a spot. The evils which have befallen mankind, from disunion either in church or state, have in many instances, been alarmingly great.

The unhappy state of Britain during the reign of the unfortunate Charles I—the divisions which rent that Kingdom—the evils which flowed from the civil war, and the awful termination of it, must all be imputed to a few designing demagogues, whose principal aim, was, the creation of an opposition party. How well they succeeded from the peculiar temper of the times, is left on record for the instruction of other governments.

The kingdom of Poland is another government, where the dreadful effects of internal dissentions were the means finally of subjecting that ancient state to be partitioned among her neighbors, casting out her name, from among the list of free and independent nations.

Scarcely 40 years have passed, since the civilized world witnessed France torn by internal dissentions—her nobles and clergy compelled to flee for their lives—her king a captive—and flaming demagogues under the false name of patriots, committing excesses, at the bare mention of which, humanity shudders. And these were the men who went about in sheep's clothing, among the ignorant populace of Paris, and other large towns, inflaming their minds, and exciting them to acts of rebellion.

We are a young government, and it is our duty, to read and reflect upon what historians have recorded. If we can by a little caution, avoid the dreaded rocks of Scylla and Carybdis, upon which wiser and older governments have almost been shipwrecked, where is the friend to his country, who will say, we should not shun them.

We believe we speak within bounds when we say that more evils have been inflicted upon mankind from disunion, than from any one source, war excepted.

Exhibiting as we have, this interesting subject, in a brief way, we cannot leave it, without inviting the attention of each of our readers, particularly to it.

[We Have Found a Haven]

Our brethren in the United States, are altogether ignorant, as regard the state and conditions of our Colony: does not prudence tell them to enquire of those who are better informed than to receive the dictation of any one of their own number, whose opportunities for information, could have been no better than theirs[?]

Source: *Liberia Herald*, April 6, 1830.

Ohio has, and Indiana shortly will adopt, laws which we predicted some months ago, that the free states would find themselves under the necessity of enacting. God forbid, that we should undertake to justify the passing and putting such into execution. As the experienced mariner foresees the approaching tornado, for hours, before it actually comes on and takes in sails and prepares for the worst, so did we foretell, and give notice of what was to be apprehended. We have found a haven, to which we invite all our race, who have the independence to think for themselves, and a courage to dare the worst, in pursuit of *Freedom*.

All new countries are subject to certain diseases which vanish as soon as the lands are cleared: from which, we have not the vanity to think, that our Colony is exempt, but where lives the man: who can say, with the least propriety that Liberia is more so, than any other. Were he a wise man, we would pronounce him ignorant in this particular; were he an ignorant man, we would know, where to place him.

To Our Readers: [Taking Stock—One Year On]

This number closes the first volume of the *Liberia Herald*. We entered on our work with diffidence having had some little experience by the way previously. We did not promise much, we could not, surrounded by pagan nations, at a distance from literary friends, from even competent mechanical assistance. Under these discouragements the *Herald* has been published for the past twelve months, and we should have desponded on our way, had we not been cheered, now and then, by a few lines of encouragement from friends and contemporaries on the other side of the Atlantic. They knew a few of the difficulties at the commencement of every new publication, even among them; and they hesitated not, to uphold our feeble hands, and for this labor of love, we think them entitled to the gratitude of every Liberian. We conceive all plans, ever put into operation to promote knowledge and civilization, incomplete without this great Archimedean lever, the press, under due and limited restraint.

We belong not to that party, who are daily exclaiming for a free press, for as fire is a very useful servant when properly cared after, but unheeded, becomes a dangerous one, so would the press be unless under the wholesome restraint of the law. Laws are intended for the mutual benefit of men in a state of social compact, and whenever circumstances shew to the contrary, they should be amended or abrogated; and the experience of past ages dem-

Source: *Liberia Herald*, February 6, 1831.

onstrates most conclusively, that no country could long exist with what is vulgarly called a free press, under the guidance of unprincipled men.

We are aware, that our sheet has often appeared with many typhograpical [sic] errors, but we were cheered with the knowledge that the most intelligent of our readers, would make many allowances for a sheet printed in *Africa*. Our Editorial head has not appeared with quality, nor quantity of matter, which we promised our readers at the commencement. The poor state of our health, and the various duties devolved upon us during the greater part of the time are our apology. The whole of a man's time should be devoted to the *Herald*, and from having other duties to perform, we have considered ourselves merely as temporary until some better qualified person could be obtained.

It is with much pleasure, we have witnessed the daily spread of the cause of Colonization. Our brethren of color also begin to view it, in a more favorable light, and though a few of them, misled themselves, have endeavoured to mislead the more ignorant to Canada, how have they succeeded? Do not the Resolutions of the Legislature of U[pper] Canada, speak volumes? Are they not seen as intruders? Will not the arbitrary laws, or rather prejudices which have been raised in Ohio, be planted and matured in Canada? It requires no prophetic eye to foretel[l] that to them and their posterity, there is no abiding place on the other side of the Atlantic. Canada will hardly afford them a temporary shelter against the bleak winds of a winter. Before God, we know of no other home for the man of color, of republican principles, than Africa. Has he no ambition? Is he dead to every thing noble? Is he contented with his condition? Let him remain in America: Let him who might here be an honor to society,—remain a sojourner in a land where it is impossible to be otherwise. His spirit is extinct, and his friends may as well bury him *now*.

In this our closing address, to our readers, we feel a freedom, which we have not for some months, and their patience must be extended, should the article appear unnecessarily long.

The changes which have taken place in the Colony during the publication of the *Herald*, are perhaps among those most worthy of notice.—Every thing has improved—our agriculture, our commerce have each shared in the blessing: Monrovia has almost assumed a new garb, and should things continue to prosper as they have, our town will certainly present the most desirable residence to a stranger, of any on the Coast of Africa. In Monrovia alone, the number of comfortable stone and wooden dwellings erected during the year has been upwards of fifty-five—and if we take into consideration, that Caldwell, Millsburg, and the recaptured towns[6] have shared equally in this prosperity, we have abundant reasons to be thankful for the showers of mercy, which have been extended to our infant Colony. Our commerce is daily extending, and we believe the day is not far distant, when our port will be the emporium of the Western Coast of Africa.

But the object which we consider of most vital importance to the future prosperity of the Colony, is Education. The subject has long lain dormant, but the late resolutions of the Board of Managers [of the ACS], and the fixed determination of our Executive to carry them into effect, give us every reason to hope that a complete[,] free school system is about being put into operation.

Every Man the Architect of His Own Fortune

Russwurm had published this stern rejection of fatalism and resignation, and call for self-reliance, self-examination, self-help, and self-improvement, more than three years earlier in the pages of Freedom's Journal *(October 31, 1828). He reprinted it, essentially, word for word. This is the most revealing indication of the creed by which Russwurm himself conducted his life. Given the hardships he had to endure since his boyhood and his remarkably lonely life, he probably adopted it from necessity rather than choice.*

"But chiefly the mould of a man's fortune is in his own hands."
Lord Bacon

"Fortune a goddess is to fools alone,
The wise are always master of their own."

Pope

It is wittily remarked by a French writer, that while the Portuguese sailors, before engaging in battle, are prostrate upon deck, imploring their saints to perform miracles in their favour, the British tars are manning their guns and working miracles for themselves. This remark, when rightly interpreted, contains a lively satire upon a species of superstition which misleads the multitude more than any other, and engenders indolence and apathy under the specious names of contentment and resignation. There may be some error, common to the vulgar, more preposterous than this, but there are few more pernicious, and not one undoubtedly in which the transaction [transition][7]

Source: *Liberia Herald*, April 22, 1831.

from speculation to conduct is so easy and unavoidable. To believe, for example, that there once were witches, who made a cockle-shell serve the purpose of a ship, and substituted a broomstick for a balloon, or that there still are fairies, who hold their gambols at midnight, among the romantic glens of Scotland, is quite a harmless superstition, whose worst effect can be to make the gossips draw closer round the winter fire, or the farmer more brief in his potations when at market. But a blind belief in fatalism, or destiny, acts as a powerful motive to indolence and indecision, and makes men sit down with their arms folded in Turkish apathy, expecting to obtain, by supernatural means, what Providence has wisely reserved as the reward of virtuous exertions. It cannot, therefore, be too early or deeply instilled into the minds of the youthful and inexperienced, that there are few difficulties which wisdom and perseverance cannot conquer; that the means of happiness, and even riches, are, in some degree, in every man's power, and that misfortune is frequently, if not generally, only another name for misconduct.

Nothing is more common, in the world, than for people to flatter their self-esteem, and excuse their indolence, by referring the prosperity of others to the caprice, or partiality of fortune. Yet few, who have examined the matter with attention, have failed to discover, that success is as general a consequence of industry and good conduct, as disappointment is the consequence of indolence and [in]decision.[8] Happiness, as Pope remarks, is truly our being's end and aim, and almost every man desires wealth as a means of happiness. But in wishing, mankind are nearly alike, and it is chiefly the striking incongruity that exists betwixt their action and thoughts that chequers society, and produces those endless varieties of character and situation which prevail in human life. Some men, with the best intention, have so little fortitude, and are so fond of present ease of pleasure, that they give way to every temptation; while others, possessed of greater strength of mind, hold out heroically to the last, and then look back with complacency on the difficulties they have overcome, and the thousands of their fellow-travelers that are lagging far behind, railing at fate, and dreaming of what they might have been. This difference in the progress which men make in life, who set out with the same prospects and opportunities, is a proof, of itself, that more depends upon conduct than fortune. And it would be good for society if, instead of envying our neighbour's lot and deploring our own, we would begin to inquire what means others have employed that we have neglected, and whether it is possible, by a change of conduct to secure a result more proportioned to our wishes. Were individuals, when unsuccessful, often to institute such an inquiry, improving the hints it would infallibly suggest, we would hear fewer complaints against the partiality of fortune, and witness less of the wide extremes of riches and poverty. But the great misfortune is, that few have courage to undertake, and still fewer candour to execute, such a system of self-examination. Conscience may perhaps whisper, that they have not done all which their circumstances permitted; but her whispers are soon stifled amidst the plaudits of self-esteem, and they remain in a happy ignorance of the exertions of others, and a consoling belief in the immutability of fortune. Others who may possess candour and firmness to undertake this inquiry, are quite appalled at the unwelcome truths it forces upon their notice. Their own industry, which they believed to be great, and their own talents, which they fancied were unequalled, are found to suffer by a comparison with those of others, and they betake themselves in despair to the refuge of indolence, and think it easier, if not better, to want wealth, than encounter the toil and trouble, of obtaining it. Thus do thousands pass through life, angry with fate when they ought to be angry with themselves; too fond of the comforts and enjoyments which riches procure ever to be happy without them, and too indolent and unsteady ever to persevere in the use of the only means by which they are obtainable.

Probably one frequent cause of disappointment in the young, may be traced to that overweening confidence in their own powers, which leads them to trust more to their own romantic anticipations, than the tried and experimental knowledge of their seniors. While the progress of learning, and the refinements of education, confer upon the present race an elegance and polish unknown to their fathers, they are too apt to magnify this merit, and regard their elders as beings of an inferior capacity. They forget completely, that a taste for literature, and the arts differ very widely from that sober and experimental knowledge which can be brought to bear upon the real business of life, and enable its possessors to preserve his place in the great crowd, where every individual is constantly endeavouring to press forward by jostling his neighbour. Even a man of very ordinary parts, who has lived long in the world, and probably, after a thousand blunders, learned to conduct himself with ability and prudence, is better qualified for imparting instructions to others, than those who, in other respects are most remarkable for their talents and attainments. Experience in this, as in every thing else, is the great mistress of wisdom, and were men guided by her safe, though often unwelcome counsels, in preference to their own fond imaginations, there would be a mighty diminution of that misery with which ignorance and obstinacy are constantly filling the world. There is little new under the sun, and the walks of life, numerous and diversified as they appear, are filled both with beacons that warn of the fate of the imprudent, and monuments that record the triumphs of the successful. That so many fail, therefore, in a task apparently so simple and easy, can only be accounted for by the false confidence which men repose in their own powers, which dispose them to slight instructions, and neglect the assistance for those charts and descriptions which have been furnished by the industry of preceding travellers.

Another circumstance, that marks the danger of the young neglecting the counsels of the old, is that revolution, which experience and the progress of knowledge necessarily produce in the opinions and impressions of every human being. He must have little acquaintance with books, and less with life; who has not remarked this of others as well as of himself. Man is not the same being to-day that he was yesterday. His mind, like his body, is in a constant state of revolution. The discovery of a new truth, or the adoption of a new opinion, often produces a total change in his views and sentiments, and gives a new turn to his most ordinary actions. This he feels and perceives, but seldom anticipates. It is the great error of his life, constantly to overrate his present knowledge and attainments; and although, at every new addition to them, he discovers his former deficiency, he still secretly flatters himself that he has at last reached perfection.—Like the torrent that rushes from the mountains, he begins his course, filled with a thousand impurities, and it is not till his knowledge has passed through the filters of the world, that error and prejudice sink to the bottom, and truth assumes its native transparency.

To this cause we must ascribe that striking diversity of feeling and sentiment which so often prevails between the pupil and preceptor, and which make the former believe that to adopt the opinions of the latter, were to doubt the evidence of his senses. To the cool and experienced, the world and its concerns have lost the master-charm of novelty, which so often leads to "bewilder, and dazzles to blind;" and hence the young find it as difficult to enter into the feeling of the old as to read with their spectacles, or walk with their crutches. But they would remember, that these hoary advisers were once young and romantic like themselves, and that it is from a knowledge of the errors into which such feelings are apt to betray us, that they caution us to be on our guard against their influence. We would not, however be understood as asserting, that there are no prejudices peculiar to age, or that the young are never in danger of being misled by instructions:—this would be hazarding too much; and it is sufficient for every purpose of instruction to affirm, that the instances in which the old are apt to feel biassed, are precisely those in which the prejudices of the young run strongest in a contrary direction; and that, at all events, there is infinitely more danger to be apprehended from their paying too little than too much deference to the opinions of others.

To Our Readers: [Let the Experiment Be Tried on Africa's Soil]

Another year has passed, and we are again brought to our last number.

The late energetic measures pursued by the parent Society, supported by approving smiles of good men of every country, is to us a source of great pleasure. We are firm in the belief that a cause which has so many advocates among the intelligent and virtuous, must be based upon the most noble principles of the human heart. The principles of the Society have now been tested for the last ten years; its motives have been called in question, and still it is every day increasing in usefulness, and making warm advocates, where previously it was looked upon, with apathy, if not suspicion.

We have ever been the advocate of freedom—we wish it to flourish wherever man exists—and if our maturer experience is against our more youthful hopes—if the soil where we thought it might in our day exist, does not bear corresponding fruit, we are sorry, and heartily invite all who are longing for it, to seek with us, or in other lands, its precious enjoyment.

We know that our native land has attractions which other lands have not though our minds and bodies groan in affliction, but it is wisdom's part to choose whether we will patiently suffer or make one effort at least to better our condition. There is such a thing as men becoming callous to the nobler feelings of the heart, and we pity them sincerely.

Spectators as we are on the arena of life, we have reason to be thankful that nothing has occurred to disturb the peace and happiness of our colony, while internal commotions have been the lot of more civilized portions of the globe. We have continued advancing in commerce and agriculture and population, and the day we hope is not far distant, when from Liberia, will issue emigrants to form other colonies on this coast, and show to the world at large that we are not quite dead to the noble objects, which the parent Society has in view.

Free schools in each of our settlements have been in operation somewhat over a year, and we have every reason to believe that great blessings have been on the rising generation by their establishment; but still our wants are great, the Recaptured Africans are unprovided for, and we stand in much need of an higher school, into which our most promising lads from the different settlements may be removed.

If our friends at home wish to see the experiment fairly tested, of a colony composed of such materials as ours, making advances in knowledge and civi-

Source: *Liberia Herald*, February 22, 1832.

lization, give us schools and competent teachers. Let the strictest economy be practiced in every other department, but let teachers be amply compensated.

The African for ages has been unjustly reproached for want of genius & incapacity to acquire the more abstruse branches of education, but let the experiment be tried on Africa's soil, and we shall see whether the descendant of Africa, in the land of his forefathers, freed from the contumely, which daily looks down upon him in America, will not satisfy the most prejudiced that all are the workmanship of one God, who has allotted to his African as well as his American children, a diversity of gifts.

In the providence of God, we trust the day is not far distant, when we shall see worthy successors to those renowned men of ancient Africa, who were born and reared on its soil. Africa has been deemed the land of monsters, henceforth let it be the land of promise to all her descendants.

[Facts Speak Louder Than Words]

From late occurrences at the South [in the United States] which we deplore as much as any man possibly can, we are led to conclude that a new impulse will be given to the noble scheme of Colonization. *Facts speak louder than words:* and when we predicted months before, that the late coercive measures pursued by the State of Ohio, would have to be adopted by all the free states, we were laughed at by many who were opposed to emigration. But how stand facts at present—Ohio has put her prohibitory laws, which were suffered to go unenforced, into operation, and the rest of the free states will shortly follow her example. And where then, will the thousands of free persons of colour; and the thousands of slaves, whose masters stand ready to free them, flee for shelter; can they *all* go to Canada[?] It is folly to think, much more to say so: can they, will they flee to Hayti: the experiment has been tried, and hundreds have returned back; with these words in their mouths, "if we are to be slaves, let us be slaves in America."

The truth is, men may disclaim as much as they please against Africa, they may circulate inflammatory papers among persons too ignorant to see through their *disinterested* motives, but we challenge them to bring facts to prove any of their assertions. To the uneducated children of Africa, their daily language is, this is your country, &c. &c. all of which is true enough; but will [any] of these men who labor from such *pure* motives, do any thing more than spout, and run from city to city, dissuading those, whose wishes are bettering their condition, from making the *attempt*. They ought surely to

Source: *Liberia Herald*, December 22, 1831 [excerpt from editorial].

be the pioneers in this march of equality, which is shortly to cover the Union, as the waters do the sea—they ought to make their dearly beloved colored brethren and sisters, not so *only* in *name* but in *fact*, and then we on this side of the Atlantic—in this land of true equality, will begin to think that there is one spark of pure disinterested benevolence in this selfseeking world.

Part C. Letters Home from Afar to a Brother

The following letters were written by Russwurm to his younger half-brother, Francis Edward Russwurm (1814–62), from Monrovia during the most embattled moment of Russwurm's time in Liberia. They shed light upon his relationship with his brother and his extended family in Maine and his thoughts as well as feelings about Monrovia.

Letter to Francis Edward Russwurm, March 31, 1834

Dear Francis E.

The departure of the Brig Anne, Langdon master for Bath, [Maine,] affords me an opportunity of dropping you a few lines. I am sorry to learn that Mr. C. Stockbridge is deceased.[9] Mr. Adam Wilson had the kindness to find me a paper containing a few lines on the subject. It is so long since I have heard from North Yarmouth that I know not but half the town may be dead. My last is from Mr. C. Stockbridge the most regular correspondent and the one who seemed to take the deepest interest in my welfare, in this distant land. Mr. J. H. Blanchard did promise to write me again, if I answered his letter directly, but I know not whether he has ever received my answer or not. Miss A. Blanchard's I also answered directly and I know not again why you all seem to forget poor me here.[10] I will not be foolish enough to impute it to the darkness of my complexion, because color is nothing in Africa: what is then the reason of so long a Silence? Since I learned that you had relinquished your liberal course of education I have been anxious to know in what line of business you purposed to employ yourself. Should it be merchandise perhaps this coast offers greater inducements than—any other at present. The reports you see published in the U. S. are much exaggerated about its unhealthiness to those who merely come on & go off in the span of 6 or 9 months.

At present our coast is completely overrun with vessels of all nations—many engaged in the Slave Trade but a respectable ~~honorable~~ number in fair trade. In the colony business is very dull and there is not much prospect of a revival until peace takes place among our natives. Our ivory trade is almost broken up and as for Gold we never did purchase but small quantities. The gold region is more to the South. At present one hardly knows what will sell but on the Coast. I have given Capt. Langdon a small invoice and it is his intention to give trade one trial at least. He belongs to Bath. He is well acquainted with Dr. Stockbridge,[11] from whom you may learn when he will sail. I shall certainly expect long letters when he returns from North Yarmouth. I did promise myself two or three months ago that I would see the U States this year but I have given over the idea as we are winding up the affairs of our firm. It is likely I shall embark on my own responsibility in commerce as early as possible after we close.[12]

Remember me to all the family; and I should feel particularly honored by a letter from Mr. or Mrs. Hawes.[13] Present my respect to Dr. Gooch & Mr. Sherman & Esq. Mellen, if he is still in N. Yarmouth.[14] Tell Mr. Cummings I hardly ever get a No [number] of the [Christian] Mirror though the [Liberia] Herald[15] is sent to him regularly. Through all vicissitudes believe me

Ever Yours Truly
Jno. B. Russwurm

P.S. Have you ever heard from J.S.R.[?] I conversed a few months ago with a Tennessee agent who told me that he was now Genl R. and lived in ---- (forgotten)[16]

Letter to Francis Edward Russwurm, September 27, 1835

Dear Francis Edward

I have written so often of late without receiving any answers that I begin to despair of hearing from you again while in Africa. I felt confident that you would receive my letters by the Brig Anne of Bath. If received, why have you all been silent so long. I wrote also to Mrs. Stockbridge & her brother W. R. Stockbridge.[17]

I should really like to know if you have attended to the commission that I gave you in reference to my note on the Stockbridge possessions.

My partner Mr Dailey is now in [the] U S and your letters can be forwarded to him at Messrs. Rogers & Co., Exchange Street, New York. By a late arrangement of the post office department all letters for Liberia, postpaid to New York, are to be forwarded by the first vessel.

For the last two years business has been uncommonly dull owing to wars in the interior but times are beginning to grow more brisk. I suppose I shall live &

Source: John Sumner Russwurm Papers, Tennessee State Library and Archives, Nashville.

die in Africa, but I hope not in Liberia; for more fanaticism, bigotry & ignorance I never saw amongst men; not excepting even the two last agents of the A. C. S.[18]

J. H. Blanchard promised if I answered offhand that he would write again. Why has he not[?] Why so much silence on the part of the family[?] I suppose they have cast me off because I am in Africa. I hope not however.

I want very much to come to America but circumstances have been so much against me that I have not been able to accomplish that most ardent wish, but I promise myself, blow high or low, upon Mr. Dailey's return[,] to cross the Atlantic again.

As you are now of age I long very much to know what business or profession you have chosen. I am fast recovering from a severe attack of the rheumatism with which I have been afflicted for the last two years.

Our George Stockbridge R is now over 13 months old & is as fine a child as you would see in any part of your happy land.[19] I have not time to write more but beg you to remember me to every member of the family individually, beginning with Mr. and Mrs. Hawes and ending with Mrs. R. Stockbridge and family. I live in Africa but my friends in America can never be forgotten.

> *Yours most affectionately*
> *Jno B. Russwurm*

Write me when you hear from J. S. R. in Tenn. My wife begs to be remembered though a stranger to all.

Part D. Governor Russwurm:
Departing from the Old and Beaten Paths

Letter Accepting Appointment as Agent and Governor of Maryland in Liberia

Excerpt of letter from Russwurm to John Latrobe (corresponding secretary, Maryland State Colonization Society), informing the Board of Managers of the Maryland State Colonization Society of his acceptance of the appointment of colonial agent and governor of Maryland in Liberia.

Monrovia, Liberia, Sept. 28, 1836

My dear Sir,

I acknowledge the receipt of yours of June 30th, 1836, notifying me of my appointment by your Board of Managers, as "agent of the Maryland State Colonization Society & Governor of Maryland in Liberia."

I cannot express my high sense of their liberality, and the flattering manner in which they have conferred the appointment. This is certainly a new era in the history of the man of color; and our community though astonished, still applaud to the skies this monument of the Board.

I accept their appointment with pleasure, and shall endeavor, by a conscientious discharge of duty to convince them and the world, "that their authority in force as in duration will not be less in Africa because it is wielded by other than a white man." And however short, I may fail in coming up to their estimate of the abilities which their representative in Africa ought to possess, yet the principles which have promoted them to action are certainly in advance of this age of liberal ideas. They have departed from the old & beaten paths, by their resolutions in my favour, and may my right hand forget "its cunning," ere I abuse their confidence. I shall enter on my duty with my whole mind engaged in it, and failure shall not arise from neglect. . . .

Source: Papers of the Maryland State Colonization Society, Maryland Historical Society, Baltimore.

Part E. Sometimes We Despond a Little: Some Candid and Private Thoughts on the Liberian Project

In these two letters, Russwurm expressed soberly and most explicitly the difficult project that the colonizationists had undertaken and his disillusionment with some of the members of the American Colonization Society (ACS). A Methodist minister at the time of his appointment in 1835, Ira Easter was the home agent of the Maryland State Colonization Society based in the Baltimore offices. Judge Samuel Wilkeson, a wealthy Buffalo businessman, had become the dynamic president of the board of managers and chairman of the executive committee of the reorganized ACS in 1838. Refusing to take a salary from the Society, he radically overhauled the debt-ridden and troubled organization, and had effectively resolved many of its financial problems by the time he resigned in 1841. Wilkeson authored A Concise History of the Commencement, Progress and Present Condition of the American Colonies in Liberia *(Washington, 1839), a useful but rather dry and legalistic pamphlet. Wilkeson had evidently written to Russwurm, who by this time had left Monrovia for Cape Palmas, seeking his frank appraisal of the key problems of the ACS colony at Monrovia.*

Letter to Rev. I. A. Easter, June 2, 1837

Dear Sir,

... You will not be surprised, that sometimes when difficulties & danger surround us, we despond a little; and think, that do our best, all our efforts will be in vain. But these are only temporary; as every day's experience gives us a better knowledge of our duty, & the practicability of establishing colonies on this coast, which in process of time, may realize all the fondest anticipations of their patrons. But such is not the labor of one or five years; time must pass—difficulties are to be met and overcome; the present generation, & perhaps the next, must pass away, before we can with justice look for prosperity to crown our efforts, or the blessing of posterity our labor. ...

It is really astonishing, how infatuated some of the people of color are in preferring bondage in [the] U.S. to freedom in Africa: all however is to be imputed to their ignorance, & the debasing state they have been in for generations.

It is certain, that the more inviting the situation of the colonists is made in Africa, the more will the respectable parts of the colored people in the U. States

Source: Papers of the Maryland State Colonization Society, Maryland Historical Society, Baltimore, Maryland.

be encouraged to emigrate at their own expense, and take up their residence here. . . .

[Of] this I am certain, that no set of men, unless actuated by higher motives than mankind generally, will be contented at first in this land, when they have so many arduous duties to perform, before they can see for what they have been toiling. We are in a heathen land, in every sense of the word; our enemies are numerous, and those who embark with the idea that they are bound to Fairy regions, make a sad mistake on the very outset. Of this, they should be disabused, and if they become dissatisfied, they will have nobody to blame but themselves.

Letter to Judge Samuel Wilkeson, January 4, 1840 [marked private]

Dear Sir,

Your highly respected favor per Saluda, came safely to hand, and I have to offer an apology for suffering it to remain so long unanswered. My heart rejoices to learn, that colonization, notwithstanding the violent opposition from the Anti-slavery party, is still gaining friends and advocates, among the great and talented of the land: that determined spirits, like yourself, leaving the comforts of a quiet and peaceful home, have come up to her aid in this her darkest hour, not only with your time and influence, but with your substance.—When we view such devotion, at this distance, we cannot doubt the motives, which impel a man to make them and we feel encouraged to pray, that God would increase their number.

Were all who called themselves Colonizationists <u>actuated</u> by a right spirit, how different would now be the face of things in Africa.—their earnest desire would have been not only to transport the people of color across the Atlantic, but to have made their home, in their fatherland, an inviting asylum to such of their brethren as were able to pay their own expenses.—and instead of having to seek Emigrants, the difficulty would now be to carry over the numbers anxious to Emigrate.

You have been the principal Agent in effecting a revolution in the management of affairs at home.—let your views cross the Atlantic and may as great a change be effected here, in the agricultural and internal improvements of your colony.

I am not located at Bassa Cove as your letter intimates, but have the honor to serve the Maryland St. Col. Society at Cape Palmas. From its first Settlement, their affairs have been managed in a manner peculiarly their own, and the result

Source: Records of the American Colonization Society, Manuscript Division, Library of Congress.

of their first six years toil, is, that they have a most flourishing and independent colony.—Capt. Waters has visited this colony, and is well qualified to judge of its effect on a stranger, compared with other colonies.

Your remark is a true one, that our destiny is in our own hands to become a great nation, but in my opinion, we can hardly dispense, yet a while, with the fostering hand of the kind parents, who have planted us on this coast. More can be done, by the Colonists than has ever yet been effected, by judicious encouragement, and the promotion of deserving men to office. Everything, however, will depend upon the principal Agent, vested as he is with sovereign power; and in filling this appointment, the patrons at home, ought to know that the Colonists are becoming too enlightened to receive and respect every one, whom the partiality of friends may think qualified.

I should not take the liberty of writing so freely, did I not believe, that you have truly the interest of the Colonies at heart; and I would add further, that my remarks refer entirely to past events, which should never be lost sight of, but rather serve as beacons for our future conduct.

I shall ever feel honored to receive a few lines from you, whenever leisure permits, and will do my best to procure such African Curiosities as are within my reach with pleasure, though my opportunities are but limited, for the present, and we have no colonial craft. My letter is a private one, and I shall feel hurt to see it in print.

Very Respectfully,
Your Obedt. Servant.
Jno. B. Russwurm.

Part F. Home from Home: A Visit to Maine and After

Russwurm, his wife, Sarah McGill Russwurm, and at least one of their children made a brief visit to the United States in August 1848. This was done primarily to provide Russwurm with the opportunity to seek medical treatment by specialists in Baltimore. One of the most striking features of these letters is the revelation of the extent to which Russwurm had become attached to his new African home, his corresponding bemused detachment from the United States, and his eagerness to return his "free home" in Liberia.

We Are Now Ready to Return to Africa: Letter to Dr. James Hall
North Yarmouth, M[ain]e.
August 21, 1848.

Dear Sir:

We arrived here last Saturday afternoon (Aug. 19th) after a tedious ride in the 7 o[']clock train from Boston. We found Mr. Stockbridge at the depot waiting to see us. We are staying at Mrs. Hawes, my old home: all appear glad to see us, not only in the family—but all my old acquaintances. Very unfortunately, her eldest daughter has been, & is still quite unwell: it grieves me much to see the old lady have so much to do in her old age, and living without one of her boys, after having raised so many. They are all away in the Western country: I shall not see my brother Francis Edward, whose health is quite poor—being inclined to consumption.

S. E. R.[20] and myself both long to see Africa again; and having seen our friends in Maine, we are now ready to return to Africa, as soon as we secure a few lines from you, informing us positively of the sailing of the packet.* The weather has been very cold, so that we have slept under 2 and 3 blankets.

I have not seen Mr. Latrobe. I have written to Messrs. Green & Brookhouse to enquire of vessels bound to the coast in October, but hardly expect a favorable answer, as each [shipping] house has despatched a vessel lately. The "N. Rich" bark, was to leave Boston on the day we left Rev. A. Russell as passenger: we wrote by him.

---

* I mean the day she will leave Baltimore for the Coast. I think we shall take passage in her. What about a vessel for your son?

Source: Papers of the Maryland State Colonization Society, Maryland Historical Society, Baltimore.

Sam. Ford[21] & myself are both troubled with diarrhea: which is quite prevalent in this region. So Dr. Burbank informs me. Dr. Burbank attends the family.

We put up at the U. States Hotel, Boston, two days for which they only charged us $19.25—oh the Yankees!

With kind respect to Miss Hall & her brother,[22]

We remain, Dear Sir,

Yours Truly

Jno. B. Russwurm.

P.S. Please also to remember us to J. B. McGill[23] & wife who will be with you by the time this arrives.

Back in Our "Free Home" in Liberia: Letter to John H. B. Latrobe
Russwurm to J. H. B. Latrobe, President, Maryland State Colonization Society.
CAPE PALMAS,

November 22, 1848.

My dear Sir:

You will be glad to hear of my safe arrival in our "free home" in Liberia, after 53 days passage to Monrovia. I arrived here on the 17th, with a heart overflowing with gratitude to that Being, who had shielded me from the dangers of the sea and land—over 10,000 miles. I have not been able to look around much on account of company and business; but I believe Dr. McGill has been assiduous in the discharge of his duty as your Agent.

The colonists and natives all appear glad to see me, and are much pleased with the kind reception I met with from our honorable Board of Managers.

My health continued to amend during the passage, and I am now much better than I was when in Baltimore. Dr. Smith's treatment has been successful, and added 12 or 15 years to my life, from my feelings.

The war is still raging in our territories to the detriment of our native trade in rice and oil; but king Freeman has been notified of my intentions to have peace once more, and has promised his aid to settle the war; he appears to be the only obstacle in the way, as the belligerents are heartily sick of starvation and imprisonment in their towns.

We at last have the bread fruit tree fairly growing in the colony: there is one on the mission lot which has lately borne fruit. The palm oil trade is just beginning, on account of the great quantity of rain which has fallen lately. It cheered

Source: *Maryland Colonization Journal* 4 (January 1849): 297–98.

my very heart to see it coming in and trade again reviving. We may now calculate upon a fair supply of rice at least for the colonists use. Should you send many emigrants, it would be well to calculate accordingly.

Twelve emigrants came to this place by the Packet, and having no provisions on hand, I have purchased a small bill from "N. Rich" barque to amount of $158, besides getting some from the Packet Co., for which I have receipted. It is thought, that if the war is not brought to an end soon, we shall have another hard year for provisions, though every colonist is making a farm, and at present, we have abundance of potatoes, but, little rice from our immediate interior.

I find our newly bought sloop "Curlew," very useful in the purchase of rice and oil, as she can run from this port to Berriby and Monrovia, being amply large.

If you send out 50 or more emigrants in the next Packet, please to order to be put on board, at least 100 barrels corn meal. I send home by this vessel two respectable colonists; each of whom is able to raise an expedition. They are old residents, and their statements can be depended on, being members of the church.

All our jacks are dead but one, and we are sadly in want of more; Dr. Fletcher[24] has no riding animal—your agent [Russwurm] rides his last mule. I enclose the semi-annual accounts up to June 30, 1848, hope they may be approved of.

With a grateful sense of your kind treatment during my visit to the U. States, for which I tender to each member of your Honorable Board my thanks, I remain as ever,

Your devoted Agent,
Jno. B. Russwurm.

The Arrival and Departure of Governor Russwurm: A Contemporary Report

Though unattributed, this report—the fullest there is of Russwurm's visit to the United States—was actually written by Dr. James Hall, general agent of the Maryland Colonization Society and editor of its journal, Maryland Colonization Journal.

The shortest voyage ever made between the Coast of Africa, and a port in the United States, was the return voyage of the Liberia Packet, which arrived off the mouth of the Chesapeake in twenty-six days from Monrovia, thus bringing Cape Palmas as near to Baltimore as Liverpool is to New York. The Packet brought to this country many of the citizens of Liberia, and among

Source: Extract from "Arrival and Departure of the Packet," *Maryland Colonization Journal* 4 (September 1848): 233–35.

others J. B. Russwurm, Esq., Governor of the colony of Maryland in Liberia. Mr. Russwurm was accompanied by Mrs. Russwurm.

Among the doubts attending the infancy of African Colonization, was the capacity of the colonists to fill the offices of Government; and although this was gradually removed, as experience showed that whenever called upon to exercise the duties of official station, the result was most honorable to themselves, and useful to the community, yet year after year passed before there was sufficient confidence entertained, to place a colored man at the head of affairs.

These doubts, however, had less weight with the Board of Managers of the [Maryland] State [Colonization] Society, than was given to them elsewhere; and in the fourth year of the colony at Cape Palmas, Mr. Holmes, the second and last white man, to have control within its limits, was recalled, and Mr. Russwurm was appointed agent of the society, and Governor of Maryland in Liberia. This was in June 1836. Since then he has more than met all the expectations of the Board of Managers. In times of difficulty, upon occasions of the most delicate emergency, in relations complicated and threatening, in the midst of savage tribes of overwhelming numbers, with discontents among the colonists, Governor Russwurm, has ever been found equal to the occasion, and by his coolness, intelligence, and judgment, has carried the colony safely through all the crises that perilled the earliest years of its existence. Of excellent education, having taken a high honor in a northern college, he has, in addition, filled the post of Governor, as an accomplished gentleman, honoring the office quite as much as the office honored him.

All the colonies on the Coast of Africa are now under the charge of coloured men: but it must not be forgotten that it was the State Society which set the example, in the appointment of Governor Russwurm, which was at a later day followed by the American Colonization Society.

The desire of Governor Russwurm to meet his friends at the north, and the early return of the Packet to Africa, prevented the board from seeing as much of him as they desired. But brief as was the opportunity, it was most gratifying to them to meet one to whom they had been so largely indebted in discharging the responsibility which has rested upon them.

As a mark of respect to Governor Russwurrn, the Board invited him to dine with them at the Exchange Hotel, where Mr. Dorsey did full justice to his high reputation as a host in the admirable repast provided on the occasion. The Board attended in force, the president of the society [John H. B. Latrobe] in the chair, and colonization lost none of its interest in the agreeable intercourse to which it thus gave rise. Toasts and sentiments and brief remarks were made by every one present. All were called upon and all responded. It would much exceed our limits to record every thing that was said, though we would be glad to have it in our power to do so. The only speech that we have room for is that of Governor Russwurm, who when his health was drunk, on the removal of the cloth, rose and said, "Mr. President and gentlemen— unaccustomed to public speaking and not anticipating the honor that has been done me, I find it difficult to express the feelings which your kindness has inspired. But I can most truly say, that I shall carry back to my home in Africa double motives from this day forth, to do my best to merit the confidence that has been reposed in me. Gentlemen I thank you."

To use the common phrase on these occasions, which is here strictly true, every thing went off admirably well.

The Packet sailed on the 6th inst. [September], with some fifty emigrants on board, and the following cabin passengers, viz: Governor Russwurm, James B. McGill, Esq., and Lady, the Hon. Samuel Benedict, the Rev. B. R. Wilson and James S. Payne, of the Methodist Episcopal Mission and Dr. James S. Smith, now one of the Colonial Physicians. The Packet cleared the port in gallant style and went to sea on the morning of the 8th. . . .

Russwurm in Baltimore: A Reminiscence by John H. B. Latrobe

The members of the Board of Managers took advantage of Governor Russwurm's presence in Baltimore to make his personal acquaintance. They gave him a dinner at the principal hotel in the city, at which there were no absentees; and there was not one present who was not impressed by the grave, courteous and dignified bearing of the agent whose wise and prudent conduct of the Society's affairs in Africa had given such satisfaction. . . .

One, with difficulty recalls, now-a-days, the sensation that the idea of this dinner to a colored man in 184[8], produced in Baltimore. It was ludicrous to see the astonishment of the Irish waiters, who surrounded the table at "Page's Hotel," when they were called upon to render the same service to a colored man that they were in the habit of rendering to the many socially prominent citizens who were his hosts.[25]

Source: John H. B. Latrobe, *Maryland in Liberia: A History of the Colony planted by the Maryland State Colonization Society under the Auspices of the State of Maryland, U.S. at Cape Palmas on the South-West Coast of Africa, 1833–1853* (Baltimore: Maryland Historical Society, 1885), p. 72.

Part G. "None in Your Employ Eat the Bread of Idleness in Africa": A Governor's Dispatches

As governor of Maryland in Africa, Russwurm submitted detailed semiannual reports outlining developments within and prospects for the colony. As the extracts from the following representative examples reveal, the reports (accompanied, generally, by detailed annexes) cover the most mundane to the most consequential questions and issues. They also indicate the challenges and setbacks as well as the progress being made. In many respects, these reports also act as barometers of Russwurm's moods at the time of writing, expressing not only his thoughts but also his feelings. The reports were addressed to Latrobe, President, M.S.C.S.

Dispatch from Harper, Cape Palmas, ca. December 1838

Dear Sir:

I had the honor of addressing you on August 20th, ult., via Monrovia; and, as there has been no opportunity of forwarding from thence, you will probably receive these lines as early, though the vessel does not proceed directly home. Then affairs appeared rather gloomy, for the reasons therein set forth; and I felt it as much duty to inform you of the dark, as I now do to give you a detail of better times and prospects.

Columbia's Emigrants.—The emigrants by this vessel have been highly favored by the fever. Not an individual has been sick enough to be considered really dangerous—consequently, we have had only two deaths, of children, since their arrival. They have had so little sickness, that I have hired a nurse only about four weeks. It is pleasant to visit them, as I was received with smiles. I have not to listen to petty grievances which I am unable to remedy. By request of Rev. J. L. Wilson, they are located on 'Bayard's Island,' in Hoffman's river. Bayard's Island contains, perhaps, 40 acres of good land. I am not much in favor of the location, but my instructions were imperative.

Farms.—The farms are now looking finely, and I speak within bounds when I assert that there is more than twice the quantity of land under cultivation this season than the last. A little pinching, scolding and petting, and driving operations on the public farm, have convinced those who had the least spark of industry that they need not starve unless they chose. A new species of potatoes has been introduced from the public farm. The seed came from Monrovia, and all are delighted with its size and productiveness.—The introduction of night guards has prevented the farms from being plundered by the natives.

Source: *African Repository and Colonial Journal* 15 (June 1839): 182–83.

The want of working cattle cramps all farming to any extent; and I feel it duty to place this subject constantly before the board. I have purchased one yoke for the Tubmans, and should have supplied them with five more, but they are not to be easily procured. A native counts his cattle as his money, to purchase wives; and nothing but dire necessity ever drives him to part with them. They know, also, that they can get better prices from vessels.

Public Farm.—Has been prosecuted with considerable energy during the past season; but, owing to its being a very unfavorable one, not much has been raised, except cassadas and potatoes. Pains were taken to have on the ground a quantity of manure, and the spot where the cotton seed was put in was well covered over. It was ploughed thrice, as it was my determination to give the seed a fair trial, but this second experiment has proved no better than the first; and if cotton is to be raised for export, it must be from the African seed, which thrives finely. The plant grows well; but when it begins to bear, there is a small insect which plays havoc among its pods, before they are fairly ready to be picked. I calculate that 200 pounds have been raised this season.—The experiment, so far as it has been tried by the colonists, proves that land should be well broken up and manured, as there was a striking difference in the several patches, and where most labor was expended in preparing the ground, there the plant was most thriving. Our cotton on the public farm was planted May 5, 1838.

Though in the rainy season, we suffered much for want of rains, as there were ten or twelve weeks in which we had none. Even the cattle suffered for want of grass, and those at work had to be fed on corn or cassadas. Notwithstanding, our corn had quite a tolerable look; but when it was harvested, the injury which it had sustained from the drought was evident, from the small quantity gathered. I planted about one acre, to show the colonists, who are daily complaining, that they could raise corn, if they would only put forth the requisite quantum of sinews. All cavilling on this head is nearly silenced, as corn has been harvested two seasons. Our leeward natives raise it so extensively as to load vessels.

Our oxen have done exceedingly well; and without them I could not get along. Besides doing all the necessary farm work, they have hauled country boards, &c., for various individuals. The pair which were first broken are still at work, and have increased in size and value.

Assistant Agent's House.—Agreeably to instructions, a comfortable house has been erected on Mount Tubman, for the permanent residence of the assistant agent, who, is now stationed there. The Tubmans and others in the vicinity are well pleased with the place, and fancy already they feel a security which they did not before. Thirty acres near will be placed under his superintendence, to test the difference between it and land exposed, as the agency farm is, to the deleterious influence of the salt air. The present missionaries at Mount Vaughan are pleased with having so good a neighbor.

The mount is being converted into a fortification, by throwing up a stockade, and digging a trench, six feet wide, around it. In it will be kept the cannon and ammunition, and it will always serve as a place of refuge for women and children in case of war or invasion. True, we fear no war or regular invasion, but we cannot tell how soon another colonist may be foolish enough to act as Parker did, or the party assaulted to take the law into his own hands.[26] On the reserve land, I have erected a comfortable dwelling for a family of respectable emigrants, during their six months' seasoning.

Free School, No. 1.—This school still continues in successful operation. The sickness and death of the teacher, O. U. Chambers, has been somewhat of a pull back to it, but I can perceive no sensible diminution in its numbers. On my late visit, forty-nine were present—average, forty-two. Not much can be said in favor of their progress, as we want a more competent teacher. As our population extends out in the bush, we shall soon be under the necessity of having another school, somewhere in the vicinity of Mount Tubman. The people there, in a praiseworthy manner, have subscribed liberally in labor towards putting up a school house. One has given a site. It is but reasonable that they should look to the society [Maryland State Colonization Society] for a teacher after it is finished. We want a fresh supply of Webster's Spelling Books, and cards of A B C. Would it not be well to give some name to Free School No. 1.?

The materials for the Ladies' School House are all ready, and I am only waiting the movements of our *only* mason, who has been engaged for the last three months at Mount Vaughan. We suffer but little inconvenience, as the house now occupied by Mr. Alleyne for his school belongs to the society. I am really pleased to have another school in operation, as the Methodist mission have discontinued theirs; and the desire to acquire knowledge is pretty general, its loss being felt sensibly by nearly all who aspire to public office. We have to raise up a class of young men for officers, as we cannot expect to find any among the emigrants duly qualified. In my opinion, the Ladies' Society, by furnishing us with a competent teacher, is conferring a blessing on this colony which will extend to our remotest posterity.

Dispatch from Harper, Cape Palmas, December 8, 1839

Dear Sir,—

I acknowledge the receipt of your last despatches, per Saluda, dated July 17th, 1839. They remained several weeks at Monrovia, for want of conveyance. All your colonists and agent, felt pleased to learn that your society was building a vessel, as packet from Baltimore to Cape Palmas.

Rice.—You will rejoice that there has been an abundant harvest of rice this season; and in consequence of our line of coast being well guarded, by British cruisers, we have had no opposition from slavers in purchasing. There has been an ample supply for the missionaries and your store, and I am now under the necessity of discontinuing to purchase any more from want of room. The natives say this is the greatest harvest known since the settlement of the colony.

Farms.—Most of the colonists have their grounds planted with potatoes and cassadas, enough for their own consumption, and a few have a goodly number of plantains and bananas under culture, but nothing to the extent that they ought. They seem incredulous about their productiveness, though they can test the question themselves. Since the offer of two premiums of $30, and $20, for the best farms on January 1st, 1840, there have been considerable efforts put forth to obtain them; and I am of the opinion, that the introduction of cotton might be greatly promoted by offering a premium also for the first hundred pounds raised by a colonist. It is almost repetition to say, that not much ought to be expected in farming till the colonists have some kind of working teams, and no sensible man can doubt, but their introduction would have a beneficial effect, and call into action many feelings which are now suffered to lie dormant. By looking at the agency farm, they see what can be done as an experiment; and certainly, they would be prepared even to surpass that, from certain data, which a longer residence and experience would give them. At present, on the agency farm, we have plenty of water-melons, canteleupes, ocra, tomatoes, egg-plants, peas, beans, pea-nuts, corn, and other garden vegetables growing, besides potatoes, cassada and plantains. The corn now growing is the second crop, and was planted in September, merely as an experiment; some of it is very fine, as the season has been an uncommon one. But the proper season for corn is when the natives plant their rice—last of March or April. The natives tell our people so, but so much wiser are they, that generally 60 or 70 days over the time elapse, before they put in their corn, and if it turns out poorly, the climate and soil are to blame.

Source: *African Repository and Colonial Journal* 16 (June 1840): 171–73.

I am sorry to say that the sugar cane at Mount Tubman is looking rather poorly. Some look passable, but nothing like the West India cane. Some of our colonists say the land is too low; I shall, therefore, experiment again in February next on different soil. Mr. Pinney, on his late visit here, said we would be sure to have good cane another year. A piece of ground has been found within sight of Mount Tubman, which the Tubman people say must produce good cotton, and as I consider them experienced in cotton, and the land is not exposed to the blighting salt air, north or south-west wind, I shall not fail to put it under cultivation. On Bayard's Island one of their people has raised quite a pretty lot, and though the quantity is small, the staple is pronounced by all to be fine. It cannot be amiss to say here, that we stand in need of light cart wheels with oaken hubs, as all we have had previously with hubs of gum, gave out without doing half service. The store is bare of farming utensils.

Supplies for the Store.—I believe I have already stated to the board that the supplies for your store, of salt beef, pork and fish are far from being equal to the demand. I wish the store to be supplied, so that the colonists may be able to purchase such articles there, and particularly those who are employed most of their time by the agent. The missionaries furnish their workmen, in some measure, with such, and I really feel hurt when unable to do as much. There could be no loss on such shipments, as they would pay equally as well as dry goods, and at the same time afford the colonists no pretext to mourn after the good things at home. My assortment of dry goods, with the reasonable supply purchased from English vessels, has been good during the past year. One article, however, I have been unable to procure, i. e. iron, I have therefore to beg you will include it in your next assortment of goods by the spring expedition. It is a first rate article of trade, besides being indispensible in a new country. I should prefer more of checks and American romauls to so much white and unbleached cottons. We need a new pair of light balances weighing 500 pounds.

Court of Monthly Sessions.—The proceedings of this court has been quite regular, during the year about to close. I should judge it to be popular, as all its decrees and judgments have been carried into effect without the least difficulty, all submit to it. Three cases of grand larceny have occurred lately, which were quite provoking. In the first, a fine cow was taken from the mission premises at Mount Vaughan, and killed, and the thieves escaped detection; in the second, a bullock was carried off from the agency farm and killed; but the thieves were not so fortunate in this case, as they are now undergoing their sentence in hard labor on the farm. This increase of crime shows, that there is some defect in the present mode of punishment. I am of the opinion, that the laws are too lenient, and that a more rigorous mode of imprisonment and employment must be adopted.

To carry this into effect it is important, that a new stone prison be erected during 1840—that it be divided into male and female wards, and that a regular jailor be employed. Our present jail is merely a log house about ten feet square, incapable of holding more than four prisoners at a time.

And while on this subject, let me inform you of the want of a court-house. It is what we cannot do without, if we wish to see justice administered with due formality; and I have been thinking that you had better appropriate a specific sum towards the erection of a stone one. I have selected an elevated site near the Presbyterian church, and as opportunity offers, shall collect the rock.

Steam Mill Site.—Under the impression that the mill will be put out this fall, I have been much put to it, to fix upon an eligible site for its location—and the reason is, the scarcity of timber in the immediate vicinity of the cape. It appears that nearly all the land within our first purchase, has been occupied by the natives for farms; and wherever this is the case, all the large trees are either cut down, or left standing to be killed by the burning of the smaller bush. Though there is but little timber up Hoffman's river, the advantages of having the mill near some running stream are too great to be lost sight of. Perhaps our neighbors from Rocktown, Grahway and Cavally may be induced to bring logs for sale for a fair compensation. Its ultimate destination must be on Cavally river, but I am dubious of the propriety of putting it there at present, until we have a settlement at Denah, or its mouth. I shall endeavor to see Baphro before its final location, to learn, if possible, if his majesty has any idea of the great advantages it would be to his town to have it erected near him.

Oberon's Emigrants.—Are all placed on their farms in comfortable houses, and if they cannot make a living, it must arise from sheer idleness. I hope the society will not lose sight of what has already been submitted to them, respecting the number of women and children without protectors, who are thus cast on their hands in a new country. They are hard subjects to deal with.

Cape Palmas People.—You must be pleased to hear that the best understanding exists between us and the Cape Palmas natives. For several months past, we have not even had a thief palaver to talk, until very lately, when king Freeman came forward and stood as security for three young lads who had robbed two American farms. The Cape Palmas people appear more industrious than we have ever known them; and instead of the daily palavers to which we have been accustomed, at this season of the year, we have nothing but peace and goodwill to cheer us on our way. It is true, the past season has been one of great plenty, and the care which consequently devolved on them to secure their crops, has occupied much of their attention. We cannot but indulge the hope, that they are falling in imperceptibly with civilized habits; as there are many symptoms which would indicate such a state, the most interesting of which, is a desire on the part of the king to do away with the abominable saswood palaver system,[27] and a more general inclination to recognize the private rights of individuals. The work of accomplishing the first, must be gradual, as the system finds strenuous advocates among all the young members of the tribe. The beneficial effects of the latter, are already visible in the increased number of canoes lining the beach undisturbed, and more vigorous efforts at fishing.

I am of the opinion that king Freeman, Yellow Will, and a few others of the leading men, have found out that honesty is the best policy in their dealings with us, and if matters depended solely on them, we should be troubled but little with palavers of any kind.

Education.—The colonial free school number one has been well attended during most of the year, as you will perceive by reference to paper marked E. At my request, after Mr. Alleyne's death, Mr. Wilson was kind enough to admit ten of the most promising boys and girls into the mission school; but so careless are the parents of this privilege, that but few have improved it by sending their children regularly. All the colonists deplore the want of education, and a few are willing to make every exertion to send their children to school, but the majority think it all sufficient, if they can stammer through a book, and scratch their names on paper. I am much in want of a good teacher for this school, as it is the only one, at present, supported by the society. Located in the country, at the intersection of three roads, it will always have plenty of scholars, if a well qualified teacher has charge. Several colonists children are attending the Mount Vaughan mission school.

Health of the Colonists.—The general health through the year must be considered as good; and I shall not enter into details, as I expect Dr. McGill will communicate with the Board by this opportunity. Dr. McDowell left here for Monrovia, December 27th, 1839 [*sic*].[28]

New Territorial Map and Plot of Harper—Have been drawn by Mr. Revey, at my request, for the use of the board. From the map you will be able to form a pretty good idea of your territory in Africa. Mr. Revey has taken considerable pains to have correct soundings of our harbor, by going over the ground himself; the want of which nearly occasioned the loss of a Hamburgh brig which struck on a sunken rock off the cape, while entering the harbor about 14 months ago.

Dispatch from Cape Palmas, December 30, 1845

Dear Sir:

My last letter of October 25, 1845, informed the Board of Managers, that I had dispatched an exploring party, consisting of Messrs. Banks, Stewart and McIntosh, to the Pah country, preparatory to an opening of the trade between that interesting people and the colony. You will be pleased to hear of their safe return, in good health, and well pleased with the country and people. Accompanying, I send you Messrs. Banks and Stewart's journals, with a chart of their route: from them you will perceive that our prospects are fair for an increase of interior trade another year. Under this head I beg leave to call your attention to the "List of arrivals" and "imports and exports" in 1845.

Since the above was penned, I learn from King Neh of Denah, personally, that a party of Pahs, in attempting to visit the colony, have had their path obstructed by the Katubohs, and have been driven back. They have returned to their country, and will doubtless attempt the same route our party went and came. Katuboh was the route marked out by Poluh their guide; but events and other advices, after ascending the river, led them fortunately to choose the path through the Eriboh country, where they were treated with great courtesy, and an old road was opened anew for them, for upwards of 20 miles. The intervening tribes can never keep the Pahs from the colony, now "our ships," as they term their visitors, have anchored in their waters. They now trade with Tabou, Bassa and Grand Berreby; and it is said, they will find their way wherever there is money to be made.

Ladies' School.—Mr. Gross has met with so little success in teaching, that I have concluded to close his school, and appropriate the house to the use of the girls' school under Mrs. Margaret Harman. It will gratify you to learn that the two schools supported by the Board are doing finely, as well as the school under the patronage of the Methodist E[piscopal] Mission. The Protestant E[piscopal] Mission have lately opened one for colonists, under the care of Mr. and Mrs. Appleby, under favorable auspices; and God grant that no palavers or other untoward events, may induce them to close it after a few months as heretofore. I shall draw on you next month for $125, in favor of Philip Gross on account of his salary. Under this head I can say that the colonists are gradually improving in education and mechanics. The Rev. Mr. Herring, with his usual good sense, has established a Debating and a Female Benevolent Society. The Debating Society meets semi-monthly, and lectures have been delivered before it by Messrs. Her-

Source: *Maryland Colonization Journal* 3 (April 1846): 146–49.

ring, McGill and Jones. The "go ahead" principle is evidently at work, and I scout at all who are willing to "rest on their oars," because of past labors or honors, and suffer their families to be raised in ignorance, contenting themselves with few of the conveniences of life, because they have always done without them. These remarks apply to many in our Colony, but they are shy of expressing themselves before me, for whether he be teacher of religion, civil or military officer, I denounce him and all such, as the great stumbling blocks in the pathway of the young and rising generation.

Though a party interested, still I avow it publicly, that the greatest stimulus ever presented to the man of color in the United States, has been the promotion of men of his race to offices of great trust and responsibility, even in Africa, by your Society, which deserves all the credit of this experiment. May she follow out her liberal principles as long as she exists; and may those in her employ remember with gratitude that she adopted her course when prejudices were rife, and many of those who termed themselves the friends of the colored man, thought it a dangerous one. But "*laus Deo*," the "Rubicon" has been crossed and the battle won, and may we not hope, that in another century, if not before, Africa will give birth to a second Tertullian, Origen and Hannibal.

Agriculture.—I can safely write, that we have planted more this season than ever—from necessity—as I determined months ago to purchase nothing of a perishable nature from those colonists who are out of debt—even for currency—for as long as I continued to do so and pay their high prices, I found perhaps 15 or more who scorned to take a hoe in hand, because they could make enough to live on by cutting plank and scantling. This threw much currency into circulation, and the bad result was it could always be bought at 50 per cent. discount. This will not be in 1846, if I can prevent it. The opening of the camwood trade, and the fair prices paid for goods, strengthened my hands, and enabled me to be more independent—here was a market which had been shut from the first, suddenly thrown open, and all who had means availed themselves of it. Prices, at which the colonists had grumbled, were given by the tradesmen without a murmur. Old debts up to 1845, can still be paid in plank at old rates—but no more shall be expended for what is not wanted for immediate use. There was much murmuring at first, but I have been able to keep my determination, with the prospects above in view.

Cotton planting on a limited scale is pretty general, since premiums have been offered for cotton and home made cloth. I have perhaps two acres planted at the farm, and around Mt. Tubman hill, doing finely—"*Nil desperandum.*" Cotton and home made cloth, we are to make in 1846, so says your agent and most of our leading colonists; but we cannot accomplish this without *cards and spinning wheels—cards and spinning wheels.*

Under this head of improvements, there has been manufactured during the past year, with the aid of Mr. Herring and his turning lathe, cart and carriage wheels, missionary carriages, fine and common chairs, and settees, bedsteads of all kinds; one loom complete, one spinning wheel, by A. Hance, for his family, coarse sewing cotton, socks and stockings, soap enough for home supply, leather now tanning in vats, by S. Smith, a corn mill, so much improved as to make fine corn meal, used daily in my family.

As Dr. Hall blamed me for ordering the light-house apparatus from Baltimore, and thus give publicity to its erection, I have to beg the Board to send out by the first vessel from New York or Boston, an iron turning lathe with tools complete, for the use of those colonists who have been taught turning by Mr. Herring, and who will be left without any on his departure. Mr. Herring's cost eighty dollars in Baltimore I believe. To encourage those who have been with Mr. Herring, my promise has been given that I would purchase one if they would learn: and the Governor's promise to colonist or native, is *sacred*. I can pay for it on arrival in oil, camwood, or bills. This goes by Capt. Lawlin home; why cannot the lathe come out in his vessel by an early application on his return? I will apply to him and he cannot refuse, knowing the benevolent object of the Board in sending it out. Do let some practical turner select the article—perhaps one that had been used but little, would answer equally as well and be cheaper. Let the article only be good and not out of repair.

New Trade Vessel.—We are delighted with the information that a company has been formed and incorporated by the liberal Legislature of Maryland, for the object of trading and carrying out passengers and freight to and from Africa. Colored men have the privilege of being stockholders, and finally may become managers of the whole concern. We see no reason the concern should not do well, as the other vessels sent to this coast, under less favorable circumstances, make money; and why not this particular one with so many interested in her welfare on the spot. Let us hope she will prove another good ship Argo, and return home, laden with the oil, camwood, ivory and gold-dust of this coast; something more substantial than the fabled "Golden fleece" of old. May a kind Providence grant to those engaged in this enterprise length of days to witness its complete working. For they can proudly exclaim, "we have taken the poor man of color, downcast and oppressed as he is in the United States—carried him to Africa—nursed and encouraged him to exertion; and now behold him, the *navigator, man of business, and professional man*."

New Home Jail.—Your attention has hitherto been drawn to the bright side of the picture let us view the dark. It. pains me to inform you, that we have frequent cases of petty crimes. We now have confined in jail for stealing and resisting the civil authority, four colonists; three are brothers—we have three more waiting trial next month, under charge of robbing the agency store. We have only one native under charge of stealing. Petty thefts are frequent, and though the natives do their part, certain colonists are not much behind; but they are old hands at the business, and have hitherto managed to keep clear of the "talons of the law." These provoking events indicate that our present jail system is too lenient; that confinement at night in a log house on the farm, and labor there during the day, they can see and converse with their relatives and friends, is looked upon as a slight punishment.

To break up this no-jail system, I have determined upon building a stone jail, about a mile further in the country. The prisoners have been engaged for several weeks in clearing the site and quarrying rock, which abounds on the spot. The stone jail will answer a double purpose in time of palaver with the natives, as it can then be easily turned into a fort, being nearly central for about 100 colonists, who could be called there in 30 minutes. Under such circumstances, I could not hesitate one minute. I intend to build it out of funds raised in the colony at an early date as possible. We want more stone masons, and are hard put to it to procure lime in large quantities.

Court of Quarterly Sessions.—For the year just closing, the experiment of having our courts *quarterly* instead of *monthly*, has been crowned with complete success, much to the satisfaction of the colonists. I think the time has arrived, when your agent can with propriety and safety be exempted from presiding as chief justice. There are, I am proud to say, some individuals in our colony who can fill that office with credit to themselves and the Society, and I would therefore earnestly beg the Board to release me, and appoint such as judges, with a small salary to be defrayed out of the Colonial Treasury, more especially the chief judge (if not already in the Society's employ) who must devote much time to preparation. The names of prominent individuals are, Dr. McGill, A. L. Jones, W. A. Prout, Thomas Jackson, and H. Hannon. Six years ago the Board were informed of my want of law books—none came and I had to expend my own funds to purchase such as I could not get along without. Our want is still unsupplied, and should the above views meet your approbation, I hope some will be sent out for the use of the newly-appointed judges. I forgot to say, as an additional reason, that the duties which now devolve on your agent are two-fold what they were two years ago, from the increase of the palm oil and opening of the camwood trade. I make all bargains personally when money is put out on trust, in my office; which I often enter between 6 and 7 A. M., and remain all day, with hardly an intermission of two or three hours for breakfast. None in your employ eat the bread of idleness in Africa. I pledge my words.

Visit to Tabou River and Bassa.—After seeing my emigrants comfortably placed in their quarters, I contemplate making a tramp on the beach as far as Tabou and Bassa, stopping some days at each, and sounding the headmen as to their inclination to annex their territories to our colony; for I am afraid they cannot stand much longer as they now do. English and French men-of-war abound on the coast, and the goodly heritage of these tribes cannot long escape their notice: it is high time, therefore, to be up and doing, before they trouble the palaver. The mania for acquiring territory in Africa is quite the siege; and every point of note, to the windward and leeward of us, favorable for trade, has been seized upon, and books, dashes and flags, given to the poor untutored natives. We want Tabou, Bassa, Little and Grand Berreby to the leeward, and Garroway and Grand Sess to the windward—but here our pathway is blocked up by the French, who claim Garroway and half the coast of Africa. Lately I have been informed, by English Captains, that the French have asserted claims to Cape Lahou, on account of some palavers with the natives, for taking possession of the goods of a vessel which was cast away on their coast.

In reviewing the events of the past year, we have abundant cause to praise our Heavenly Father, that our course has been still onward in the acquisition of the arts and sciences of civilized life. With war raging in our territory, we have been permitted to live in peace, and to pass through contending parties and no harm befall us. His arm has been around us when the forked lightening played around our bed at midnight, and rent asunder the workmanship of man's hands within two feet of our head, and when the lofty monarchs of the forest have fallen on our right and left.

Notes

The following are abbreviations used in the notes:

MSCSP   Papers of the Maryland State Colonization Society, Maryland Historical Society, Baltimore.

RACS   Records of the American Colonization Society, Manuscript Division, Library of Congress, Washington, DC.

Russwurm Collection   John Brown Russwurm Collection, George J. Mitchell Department of Special Collections & Archives, Bowdoin College Library, Brunswick, ME.

Sumner Russwurm Papers   John Sumner Russwurm Papers, Manuscript Section, Tennessee State Library and Archives, Nashville.

PREFACE AND ACKNOWLEDGMENTS

1. Winston James, *Holding Aloft the Banner of Ethiopia: Caribbean Radicalism in Early Twentieth-Century America* (London and New York: Verso, 1998); the paper was presented as a keynote address at an international conference at the University of Paris (Sorbonne) in October, 2000. An abbreviation of a longer, written version was published as "The Wings of Ethiopia: The Caribbean Diaspora and Pan-African Projects—From John Brown Russwurm to George Padmore," in Geneviève Fabre and Klaus Benesch, eds., *African Diasporas in the New and Old Worlds: Consciousness and Imagination* (Amsterdam and New York: Rodopi, 2004), pp. 133–172.

PART ONE

PROLOGUE

1. Imanuel Geiss, *The Pan-African Movement,* trans. Ann Keep (London: Methuen, 1974); Oruno Lara, *La naissance du Panafricanisme: Les racines caraïbes, américaines et africaines du mouvement au XIXe siècle* (Paris: Maisonneuve and Larose, 2000).

2. P. Olisanwuche Esedebe, *Pan-Africanism: The Idea and Movement, 1776–1963* (Washington, DC: Howard University Press, 1982), p. 15.

3. George Padmore, *Pan-Africanism or Communism? The Coming Struggle for Africa* (London: Dennis Dobson, 1956), p. 47.

4. Edward Wilmot Blyden (1832–1912) revisited his native St. Thomas (Virgin Islands) only once (in 1862) and then only on a recruiting trip to win emigrants to his new home, Liberia. Hollis Lynch, *Edward Wilmot Blyden: Pan-Negro Patriot, 1832–1912* (London: Oxford University Press, 1967), p. 33.

5. Mary Sagarin, *John Brown Russwurm: The Story of "Freedom's Journal," Freedom's Journey* (New York: Lothrop, Lee and Shepard, 1970), is the closest there is to a biography of Russwurm. But though generally well researched, it is a short book written mainly for a juvenile audience,

without the usual scholarly apparatus. Janice Borzendowski's *John Russwurm: Publisher* (New York: Chelsea House, 1989), published in the Black Americans of Achievement series, carries some useful illustrations but is even more explicitly geared to children. For good overviews of Russwurm's life, see Clarence Contee, "John Brown Russwurm," in *Dictionary of American Negro Biography,* ed. Rayford Logan and Michael Winston (New York: Norton, 1982), pp. 538–39, and Penelope Campbell, "John Brown Russwurm," American National Biography Online, February 2000, www.anb.org/articles/04/0400877.html. There are, however, two recent and noteworthy contributions: Amos J. Beyan, *African American Settlements in West Africa: John Brown Russwurm and the American Civilizing Efforts* (New York: Palgrave Macmillan, 2005), which is, unfortunately, seriously flawed, and especially Jacqueline Bacon, *Freedom's Journal: The First African-American Newspaper* (Lanham, MD: Lexington Books, 2007), which, as its title suggests, is concerned with Russwurm's time as editor of *Freedom's Journal.* For an earlier attempt to locate Russwurm within the wider Caribbean and Pan-Africanist traditions, see Winston James, "The Wings of Ethiopia: The Caribbean Diaspora and Pan-African Projects From John Brown Russwurm to George Padmore," in *African Diasporas in the New and Old Worlds: Consciousness and Imagination,* ed. Geneviève Fabre and Klaus Benesch (Amsterdam: Rodopi, 2004), pp. 133–72.

1. FROM BOY TO MAN

1. "Monument to Governor Russwurm," *Maryland Colonization Journal,* n.s., 6 (March 1853): 350; Nehemiah Cleaveland and Alphaeus S. Packard, *History of Bowdoin College* (Boston: James R. Osgood, 1882), p. 352; J. T. Hull, "John Russwurm—His Son John B. Russwurm," paper presented at the proceedings of the Maine Genealogical Society, n. d. (ca. late nineteenth century), clipping, Russwurm Collection, box 1, folder 5; "An African Governor from the State of Maine," *Portland Transcript,* September 16, 1848.

2. See Sandra Sandiford Young, "John Brown Russwurm's Dilemma: Citizenship or Emigration?" in *Prophets of Protest: Reconsidering the History of American Abolitionism,* ed. Timothy Patrick McCarthy and John Stauffer (New York: New Press, 2006), p. 92, where the housekeeper status has been attributed.

3. The guide to the Sumner Russwurm Papers describes John Brown Russwurm's mother as a "Jamaican Negro," which can mean anything, given the American "one-drop rule," from near white to black in complexion. Richard L. Hall, *On Afric's Shore: A History of Maryland in Liberia, 1834–1857* (Baltimore: Maryland Historical Society, 2003), p. 137.

4. Janice Borzendowski, *John Russwurm: Publisher* (New York: Chelsea House, 1989), p. 17. More authoritatively, an 1848 profile in the *Portland Transcript,* unattributed but evidently written by someone who had attended Bowdoin "a few years after Mr. Russwurm graduated" and who knew his associates and probably relatives, reported: "The mother died when the boy was quite young" ("African Governor").

5. Edward Long, *The History of Jamaica,* 3 vols. (1774; repr., London: Frank Cass, 1970), vol. 2, p. 332. For two valuable studies of this group in Jamaican slave and postslave society, see Gad Heuman, *Between Black and White: Race, Politics and the Free Coloreds in Jamaica, 1792–1865* (Oxford: Clio Press, 1981), and Mavis Campbell, *The Dynamics of Change in a Slave Society: A Socio-Political History of the Free Coloureds of Jamaica, 1800–1865* (London: Associated Universities Press, 1976). For a good overview of the position within the Americas as a whole, see D. Cohen and J. Greene, eds., *Neither Slave nor Free: The Freedmen of African Descent in the Slave Societies of the New World* (Baltimore: Johns Hopkins University Press, 1972).

6. Mary Sagarin asserts that in 1810 he owned some fifty-four slaves with a business partner (a claim repeated by Elizabeth Chittenden), but Sandra Young adduces evidence to suggest that he was more accurately an agent and factor rather than a plantation owner. Mary Sagarin, *John Brown Russwurm: The Story of "Freedom's Journal," Freedom's Journey* (New York: Lothrop, Lee

and Shepard, 1970), p. 14; Elizabeth F. Chittenden, "John Brown Russwurm, 1799–1851: Bowdoin's First Black Graduate," *Down East Magazine*, June 1972, p. 62; Sandra Sandiford Young, "A Different Journey: John Brown Russwurm, 1799–1851" (PhD diss., Boston College, 2004), pp. 5–9. The stepdaughter of Russwurm's American wife wrote: "I have heard mother [the former Mrs. Russwurm] say, that, to hold property in the West Indies, Mr. Russwurm had married a colored woman, and a son, John Brown Russwurm, was the issue." Sarah Elizabeth (Hawes) Cutter, "The Hawes Family," *Old Times in North Yarmouth*, 6 (April 1882): 843.

7. The Russwurm family history and family tree are provided in the Sumner Russwurm Papers. (John Brown Russwurm was the cousin of John Sumner Russwurm [1793–1860].) See also the helpful overview provided by Sagarin, *John Brown Russwurm*, pp. 13–21. The repeated claim that the father named the son after himself is undermined, however, by his widow's testimony that the boy was named John Brown after John Russwurm's best friend in Jamaica, a physician. See "Monument to Governor Russwurm," p. 350.

8. Cutter, "Hawes Family," p. 844, repeated by Hull in "John Russwurm."

9. Information on the Russwurm family and its business affairs may be gleaned from the Sumner Russwurm Papers. In 1780, Massachusetts became the first state in the Union to abolish slavery. John Daniels, *In Freedom's Birthplace: A Study of the Boston Negroes* (Boston: Houghton Mifflin, 1914), pp. 8–9. But as modern scholarship has established, abolition in Massachusetts, as in the rest of New England, was by no means immediate; rather, it was attained over a period of twenty years. See especially Joanne Pope Melish, *Disowning Slavery: Gradual Emancipation and "Race" in New England, 1780–1860* (Ithaca: Cornell University Press, 1998), esp. pp. 64–65.

10. Susan Blanchard Russwurm was born in Weymouth, Massachusetts, on December 18, 1788. She married John R. Russwurm (b. 1761) on March 4, 1813. She was twenty-four and he was fifty-two. See Cutter, "Hawes Family," pp. 842–43, for dates of birth and marriage.

11. "Monument to Governor Russwurm," p. 350.

12. The archives are silent about Russwurm's seven years in Quebec. All that we know is that he was fluent in the French he learned there. We do not know the name of the school or anything about his boarding arrangements while there. Did he board with a family, or did he live in dormitories, as boys at elite French and British "public" schools did (and do)? He makes no mention of his time in Canada either in his journalism or in his private correspondence. In fact, we know about his Quebec days only because his close friend, James Hall, mentioned them in his obituary of Russwurm. His consistent antipathy toward the French (at least the government) may have stemmed from unpleasant experiences in Quebec as much as from his hatred of French imperialism in the Caribbean (especially as it related to his beloved Haiti) and West Africa.

13. Quotations from J. T. H[ull], "Russwarm *[sic]* Family," *Portland Daily Press*, February 21, 1878, reprinted in *Old Times in North Yarmouth* 5 (October 1881): 782, and Hull, "John Russwurm."

14. Hull mistakenly claimed in two submissions on the subject that John had accompanied his father when he arrived in Maine in 1812. See Hull, "Russwarm *[sic]* Family," and Hull, "John Russwurm." His widow, who should know, categorically declared that John Russwurm arrived in Portland on his own and later sent for the boy. "Mr. R.," she wrote, "lived several months after John came home." See "Monument to Governor Russwurm," p. 350.

15. John inherited two thousand dollars willed by his father. But Susan Blanchard Russwurm wrote: "We had much difficulty settling the estate, and most of the legacy to him was lost." "Last Will and Testament of John Russwurm late of Port Antonio within the Island of Jamaica but now of Westbrook within the County of Cumberland and the Commonwealth of Massachusetts," LOS 92, Folio 124, File #1239/03, Jamaica National Archives, Spanish Town, Jamaica, quoted in Young, "Different Journey," pp. 28–29; "Monument to Governor Russwurm," p. 350.

16. Russwurm to John Sumner Russwurm, July 19, 1819, and January 9, 1826, both in Sumner Russwurm Papers, box 2, folder 7. Susan Hawes to John Sumner Russwurm, November 10,

1826, Sumner Russwurm Papers, box 1, folder 3. The dispute over the will dragged on for over a decade. Despite the rift between Russwurm and his cousin, over the years both men continued to inquire after each other, though only through third parties.

17. James H. Blanchard to John Sumner Russwurm, June 14, 1850, box 1, folder 1, Sumner Russwurm Papers.

18. Hull, *Portland Daily Press*, February 21, 1878.

19. Francis Edward Russwurm was actually born on July 23, 1814. Like his elder brother, he attended Bowdoin (1830–33), but for unknown reasons he abandoned college before graduating. His big brother wrote to him from Monrovia, Liberia, expressing disquiet at his relinquishing his studies. Russwurm invited Francis to join him in Monrovia, where he could operate as a merchant. Francis, who suffered from ill health, declined the offer and subsequently worked as a teacher in Maine, Mississippi, and last near the Mexican border in Campo, California, where he died in 1862. *General Catalogue of Bowdoin College and the Medical School of Maine, 1794–1912* (Brunswick, ME: Bowdoin College, 1912), pp. 457, 668; Russwurm to Francis Edward Russwurm, March 31, 1834, box 2, folder 6, Sumner Russwurm Papers.

20. "Monument to Governor Russwurm," pp. 350–51, quotation on p. 350.

21. The best overview of the black experience in Canada remains Robin W. Winks, *The Blacks in Canada: A History*, 2nd ed. (Montreal: McGill-Queen's University Press, 1997).

22. His interest in and connection to Jamaica and the Caribbean generally are evident in his later writings in *Freedom's Journal* and his personal correspondence. See especially Russwurm to J. H. B. Latrobe, February 23, 1834, MSCSP, reel 2. Some of his Caribbean references were quite subtle and implicit, such as his delight in seeing breadfruit trees on a trip to Cape Coast, Gold Coast (today's Ghana) in 1848 and his discussion of the acquisition and propagation of the plant. Russwurm to James Hall, May 4, 1848, MSCSP, reel 5.

23. "Monument to Governor Russwurm," p. 350.

24. Ibid., pp. 350–51.

25. "Colonization: Tribute of Respect to the Memory of Governor Russwurm," *Maryland Colonization Journal* 6 (April 1852): 164.

26. Susan Blanchard Russwurm had married William Hawes in North Yarmouth, Maine, on May 4, 1817. Cutter, "Hawes Family," p. 841. Thus Russwurm was in Jamaica some weeks, and more likely months, before May 1817. He left possibly at the end of 1816 but more likely in early 1817.

27. "Monument to Governor Russwurm," pp. 350–51; see Rev. Joseph Stockbridge, U.S. Navy, "The Stockbridge Family," *Old Times in North Yarmouth* 6 (January 1882): 806–9, quotation on pp. 808–9. See also Joseph Stockbridge, "North Yarmouth," *Old Times in North Yarmouth* 5 (January 1881): 608–9; George Thomas Little, ed., *Genealogical and Family History of the State of Maine* (New York: Lewis Historical Publishing, 1909), vol. 2, pp. 885–87.

28. Russwurm to Francis Edward Russwurm, March 31, 1834, Sumner Russwurm Papers, box 2, folder 7.

29. Henry S. Burrage, *History of the Baptists in Maine* (Portland, ME: Marks Printing House, 1904), pp. 162–66, quotation on p. 163.

30. Hebron Academy's records are incomplete for the early years of its formation. But there is no doubt that Russwurm attended the school. In the same letter addressed to his school friend and fellow Hebronite, John Otis, he explained why he had missed the "last quarter" of the school year and described his plans to attend another educational institution, Gorham Academy. See Russwurm to John Otis, June 22, 1819, Russwurm Collection, box 1, folder 1; Harold E. Hall (alumni secretary, Hebron Academy) to Robert M. Cross (editor, *Bowdoin Alumnus*), June 10, 1965, Cross to Hall, June 16, 1965, and Hall to Cross, July 2, 1965, all in Russwurm Collection, box 1, folder 6.

31. Josiah Goold to John S. Russwurm, November 19, 1819, Sumner Russwurm Papers, box 1, folder 3.

32. In 1820, around the time Russwurm left Maine, of the state's almost 300,000 people, less than 1,000 were classified as "Negro" a proportion of 0.3 percent, the lowest of all the New England states and one of the lowest in the nation. In 1910 the proportion dropped to 0.2 percent, less than 1,400 out of a population of over 740,000. U.S. Bureau of the Census, *Negro Population, 1790–1915* (Washington, DC: Government Printing Office, 1918), tables 3, 13, and 5, pp. 45, 49, and 51. It has been suggested that there is "no indication" that Russwurm had "any contact with the blacks of Portland," which numbered just over two hundred at the time. Young, "Different Journey," p. 27. But there is at least indirect evidence that he did. When he started *Freedom's Journal* in March 1827, the first name listed among the paper's "authorized agents" was that of Reuben Ruby, a leading member of the African American community in the town. Ruby would hold this position for over a year. And when he stepped down on April 18, 1828, his position was taken by another distinguished African American, Isaac Talbot, who would serve in this capacity until the paper ceased publication in March 1829. This suggests prior contact with these men and no doubt others of the black community before Russwurm left Maine in 1820. See *Freedom's Journal*, March 16, 1827 to April 18, 1828, and March 28, 1829. For more on these men and their families, see Benjamin Quarles, *Black Abolitionists* (New York: Oxford University Press, 1969), p. 21, and H. H. Price and Gerald E. Talbot, eds., *Maine's Visible Black History: The First Chronicle of Its People* (Gardiner, ME: Tilbury House, 2006), esp. pp. 43–45.

33. "Monument to Governor Russwurm," p. 351.

34. Charles H. Wesley, "The Negro's Struggle for Freedom in Its Birthplace," *Journal of Negro History* 30 (January 1945): 69; Arthur O. White, "The Black Leadership Class and Education in Antebellum Boston," *Journal of Negro Education* 42 (Autumn 1973): 510–11; George A. Levesque, "Before Integration: The Forgotten Years of Jim Crow Education in Boston," *Journal of Negro Education* 48 (Spring 1979): 122.

35. For profiles of Saunders, see Arthur O. White, "Prince Saunders: An Instance of Social Mobility among Antebellum New England Blacks," *Journal of Negro History* 60 (October 1975): 526–35, and Frank Bayard, "Prince Saunders," in *Dictionary of American Negro Biography*, ed. Rayford W. Logan and Michael R. Winston (New York: Norton, 1982), pp. 541–42. Saunders also figures in Earl Leslie Griggs and Clifford H. Prator, eds., *Henry Christophe and Thomas Clarkson: A Correspondence* (Berkeley: University of California Press, 1952), which includes some of his correspondence; and Hubert Cole, *Christophe: King of Haiti* (New York: Viking Press, 1967).

36. See Sheldon H. Harris, *Paul Cuffe: Black America and the African Return* (New York: Simon and Schuster, 1972), and Lamont D. Thomas, *Rise to Be a People: A Biography of Paul Cuffe* (Urbana: University of Illinois Press, 1986).

37. *Boston Centinel* report, repr. in *Weekly Recorder*, July 31, 1816.

38. White, "Prince Saunders," pp. 529–30.

39. Quoted in Cole, *Christophe*, p. 239.

40. Prince Sanders [sic], *Haytian Papers: A Collection of Very Interesting Proclamations and Other Official Documents; Together with Some Account of the Rise, Progress, and Present State of the Kingdom of Hayti* (London: W. Reed, Law, 1816).

41. Cole, *Christophe*, p. 240.

42. Prince Saunders, *Haytian Papers* (Boston: Caleb Bingham, 1818).

43. Prince Saunders, *A Memoir Presented to the American Convention for Promoting the Abolition of Slavery, and Improving the Condition of the African Race, December 11th 1818* (Philadelphia: Dennis Heartt, 1818), repr. in Dorothy Porter, ed., *Early Negro Writing, 1860–1837* (Baltimore: Black Classic Press, 1995), pp. 269–80.

44. Saunders, *Memoir*, p. 272.

45. Saunders to Thomas Clarkson, July 14, 1821, in Griggs and Prator, *Henry Christophe*, pp. 226–28; White, "Prince Saunders," p. 535.

46. White, "Prince Saunders," p. 534, where the claim is made, but without supporting evidence. None of the contemporary reports mention Saunders among those accompanying Paul.

47. Letter to the editor, Boston, July 1, 1824, *Columbian Centinel*, July 3, 1824.

48. James Oliver Horton and Lois E. Horton, *Black Bostonians: Family Life and Community Struggle in the Antebellum North* (New York: Holmes and Meier, 1999), p. 100. All the contemporary obituaries reported that Paul died in Boston surrounded by his family. The most substantial was carried by the *American Baptist*, July 1831, pp. 221–23; also see the *Liberator*'s, April 16, 1831. The family is profiled in J. Marcus Mitchell, "The Paul Family," *Old-Time New England* 63 (January–March 1972): 73–77.

49. *Boston Centinel*, August 25, 1825, repr. in the *Western Luminary*, September 21, 1825; emphasis in original.

50. Cutter, "Hawes Family," p. 843.

51. Anne Catherine got married in 1824, the same year Russwurm left Boston for Bowdoin College; Susan Paul remained single and was engaged to be married when she died in April, 1841, at the age of thirty-two. See Mitchell, "Paul Family," p. 75; and the *Liberator*, April 23, 1841, for Susan Paul's obituary.

52. "Monument to Governor Russwurm," p. 351; William Brewer, "John B. Russwurm," *Journal of Negro History* 13 4 (October 1928): 413–22; Philip Foner, "John Browne Russwurm: A Document," *Journal of Negro History* 54 (October 1969): 393–97; Floyd Miller, *The Search for a Black Nationality: Black Emigration and Colonization, 1787–1863* (Urbana: University of Illinois Press, 1975), pp. 84–85. Long thought to be the first black graduate of an American college, Russwurm was in fact the third documented case: Alexander L. Twilight graduated from Middlebury College (Vermont) in 1823, and Edward Jones (who later became close friends with Russwurm) graduated two weeks (August 23, 1826) before him from Amherst College. Athern P. Daggett (professor of government and acting president, Bowdoin College) to William S. Burton, May 3, 1968, Russwurm Collection, box 1, folder 6. Clarence Contee, "John Brown Russwurm," in *Dictionary of American Negro Biography*, ed. Rayford Logan and Michael Winston (New York: Norton, 1982), pp. 538–39.

53. A detailed curriculum for each term and year is provided in *Catalogue of the Officers and Students of Bowdoin College, and the Medical School of Maine. February, 1824* (Brunswick, ME: Joseph Griffin, 1824).

54. "Monument to Governor Russwurm," p. 352, emphasis in original.

55. Cleaveland and Packard, *History of Bowdoin College*, pp. 352–54. For Cleaveland's and Packard's links to Bowdoin, see Nehemiah Cleaveland Papers, 1806–77, and Alpheus Spring Packard Papers, 1819–86, both at George J. Mitchell Department of Special Collections and Archives, Bowdoin College Library.

56. Henry G. Russell, "Chapel Talk on John Brown Russwurm," delivered at Bowdoin College, November 10, 1947, Russwurm Collection, box 1, folder 7.

57. Helen B. Johnson (registrar, Bowdoin College) to R. Grann Lloyd (managing editor, *Negro Educational Review*), December 4, 1961, Russwurm Collection, box 1, folder 6.

58. He actually signed the note "John Browne Russwurm." For unknown reasons he seem to have consistently spelt Brown with an "e" while at Bowdoin; the same spelling of the name appears on his commencement address. But the official college documents all spell it as Brown. In subsequent years, he simply signed his name "John B. Russwurm." It is a minor and strange enigma that remains unsolved, though, following convention, I have decided to spell it without the "e." Russwurm to G. Y. Sawyer (secretary, Athenaean Society), October 30, [1824], Russwurm Collection, box 1, folder 2. Also see Sagarin, *John Brown Russwurm*, pp. 32–40.

59. If he did not harbor racist views at that point, Hawthorne certainly did in subsequent years, though he was mildly antislavery, a self-described "moderate friend of emancipation." See Patrick Brancaccio, "'The Black Man's Paradise': Hawthorne's Editing of the *Journal of*

an African Cruiser," *New England Quarterly* 53 (March 1980): 23–41, quotation on p. 28; also Brenda Wineapple, *Hawthorne: A Life* (New York: Alfred Knopf, 2003). It should be said that both Hawthorne and Bridge held Russwurm, *as an individual,* in high regard, while he was at Bowdoin and subsequently.

60. Horatio Bridge, *Personal Recollections of Nathaniel Hawthorne* (1893; repr., New York: Haskell House, 1968), p. 30. However, Bridge, who served as an officer in the African Squadron of the U. S. Navy, noted that twenty years later "I renewed the acquaintance pleasantly in Africa, where as Governor of Cape Palmas he received, with dignity and ease, the Commodore and officers of our squadron, myself all the more cordially because we had been college associates and fellow-Athenaeans" (p. 30). Bridge had also recorded his encounter with Russwurm in Liberia in his *Journal of an African Cruiser* (1845; repr., London: Dawson's of Pall Mall, 1968), pp. 14, 37, 174. Soon after the book's appearance in 1845, extensive extracts were approvingly reprinted in the *Maryland Colonization Journal* (see, for instance, vol. 3, September 1845, and vol. 3, November 1845), as well as the *African Repository*.

61. "Monument to Governor Russwurm," p. 352. Though unattributed on publication in the *Maryland Colonization Journal*, the profile was actually written by James Hall. See James Hall to A. Cleveland, Esq., November 15, 1853, Russwurm Collection, box 1, folder 5. In his obituary Hall mistakenly gave the year of Russwurm's marriage as 1835; it was actually 1833.

62. Russwurm to Col. John S. Russwurm, January 9, 1826, Sumner Russwurm Papers, Family Correspondence, box 2, folder 7.

63. See [John Brown Russwurm], "Toussaint L'Overture, the Principal Chief in the Revolution of St. Domingo," ca. 1825, quotation on p. 22, African-American History Collection, William L. Clements Library, University of Michigan, Ann Arbor. Although the manuscript was originally attributed to Russwurm, the library later marked the author as "anonymous." This was because, the library explained, Russwurm's name does not appear on the manuscript itself: "The actual document has no signature or date." Thus it was the library's mistake to have originally attributed the essay to Russwurm. Even though when the item was bought at an auction in 1995 and the auction catalog listed the item as authored by "John Brown Russwurm, Bowdoin College, Me., ca. 1825," because Russwurm's name did not appear on the handwritten manuscript itself it was thought best to list the author as "Anonymous" (Janet Bloom, William L. Clements Library, pers. comm., December 1 and 2, 2008.) The reasoning is understandable, but the handwriting, the provenance, the year, and Russwurm's 1826 commencement address (discussed below) make the essay unmistakably the work of Russwurm. I am grateful to Professor Julius Scott (Department of History, University of Michigan) for informing me of the existence of this manuscript. Cora Kaplan, "Black Heroes/White Writers: Toussaint L'Ouverture and the Literary Imagination," *History Workshop Journal*, no. 46 (1998): 33–62, is an illuminating analysis of Toussaint's treatment particularly by British romantic writers, including Wordsworth, author of the most famous and enduring poetic tribute to Toussaint Louverture, "To Toussaint L'Ouverture" (1803).

64. Russwurm's facility with the French language is explicitly noted by James Hall; see "Monument to Governor Russwurm," p. 350. The book on which Russwurm's essay heavily relies is *The History of the Island of St. Domingo, from Its First Discovery by Columbus to the Present* (Edinburgh and London: Archibald Constable; Rest Fenner, 1818; and New York: Mahlon Day, 1824). In 1826 the anonymous author was revealed to have been Admiral Sir James Barskett; see Robert I. Rotberg's preface to the Frank Cass edition, published in London in 1971. Russwurm drew most heavily from chs. 7 and 8 of Barskett's book. The implication of plagiarism should be considered with caution since Russwurm never published this essay, and it is not even clear that it was submitted as work for a class at Bowdoin. He probably wrote it for his own edification—a meditation on Haiti and Toussaint drawing upon Barskett's book, almost like note taking.

65. *Eastern Argus*, September 12, 1826.

66. Russwurm, "The Condition and Prospects of Hayti," Russwurm Collection, box 1, folder 3. He had made a similar point in the earlier essay on Louverture, which opened with the observation that "civil wars and revolutions afford favourable opportunities for the expansion of latent talent, and often elevate to stations of importance those who seemed little qualified to perform any duties except those of a subordinate character." Russwurm, "Toussaint L'Overture," p. 1.

67. See Jacques Nicolas Léger, *Haiti: Her History and Her Detractors* (New York: Neale, 1907); Alfred N. Hunt, *Haiti's Influence on Antebellum America: Slumbering Volcano in the Caribbean* (Baton Rouge: Louisiana State University Press, 1988); and J. Michael Dash, *Haiti and the United States: National Stereotypes and the Literary Imagination* (Basingstoke: Macmillan Press, 1988), ch. 1.

68. *Eastern Argus*, September 12, 1826.

69. Quotation from the *Boston Commercial Gazette*, September 14, 1826.

70. *Eastern Argus*, September 12, 1826; *Genius of Universal Emancipation*, October 14, 1826; Calvin Stockbridge to Ralph Gurley, October 23, 1826, RACS, reel 1; "African Governor"; H. H. Price and Gerald E. Talbot, eds., *Maine's Visible Black History,: The First Chronicle of Its People* (Gardiner: Tilbury House, 2006), p. 227.

71. Stockbridge to Gurley, October 23, 1826.

72. Sagarin, *John Brown Russwurm*, p. 41.

73. Stockbridge to Gurley, October 23, 1826.

74. Russwurm to R. R. Gurley, February 26, 1827, in "Letters to the American Colonization Society," *Journal of Negro History* 10 (April 1925): 156.

2. FREEDOM'S JOURNAL

1. For more on Cornish, see David E. Swift, *Black Prophets of Justice: Activist Clergy before the Civil War* (Baton Rouge: Louisiana State University Press, 1989), esp. chs. 3, 4 and 5; Jane H. Pease and William H. Pease, "The Negro Conservative: Samuel Eli Cornish," in *Bound with Them in Chains: A Biographical History of the Antislavery Movement* (Westport, CT: Greenwood Press, 1972), pp. 140–61; see also, by the same authors, "Samuel Eli Cornish," in *Dictionary of American Negro Biography*, ed. Rayford Logan and Michael Winston (New York: Norton, 1982), pp. 134–35, Frankie Hutton, *The Early Black Press in America, 1827 to 1860* (Westport, CT: Greenwood Press, 1993), pp. 4–9, and Graham Russell Hodges, "Samuel Eli Cornish," *American National Biography Online*, February 2000, www.anb.org/articles/15/15-00147.html.

2. "Monument to Governor Russwurm," *Maryland Colonization Journal*, n.s., 6 (March 1853): 352; Russwurm to Gurley, July 3, 1829, RACS, reel 5. Describing the bond between them, Russwurm told Hall less than two years before he died, "I have no friend living whom I esteem more highly & to whom I feel under greater obligations." Russwurm to Hall, October 18, 1849, MSCSP, reel 6; "Mr. Gerrit Smith on Colonization," *African Repository and Colonial Journal* 11 (April 1835): 115; for the prior relationship with Russwurm (and Cornish), see *Freedom's Journal*, March 23, 1827; Gerrit Smith to editors of Freedom's Journal, March 31, 1827, letter book 1; Cornish and Russwurm to Gerrit Smith, April 16, 1827, box 32, Gerrit Smith Papers, Special Collection Research Center, Syracuse University; John Stauffer, *The Black Hearts of Men: Radical Abolitionists and the Transformation of Race* (Cambridge, MA: Harvard University Press, 2002), pp. 93–94; Jacqueline Bacon, *Freedom's Journal: The First African-American Newspaper* (Lanham, MD: Lexington Books, 2007), pp. 47–50.

3. According to Hall, Russwurm "*ultimately* became a devout member of the Protestant Episcopal Church." "Monument to Governor Russwurm," p. 352, emphasis mine. The Reverend Ralph Gurley, who had known Russwurm since his graduation from Bowdoin, and who saw the governor only a couple years before his death, was "happy" to report that Russwurm had "*within the last few years*, become connected with the Episcopal Church." See obituary by Ralph

Gurley (reprinted from the *Christian Statesman*), "Death of Governor Russwurm," *Maryland Colonization Journal* 6 (November 1851): 82–84, quotation on p. 83, emphasis mine. The article was also republished as "The Late Governor Russwurm," *African Repository and Colonial Journal* 27 (December 1851): 356–58, but without attribution. Russwurm probably formally joined the church around 1849. The Rev. Jacob Rambo, a missionary of the Protestant Episcopal Church, in a letter from Cape Palmas dated April 19, 1849, remarked: "The Governor [Russwurm] is an excellent Christian gentleman, a member of our Church here." Rev. J. Rambo to "Dear Brethren," April 19, 1849, extract published in *Maryland Colonization Journal*, n.s., 5 (July 1849): 12.

4. [Russwurm], "To the Senior Editor, No. III," *Freedom's Journal*, August 17, 1827. The attribution to Russwurm is discussed later.

5. *Freedom's Journal*, March 16, 1827. See I. Garland Penn, *The Afro-American Press and Its Editors* (Springfield, MA: Wiley, 1891), pp. 25–28; Bella Gross, "*Freedom's Journal* and *The Rights of All*," *Journal of Negro History* 17 (July 1932): 241–86, esp. 241–46; and Bacon, *Freedom's Journal*, esp. pp. 38–41, for the hostile ideological context that resulted in the birth of the *Journal*.

6. *Freedom's Journal*, March 16, 1827.

7. Haiti its history, heroes, and contemporary development, including the experience of African American emigrants to the country was one of the most extensively covered subjects in *Freedom's Journal*.

8. [Russwurm], "The Mutability of Human Affairs," parts 1–3, *Freedom's Journal*, April 6, 13, and 20, 1827, respectively. Though the essay was published unattributed, its authorship was revealed by Russwurm more than a year and a half later, in December 1828. In response to apparent criticism for not carrying enough on ancient Africa, Russwurm wrote: "We acknowledge, that with the exception of the article upon 'Mutability of Human Affairs,' we have not written any thing relating to Africa centuries ago." His explicit claiming of authorship was partly because "we cannot refrain from expressing our contempt of those individuals, who would rob us of our hard earned labours by running about, and filling the ears of some with a long list of their contributions to the *Journal*. . . . We wish to claim no more than what has really emanated from our pen. . . . We intend publishing a list of contributors to our columns at the close of our labours; when no doubt, many who now wear borrowed plumes, will appear in their true feathers." (He did not, alas, publish this list.) "Our Labours," *Freedom's Journal*, December 5, 1828. Bruce Dain, in "Haiti and Egypt in Early Black Racial Discourse," *Slavery and Abolition* 14 (December 1993): 139–61, and in his book *A Hideous Monster of the Mind: American Race Theory in the Early Republic* (Cambridge, MA: Harvard University Press, 2002), p. 135, recognizes the importance of the essay but does not attribute authorship to Russwurm. He thinks the "we" makes the claim ambiguous. But the context, as well as Russwurm's habitual use of the royal "we" in his editorials—he invariably used the collective pronoun—long after Cornish had gone, sustains the claim. Moreover, the repeated use of the authorial personal pronoun in the essay makes it clear to the reader that this is an individual and very personal meditation. Gross, in "*Freedom's Journal*," implies (but does not claim outright, as Dain suggests, "Haiti and Egypt," p. 159 n.) that it was written by Cornish (p. 246), in keeping with her unsustained notion that everything good in the *Journal* is attributable to Cornish. She makes no mention of the December 1828 editorial. Mia Bay, *The White Image in the Black Mind: African American Ideas about White People, 1830–1925* (New York: Oxford University Press, 2000), pp. 26–36, correctly gives the authorship to Russwurm, although she does not say why. Jacqueline Bacon rather cavalierly attributes it to both Cornish and Russwurm, going so far as to give (without explanation or caveat) "Samuel E. Cornish and John B. Russwurm" as the authors in her footnotes, when in fact no attribution of authorship is given in *Freedom's Journal* itself. See Bacon, *Freedom's Journal*, pp. 150–51, p. 171 n. 11.

9. [Russwurm], "Mutability," part 1.

10. See especially Cheikh Anta Diop, *African Origins of Civilization: Myth or Reality?* trans. Mercer Cook (Westport, CT: Lawrence Hill, 1974); Martin Bernal, *Black Athena: The Afroasiatic*

Roots of Classical Civilization, vol. 1, *The Fabrication of Ancient Greece, 1785–1985* (London: Free Association Books, 1987).

11. [Russwurm], "Mutability," part 2.

12. [Russwurm], "Mutability," part 3.

13. Dain, "Haiti and Egypt," esp. pp. 147–50; Wilson Jeremiah Moses, *Afrotopia: The Roots of African American Popular History* (Cambridge: Cambridge University Press, 1998), ch. 3, esp. pp. 51–55; Bay, *White Image*, pp. 26–36.

14. *Freedom's Journal*, March 16, 1827. There is extensive commentary on *Freedom's Journal* stretching back to the late nineteenth century. But see in particular Penn, *Afro-American Press*, pp. 25–31; Gross, "*Freedom's Journal*,"; Lionel C. Barrow Jr., "'Our Own Cause': *Freedom's Journal* and the Beginning of the Black Press," *Journalism History* 4 (Winter 1977–78): 118–22; Kenneth D. Nordin, "In Search of Black Unity: An Interpretation of the Content and Function of *Freedom's Journal*," *Journalism History* 4 (Winter 1977–78): 123–28; Hutton, *Early Black Press*; Dickson D. Bruce, *The Origins of African American Literature, 1680–1865* (Charlottesville: University of Virginia Press, 2001), ch. 4; Jacqueline Bacon, "The History of *Freedom's Journal*: A Study in Empowerment and Community," *Journal of African American History* 88 (Winter 2003): 1–20; Bacon, *Freedom's Journal*; see also George E. Walker, *The Afro-American in New York City, 1827–1860* (New York: Garland, 1993), for a detailed analysis of the wider context within which the paper operated. See also Craig S. Wilder, *In the Company of Black Men: The African Influence on African American Culture in New York City* (New York: New York University Press, 2001), and Leslie M. Harris, *In the Shadow of Slavery: African Americans in New York City, 1626–1863* (Chicago: University of Chicago Press, 2003), chs. 3 and 4.

15. The announcement of "Mr. W. R. Gardiner, Port-au-Prince, Hayti," among the "authorised agents" was made in the second issue of the paper. See *Freedom's Journal*, March 23, 1827.

16. David Walker, "Address Delivered before the General Colored Association of Boston," *Freedom's Journal*, December 19, 1828.

17. The most authoritative edition of the *Appeal* is Peter Hinks, ed., *David Walker's Appeal to the Colored Citizens of the World* (University Park: Pennsylvania State University Press, 2000). Hinks, in his fine study of Walker, suggests that the articles carried in *Freedom's Journal*, especially those on African civilizations and culture, had a significant impact on Walker's intellectual formation and the formulation of his *Appeal*. See Peter Hinks, *To Awaken My Afflicted Brethren: David Walker and the Problem of Antebellum Slave Resistance* (University Park: University of Pennsylvania Press, 1997), pp. 179–95.

18. P. J. Staudenraus's *The African Colonization Movement, 1816–1865* (New York: Columbia University Press, 1961) remains the most authoritative history of the ACS and its early efforts; also see Archibald Alexander, *A History of Colonization on the Western Coast of Africa* (Philadelphia: William S. Martien, 1846); Early Lee Fox, *The American Colonization Society, 1817–1840* (Baltimore: Johns Hopkins Press, 1919); H. N. Sherwood, "The Formation of the American Colonization Society," *Journal of Negro History* 2 (July 1917): 209–28; Frederic Bancroft, "The Early Antislavery Movement and African Colonization," in *Frederic Bancroft: Historian*, ed. Jacob E. Cooke (Norman: University of Oklahoma Press, 1957), pp. 147–91; George M. Fredrickson, *The Black Image in the White Mind: The Debate on Afro-American Character and Destiny, 1817–1914*, 2nd ed. (Middletown: Wesleyan University Press, 1987), ch. 1; Douglas R. Egerton, "'Its Origin Is Not a Little Curious': A New Look at the American Colonization Society," *Journal of the Early Republic* 5 (Winter 1985): 463–80; Eric Burin, *Slavery and the Peculiar Solution: A History of the American Colonization Society* (Gainesville: University Press of Florida, 2005).

19. *Freedom's Journal*, January 25, 1828.

20. *Freedom's Journal*, August 17, 1827.

21. *Freedom's Journal*, September 21, 1827.

22. *Freedom's Journal*, September 14, 1827.

23. Russwurm actually traveled from New York to Massachusetts between July and August 1827, stopping for varying lengths of time in New Haven, Hartford, Worcester, Boston, and Salem. He probably went even further north, most likely as far as Maine to see relatives, but there is no direct evidence that he actually did so. His dispatches from Connecticut, datelined July, were published in *Freedom's Journal* in consecutively numbered parts on August 3, 10, 17, and 31, 1827. Probably because of the furor caused by the first four parts, the pressure on space in the paper, and Cornish's resignation on September 14, the other two parts, titled "Letter No. V," and "Letter No. VI" and addressed this time "To Rev. Samuel E. Cornish," were not published until November 2 and 9, respectively. They were datelined "Boston, August." In the first of these latter two, Russwurm opened with the sentence: "As you are aware of the reasons which have delayed the remaining letters of this series, I shall proceed without making any unnecessary apologies."

24. *Freedom's Journal*, September 7 and 21, 1827. See also issues for October 12 and 26, 1827.

25. [Russwurm], "To the Senior Editor, No. III," *Freedom's Journal*, August 17, 1827.

26. "Wilberforce," letter to the editor, *Freedom's Journal*, September 7, 1827.

27. [Russwurm], "Wilberforce," *Freedom's Journal*, September 7, 1827.

28. Rev. Dr. Samuel Miller, letter to *New York Observer*, repr. in *Freedom's Journal*, September 21, 1827.

29. Russwurm, reply to Rev. Dr. Samuel Miller, *Freedom's Journal*, September 21, 1827.

30. Rev. Dr. Samuel Miller quoted in *Freedom's Journal*, October 26, 1827.

31. Miller explained the circumstances under which he came to transmit Wilberforce's letter. He was already preparing a letter to the editors of *Freedom's Journal* cancelling his subscription when "a highly respected gentleman of my acquaintance, who is, at the same time, as cordial a friend to African rights and improvements as any man in the land, and as much dissatisfied with 'Freedom's Journal' as myself, happening to step into my study, and learning my purpose, informed me that he had prepared a communication under the signature of 'Wilberforce,' which on account of peculiar circumstances, he could not conveniently transmit to the Editor himself, and which he requested me to inclose with the letter which I had prepared. Fully approving the substance of the piece, . . . I did not hesitate to comply with his request." Samuel Miller (1769–1850) was the second professor appointed at Princeton Theological Seminary, joining Alexander in 1813. He and Alexander spent the rest of their careers at the seminary. The relationship between Alexander and Miller was so close that the biography of Alexander, written by his son, James Alexander, is in many was a joint biography of the two men. Alexander, his son revealed, "maintained the most pleasing and harmonious intimacy" with Dr. Miller. James Alexander wrote of the "inviolable sacredness of fraternal regard which for nearly forty years subsisted between [them.]" He elaborated: "During this long period the thread of their lives had been entwined together, with increasing closeness. They were mutual advisers and confidential friends, and in each other's progress, happiness, and acceptance with the church." With some justification Alexander's son believed that the father should be ranked among the early founders of the colonization movement. Noting that "the name of Dr. Alexander has long been associated with the American Colonization Society," he went on to suggest that "if those who were of the councils which projected it, and early committed themselves in its favour, are to be ranked as its founders, he assuredly deserves a name among them." He pointed out that the Rev. Robert Finley, "the real father of the movement in its modern form," a native of Princeton and an alumnus of the seminary, was an "intimate friend" of Alexander. James Alexander "remembered the long and anxious interviews" that Finley and his father had held upon this subject. Not many months after one of these conversations, Finley disclosed to Alexander his plan "of a colony of free blacks on the western coast of Africa." The scheme struck most as "chimerical," but Finley was "immovable," and "from the very outset Dr. Alexander was as sanguine as he. The first public meeting which ever took place in the country to consider this

matter was held in the borough of Princeton; where Dr. Finley gave an exposition of his plan. The meeting was small, but among those present were the professors and most of the students of the Theological Seminary." See *Freedom's Journal*, September 21, 1827; James W. Alexander, *The Life of Archibald Alexander, D. D., First Professor in the Theological Seminary, at Princeton, New Jersey* (New York: Charles Scribner, 1854), quotations on pp. 417, 578, 450; his resemblance to Wilberforce is discussed on p. 575; "the Rev. Theodore Wright, a man of colour," is explicitly mentioned as one of Alexander's former students (p. 417). Alexander and Miller were in fact the only two teachers the seminary had at the time. See also A. Alexander, *History of Colonization*, where Alexander remembered Russwurm's warm opposition to the colonizationists but forgave him: "[Russwurm] undertook to publish a paper for the coloured people in the city of New York, in connexion with the Rev. Mr. Cornish. The sentiments expressed in this paper were in opposition to the principles of the Colonization Society, and were often expressed with a violence that was offensive to many. But Mr. Russwurm was the enemy of this noble enterprise only because he did not understand its real principles. As soon as he had opportunity of a full examination of the subject, he declared himself the convert to the principles of the colonizationists" (pp. 283–84). Elsewhere in the book he discussed and praised Russwurm's work in Liberia. Wright is quoted from "Address of the Rev. Theodore S. Wright before the Convention of the New York State Anti-Slavery Society, on the Acceptance of the Annual Report, held at Utica, Sept. 30 [1837]," *Colored American*, October 14, 1837. Wright, I believe dishonestly, attributes to Cornish the reply to Miller. I say dishonestly, because Wright knew better and I doubt that he forgot: he was at the time the *Journal's* agent in Princeton, a role in which he served right up to the demise of the paper. (His name is listed among the agents in the very issue, September 21, 1827, in which Russwurm had his exchange with Miller. See also the agents listed in the final issue, March 28, 1829.) And Russwurm proudly announced Wright's ordination in Albany, an event that Russwurm probably attended, in one of the last issues of the *Journal* (March 14, 1829). But since Russwurm had embraced colonization and had emigrated to Liberia, he was anathema—hence Wright's (and others') attempt to write Russwurm out of the history of the black struggle in America. It is a practice taken to its extreme by Bella Gross in the 1930s and followed by so many others since.

32. [Samuel Cornish], "Colored People Always Opposed Colonization," *Colored American*, May 13, 1837.

33. Editorial, *Georgetown Columbian and District Advertiser*, May 29, 1827, quoted in editorial, *Freedom's Journal*, June 8, 1827.

34. Editorial, *Freedom's Journal*, June 8, 1827. This and the earlier passage quoted were not carried in the *Colored American* extract.

35. *New York Observer*, June 6, 1829.

36. [Samuel Cornish], "An Error Corrected," *Rights of All*, June 12, 1829; also see "The Old Hobby, Colonization," *Rights of All*, September 18, 1829.

37. Swift, *Black Prophets of Justice*, provides a detailed analysis of the relationship between Cornish and Wright. In 1834 the Episcopalian hierarchy forced a humiliating public renunciation of the abolitionists by the distinguished African American clergyman, the Rev. Peter Williams, a friend to both Cornish and Russwurm, at a time when the abolitionist movement was much stronger. Bishop Benjamin Onderdonk closed Williams's New York church and wrote in a public rebuke to Williams: "Let me advise you to resign, at once, your connexion, in every department, with the Anti-Slavery Society, and to make public your resignation. I cannot now give you all my reasons. Let me see you as soon as you can." Remarkably, Williams complied, though without renouncing the Anti-Slavery Society. See "Correspondence between Rev. Bishop Onderdonk and Rev. Peter Williams," *African Repository and Colonial Journal* 10 (August 1834): 185–88.

38. Samuel E. Cornish and Theodore S. Wright, *The Colonization Scheme Considered* (Newark, NJ: Aaron Guest, 1840).

39. These matters are expanded upon below.

40. Forten's letters are carried in *Freedom's Journal*, May 18 and June 3, 1827.

41. Cornish identified the "Man of Colour" in the *Colored American*, May 13, 1837.

42. Rev. Richard Allen, letter to *Freedom's Journal*, November 2, 1827. For Allen's remarkable life and career, see Richard S. Newman's fine biography, *Freedom's Prophet: Bishop Richard Allen, the AME Church, and the Black Founding Fathers* (New York: New York University Press, 2008).

43. *Freedom's Journal*, September 14, 1827.

44. Cornish, who had been brought up on the land in Delaware, was a keen advocate of the wholesomeness of rural life, preached the economic wisdom of land ownership, and recommended farming to America's urban black population. "We decidedly recommend an agricultural life to our brethren, it is more adapted to their situation and interest, than any other," he wrote in 1829. Almost a decade later he asked rhetorically, "What is more honorable than husbandry? To till the soil, to be a producer of corn and wheat, and a grower of flocks and herds, has something in it paradisiacal. If there be any calling in this world, allied to primitive innocency, it is husbandry. There is more independence of circumstances—more safety from the common calamities of life in the business of a farmer, than in any other occupation." He had "often lamented the apparent aversion to farming" among African Americans. "This is decidedly the worst feature of our domestic character." He went so far as to declare: "Nothing else can possibly procure for us so much independence and importance in this country, as husbandry, and nothing is more easy." [Samuel E. Cornish], "Agriculture," *Rights of All*, May 29, 1829, and "Agricultural Pursuits," *Colored American*, November 4, 1837; see also his editorial "The Importance of Agricultural Pursuits," *Colored American*, April 15, 1837. See Pease and Pease, "Negro Conservative," for Cornish's activities after leaving the *Journal*.

45. These matters are returned to later.

3. QUITTING AMERICA AND ITS COST

1. *Freedom's Journal*, August 17 and 31, 1827.

2. *Freedom's Journal*, February 14, 1829.

3. Ibid.

4. Quoted in William Brewer, "John B. Russwurm," *Journal of Negro History* 13 4 (October 1928): 421.

5. Terry Alford suggests that Russwurm's meeting with the African prince Abd Rahman Ibrahima was the catalyst. Ibrahima had been captured and sold to the slave traders in Futa Jallon, ending up as a slave in Natchez, Mississippi. He regained his freedom some forty years later in 1828 and went to Liberia under the auspices of the ACS. Before the prince returned to Africa, Russwurm met him, and the old man and the young editor became good friends. Russwurm became a tireless advocate for Ibrahima and campaigned through the pages of *Freedom's Journal* to raise funds to purchase the freedom of his family members who remained in bondage. But there is no evidence to suggest that this led to Russwurm's conversion to colonization. Terry Alford, *Prince among Slaves: The True Story of an African Prince Sold into Slavery in the American South* (New York: Oxford University Press, 1977), pp. 168–79. After reaching Liberia in 1829, where he saw the many deaths of African American emigrants, Ibrahima actually sent a message back to the United States discouraging others from going to Liberia and specifically warning Russwurm not to go there because he "certainly will be a dead man, he must stay where he is." Quotation from extract of Ibrahima's letter, printed in "Important from Africa," *Rights of All*, July 17, 1829. For Russwurm's moving response to his first meeting with Ibrahima, see his "Travelling Scraps," *Freedom's Journal*, August 29, 1828.

6. Russwurm sent six unsigned articles in the form of letters addressed to Cornish: *Freedom's Journal*, August 3, 10, 17, and 31, and November 2 and 9, 1827. He also wrote a series of five

articles the following summer, entitled "Travelling Scraps," describing his trip from New York City to Washington, D.C., in *Freedom's Journal*, June 27, July 11, and 25, August 15 and 29, 1828. For the responses of Blyden, Campbell, Claude McKay, and other twentieth-century Caribbean immigrants to the United States, see Hollis Lynch, *Edward Wilmot Blyden: Pan-Negro Patriot, 1832–1912* (London: Oxford University Press, 1967); Richard Blackett, "Robert Campbell and the Triangle of the Black Experience," in *Beating against the Barriers: The Lives of Six Nineteenth-Century Afro-Americans* (Ithaca: Cornell University Press, 1989); Winston James, *Holding Aloft the Banner of Ethiopia: Caribbean Radicalism in Early Twentieth-Century America* (London: Verso, 1998), and Winston James, "The Wings of Ethiopia: The Caribbean Diaspora and Pan-African Projects from John Brown Russwurm to George Padmore," in *The African Diaspora in the New and Old Worlds: Consciousness and Imagination,* ed. Geneviève Fabre and Klaus Bonesch (Amsterdam: Rodopi, 2004).

7. In the third part of his travelogue from Connecticut written in July 1827, Russwurm noted: "In traveling in the stage, I have ever considered myself, so far as money would go, as good as the best; and holding this opinion, have ever been unwilling to accept any other treatment than the best." *Freedom's Journal*, August 17, 1827. See the objections of "Wilberforce" (who explicitly cited this passage) and Samuel Miller, along with Russwurm's forceful riposte in *Freedom's Journal*, September 7, and 21, 1827. Russwurm, like Frederick Douglass after him, could never get used to the racist indignities encountered in traveling as a black man in the United States. Six months before he finally gave up on the United States, he observed: "Prejudices at present are so great, that if we consulted convenience and comfort alone, it would always be best to travel under the assumed name of Governor Troup's or Gen. Woolfolk's body servant, than as a free man on your own private affairs. But where is the man who would assume even for a few days, the name of a great man's valet-de-chambre for the sake of convenience or comfort? He must surely be wanting in all the finer feelings of our nature—in all that should adorn a man. Let me rather be tortured or gibbeted by piecemeals, traveling as a free man." "Travelling Scraps," *Freedom's Journal*, June 27, 1828.

8. *Freedom's Journal*, August 3, 1827.

9. *Freedom's Journal*, March 7, 1829.

10. Russwurm to R. R. Gurley (secretary, American Colonization Society), February 24, 1829, RACS, reel 5. In 1521 Martin Luther, summoned by the Diet of Worms, was asked to withdraw his teachings condemned by the pope. Despite enormous pressure, he refused. According to tradition, he ended his statement of defense with the words: "Here I stand. I cannot do otherwise. God help me. Amen."

11. Russwurm to Gurley, May 7, 1829, RACS, reel 5.

12. Russwurm to Gurley, February 24, 1829.

13. *Rights of All*, May 29, 1829.

14. C. C. Andrews to Gurley, July 1, 1829, RACS, reel 6. Andrews added a note to this letter, dated July 2, specifically reporting his conversation with Cornish: "I have had the pleasure of an interview with Revd. Mr. Cornish, from whom I learn, that he considers Mr. R[usswurm] worthy of all confidence, and is willing to bear full testimony as to R[usswurm]'s correct habits and exemplary deportment." Gurley, apparently, did not contact Cornish directly for a reference. There is no correspondence between the two men.

15. Williams's speech, delivered on July 4, 1830, repr. in Carter G. Woodson, ed., *Negro Orators and Their Orations* (Washington, DC: Associated Publishers, 1925), pp. 77–81, quotation on p. 80.

16. See, for instance, *Freedom's Journal*, January 11, 1828, where it is reported that at a joint meeting of New York Manumission Society, and Trustees of the African Schools chaired by Peter Williams, Russwurm volunteered to canvas the nineteenth district to try and ascertain why the black children were not attending school in the numbers expected despite the avail-

ability of places. Samuel Cornish was also there in his capacity of general agent of the trustees of the New York African School.

17. "Correspondence between Rev. Bishop Onderdonk and Rev. Peter Williams," *African Repository and Colonial Journal* 10 (August 1834): 185–88. Andrews had sent Russwurm a glowing letter of thanks in November 1827 for his donating copies of the *Journal* to the library of the New York African Free School (*Freedom's Journal*, November 9, 1827). Russwurm acknowledged the help of both Williams and Andrews: Russwurm to Gurley, July 3 and 24, 1829, RACS, reel 5; see also Andrews to Gurley, July 1, 1829, RACS, reel 6.

18. *Freedom's Journal*, April 25, 1828; Russwurm to Gurley, February 24, 1829.

19. When Russwurm taught at the African Free School in Boston before going to college, he earned $300 per annum; seven years later, in 1829, the ACS offered him $450 per annum to work as superintendent of schools hardly enough, if money was the only object in mind.

20. *Freedom's Journal*, March 14, 1829.

21. *Freedom's Journal*, March 28, 1829.

22. *Freedom's Journal*, March 28, 1829.

23. "R," letter to the editor, *Liberator*, April 16, 1831.

24. "C.D.T. A Philadelphian," letter to the editor, *Liberator*, April 30, 1831.

25. *Christian Mirror*, editorial, "John B. Russwurm," April 21, 1831; *Liberator*, May 7, 1831. Asa Cummings (1790–1856), editor of the *Mirror* (1826–55), evidently knew Russwurm and his family well. He was a resident of North Yarmouth (where he was a pastor) during Russwurm's time there and also had strong connections with Bowdoin, serving as a tutor and overseer (1821–49) and trustee (1849–56). He was also a life member of the ACS. See Joseph Griffin, *History of the Press of Maine* (Brunswick, ME: J. Griffin, 1872), pp. 64–66; Nehemiah Cleaveland and Alphaeus S. Packard, *History of Bowdoin College* (Boston: James R. Osgood, 1882), pp. 65–68; for his life membership in the ACS, see for instance, *Eleventh Annual Report of the American Society for Colonizing the Free People of Colour in the United States* (Washington, DC, 1828), p. 53.

26. *American Spectator and Washington City Chronicle,* quoted in the *Liberator*, May 21, 1831, with Garrison's response. Garrison referred to this publication as the "Washington Spectator" as well the "American Spectator." But its proper title is as given above. It was published by the African Education Society (formed in December 1829) and was edited by the Rev. Isaac Orr, who knew Russwurm. Ralph Gurley was the moving force behind the formation of AES. Orr was its secretary, and Gurley served on its board of managers. See *Report of the Proceedings at the Formation of the African Education Society* (Washington, DC, 1830). Though not entirely unfounded, Russwurm's appointment by the ACS was more complicated than the *Spectator* made out. The *Spectator's* was a forceful rejection of the notion of a bribe. But I, too, have seen the documents, and they reveal that it was Russwurm who contacted the ACS and willingly retracted his earlier position. There were definitely members of the ACS board who remained angry with Russwurm, which explains the drawn-out nature of his final appointment. See discussion below.

27. *Colored American*, January 27, 1838.

28. Russwurm to Gurley, July 3, 1829.

29. *Freedom's Journal*, March 14, 1829.

30. Russwurm to Gurley, February 24, 1829.

31. Russwurm to Gurley, May 7, 1829, RACS, reel 5.

32. Philip Staudenraus, *The African Colonization Movement, 1816–1865* (New York: Columbia University Press, 1961), ch. 7; Penelope Campbell, *Maryland in Africa: The Maryland State Colonization Society, 1831–1857* (Urbana, University of Illinois Press [1971]), pp. 103–6; Ira Berlin, *Slaves without Masters: The Free Negro in the Antebellum South* (New York: Pantheon Books, 1974), ch. 6; Jeffrey B. Allen, "'All of Us Are Highly Pleased with the Country': Black and

White Kentuckians on Liberian Colonization," *Phylon* 43 (Summer 1982): 97–109; Marie Tyler McGraw, "Richmond Free Blacks and African Colonization, 1816–1832," *Journal of American Studies* 21 (August 1987): 207–24; James Oliver Horton and Lois E. Horton, *In Hope of Liberty: Culture, Community and Protest among Northern Free Blacks, 1700–1860* (New York: Oxford University Press, 1997), ch. 8.

33. Gurley first approached Russwurm with the offer of a job in a letter dated December 25, 1826. After soliciting the advice of his friends around the country, Russwurm turned down the "liberal offer" of the ACS, pointing out that "among the number consulted is Mr. C. Stockbridge of Maine; whose views are considerably altered, since his address to you." Stockbridge, concerned about the dim prospects of his former charge in a racist United States, wrote to Gurley a month after Russwurm's graduation informing him that Russwurm might be willing to consider a teaching position in Liberia or one as an assistant to the governor. Russwurm to Gurley, February 26, 1827, reprinted in "Letters to the American Colonization Society," p. 156; Stockbridge to Gurley, October 23, 1826, RACS, reel 1.

34. Russwurm to Gurley, February 24, 1829.

35. Russwurm to Gurley, January 26 and July 24, 1829; *African Repository and Colonial Journal* 4 (February 1829): 376–77.

36. See Russwurm's letters to Gurley between January 26 and August 16, 1829, RACS, reels 5 and 6; quotations from Russwurm to Gurley, February 24 and July 24, 1829.

37. The MA from Bowdoin College was largely honorific, rather like that awarded by many European universities, such as Cambridge. According to the *Laws of Bowdoin College*: "Every Bachelor, who, in the third year after the first degree given to his class, having preserved a good moral character, shall attend at the commencement and perform the appointed public exercises, unless excused, may receive the degree of Master of Arts." It is not clear that Russwurm actually attended, but as Bowdoin's archivist, Richard Lindemann, in a letter to the author, points out: "We can't prove that Russwurm was present at Bowdoin to receive his M.A. except through negative evidence: the by-laws require the degree recipient's attendance 'unless excused' and there is no record in the Faculty Board minutes excusing him; the vote conferring the M.A. to Russwurm is recorded; the degree was conferred on September 1, 1829. We have no record of his 'part,' nor its title, presuming he delivered one." Richard H. F. Lindemann (director, George J. Mitchell Department of Special Collections and Archives, Bowdoin College Library), pers. comm., July 8, 2004. The *General Catalogue of Bowdoin College and the Medical College of Maine, 1794–1912* (Brunswick, ME: Bowdoin College, 1912), p. 76, confirms the awarding of the "A. M." degree. This should clear up some of the confusion in the extant literature about Russwurm's postbaccalaureate degree; see Bella Gross, "*Freedom's Journal* and the *Rights of All*," *Journal of Negro History* 17 (July 1932): 248 n.; Richard L. Hall, *On Afric's Shore: A History of Maryland in Liberia, 1834–1857* (Baltimore: Maryland Historical Society, 2003), pp. 141, 551 n.

38. Russwurm to Gurley, February 24 and April 8, 1829.

39. *Rights of All*, August 7–14, 1829.

40. *Freedom's Journal*, December 5, 1828, and March 28, 1829. By 1829 Russwurm had become increasingly impatient with the unreasonable behavior of some of the *Journal's* correspondents, who expected him to pay their postage to the paper. In the very last issue, he addressed a note "To Correpondents," which announced: "For the benefit of our successor, we inform our Hudson Correspondent, that printers are generally paid for the insertion of marriages, instead of having postage to pay—we therefore consign his document to our stove.—F. E. G. of Utica cannot b[e] inserted, as the postage was unpaid—Correspondents should remember that their communications if ever so worthy of insertion, are generally neglected, if the editors are burdened with postage." *Freedom's Journal*, March 28, 1829. Benjamin Quarles has documented the financial difficulties of antislavery and black publications in the antebellum period. Quarles, *Black Abolitionists* (New York: Oxford University Press, 1969), pp. 86–89.

41. The titles of editor and proprietor are mentioned several times in the *Journal*: see, for instance, the "Prospectus" in *Freedom's Journal*, April 25, 1828. Gross claims that after leaving the paper Cornish served as "one of its leading directors." But the paper never had directors, "leading" or otherwise, and she provides no evidence that it ever did. Gross, "*Freedom's Journal*," p. 242.

42. Rather imaginatively, Russwurm started a subscribers' evening school in November 1828. He taught reading, writing, arithmetic, English grammar, and geography. Terms, the advertisement promised, would be "moderate." It is not clear how many took up the offer, but he would not have made much from the exercise. The African Free School, run by the New York Manumission Society, was offering free education to poor black children, and for those whose parents could afford it, they charged twenty-five cents per quarter. Advertisements for both Russwurm's subscribers' evening school and the African Free School are carried in *Freedom's Journal*, November 14, 1828. For a history of the school, see Charles C. Andrews, *The History of the New-York African Free-Schools, From Their Establishment in 1787, to the Present Time* (New York: Mahlon Day, 1830).

43. For the nature and evidence of some of this support, see Jacqueline Bacon, "History of *Freedom's Journal*: A Study in Empowerment and Community," *Journal of African American History* 88 (Winter 2003): 5–6.

44. Russwurm to Gurley, January 26 and February 24, 1829.

45. *Freedom's Journal*, March 28, 1829. Russwurm told Gurley that he had little time for editorial work, as "my two boys and myself do all the printing, prep-work, &c. for our paper." Russwurm to Gurley, February 24, 1829.

46. "Our Labours," *Freedom's Journal*, December 5, 1828.

47. This based on the fact that Cornish claimed eight hundred subscribers for his new paper, the *Rights of All* (August 7–14, 1829), which would have drawn largely upon those who had previously subscribed to the then-defunct *Freedom's Journal*. Jacqueline Bacon, *Freedom's Journal: The First African-American Newspaper* (Lanham, MD: Lexington Books, 2007), pp. 51–54.

48. *Rights of All*, August 7–14, 1829. Jennings and Williams's appeal, on "behalf of stockholders," also appeared in the August 7–14, 1829, issue. They wrote: "Unless you come forward and contribute to its support, it must stop. Will you suffer this? We hope not." The issue, dated October 9, 1829, is generally believed to have been the last. Armistead S. Pride, "*Rights of All*: Second Step in the Development of Black Journalism," *Journalism History* 4 (Winter 1977–78): 131.

49. Bacon, "History of *Freedom's Journal*," p. 6.

50. Russwurm to Gurley, July 3, 1829, RACS, reel 5.

51. *Freedom's Journal*, March 14, 1829.

52. Kenneth D. Nordin, "In Search of Black Unity: An Interpretation of the Content and Function of *Freedom's Journal*," *Journalism History* 4 (Winter 1977–78): 128.

53. Russwurm to Gurley, February 24, 1829.

54. *Freedom's Journal*, March 28, 1829.

55. *Freedom's Journal*, March 28, 1829.

4. "WE HAVE FOUND A HAVEN"

1. Russwurm to A. R. Plumley (agent of the ACS), November 18, 1829, extract printed under the title "Liberia," in *Boston Recorder and Religious Telegraph*, April 28, 1830.

2. Wilson Jeremiah Moses has cogently and extensively analyzed this tendency, which he aptly dubbed "civilizationism." See especially his *The Golden Age of Black Nationalism, 1850–1925* (1978; repr., New York: Oxford University Press, 1988) and the magisterial *Alexander Crummell: A Study of Civilization and Discontent* (New York: Oxford University Press, 1989). Blyden's story is told by Hollis Lynch, *Edward Wilmot Blyden: Pan-Negro Patriot, 1832–1912* (London: Oxford University Press, 1967), which remains the definitive biography of the man.

3. Russwurm to A. R. Plumley, November 18, 1829.

4. Russwurm to Plumley, November 18, 1829.

5. The Dailey and Russwurm commission business was started on January 1, 1831, and was apparently quite successful, despite the periodic disruption of trade caused by internecine wars in the interior. The partnership lasted until 1835, though it was not officially dissolved until the following year. Dailey blamed the influence of Governor Mechlin, his nemesis, on Russwurm for the ending of the partnership, but the matter was more complex than that. See *Liberia Herald*, February 6, 1831, for the announcement of the partnership and the impressive list of references; the "marine list," carried in the same issue, as well as others, indicates that Dailey and Russwurm had a substantial business enterprise. Joseph R. Dailey to Robert Purvis, April 12, 1833, repr. in C. Peter Ripley, ed., *The Black Abolitionist Papers*, vol. 3, *The United States, 1830–1846* (Chapel Hill: University of North Carolina Press, 1991), pp. 74–77; "Monument to Governor Russwurm," *Maryland Colonization Journal*, n.s., 6 (March 1853): 351–52; Russwurm to Francis E. Russwurm, March 31, 1834, and September 27, 1835, both in Sumner Russwurm Papers, box 2, folder 6; Russwurm to Gurley, May 5, 1834, RACS, reel 153; Russwurm to Latrobe, June 22, 1837, MSCSP, reel 3; Julie Winch, *A Gentleman of Color: The Life of James Forten* (New York: Oxford University Press, 2002), pp. 249–50.

6. *African Repository and Colonial Journal* 18 (June 1842): 185.

7. [Russwurm], "To Our Readers," *Liberia Herald*, February 6, 1831.

8. An earlier newspaper called *Liberia Herald* was begun in 1826 by the newly arrived emigrant Charles Force, but the paper died soon after it began with the death of its founder in the same year. No copy of the paper has apparently survived. On the basis of an absence of copies, especially among the ACS papers, Carl Burrowes doubts that it ever existed. But the evidence against his position is strong. Certainly Russwurm knew of the previous effort before he went to Liberia and asked Gurley to send a spare copy so he might see it. He apparently did not get a copy. However, the *American Baptist Magazine* of July 1826 provides definitive proof that the paper had appeared, carrying an article from the first number of the *Herald*. In the article, Force thanked the donors for the press, which along with his salary came to $1,000. "But," he wrote, "they will best understand our feelings when we inform them that nearly $200 have been subscribed by our citizens towards the immediate issue and support of a publick Newspaper." Appended to the article is a melancholy note by the editor of the *American Baptist Magazine*, which reads: "We regret to state, that the Publisher, Mr. Charles L. Force, had only issued three papers, before he was removed by death." The Rev. Calvin Holton, who had gone out in the party of forty Baptists, which included Force, narrowly survived and was barely able to report home of the devastation. The party had sailed from Boston on January 4, 1826 and arrived in Monrovia on February 7. But by April 24, when Holton wrote to the magazine, eleven or twelve were dead, including Force, primarily from the fever. *American Baptist Magazine* 4 (March 1826): 92–93, 6 (July 1826): 214–15, and 6 (September 1826): 272–73; Charles Huberich, *The Political and Legislative History of Liberia*, 2 vols. (New York: Central Book, 1947), vol. 1, pp. 344, 392–93; Burrowes, "Press Freedom in Liberia, 1830–1847: The Impact of Heterogeneity and Modernity," *Journalism and Mass Communication Quarterly* 74 (Summer 1997): 333, 344 n. 23; Russwurm to Gurley, April 8, 1829, RACS, reel 5.

9. *Freedom's Journal*, August 3, 1827. During the following summer, Russwurm spent time in Philadelphia on his trip to Washington. He admired the African American population of the city and its enterprise and relative prosperity. "Should a stranger desire to see the elite of our people," Russwurm declared, "he must visit Philadelphia, which contains a larger number of them than any other city." But in general he found Philadelphia dull compared to the "busy hum of New York." It had one attribute that excited Russwurm: the advancement in education among its black population. He evidently visited every school in the city catering to African American children and offered his appraisal of each. He devoted most of his two dispatches on

Philadelphia to these schools. He was most "delighted" by the newly established infant school, in whose future welfare he felt "the deepest solicitude." Russwurm took the opportunity to once again drive home his point about the centrality of education: "In this day of general illumination, the 'Schoolmaster with his Primer' should be an object of the first importance in every well regulated community." This was a key component of the philosophy that he took with him to Liberia the following year. [Russwurm], "Travelling Scraps," *Freedom's Journal*, June 27 and July 11, 1828.

10. *Liberia Herald*, March 6, 1830; cf. Garvey's remarks on education in Winston James, *Holding Aloft the Banner of Ethiopia: Caribbean Radicalism in Early Twentieth-Century America* (London: Verso, 1998), p. 79.

11. *Liberia Herald*, July 22, 1831. See also *Liberia Herald*, February 6, April 22, November 22, and December 22, 1831, and February 22, 1832.

12. *Liberia Herald*, February 6, 1831.

13. *Liberia Herald*, November 22, 1831.

14. [Russwurm], "To Our Readers," *Liberia Herald*, February 22, 1832.

15. It is possible that Russwurm made the demand for a high school for girls, but it does not appear in the extant copies of the *Herald*. For more progressive ideas on women, see Russwurm's 1827 report from New Haven, "To the Senior Editor, No. III," *Freedom's Journal*, August 17, 1827, "Ascent of a Female to Mount Blanc," *Freedom's Journal*, February 14, 1829, and his poem "Stanzas on Woman," *Liberia Herald*, June 5, 1830.

16. [Russwurm], "To Our Readers," *Liberia Herald*, February 22, 1832.

17. See *Liberia Herald*, February 22, 1832, and April 22, 1831, respectively; *Freedom's Journal*, October 31, 1828.

18. *Liberia Herald*, April 22, 1831; *Freedom's Journal*, August 31, 1827.

19. Quotations from "Kosciusko," *Liberia Herald*, November 22, 1831, and "Funeral of Bolivar," *Liberia Herald*, May 23, 1831.For the other topics mentioned, see *Liberia Herald*, June 5, 1830; February 6, April 22, May 23, June 22, July 22, and November 22, 1831. During the revolutionary war, Kosciuszko, who served as an officer in the Continental Army, developed a close bond over a period of four years with his black orderly, Agrippa Hull. Kosciuszko became an abolitionist. His close friend Thomas Jefferson agreed to serve as the executor of his will. Kosciuszko willed his considerable American estate to purchase the freedom of Jefferson's slaves. After Kosciuszko's death in 1817, Jefferson challenged Kosciuszko's will in the Virginia courts and refused to manumit his slaves, who remained in bondage and were sold at auction after Jefferson's death in 1826. See Gary B. Nash and Graham Russell Gao Hodges, *Friends of Liberty: A Tale of Three Patriots, Two Revolutions, and the Betrayal That Divided a Nation: Thomas Jefferson, Tadeusz Kosciuszko, and Agrippa Hull* (New York: Basic Books, 2008); see also Charles Mackenzie, *Notes on Haiti, Made during a Residence in that Republic*, 2 vols. (London: Henry Colburn and Richard Bentley, 1830).

20. *Liberia Herald*, April 6, 1830. For more on the "Black Laws" in Ohio and on the Cincinnati crisis of 1829 and its aftermath, see Carter G. Woodson, "The Negroes of Cincinnati Prior to the Civil War," *Journal of Negro History* 1 (January 1916): 1–22; Richard C. Wade, "The Negro in Cincinnati, 1800–1830," *Journal of Negro History* 39 (January 1954): 343–57. Wade is at pains to claim that there was no riot in Cincinnati, but his own evidence contradicts his assertion (esp. pp. 55–56). He does, however, provide disturbing evidence of the role played by the Cincinnati Colonization Society, evidence that Russwurm was either unaware of or chose to ignore. Robin W. Winks, *The Blacks in Canada: A History*, 2nd ed. (Montreal: McGill-Queen's University Press, 1997), chs. 5 and 6.

21. *Liberia Herald*, February 6, 1831.

22. *Liberia Herald*, December 22, 1831.

23. *Liberia Herald*, February 6, 1831, emphasis in the original.

24. Russwurm reported in an editorial the arrival, on February 11, 1832, of twenty-two emigrants, most of whom came from Ohio. *Liberia Herald*, February 22, 1832. But one demographer calculates that of the 4,472 emigrants who left the United States for Liberia between 1820 and 1843, only 19 came from Ohio. Antonio McDaniel, *Swing Low, Sweet Chariot: The Mortality Cost of Colonizing Liberia in the Nineteenth Century* (Chicago: University of Chicago Press, 1995), table C1, pp. 160–61. Most black Ohioans at the time, however, were born in Kentucky, and some of those might very well have been included among the 195 who gave their state of origin as Kentucky. Still, the number remains relatively small.

25. Russwurm to Gurley, January 26 and February 24, 1829, emphasis in original.

26. The expression is that of Joseph Dailey (quoted in Ripley, *Black Abolitionist Papers*, vol. 3, p. 71), about whom more will be said.

27. "Mr. Russwurm's Letter" [March 20, 1830], *African Repository and Colonial Journal* 6 (April 1830): 61. Although the *Repository* does not disclose the addressee, stating only that he is "a young man of colour, now preparing himself for missionary efforts in Africa" (p. 60), Edward Jones was certainly the recipient of the letter. Cf. Ripley, *Black Abolitionist Papers*, p. 79.

28. Russwurm to Gurley, June 23, 1828, RACS, reel 4. Russwurm had visited Gurley during his trip to Washington earlier in June, 1828. Despite their differences, the two men had always respected each other. Russwurm openly revealed that he had "always entertained the highest sentiments" for Gurley. He considered him, "in every respect, a man of superior intellect without whose assistance the [ACS] would shortly descend to the 'tomb of the Capulets.'" [Russwurm], "Travelling Scraps," *Freedom's Journal*, August 29, 1828. It appears that, either during their conversation in Washington or soon after his return to New York, Gurley made Russwurm another offer (the first was in December 1826) to go to Liberia. It was once again rejected by Russwurm but would be acceptable to Jones: "Since my return, I have conversed repeatedly with Mr. Edward Jones concerning the communication I had the honour of making to you. He thinks very favourably of it, and I am certain were the same offer which was tendered to me, made to him, it would be accepted with pleasure." Russwurm to Gurley, June 23, 1828.

29. See "Constitution of the African Mission School Society," *African Repository and Colonial Journal* 4 (September 1828): 205–8; "Report of the Board of Directors of the African Mission School Society, Presented to the Society at Hartford, Aug. 6th, 1830," *African Repository and Colonial Journal* 6 (November 1830): 260–64; Hugh Hawkins, "Edward Jones," in Logan and Winston, *Dictionary of American Negro Biography*, p. 364; Nemata A. Blyden, "Edward Jones: An African American in Sierra Leone," in *Moving On: Black Loyalists in the Afro-Atlantic World*, ed. John W. Pulis (New York: Garland, 1999); *Freedom's Journal*, March 7, 1829; Vincent P. Franklin, "Education for Colonization: Attempts to Educate Free Blacks in the United States for Emigration to Africa, 1823–1833," *Journal of Negro Education* 43 (Winter 1974): 94–95. For Sierra Leone as model for the early colonizationists, see Philip Staudenraus, *The African Colonization Movement, 1816–1865* (New York: Columbia University Press, 1961), chs. 1 and 2, esp. pp. 20–21; for the ideological foundations of the colony, see Stephen J. Braidwood, *Black Poor and White Philanthropists: London's Blacks and the Foundation of the Sierra Leone Settlement, 1786–1791* (Liverpool: Liverpool University Press, 1994); and for the colony's general history, Christopher Fyfe's *The History of Sierra Leone* (Oxford: Oxford University Press, 1962) remains unsurpassed.

30. Russwurm to Rev. I. A. Easter, June 2, 1837, MSCSP, reel 3.

31. *Freedom's Journal*, March 14, 1829.

32. Russwurm to Gurley, January 26, 1829.

33. William Cornish to Samuel Cornish, June 25, 1846, repr. in *African Repository and Colonial Journal* 22 (October 1846): 303.

34. See "Marriages in MD. in Liberia, in 1849"; W. Prout (Chairman), Wm. C. Cornish et al., "The Honorable, the Board of Managers Maryland State Colonization Society, Balt.," October

1, 1850; and "Schools in Maryland in Liberia," all in *Maryland Colonization Journal* n. s., 5, (November 1850): 19, 34–40, 40, respectively.

35. McDaniel, *Swing Low, Sweet Chariot*, table C1, pp. 160–61; Richard L. Hall, *On Afric's Shore: A History of Maryland in Liberia, 1834–1857* (Baltimore: Maryland Historical Society, 2003), p. 346.

36. Quoted in Mary Sagarin, *John Brown Russwurm: The Story of "Freedom's Journal," Freedom's Journey* (New York: Lothrop, Lee and Shepard, 1970), p. 90. There is a substantial body of literature on the free people of color in antebellum America. For some good analyses of their condition, North and South, see Leon Litwack, *North of Slavery: The Negro in the Free States, 1790–1860* (Chicago: University of Chicago Press, 1961); Ira Berlin, *Slaves without Masters: The Free Negro in the Antebellum South* (New York: Pantheon Books, 1974); James Horton, *Free People of Color: Inside the African American Community* (Washington, DC: Smithsonian Institution, 1993).

37. Russwurm to Easter, June 2, 1837.

38. *Liberia Herald*, December 22, 1831.

39. Russwurm to Latrobe, June 26, 1843, MSCSP, reel 4.

40. Russwurm to Francis E. Russwurm, September 27, 1835, Sumner Russwurm Papers, box 2, folder 6.

41. Russwurm to Gurley, August 6, 1833, quoted in Penelope Campbell, *Maryland in Africa; The Maryland State Colonization Society, 1831–1857* (Urbana, University of Illinois Press [1971]), p. 51.

42. Dr. James Hall, "My First Visit to Liberia [Concluded]," *African Repository and Colonial Journal* 62 (January 1886): 1–2, emphasis in original.

43. Russwurm to Gurley, May 5, and 16, 1834, RACS, reel 153; the $1,000 bill is mentioned by Russwurm again in Russwurm to Latrobe, May 9, 1834, MSCSP, reel 2.

44. Russwurm to Gurley, May 5, 1834, emphasis in original; Russwurm to Latrobe, May 9, 1834.

45. Quotations are taken from Russwurm to Latrobe, July 18, 1832, February 5, 1833, and May 9, 1934, MSCSP, reels 1 and 2; Russwurm to Gurley May 5, and 16, 1834; Russwurm to Judge [Samuel] Wilkeson, January 4, 1840, RACS, reel 154.

46. Russwurm to Gurley, May 5, and 16, 1834, RACS, reel 153. Early Lee Fox, *The American Colonization Society, 1817–1840* (Baltimore: Johns Hopkins University Press, 1919), ch. 2, is, despite the author's racism, good on many of the organizational, financial, and administrative problems of the ACS at the time. See also Staudenraus, *African Colonization Movement*, esp. ch. 17, and Eric Burin, *Slavery and the Peculiar Solution: A History of the American Colonization Society* (Gainesville: University Press of Florida, 2005), pp. 19–27, for the wider context of crisis in the ACS in the 1830s.

47. Both Ashmun and the ACS board resisted the democratizing measures put forward by Gurley (who was sent out to Liberia to deal with the crisis), but both quickly came around to recognizing their popular appeal and efficacy. Ralph Randolph Gurley, *Life of Jehudi Ashmun, Late Colonial Agent in Liberia* (1835; repr., New York: Negro Universities Press, 1969), pp. 182–223; Fox, *American Colonization Society*, pp. 71–75; Miles Mark Fisher, "Lott Cary, the Colonizing Missionary," *Journal of Negro History* 7 (October 1922): 398–401; Staudenraus, *African Colonization Movement*, pp. 91–97.

48. Russwurm to Judge Wilkeson, January 4, 1840.

49. Brown to Board of Managers, ACS, May 1835, quoted in Tom W. Shick, *Behold the Promised Land: A History of Afro-American Settler Society in Nineteenth-Century Liberia* (Baltimore: Johns Hopkins University Press, 1980), p. 39.

50. Joseph R. Dailey to Robert Purvis, April 12, 1833, in Ripley, *Black Abolitionist Papers*, vol. 3, pp. 74–77, quotation on p. 76; second quotation from Dailey to James M'Crummell, Septem-

ber 6, 1840, published in *Colored American*, December 5, 1840. As Floyd Miller has shown, the struggle for black empowerment in the Liberian enterprise began even before the first colonists landed, manifesting itself on the very first voyage out, and continued right up to independence in 1847. Floyd Miller, *The Search for a Black Nationality: Black Emigration and Colonization, 1787–1863* (Urbana: University of Illinois Press, 1975), esp. ch. 3.

51. Campbell, *Maryland in Africa*, p. 48.

52. Ibid., p. 48; Staudenraus, *African Colonization Movement*, p. 167; Hall, *On Afric's Shore*, p. 33. The fact that Mechlin scandalized the ACS board and the colony by having a "mulatto child" with the wife of a colonist did not help his case.

53. For Blyden's assessment of Russwurm, see Edward W. Blyden, "Latrobe's *Maryland in Liberia,*" *African Repository and Colonial Journal* 63 (July 1887): 78. Blyden had probably forgotten about Edward Jones, who in the 1830s was living in Sierra Leone. On Russwurm being overlooked for the governorship, see Hall, *On Afric's Shore*, p. 141; also Campbell, *Maryland in Africa*, pp. 90–92, and Sagarin, *John Brown Russwurm*, p. 99.

54. Russwurm to Gurley, October 5, 1835, RACS, reel 153.

55. George McGill to Board of Managers, ACS, October 8, 1835, RACS, reel 153, where he twice refers to Pinney as deranged; see also Shick, *Behold the Promised Land*, p. 39.

56. J. W. Prout to "Respected Friend," May 14, 1835, Prout to Gurley May 13, 1835, and H. Teage to Gurley, May 15 and July 1, 1835, all in RACS, reel 153.

57. Skinner to Gurley, August 24 and 27, 1835, and September 21, 1835, Russwurm to Gurley, October 5, 1835, and George McGill to Board of Managers, ACS, October 8, 1835, all in RACS, reel 153. Hall (*On Afric's Shore*, p. 143) mistakenly claims that Russwurm ran again and lost; he did not. The literature on the early Liberian press and its relation to the colonial government is strewn with errors when it comes to Russwurm's career in Monrovia. In an influential essay, Momo K. Rogers, "The Liberian Press: An Analysis," *Journalism Quarterly* 63 (Summer 1986): 273–81, even has Russwurm as an ally of "the conservative group led by Mechlin and Dr. Todsen, the Colonial Physician." He also got wrong the details and wider issue at stake when the mob attacked the *Herald* in 1834 (pp. 276–77); Carl Burrowes's account is only slightly less garbled. See Burrowes, "Press Freedom in Liberia," pp. 333–34. Much of the error stemmed from Huberich's pioneering 1947 work, *Political and Legislative History*, vol. 1, where many of these mistakes were first made and uncritically repeated by others who followed.

58. Skinner to Gurley, August 27, 1835, RACS, reel 153, emphasis in original.

59. McGill to Board of Managers, ACS, October 8, 1835.

60. Russwurm to Gurley, October 5, 1835, emphasis in original.

61. Russwurm to Francis E. Russwurm, September 27, 1835, Sumner Russwurm Papers, box 2, folder 6.

62. Russwurm to Gurley, October 5, 1835; Sagarin, *John Brown Russwurm*, pp. 96–98.

63. "Monument to Governor Russwurm," p. 352.

64. See Russwurm family tree in Sumner Russwurm Papers; Russwurm to Francis Edward Russwurm, September 27, 1835, box 2, folder 6, Sumner Russwurm Papers; Russwurm to Hall, August 21, and November 24, 1848, MSCSP, reel 5; James Hall to A. Cleveland, November 15, 1853, Russwurm Collection, box 1, folder 5; Sarah Elizabeth (Hawes) Cutter, "The Hawes Family," *Old Times in North Yarmouth* 6 (April 1882): 843; J. T. Hull, "John Russwurm—His Son John B. Russwurm," Russwurm Collection, box 1, folder 5; Sagarin, *John Brown Russwurm*, p. 131; J[ohn] T. H[ull], "Russwarm [sic] Family," *Portland Daily Press,* February 21, 1878, repr. in *Old Times in North Yarmouth* 5 (October 1881): 782.

65. Hall, *On Afric's Shore*, pp. 265–66; Leroy Graham, *Baltimore: The Nineteenth Century Black Capital* (Washington, DC: University Press of America, 1982), pp. 77–79; quotation of Samuel McGill from Samuel F. McGill to Moses Sheppard, May 16, 1854, in Graham, *Baltimore*, p. 78. In addition to Graham's book, for a good portrait of black Baltimore during McGill's time

there, see Christopher Phillips, *Freedom's Port: The African American Community of Baltimore, 1790–1860* (Urbana: University of Illinois Press, 1979), esp. chs. 1–5. Wood, a blacksmith, went to New York instead of Baltimore. Unlike McGill he gave Haiti a second try in 1824 but left again and returned to Baltimore. With his wife and infant son, Wood accompanied his friend George McGill to Liberia on the *Doris* in 1827. Like McGill, Wood also settled at Cape Palmas, where he served in Russwurm's government.

66. *African Repository and Colonial Journal* 3 (September 1827): 210. Huberich's pioneering work seems to have been the source of the assertion that McGill emigrated with his family in 1827. See Huberich, *Political and Legislative History*, vol. 1, p. 441, where he also mistakenly asserts that the *Doris*, which took McGill to Liberia, arrived on August (instead of April) 11, 1827. See *African Repository and Colonial Journal* 3 (September 1827): 208.

67. *African Repository and Colonial Journal* 3 (December 1827): 300–308.

68. *African Repository and Colonial Journal* 6 (October 1830): 246–47.

69. Latrobe quoted in "Colonization Meeting," *Maryland Colonization Journal*, n.s., 1 (November 15, 1842): 274–75; Hall to Cleveland, November 15, 1853; see also Graham, *Baltimore*, pp. 107–8.

70. For evidence of her business activity, see Hall, *On Afric's Shore*, p. 594.

71. Russwurm to Hall, October 18, 1849, MSCSP, reel 5.

72. Russwurm to Latrobe, February 23, 1834, MSCSP, reel 2.

73. For evidence regarding the Russwurms' relationship, see, for instance, Russwurm to Hall, November 24, 1848, and October 18, 1849, MSCSP, reel 5. In a letter dated April 9, 1852, to Jacob Loring (the family's attorney in Maine), written jointly by Samuel McGill and Sarah Russwurm as administrators of the Russwurm estate, they wrote: "Mrs. R. is now about to embark for Monrovia where she will in future reside." The "Shipping Intelligence" from the *Liberia Herald* listed "Mrs. Russwurm and family" among those who arrived from Cape Palmas on May 9, 1852. See McGill and Russwurm to Loring, April 9, 1852, and Sarah Russwurm to James Hall, dated Monrovia, June 4, 1853; "Shipping Intelligence" from *Liberia Herald*, reprinted in *Maryland Colonization Journal*, n.s., 6 (July 1852): 211. For a brief biographical sketch of Augustus Washington along with a sample of his writings, see Wilson Jeremiah Moses, ed., *Liberian Dreams: Back-to-Africa Narratives from the 1850s* (University Park: Pennsylvania State University Press, 1998), pp. 179–224. For Washington as a daguerreotypist, see the splendid exhibition catalog *A Durable Memento: Portraits by Augustus Washington, African American Daguerreotypist*, ed. Ann M. Shumard (Washington, DC: National Portrait Gallery, Smithsonian Institution, 1999), quotation on p. 12.

74. Russwurm to Hall, September 16, 1850, where Russwurm discusses the financial arrangements for the boys' schooling and boarding. Details of George and Francis Russwurm's time in North Yarmouth (as well as of the Russwurm estate) are contained in the John Russwurm Correspondence, Maine Historical Society, Portland. See in particular, Russwurm to Jacob G. Loring, February 7, 1851; Loring to Russwurm, July 11, 1851; Samuel McGill and Sarah E. Russwurm to Loring, September 19, 1851; Loring to James Hall, December 22, 1851; McGill and Sarah E. Russwurm to Loring, April 9, 1852 (which is quoted above); Hall to Loring, October 31, 1853. See also Hall to Cleveland, November 15, 1853 (which is quoted above); *Catalogue of the Officers and Students of North Yarmouth Academy* (Portland, ME: Thurston) for the academic years 1850–51 and 1851–52; Cutter, "Hawes Family," pp. 841–44; Hull, "John Russwurm"; H. H. Price and Gerald E. Talbot, *Maine's Visible Black History: The First Chronicle of Its People* (Gardiner, ME: Tilbury House, 2006), p. 165; Alex Lear, "Crossing the Color Line: Historic Yarmouth Shares Ties with African Republic," *Community Leader* (Maine), December 7, 2006.

75. Hull, "John Russwurm"; Hull, "Russwarm Family," p. 782; Cutter, "Hawes Family," p. 844.

76. Sagarin, *John Brown Russwurm*, p. 131.

77. Russwurm to Hall, August 21 and November 24, 1848. I arrived at the approximate age of Samuel Ford by means of an entry to the journal of the Rev. John Payne, a missionary of the

Episcopal Church in Maryland in Liberia. In his entry for June 5, 1845, Payne registered that, "at the request of the parents, I baptized the infant son of Gov. Russwurm." I therefore assume that Sam was born in early 1845. "Journal of the Rev. J. Payne, Missionary at Cavalla, Western Africa," extract published in *Maryland Colonization Journal*, n.s., 3 (January 1846): 110–11, quotation on p. 111.

78. Russwurm to Francis Edward Russwurm, September 27, 1835; "Monument to Governor Russwurm," p. 352.

5. GOVERNOR RUSSWURM

1. Quotations from John H. B. Latrobe, *Maryland in Liberia: A History of the Colony Planted by the Maryland State Colonization Society under the Auspices of the State of Maryland, U.S. at Cape Palmas on the South-West Coast of Africa, 1833–1853* (Baltimore: Maryland Historical Society, 1885), pp. 19–20; and from an extract of an 1879 unpublished autobiographical sketch by Latrobe in John E. Semmes, *John H. B. Latrobe and His Times, 1803–1891* (Baltimore: Norman, Remington, 1917), p. 144. (Latrobe, himself an influential mason, also mentioned the important role of this group in the initial formation of the MSCS; see Semmes, *John H. B. Latrobe,* p. 143.) P. J. Staudenraus's *The African Colonization Movement, 1816–1865* (New York: Columbia University Press, 1961), pp. 232–34, also noted the antislavery impulses of the MSCS, and Masonic connections (pp. 111–12). In his survey of the early colonization movement, Frederic Bancroft noted that "Maryland was an exception among the slave states, in being energetic and not afraid of an antislavery trend." Frederic Bancroft, "The Early Antislavery Movement and African Colonization," in *Frederic Bancroft: Historian,* ed. Jacob E. Cooke (Norman: University of Oklahoma Press, 1957), p. 182. Maryland in Liberia maintained a separate identity until it amalgamated with Liberia proper (the Republic of Liberia) in 1857. There are two comprehensive histories of the colony: Penelope Campbell, *Maryland in Africa: The Maryland State Colonization Society, 1831–1857* (Urbana: University of Illinois Press, [1971]), and Richard L. Hall, *On Afric's Shore: A History of Maryland in Liberia, 1834–1857* (Baltimore: Maryland Historical Society, 2003). Jane Martin's 1968 study remains the most comprehensive and authoritative on the subject of the indigenous Africans, primarily the Glebo (often referred to as Grebo) people, who lived in and around Cape Palmas at the time the colony was established in 1834. See Jane Jackson Martin, "The Dual Legacy: Government Authority and Mission Influence among the Glebo of Eastern Liberia, 1834–1910" (PhD diss., Boston University, 1968). Latrobe, *Maryland in Liberia,* is the story from the perspective of the prime mover behind the whole project. See also Harry Johnston, *Liberia,* 2 vols. (London: Hutchinson, 1906).

2. The young and idealistic Latrobe, officially the MSCS's corresponding secretary but in fact the "factotum," as he reflected many years later, was given the job of drafting the constitution of the new colony. Not quite thirty at the time, Latrobe recognized that it was, as he put it, "a rare opportunity to a young lawyer to lay the foundations of what might grow to be a great nation." Guided by liberal and democratic sensibilities, Latrobe took the job very seriously. As he recalled half a century later: "I prepared a charter containing a Bill of Rights, to begin with. I studied the charters and constitutions of the different states of the United States and selected the best, or made up one from the best of them. I then took Nathan Dane's ordinance of 1787 for the government of the Northwest Territory and modified it until I fancied it would do for the Maryland colony." Quoted in Semmes, *John H. B. Latrobe,* pp. 146–47. The constitution was adopted unanimously by the board of managers of the MSCS on November 22, 1833. See "Constitution of Maryland in Liberia," repr. in *Fourth Annual Report of the Maryland State Colonization Society* (Baltimore: John D. Toy, 1836), pp. 62–66. One of the major differences between the constitution of the colony and that of the United States was that the former (Article 7.19) explicitly outlawed slavery and involuntary servitude.

3. See *Seventh Annual Report of the Board of Managers of the Maryland State Colonization Society* (Baltimore: John D. Toy, 1839), p. 27, for list of officers in 1838 and the method of its determination; "Fourteenth Annual Report of the Board of Managers of the Maryland State Colonization Society," reprinted in *Maryland Colonization Journal*, n.s., 3 (March 1846): 135; Edward W. Blyden, "Latrobe's *Maryland in Liberia*," *African Repository and Colonial Journal* 63 (July 1887): 87.

4. Campbell, *Maryland in Africa*, p. 67; James Hall quoted in Latrobe, *Maryland in Liberia*, p. 26; Hall, *On Afric's Shore*, p. 61.

5. Latrobe to Russwurm, June 30, 1836. I have come across no case of wife beating mentioned by Russwurm in his dispatches. It probably occurred rarely, if at all, by the time Russwurm took charge of the colony, given the deterring effect of Hall's exemplary treatment of offenders. The initial provisions for new colonists are elaborated upon by Latrobe in "Fourteenth Annual Report," p. 136; Campbell, *Maryland in Africa*, p. 69.

6. Whereas the MSCS appointed a black governor within two years of the establishment of Maryland in Liberia, the ACS took twenty-one years after the founding of Liberia to appoint a black governor, Joseph Roberts, in 1841. Established in 1787, Sierra Leone did not have a black governor (William Fergusson) until 1845.

7. "The Maryland State Colonization Society," *African Repository and Colonial Journal* 13 (April 1837): 118.

8. Capt. J. I. Nicholson to Hon. Mahlon Dickerson, Secretary of the Navy, January 8, 1837, published in "Capt. Nicholson's Report," *African Repository and Colonial Journal* 13 (April 1837): 105–9, quotation on 108.

9. Nicholson to Latrobe, March 3, 1837, and Nicholson to Russwurm, December 17, 1836, both in MSCSP, reel 3.

10. "Capt. Nicholson's Report," p. 109.

11. "Maryland State Colonization Society," p. 118.

12. Latrobe to Russwurm, June 30, 1836, MSCSP, reel 24. See also the announcement of Russwurm's appointment in the *Fifth Annual Report of the Board of Managers of the Maryland State Colonization Society* (Baltimore: John D. Toy, 1837), pp. 7–8. For more on Latrobe, in addition to his own writings and administrative role extensively referred to in what follows, see Semmes, *John H. B. Latrobe,* and Hall, *On Afric's Shore.*

13. Russwurm to Latrobe, September 28, 1836, MSCSP, reel 2.

14. *Seventh Annual Report of the Board of Managers of the Maryland State Colonization Society* (Baltimore: John D. Toy, 1839), pp. 8–9.

15. Hall in letter to the MSCS's board of managers quoted in Archibald Alexander, *A History of Colonization on the Western Coast of Africa* (1846; repr., New York: Negro Universities Press, 1969), pp. 432–33.

16. Russwurm had procured twenty-four young breadfruit plants during a visit to Cape Coast, Gold Coast, and shipped them back to Cape Palmas. Russwurm to Hall, May 4, 1848, and Russwurm to Latrobe, November 22, 1848, both in MSCSP, reel 5. Russwurm to Latrobe, December 8, 1839, published in *African Repository and Colonial Journal* 16 (June 1, 1840): 171; William Allen and T. R. H. Thomson, *A Narrative of the Expedition Sent by Her Majesty's Government to the River Niger in 1841,* 2 vols. (London: Richard Bentley, 1848), vol. 1, p. 111.

17. Apart from the Campbell *(Maryland in Africa)* and Hall *(On Afric's Shore)* volumes, there are two especially fine analyses of some of Russwurm's major achievements as governor: Samuel W. Laughon, "Administrative Problems in Maryland in Liberia: 1836–1851," *Journal of Negro History* 26 (July 1941): 325–64; and Charles A. Earp, "The Role of Education in the Maryland Colonization Movement," *Journal of Negro History* 26 (July 1941): 365–88; quotation from Russwurm to Latrobe, December 30, 1845, published in *Maryland Colonization Journal* 3 (April 1846): 146–49. Russwurm offered his resignation in 1838 and again in 1841. On both occasions he was

prevailed upon by the MSCS's board, especially its president (Latrobe), to remain. Everyone recognized that he was the best person for the job. See especially Russwurm to Latrobe, June 24 and September 22, 1841, MSCSP, reel 4; Latrobe to Russwurm, December 18, 1841, MSCSP, reel 17. The tendering of his resignation in 1841 was made public; see the statement released by the office of MSCS, December 12, 1841, published in *Maryland Colonization Journal*, n.s., 1 (December 15, 1841): 112. Apparently Russwurm formally withdrew the resignation only after more than a year; see "The Eleventh Annual Report of the Board of Managers of the Maryland State Colonization Society," published in *Maryland Colonization Journal*, n.s., 1 (January 15, 1843): 309. See also Hall, *On Afric's Shore*, pp. 189–90, 204–8.

18. Russwurm to Latrobe, April 26, 1838, quoted in Laughon, "Administrative Problems," p. 353.

19. Dr. Samuel McGill to Latrobe, January 24, 1846, published in *Maryland Colonization Journal* 3 (April 1846): 150–51. Samuel McGill studied medicine in Washington and Dartmouth Medical School under the auspices of the MSCS before serving as the colony's physician. But Russwurm and his brother-in-law, who was far keener on mercantile trade and not paying his taxes (Russwurm saw to it that he paid), seldom got on together in later years. McGill became acting governor after Russwurm's death before moving to Monrovia, where he functioned as a merchant in a company owned by himself and his brothers, McGill Brothers.

20. Hall, *On Afric's Shore*, p. 348.

21. Russwurm to Latrobe, December 30, 1845, published in *African Repository and Colonial Journal* 22 (July 1846): 202–3.

22. *Maryland Colonization Journal* 2 (December 1844): 259; journal quoted in J. W. Lugenbeel to Dr. James Hall, May 26, 1846, published in *African Repository and Colonial Journal* 22 (August 1846): 244–45. See also the remarkably complimentary letters written by two U. S. Navy officers published in *Maryland Colonization Journal*, n.s., 1 (July 15, 1841): 19–24.

23. *Maryland Colonization Journal* 5 (November 1850): 39.

24. Russwurm to Latrobe, December 30, 1845, p. 202; *Maryland Colonization Journal* 5 (November 1850): 39; Earp, "Role of Education," pp. 386–87; Hall, *On Afric's Shore*, pp. 348, 599 n.

25. W. A. Prout to James Hall, April 29, 1848, published in *Maryland Colonization Journal* 4 (July 1848): 203. Earp, "Role of Education," p. 386; Hall, *On Afric's Shore*, p. 348.

26. Prout was largely educated by and also might have been literally adopted by Russwurm. The *Maryland Colonization Journal* reported that Prout had been "early adopted and educated" by Russwurm. See *African Repository and Colonial Journal* 30 (October 1854): 289.

27. Earp, "Role of Education," p. 387; Hall, *On Afric's Shore*, pp. 349–53.

28. Blyden, "Latrobe's Maryland in Liberia," p. 87.

29. McGill to Latrobe, January 24, 1846, p. 151.

30. John H. B. Latrobe, "Fifteenth Annual Report of the Board of Managers of the Maryland State Colonization Society," *Maryland Colonization Journal*, n.s., 3 (June 1847): 369–73; quotation on p. 370.

31. Russwurm to Latrobe, June 26 and July 31, 1843. A particularly touching example of the solicitude with which Russwurm cared for the colonists is contained in another letter he wrote to Latrobe, June 28, 1843; all in MSCSP, reel 4.

32. For an analysis of Mechlin's methods in dealing with indigenous Africans, see Claude Andrew Clegg, *The Price of Liberty: African Americans and the Making of Liberia* (Chapel Hill: University of North Carolina Press, 2004), pp. 103–12.

33. Martin, "Dual Legacy," pp. 107–9; Campbell, *Maryland in Africa*, pp. 129–30; Hall, *On Afric's Shore*, pp. 181–91, 207–8.

34. "Monument to Governor Russwurm," *Maryland Colonization Journal*, n.s., 6 (March 1853), p. 352.

35. "Letter from Dr. McGill," *Maryland Colonization Journal*, n.s., 2 (December 1844): 283–85, quotation on p. 284.

36. *African Repository and Colonial Journal* 20 (May 1844): 140.

37. Blyden, "Latrobe's *Maryland in Liberia*," p. 79. Throughout his life Russwurm emphasized the merits of union. "From our boyhood," he revealed in the *Liberia Herald*, "we have often reflected upon the fable of the old man, who had several sons, and the bundle of sticks. It is in our humble opinion, a fine illustration of Union in a family, church, or State." *Liberia Herald*, June 5, 1830. This is almost certainly the same parable related to Blyden.

38. *African Repository and Colonial Journal* 19 (October 1843): 316–18, quotation on p. 317.

39. "Monument to Governor Russwurm," p. 352. Blyden ("Latrobe's *Maryland in Liberia*," p. 80) rather uncritically subscribed to the view that Russwurm was too soft on the Africans. Russwurm confessed in one of his letters to Latrobe that "perhaps the indolent receive more pity than they merit" under his governorship. Russwurm to Latrobe, June 26, 1843, MSCSP, reel 4. After he died, some colonists criticized Russwurm, rather hypocritically, for having given out too much charity, which they said had fostered the stagnation of the community. Hall, *On Afric's Shore*, p. 316. Russwurm's apparent excessive generosity may have its roots in his own experience of hardship as a youth in Maine.

40. Hall revealed to Latrobe that, as a part of the deal in purchasing the first piece of land for the settlement at Cape Palmas, he had passed on to King Freeman "800 lbs of Tobacco which was so bad that I could never trade it off." Pleased with himself, Hall admitted to Latrobe that he had "*put it into them* pretty well" in making the deal. Hall to Latrobe, October 15, 1834, quoted in Hall, *On Afric's Shore*, p. 77, emphasis in original. Russwurm to Latrobe, July 31, 1843, MSCSP, reel 4. Russwurm never took a liking to missionaries as a group, especially the American ones with whom he had dealings in Africa. He contrasted the American ones unfavorably with British missionaries at Cape Coast in the Gold Coast (Ghana), whom he thought were free of racism. Russwurm to Hall, November 22, 1848, MSCSP, reel 5.

41. Martin, "Dual Legacy," pp. 96–97; Hall, *On Afric's Shore*, esp. pp. 225–46; see also Harrison Ola Abingbade, "The Settler-African Conflicts: The Case of the Maryland Colonists and the Grebo, 1840–1900," *Journal of Negro History* 66 (Summer 1981): 93–109, though it is rather unreliable in places. One of the many errors of fact and interpretation in Amos J. Beyan's book is the outlandish notion that Russwurm had planned to emulate Andrew Jackson's "extermination policy toward American Indians" by applying it to the Gleboes. Beyan does not reveal to his readers that this calumny against Russwurm was spread by racist missionaries who had effectively been expelled from Maryland in Liberia by Russwurm with the backing of the MSCS. Amos J. Beyan, *African American Settlements in West Africa: John Brown Russwurm and the American Civilizing Efforts* (New York: Palgrave Macmillan, 2005), pp. 103–4.

42. Russwurm to Latrobe, May 31, 1841, MSCSP, reel 4. The problem of natives stealing from the colonists was a perennial and perplexing problem for all the settlements in Liberia, especially in the early years. James Hall came to the conclusion that among the Africans in the vicinity of Cape Palmas at least, "theft was tolerated, and even considered praiseworthy, in case the affair was managed adroitly." But he came up with nonviolent and imaginative measures that reduced its occurrence. See James Hall's communication on the problem in the MSCS's *Fifth Annual Report*, pp. 22–23.

43. "Letter from Dr. McDowell to the Rev. Mr. Easter," January 15, 1839, published in *African Repository and Colonial Journal* 15 (August 1839): 213.

44. Russwurm to Latrobe, September 24, 1841; Blyden, "Latrobe's *Maryland in Liberia*," pp. 79–81.

45. "Address of the Board of Managers of the Maryland State Colonization Society to the Citizens of Maryland in Liberia," October 21, 1851, repr. in *Maryland Colonization Journal*, n.s., 6 (October 1851): 67–68. See also Charles W. Thomas, *Adventures and Observations on the West Coast of Africa, and Its Islands* (New York: Derby and Jackson, 1860), pp. 177–79.

46. See, for instance, Russwurm to Latrobe, June 26 and July 31, 1843.

47. Hall, *On Afric's Shore*, pp. 211–12; see also Campbell, *Maryland in Africa*, pp. 132–39.

48. Russwurm to Latrobe, August 24, 1844, MSCSP, reel 5; Laughon, "Administrative Problems," pp. 358–60; Campbell, *Maryland in Africa,* pp. 154–55.

49. Russwurm to Latrobe, February 12, 1842, MSCSP, reel 4; Martin, "Dual Legacy," pp. 121–60, Wilson quoted on 127; Hall, *On Afric's Shore,* pp. 177–78, 207, 212.

50. See, however, his letter to Judge Wilkeson, January 4, 1840, RACS, reel 154; he took care to mark it private and within the body of the letter itself again told Wilkeson to regard it as confidential.

51. Edward Wilmot Blyden, "A Voice from Bleeding Africa" [1856], in *Black Spokesman: Selected Published Writings of Edward Wilmot Blyden,* ed. Hollis R. Lynch (London: Frank Cass, 1971), p. 10, emphasis in original.

52. Russwurm wrote less than a year before he died: "I am not opposed to annexation to the Republic on fair terms, whenever the [MSCS] Board deem it expedient. We ought to join as a sovereign state, and I believe, objections to this will be the great difficulty in the way. Annexation would improve our coasting trade, by keeping foreigners from putting factories on shore, without permits and duties." Russwurm quoted in "Latest from Cape Palmas and the Republic," *Maryland Colonization Journal,* n.s., 5 (November 1850): 19. See also "Latest from the Republic and the Colony," *Maryland Colonization Journal,* n.s., 5 (January 1850): 113–14; Hall, *On Afric's Shore,* pp. 306–7.

53. The tragic vicissitudes of Maryland in Liberia after Russwurm's death are outlined and analyzed in detail in Campbell, *Maryland in Africa,* chs. 8 and 9; and Hall, *On Afric's Shore,* chs. 17–21. Also see Thomas, *Adventures and Observations,* pp. 179–82. Latrobe (*Maryland in Liberia,* pp. 81–84) noted that because Russwurm's successors as governor of Maryland in Liberia lacked his "cautious and sagacious and patient temper" (p. 83), bloody conflict with the indigenous Africans resulted.

54. For the text of the land deeds to Maryland in Liberia before it was absorbed by Liberia, see Latrobe, *Maryland in Liberia,* pp. 95–125.

55. Russwurm to Latrobe, December 30, 1845, published in *Maryland Colonization Journal* 3 (April 1846): 149.

56. Russwurm to Latrobe, May 9, 1834, MSCSP, reel 2.

57. Jocelyn quoted in Jacqueline Bacon, *Freedom's Journal: The First African-American Newspaper* (Lanham, MD: Lexington Books, 2007), p. 254.

58. W. A. Prout to Latrobe, July 16, 1851, MSCSP, reel 6.

59. *Maryland Colonization Journal* 6 (October 1851): 67.

60. Hall, *On Afric's Shore,* p. 284.

61. "Arrival of the Liberia Packet," *Maryland Colonization Journal,* n.s., 4 (August 1848): 217–18; "Arrival and Departure of the Packet," *Maryland Colonization Journal,* n.s., 4 (September 1848): 232–35. His detractors in Philadelphia would have been surprised to learn that Russwurm, not the MSCS, financed the whole trip of himself, his wife, and his son to the United States. He complained afterwards of depleted savings. The payment of his salary was often years in arrears, but he made little fuss about it, bringing the matter up only when he needed the money, which evidently was not very often. (When he died, he was still owed an undisclosed but clearly substantial sum by the estate of Calvin Stockbridge, with whom he had evidently done business, and his brother Francis still owed him almost ten thousand dollars that he had lent him over a decade earlier.) In September 1850, less than a year before he died, he thanked James Hall for collecting the balance on his salary up to January 1, 1848. This suggests that he had not collected his salary for the whole of 1848, 1849, and the nine months up to September 1850. (The MSCS's annual report for 1842 stated that Russwurm was paid $5,178.89 without indicating what the payment was for. It probably was a combination of several years' salary plus other money owed to him by the Society. Russwurm was appointed at $1,000 per year in 1836, and there is no indication that his salary ever increased beyond that, let alone substantially.) He

knew the financial difficulty that the MSCS was in—despite its $10,000 per year state fund—
and as late as February 1851 he instructed his attorney, "Don't press if the Society doesn't have
the money." He never pressured his brother either, or the Stockbridges: "Stockbridge's Estates is
not to be pressed for settlement." (He never forgot the kindness of Calvin Stockbridge and his
family.) Despite his misgivings about the ACS regime in Monrovia, when Russwurm accepted
the governorship of Maryland in Liberia in 1836 he sacrificed material wealth for himself and
his family. As John Latrobe told an African American audience in Baltimore at a memorial in
Russwurm's honor, Russwurm "sacrificed a lucrative business at Monrovia by his acceptance of
this post." A few months before he was appointed at Cape Palmas, Russwurm was chosen as the
"commercial agent for the English insurance house of Lloyds." Russwurm in fact had established an extensive international commercial network, including along the West African coast,
especially in Sierra Leone and the Gold Coast. (At the time of the winding up of his partnership
with Joseph Dailey, he was co-owner of at least one schooner.) In effect, Russwurm not only
forewent the further accumulation of wealth; he subsidized the MSCS. See "Eleventh Annual
Report of the Board of Managers of the Maryland State Colonization Society," in *Maryland Colonization Journal*, n.s., 1 (January 15, 1843): 314; Latrobe, *Maryland in Liberia*, p. 54; Russwurm
to Hall, January 20, 1849 and September 16, 1850, MSCSP, reels 5 and 6; matters pertaining to
Russwurm's estate can be gleaned from the extensive correspondence between his Maine agent,
Jacob Loring, Sarah Russwurm and James Hall in the John Russwurm Correspondence, Maine
Historical Society, Portland (quotation from Russwurm to Loring, February 7, 1851); "Colonization: Tribute of Respect to the Memory of Governor Russwurm," *Maryland Colonization Journal*
6 (April 1852): 164; "Monument to Governor Russwurm," p. 352.

    62. Latrobe, *Maryland in Liberia*, p. 72.

    63. Quoted in "Arrival and Departure," p. 234.

    64. Latrobe, *Maryland in Liberia*, p. 72; "Arrival and Departure," pp. 232–35. The latter report
in the *Journal* gave the name of the venue of the event as the Exchange Hotel. The anomaly is
easily resolved: the Exchange Building (which was designed by Latrobe's father, the renowned
Benjamin Latrobe), of which the Exchange Hotel was a part, opened in 1820, but by the time of
Russwurm's visit it was known as Page's Hotel. It had been refurbished under new ownership
and apparently assumed the new name in 1835, when its facilities were advertised in the press.
See Maryland Historical Society, "Baltimore Architecture Then and Now," 2004www.mdhs.
org/library/baltarch/Page11.html; Matchett's Baltimore Director for 1835, vol. 493, preface 2,
Advertisements, Maryland State Archives, www.mdarchives.state.md.us/megafile/msa/speccol/
sc2900/sc2908/000001/000493/html/am493p--2.html.

    65. "Arrival and Departure," p. 234; Russwurm to Hall, August 21, 1848, MSCSP, reel 5; James
H. Blanchard to John Sumner Russwurm, June 14, 1850, box 1, folder 1, Sumner Russwurm Papers.

    66. Russwurm to Hall, August 21, 1848, MSCSP, reel 5.

    67. *General Catalogue of Bowdoin College and the Medical School of Maine, 1794–1912* (Bruns-
wick, ME: Bowdoin College, 1912), pp. 457 and 668.

    68. Sagarin, *John Brown Russwurm*, pp. 134–35; In September 1850, Russwurm told Hall that he
had not heard a word from Boston about the college. In any case, he said, "The office would not
suit." But he gave the project his blessings and support, "willing to lend my aid to the Ex[ecutive]
Com[mit]tee. It is a fine undertaking, & they seem in earnest." Nothing, apparently, came of the
idea. Russwurm to Hall, September 16, 1850, MSCSP, reel 6; Hall, *On Afric's Shore*, p. 291.

    69. "Arrival of the Liberia Packet" stated that Russwurm intended to visit Bowdoin during
commencement (p. 217); Russwurm to Hall, August 21, 1848. Sagarin (*John Brown Russwurm*, p.
133) wrote that during the visit Russwurm's "black friends and colleagues from the old days of
Freedom's Journal, even when they could be found, gave him a cold welcome. To them, he was
not a homecoming hero, but a man who held an office to which he had been appointed by officials in the slave state of Maryland." This is not implausible, but there is no evidence to support

the claim. Indeed, there is evidence from Boston to the contrary, as Russwurm's letter to Hall indicates. He probably was still persona non grata in certain circles in New York and Philadelphia, but he never even stopped in those cities, and there is no evidence that he contacted former friends and colleagues in either place.

70. "Arrival and Departure," p. 234. Hall (*On Afric's Shore*, p. 291) claims that Russwurm visited Bowdoin (where the offer of the presidency of the prospective black college was made), but there is no evidence to suggest that he did. He certainly did not attend the commencement exercise and he probably did not go there at all. The black college idea was, however, definitely put to Russwurm while in Boston.

71. "Arrival of the Packet, and Advices from the Colony," *Maryland Colonization Journal*, n.s., 4 (January 1849): 297–98; see also Russwurm to Hall, January 18, 1849, where Russwurm delights in and boasts about "our free home in Africa." MSCSP, reel 5, emphasis in original; Sagarin, *John Brown Russwurm*, pp. 132–35.

72. Samuel McGill to Latrobe, July 11, 1851, and W. A. Prout to Latrobe, July 16, 1851, both in MSCSP, reel 6. Hall, *On Afric's Shore*, pp. 309–10.

73. Josh H. Stewart to Board of Managers, Maryland Colonization Society, undated (but contains the report and petition from a meeting of citizens that took place on August 2, 1851), MSCSP, reel 6.

74. Hall, *On Afric's Shore*, pp. 310–11.

75. Quoted in ibid., p. 311.

76. Johnston, *Liberia*, vol. 1, pp. 190 and 232.

77. M. C. Perry (Commander of the U.S. Naval Forces, Western Coast of Africa) to Hon. David Henshaw (Secretary of the Navy), January 29, 1844, published in *African Repository and Colonial Journal* 20 (June 1844): 166–68, quotation on p. 167.

78. "Address of the Board," pp. 67–68.

79. See Russwurm's letter in "Latest from the Republic and the Colony," p. 114, where Russwurm explicitly mentions Gurley's visit.

80. [Ralph Gurley], "The Late Governor Russwurm," repr. in *African Repository and Colonial Journal* 27 (December 1851): 356–58, quotation on p. 357. See also "Death of Governor Russwurm," *Maryland Colonization Journal* 6 (October 1851): 82–84.

81. C. Abayomi Cassell, *Liberia: History of the First African Republic* (New York: Fountainhead, 1970), p. 169; Antonio McDaniel, *Swing Low, Sweet Chariot: The Mortality Cost of Colonizing Liberia in the Nineteenth Century* (Chicago: University of Chicago Press, 1995), p. 61.

82. The best analysis of the Compromise of 1850, of which the Fugitive Slave Law was an important and the most controversial component, is Holman Hamilton, *Prologue to Conflict: The Crisis and Compromise of 1850* ([Lexington]: University of Kentucky Press, 1964). The law's impact on the development of black nationalism and emigrationism in the United States is discussed at length in Floyd Miller, *The Search for a Black Nationality: Black Emigration and Colonization, 1787–1863* (Urbana: University of Illinois Press, 1975); Clegg, *Price of Liberty*, ch. 6, discusses its impact on black North Carolinians.

83. Wilson Jeremiah Moses, *Alexander Crummell: A Study of Civilization and Discontent* (New York: Oxford University Press, 1989); Hollis Lynch, *Edward Wilmot Blyden: Pan-Negro Patriot, 1832–1912* (London: Oxford University Press, 1967).

EPILOGUE

1. Arthur Schomburg, "Our Pioneers," *New York Amsterdam News*, September 19, 1936.

2. Julie Winch, *A Gentleman of Color: The Life of James Forten* (New York: Oxford University Press, 2002), p. 205. In contrast, Terry Alford, *Prince among Slaves: The True Story of an African Prince Sold into Slavery in the American South* (New York: Oxford University Press, 1977), p. 168,

adjudged Russwurm's embrace of colonization to have been sincere, while Kenneth D. Nordin, "In Search of Black Unity: An Interpretation of the Content and Function of *Freedom's Journal*," *Journalism History* 4 (Winter 1977–78): 123–28, esp. 127–28, and Jacqueline Bacon, "The History of *Freedom's Journal*: A Study in Empowerment and Community," *Journal of African American History* 88 (Winter 2003): 1–20, esp. pp. 12–16, provide a good corrective to the erroneous ideas about Russwurm's conversion.

    3. *Liberator*, May 21, 1831.

    4. *Liberator*, May 7, 1831.

    5. Bella Gross, "*Freedom's Journal* and the *Rights of All*," *Journal of Negro History* 17 (July 1932): 241–86. Subsequent page citations to this article are given parenthetically in the text.

    6. As recently as 1977, Lionel C. Barrow Jr., dean of the School of Communication at Howard University, referred to Gross's article as "probably the most extensive and scholarly review of *Freedom's Journal* available." Extensive it is; scholarly it is not. See Lionel C. Barrow, "'Our Own Cause': *Freedom's Journal* and the Beginning of the Black Press," *Journalism History* 4 (Winter 1977–78): 122.

    7. See earlier discussion and *Liberia Herald*, February 6 and December 22, 1831, especially.

    8. George E. Walker, *The Afro-American in New York City, 1827–1860* (New York: Garland, 1993), p. 80.

    9. See for instance, Pease and Pease, "The Negro Conservative: Samuel Eli Cornish," in Jane H. Pease and William H. Pease, *Bound with Them in Chains: A Biographical History of the Antislavery Movement* (Westport, CT: Greenwood Press, 1972), pp. 140-61.

    10. Russwurm, "Colonization," *Freedom's Journal*, March 14, 1829.

    11. For her outrageous assertion, Gross gave as reference the following: "*Liberator*, vol. I, contains many letters and resolutions. Woodson, *Mind of the Negro*." Of course the *Liberator* carried "many letters and resolutions." So what? Where is the evidence that Russwurm "sold" settlers "into the hands of their enemies," as she asserts? Woodson's *Mind of the Negro* cannot help her either, for there is nothing there of the kind. Hence there is not even a page reference to support her, so she cites the book and pretends that that is good enough—even though there is nothing in its almost seven hundred pages to uphold her claim.

    12. Schomburg, "Our Pioneers."

    13. Rev. A. R. Russell to Rev. John Seys, July 13, 1852, published in *Maryland Colonization Journal*, n.s., 6 (December 1852): 296–98, quotation on pp. 297–98. Russell went to Liberia as a child, was educated there, and was ordained in the United States as a minister of the Methodist Episcopal Church in 1848. At the time of writing he was a senator in the Liberian parliament.

    14. [Samuel Cornish], "Our Trust Is in God," *Colored American*, July 14, 1838.

    15. *Liberia Herald*, December 22, 1831, emphasis in the original.

    16. Early Lee Fox, *The American Colonization Society, 1817–1840* (Baltimore: Johns Hopkins University Press, 1919), ch. 1; Philip Staudenraus, *The African Colonization Movement, 1816–1865* (New York: Columbia University Press, 1961), chs. 1 and 2; Claude Andrew Clegg, *The Price of Liberty: African Americans and the Making of Liberia* (Chapel Hill: University of North Carolina Press, 2004), ch. 1; Eric Burin, *Slavery and the Peculiar Solution: A History of the American Colonization Society* (Gainesville: University Press of Florida, 2005), esp. chs. 2, 4, and 6. Russell to Seys, July 13, 1852, p. 298.

    17. See Stephen B. Weeks, *Southern Quakers and Slavery: A Study in Institutional History* (Baltimore: Johns Hopkins Press, 1896), esp. ch. 9; and the fine essay by P. M. Sherrill, "The Quakers and the North Carolina Manumission Society," in *Historical Papers*, Published by the Trinity College Historical Society, Series X (1914): 32-51. (Trinity College later became Duke University.) See also Clegg, *Price of Liberty*, ch. 1, and Burin, *Slavery*, pp. 34–37.

    18. "Letter from Jeremiah Hubbard," *African Repository and Colonial Journal* 10 (April 1834): 33–43, quotation on 41–42. Little is known about Hubbard, but it is noteworthy that he was said

to have been "one-fourth Indian"; Weeks, *Southern Quakers*, p. 138; similarly, Sherrill, "Quakers and North Carolina Manumission Society," thought it significant to mention that Hubbard had "Indian blood in his veins," p. 35. According to one obituary, he was born in Virginia in 1777 but grew up in North Carolina where he taught school. In 1837, Hubbard, like many other North Carolina Quakers in the 1830s, moved to the "Western Country." In Hubbard's case, the destination was Richmond, Indiana. He died in Indiana in 1849. *Friends' Review: A Religious, Literary and Miscellaneous Journal*, 7 (Twelfth Month [December] 10, 1853): 195–97. Hubbard was the delegate from the Society of Friends of North Carolina to the ACS's annual meeting in 1832: *Fifteenth Annual Report of the American Society for Colonizing the Free People of Colour of the United States* (Washington, DC, 1832), p. iv. As Staudenraus and Fox also document, Quaker influence was also strong elsewhere in the movement, especially in Pennsylvania, where Elliot Cresson, a wealthy but devout Quaker, was the leading force.

19. Antonio McDaniel, *Swing Low, Sweet Chariot: The Mortality Cost of Colonizing Liberia in the Nineteenth Century* (Chicago: University of Chicago Press, 1995), pp. 60–61; Clegg, *Price of Liberty*, pp. 88–196; Campbell, *Maryland in Africa*, p. 242; Jeffrey B. Allen, "'All of Us Are Highly Pleased with the Country': Black and White Kentuckians on Liberian Colonization," *Phylon* 43 (Summer 1982): 97–109; Burin, *Slavery and the Peculiar Solution*, esp. chs. 2, 3 and 4.

20. Marie Tyler McGraw has persuasively shown that up to the end of the 1820s, the Richmond Colonization Society (which later expanded into the Virginia State Colonization) was relatively enlightened in its policies and practices and received considerable support from the free people of color. However, by the end of the decade and especially after Nat Turner's revolt in 1831, the slaveholding class became more hegemonic and hostile, thus alienating black support. Marie Tyler McGraw, "Richmond Free Blacks and African Colonization, 1816–1832," *Journal of American Studies* 21 (August 1987): 207–24. Colonization was largely a northern and upper southern phenomenon. The states of the Lower South, such as South Carolina, Alabama, and Georgia, had little time for the colonizationists, whom they perceive as abolitionists in disguise, and colonization a "nest egg" of abolitionists wishing to hatch "anxiety, inquietude and troubles to which there could be no end." Ira Berlin, *Slaves without Masters: The Free Negro in the Antebellum South* (New York: Pantheon Books, 1974), pp. 212–14; Staudenraus, *African Colonization Movement*, pp. 74–76, 146–48, quotation on p. 75.

21. *Second Annual Report of the American Society for Colonizing the Free People of Colour of the United States* (Washington, DC, 1819), p. 9; see also Staudenraus, *African Colonization Movement*, pp. 75–76.

22. Quoted in Staudenraus, *African Colonization Movement*, p. 76.

23. H. N. Sherwood, "The Formation of the American Colonization Society," *Journal of Negro History* 2 (July 1917): 211. Lundy to the end in fact remained committed to colonization. He differed with the ACS primarily over the prospective homeland for African Americans; he sought one in the New World, preferably Mexico. See Pease and Pease, *Bound with Them*, ch. 5.

24. The text of the speech is reproduced in Wendell P. Garrison and Francis J. Garrison, *William Lloyd Garrison, 1805–1879: The Story of His Life Told by His Children*, 4 vols. (New York: Century, 1885–89), vol. 1, pp. 127–37, quotation on p. 137. The passage quoted has been neatly suppressed, no doubt by Garrison himself or with his approval, in the version of the speech published in *Selections from the Writings and Speeches of William Lloyd Garrison* (New York: New American Library, 1969), pp. 44–61, which was first published in 1852—a less than gentle attempt to rewrite history.

25. Garrison and Garrison, *William Lloyd Garrison*, vol. 1, pp. 124 and 137.

26. Samuel Cornish, "Colored People Always Opposed to Colonization," *Colored American*, May 13, 1837.

27. Benjamin Quarles, *Black Abolitionists* (New York: Oxford University Press, 1969), chs. 1 and 2; Staudenraus, *African Colonization Movement*, esp. chap. 15; George A. Levesque, "Black

Abolitionists in the Age of Jackson: Catalysts in the Radicalization of American Abolition," *Journal of Black Studies* 1 (December 1970): 187–201; Winch, *Gentleman of Color*, ch. 10.

28. Not the presidents and vice presidents of the ACS, but "the secretaries and the boards of managers and directors . . . [who] were the molders of policy," Fox (*American Colonization Society*, p. 74) argues. Staudenraus, *African Colonization Movement*, pp. 202–6; Bruce Rosen, "Abolition and Colonization, the Years of Conflict: 1829–1834," *Phylon* 33 (June 1972): 187–88.

29. Frederic Bancroft, "The Early Antislavery Movement and African Colonization," reprinted in *Frederic Bancroft: Historian*, ed. Jacob E. Cooke (Norman: University of Oklahoma Press, 1957), pp. 147–91, quotation on pp. 159, 163–64, 166–67; Latrobe to Gurley, January 27, 1827, quoted in Fox, *American Colonization Society*, p. 83.

30. Campbell does not say this, but reports of conditions in Maryland in Liberia, written primarily by Russwurm and published in the *Maryland Colonization Journal*, are extraordinarily open about problems and challenges in the colony, as they would not have been had the Society aimed at pulling the wool over people's eyes. Ironically, the criticism of the abolitionists of Liberia contributed to improving conditions there for emigrants, thus making it more attractive to would-be emigrants, not less, as the abolitionist had intended.

31. Penelope Campbell, *Maryland in Africa: The Maryland State Colonization Society, 1831–1857* (Urbana, University of Illinois Press [1971]), pp. 242–43; John H. B. Latrobe, *Memoir of Benjamin Banneker* (Baltimore: Maryland Historical Society, 1845), which was first presented to the Maryland Historical Society on May 1, 1845, published in the *Maryland Colonization Journal* the same month and also in the *African Repository and Colonial Journal*, 21 (November 1845): 321–32. Russwurm wrote to Latrobe: "You merit the thanks of our whole race for your able memoir of B. Banneker—be pleased to accept mine." Russwurm to Latrobe, January 24, 1846, repr. in *Maryland Colonization Journal*, n.s., 3 (April 1846): 150. For more recent appreciation of Banneker, see Silvio A. Bedini, *The Life of Benjamin Banneker: The First African-American Man of Science*, 2nd ed. (Baltimore: Maryland Historical Society, 1999); Charles A. Cerami, *Benjamin Banneker: Surveyor, Astronomer, Publisher, Patriot* (New York: Wiley, 2002). For biographical portraits of Latrobe, see his obituary, "John H. B. Latrobe, Esq.," *African Repository and Colonial Journal*, 67 (October 1891): 97–98; John E. Semmes, *John H. B. Latrobe and His Times, 1803–1891* (Baltimore: Norman, Remington, 1917).

32. Hall to Jacob Loring, August 4, 1853, John Russwurm Correspondence, Maine Historical Society, Portland; Hall, *An Address to the Free People of Color of the State of Maryland* (Baltimore: John D. Toy, 1859), quotations on pp. 1–2; "Communication from Dr. Hall," May 1, 1836, reprinted in *Fifth Annual Report of the Board of Managers of the Maryland State Colonization Society* (Baltimore: John D. Toy, 1837), pp. 20–31, quotation on pp. 24–25. For more on Yellow Will, see also Jane Jackson Martin, "The Dual Legacy: Government Authority and Mission Influence among the Glebo of Eastern Liberia, 1834–1910" (PhD diss., Boston University, 1968), pp. 98–100.

33. John H. B. Latrobe, "Dr. James Hall," *African Repository and Colonial Journal*, 65 (October 1889): 117–19, quotation on pp. 117 and 118; Sarah Russwurm and Samuel McGill to Jacob Loring, September 19, 1851, Russwurm Correspondence; Blyden to Hall, November 23, 1868, quoted in Martin, "Dual Legacy," p. 70. Latrobe, "Cape Palmas, Liberia," *African Repository and Colonial Journal*, 61 (January 1885): 1–8, documents Hall's achievements as the first governor of Maryland in Liberia that Hall himself was too modest to relate in Hall, "Cape Palmas, Liberia," *African Repository and Colonial Journal*, 60 (October 1884): 97–108.

34. The literature on the subject is vast, but see Benjamin Quarles, "The Breach between Douglass and Garrison," *Journal of Negro History* 23 (April 1938): 144–54; William H. Pease and Jane H. Pease, "The Boston Garrisonians and the Problem of Frederick Douglass," *Canadian Journal of History* 2 (September 1967): 29–48, who quoted Bradburn (p. 33); Tyrone Tillery, "The Inevitability of the Douglass-Garrison Conflict," *Phylon* 37 (Spring 1976): 137–49; John R. McKivigan, "The Frederick Douglass-Gerrit Smith Friendship and Political Abolitionism in the

1850s," in *Frederick Douglass: New Literary and Historical Essays*, ed. Eric J. Sunquist (Cambridge: Cambridge University Press, 1990); Waldo E. Martin, *The Mind of Frederick Douglass* (Chapel Hill: University of North Carolina Press, 1984); William S. McFeely, *Frederick Douglass* (New York: W. W. Norton, 1991). Apart from the polemics against the Garrisonians in his newspapers (the *North Star*, and *Frederick Douglass's Paper*), Douglass reflects upon the break with his "Boston friends" in his *My Bondage and My Freedom* (1855; repr., New York: Dover Publications, 1969), ch. xxv, and again in his *Life and Times of Frederick Douglass, Written by Himself* (1881; New York: Citadel Press, 1983), ch. vii.

35. George M. Fredrickson, *The Black Image in the White Mind: The Debate on Afro-American Character and Destiny, 1817–1914*, 2nd ed. (Middletown: Wesleyan University Press, 1987), pp. 12–13.

36. Peter Hinks, *To Awaken My Afflicted Brethren: David Walker and the Problem of Antebellum Slave Resistance* (University Park: University of Pennsylvania Press, 1997), esp. pp. 181–95. Dickson D. Bruce, *The Origins of African American Literature, 1680–1865* (Charlottesville: University Press of Virginia, 2001), pp. 154–55, also noted the antiracist role of the *African Repository*. Bruce Dain more recently wrote, "Certain sincere colonizationists became the first major American figures to explicitly and unequivocally to see blacks as in effect fully equal and undegenerate, in Africa and as Negroes—that is as distinct, different, and separate, but still equal, and connected to the West and Christianity." He, however, disfigured his analysis of the ACS by claiming unconvincingly that the celebration of Africa found in the *African Repository* was done to "fend off emigration to Haiti," forgetting that the ACS was not univocal but constituted a cacophony—many voices with different motives. In any case, ACS auxillary societies in New York, Philadelphia, Boston, Maryland and elsewhere sponsored the emigration of hundreds, if not thousands, of African Americans to Haiti. In North Carolina alone, 119 African Americans sailed to Haiti in 1826 under the auspices of a society with affiliation to the ACS. Bruce Dain, *A Hideous Monster of the Mind: American Race Theory in the Early Republic* (Cambridge, MA: Harvard University Press, 2002), pp. 105 and 123. The ACS celebration of Africa extended to the de facto permanent exhibition of African artefacts and items of material culture at their offices on Pennsylvania Avenue in Washington. Russwurm, who visited their offices in the summer of 1828, reported that they contained "many articles of African ingenuity from Liberia and the surrounding country, worthy of inspection. There I saw various specimens of cloth manufactured by the untutored natives; various implements of war, some of iron, and the skin of the tiger, a description of which was given in one of the numbers of the *Repository*." [Russwurm], "Travelling Scraps," *Freedom's Journal*, August 29, 1828.

37. Peter Hinks, ed., *David Walker's Appeal to the Coloured Citizens of the World* (University Park: Pennsylvania State University Press, 2000), p. 72.

38. See Walker's attack on colonization and the ACS in ibid., pp. 70–72.

39. Ibid., p. 70. I have never seen this passage quoted in any of the many commentaries on Walker's *Appeal*. Not even Hinks, in his fine study, *To Awaken*, mentions it.

40. *Freedom's Journal*, December 19, 1828.

41. Hinks came to a similar conclusion on the question, noting that "Walker had some ambivalence about the impulses behind colonizationism" (*To Awaken*, pp. 184–85 n). But the evidence, including Hinks's own, suggests something else. Walker recognized and divided the impulses, noting that some were good and others bad, while still condemning colonization as a project. Such a position does not amount to "ambivalence" in any meaningful sense of the term.

42. Quoted in Fox, *American Colonization Society*, p. 137.

43. See especially William Loren Katz, "The Earliest Responses of American Negroes and Whites to African Colonization," in William Lloyd Garrison, *Thoughts on African Colonization* (New York: Arno Press, 1968), pp. i–xi; Allen, "'All of Us'"; McGraw, "Richmond Free Blacks."

44. Quoted in Hall, *On Afric's Shore*, pp. 354–55. (Spelling and punctuation as they appear in the original.) For similar testimony of emigrants to Liberia, see Bell Wiley, ed., *Slaves No More:*

Letters from Liberia, 1833–1869 (Lexington: University Press of Kentucky, 1980), and Randall M. Miller, ed., *"Dear Master": Letters of a Slave Family*, 2nd ed. (Athens: University of Georgia Press, 1990); also see Wilson Jeremiah Moses, ed., *Liberian Dreams: Back-to-Africa Narratives from the 1850s* (University Park: Pennsylvania State University Press, 1998). Both the *African Repository* and the *Maryland State Colonization Journal* carried extensive testimonies of emigrants.

45. The interest in and writings about Liberia by Blyden, Crummell, and Garvey are well known. Less so are those of Padmore and Azikiwe. See George Padmore, *Pan-Africanism or Communism? The Coming Struggle for Africa* (London: Dennis Dobson, 1956), chs. 1–3; Ben N. Azikiwe, "In Defense of Liberia," *Journal of Negro History* 17 (January 1932): 30–50; Ben N. Azikiwe [as Nnamdi Azikiwe], *Liberia in World Politics*, 2 vols. (London: 1934), and *My Odyssey: An Autobiography* (New York: Praeger, 1970); Imanuel Geiss, *The Pan-African Movement*, trans. Ann Keep (London: Methuen, 1974); P. Olisanwuche Esedebe, *Pan-Africanism: The Idea and Movement, 1776–1963* (Washington, DC: Howard University Press, 1982); J. Ayodele Langley, *Pan-Africanism and Nationalism in West Africa, 1900–1945* (Oxford: Clarendon Press, 1973).

46. On Russwurm and the Negro Convention Movement, see Bacon, "History of *Freedom's Journal*"; Nordin, "In Search of Black Unity"; Howard H. Bell, "Free Negroes of the North, 1830–1835: A Study in National Co-operation," *Journal of Negro Education* 26 (Autumn 1957); Howard H. Bell, ed., *Minutes of the Proceedings of the National Negro Conventions, 1830–1864* (New York: Arno Press, 1969).

47. "C. D. T., a Philadelphian," letter to the editor, *Liberator*, April 30, 1831.

48. For a historical overview and analysis of the Caribbean contribution, see Winston James, "The Wings of Ethiopia: The Caribbean Diaspora and Pan-African Projects From John Brown Russwurm to George Padmore," in *African Diasporas in the New and Old Worlds: Consciousness and Imagination*, ed. Geneviève Fabre and Klaus Benesch (Amsterdam: Rodopi, 2004), pp. 133–72.

PART TWO

1. EARLY WRITINGS

1. Russwurm to Col. John S. Russwurm, January 9, 1826, Family Correspondence, box 2, folder 7, Sumner Russwurm Papers.

2. See [John Brown Russwurm], "Toussaint L'Overture, the Principal Chief in the Revolution of St. Domingo," ca. 1825 (quotation on p. 22), African-American History Collection, William L. Clements Library, University of Michigan, Ann Arbor.

3. Chief figures in the Haitian Revolution (1791–1804): Toussaint Louverture (1743–1803), Jean-Jacques Dessalines (1758–1806), and Henri Christophe (1767–1820).

4. Hernán Cortés de Monroy y Pizarro (1485–1547) and Francisco Pizarro González (ca. 1471–1541), Spanish invaders and conquerors of the Aztec and Inca empires, respectively.

5. Jean-Pierre Boyer (1776–1850), president of the Republic of Haiti (1818–43); Henri Christophe had declared himself king of Haiti in 1811 and had established a royal court. After Dessalines's assassination in 1806, Christophe controlled the north of Haiti, and Petíon, followed by Boyer, controlled the south. After Christophe's suicide in 1820, Haiti was reunified under Boyer's rule.

2. WRITINGS FROM *FREEDOM'S JOURNAL*

1. Dixon Denham (1786–1828) and Hugh Clapperton (1788–1827) were British explorers of West and Central Africa. They have been credited as the first Europeans to have direct experience of the Hausa states and to see Lake Chad. They (along with their ill-fated fellow explorer Walter Oudney) wrote of their experiences in *Narrative of Travels and Discoveries in Northern and Central Africa in the Years 1822–1823 and 1824*, first published in London in 1826.

2. "There is no doubt that the Ethiopians are burnt by the heat of the sun and are born with a burnt appearance and with curly beards and hair." The passage is from Pliny (the Elder), *Natural History*, bk. 2, ch. 78.

3. Homer, *The Iliad*, bk. 1, as translated by Alexander Pope.

4. Thomas Buxton (1786–1845), leading British abolitionist and parliamentarian.

5. Daniel Webster (1782–1852), then a congressman from Massachusetts. The speech was delivered in the House of Representatives on January 19, 1824. *Annals of Congress*, House of Representatives, 18th Cong., 1st sess., cols. 1085–99, quotation from col. 1094.

6. Lord Althorp (3rd Earl Spencer, 1782–1845), British liberal parliamentarian.

7. Henry Peter Brougham (1778–1868), distinguished British abolitionist and parliamentarian.

8. Thomas Clarkson (1760–1846), one of Britain's leading abolitionists. Russwurm is here referring to Clarkson's influential pamphlet, *Thoughts on the Necessity of Improving the Condition of the Slaves in the British Colonies, with a View to Their Ultimate Emancipation* (London, 1823).

9. Cornish had, by the time the letter was published, resigned from *Freedom's Journal*. Accordingly, Russwurm no longer addressed this final letter to the "Senior Editor," as he had with the previous four; instead he addressed it to Rev. Cornish by name.

10. Drawn from Horace, *Ode* 3.30: "Exegi monumentum aere perennius regalique situ pyramidum altius" (I have erected a monument more durable than bronze, loftier than the regal pile of Pyramids).

11. The item in question went under the title "WORTHY OF NOTICE" and reads in full: "During the past week, we have heard of several persons being arrested as runaways from the South. It would be well if all our brethren who have been so lucky as to escape from bondage, would pay particular attention to this notice, and leave the city, or the more frequented parts of it, for awhile, at least, as there are many from the South now in daily search of them." *Freedom's Journal*, October 31, 1828.

12. John Milton, *Paradise Lost*, 12.64–71.

13. Lucius Tarquinius Superbus, seventh king of Rome, who reigned from 535 B.C. to 496 B.C. Legend has it that he purchased three books of prophecy from the Cumaean Sibyl, which were secured in the fortress temple of Jupiter.

14. George Troup (1780–1856), governor of Georgia (1823–27), was a staunch supporter of slavery and "states' rights" who organized the removal of Creek Indians from western Georgia. He later represented Georgia in the U.S. Senate (1829–33). Austin Woolfolk was Maryland's largest and wealthiest slave trader at the time, based in Baltimore. He was notoriously cruel, and feared and hated in equal measure. Most of his money came from trading slaves to the Deep South. Benjamin Lundy, the pioneering abolitionist, was severely beaten by Woolfolk.

15. Anthony Benezet (Antoine Bénézet, 1713–84) was a French-born pioneer Quaker abolitionist and advocate and practitioner of black and female education. In 1731 he migrated to Pennsylvania, where he lived for the rest of his life.

16. See "Philadelphia Report," *Freedom's Journal*, July 18 and 25, 1828.

17. Abd al-Rahman Ibrahima (1762–1829), son of the King of Timbo (now part of the Republic of Guinea), had been captured and sold to slave traders in Futa Jallon, ending up as a slave in Natchez, Mississippi. He regained his freedom some forty years later in 1828 and went to Liberia under the auspices of the ACS, where he died five months after his arrival, never reaching his homeland.

18. The item referred to was a report from a British newspaper with the dateline, Bristol, December 27 [1828]: "By the brig Tom Cod, which arrived at this port yesterday from Africa, we have the following intelligence from Cape Mensurado [sic]. On the 18th. November last, an expedition was preparing by the American settlers at that place, to destroy a French slave ship and factory at Digby, about thirty miles distant, where during the night the magazine in which they were making cartridges, blew up, & horrible to relate, Mr. Lot Carey, the Governor, and

nine of his people, were destroyed." Lott Cary or Carey (1780–1828), one of the earliest African Americans to settle in Liberia, was born a slave in Virginia and purchased his freedom and that of his family. He became a Baptist minister and at the time of his death was acting governor of Liberia after the sudden death of the white governor, Jehudi Ashmun.

3. WRITINGS FROM LIBERIA

1. Dr. Joseph Mechlin, colonial agent, 1829–33.

2. Appointed colonial agent in September 1828, Dr. Richard Randall (1796–1829) arrived in Liberia on December 22 and immediately took up his duties. He died of fever in April 1829 and was succeeded by Dr. Mechlin.

3. See chapter 2, note 15.

4. David Brainerd (1718–47) and Charles Elliot (1792–1869) were distinguished Christian missionaries who worked among Native Americans.

5. Francis Devany (1797–1833) was sheriff of Liberia. Born into slavery in South Carolina, he acquired some education and obtained his freedom. He moved to Philadelphia in his teens and became an apprentice sailmaker under James Forten, the wealthy African American sailmaker and abolitionist. Accompanied by his wife and two children, Devany left for Liberia in 1823. He became a merchant in Monrovia, and his personal wealth was estimated to be in excess of $20,000 by the end of the 1820s. He died in Monrovia.

6. Towns comprising those liberated from slave ships, chiefly by the U.S. Navy and the British Navy in an effort to suppress the slave trade. Such rescued persons were generally referred to as "recaptured" Africans or slaves.

7. In the earlier version, published in *Freedom's Journal, transition* instead of *transaction* was used. The latter might have been a typographical error, since *transition* is a more suitable word.

8. The *Freedom's Journal* version has *indecision,* which appears to be what was intended here also, given his earlier condemnation of indecision.

9. Calvin Stockbridge (1784–1834), Russwurm's guardian.

10. James H. Blanchard and Ann Blanchard, siblings and Russwurm's stepbrother and stepsister (children of Susan Hawes, Russwurm's stepmother, from her first marriage).

11. William Stockbridge, MD (1813–53), son of William R. Stockbridge (1782–1850), brother and business partner of Calvin Stockbridge.

12. Russwurm is here referring to his commission business partnership, J. R. Dailey and John B. Russwurm, which was established on January 1, 1831. (See announcement in *Liberia Herald,* February 6, 1831.) It was not formally dissolved until 1836.

13. William Hawes and Susan Hawes. Susan Hawes was widowed by Russwurm's father, John R. Russwurm, in 1815. She married William Hawes two years later. Susan Hawes had raised John as one of her own, even after the death of her husband and her marriage to Hawes.

14. Genville Mellen (1799–1841), lawyer and poet, who practiced in North Yarmouth between 1823 and 1828; son of Prentiss Mellen (1764–1840), former senator for Massachusetts, first chief justice of the state of Maine, and trustee of Bowdoin College at the time Russwurm attended.

15. Asa Cummings, editor of the *Christian Mirror.* Russwurm founded and edited the *Liberia Herald* from 1830 to 1835, when he resigned from the paper.

16. John Sumner Russwurm (1793–1860), Russwurm's first cousin. He served as inspector general of Tennessee during the long and entire tenure of Governor William Carroll, 1821 to 1827, and 1829 to 1835; thus the title of "General," which was completely nonmilitary in this case. At the time of the letter, J. S. Russwurm lived in Murfreesboro, Rutherford County, Tennessee, the name of which town Russwurm had forgotten.

17. Russwurm is here presumably referring Calvin Stockbridge's widow and her brother-in-law (not her brother) William R. Stockbridge.

18. The last two agents of the ACS referred to here are Rev. John B. Pinney (agent from October 1833 to summer 1834) and Dr. Ezekiel Skinner (January 1835 to September 1836). Russwurm had major disagreements and struggles with both.

19. George Stockbridge Russwurm was Russwurm and Sarah McGill Russwurm's first child.

20. His wife, Sarah Elizabeth Russwurm.

21. John and Sarah Russwurm's last son. The couple reportedly had five children: George Stockbridge (1834); James Hall (1836), who apparently died in infancy; Francis Edward (Frank) (1839); a fourth son, who according to Mary Sagarin "also survived, but his name does not seem to have been recorded anywhere" (Mary Sagarin, *John Brown Russwurm: The Story of "Freedom's Journal," Freedom's Journey* [New York: Lothrop, Lee and Shepard, 1970], p. 131), was in fact Samuel Ford; and one daughter, apparently their fourth child, Angelina.

22. Hall's daughter and son.

23. James McGill, Russwurm's brother-in-law, Sarah Russwurm's brother.

24. Dr. Dempsey Fletcher, an African American settler who went to Liberia as a child, was brought from Cape Palmas to the United States by the MSCS to be educated as a physician. He graduated from Dartmouth Medical School and then returned to the colony. He became deputy to Dr. Samuel McGill (also a Dartmouth graduate), colonial physician. For years prior to his medical training in the United States, Fletcher served as the colony's apothecary while receiving some medical education under Dr. McGill. See John H. B. Latrobe, "Thirteenth Annual Report of the Board of Managers of the Maryland State Colonization Society," *Maryland Colonization Journal* 2 (April 1845): 340; H. B. Latrobe, "Fifteenth Annual Report of the Board of Managers of the Maryland State Colonization Society," *Maryland Colonization Journal* 3 (June 1847): 371; G. S. Stockwell, *The Republic of Liberia: Its Geography, Climate, Soil, and Productions, with A History of Its Early Settlement* (New York: A. A. Barnes, 1868), pp. 173–74.

25. This, the second, paragraph actually appeared in Latrobe's text as a footnote to the first paragraph. The report in the *Maryland Colonization Journal* gave the name of the venue of the event as the Exchange Hotel. The anomaly is easily resolved: the Exchange Building (which was designed by Latrobe's father, the renowned Benjamin Latrobe), of which the Exchange Hotel was a part, opened in 1820, but by the time of Russwurm's visit it was known as Page's Hotel. It had been refurbished and apparently assumed the new name in 1835. See Maryland Historical Society, "Baltimore Architecture Then and Now," 2004, www.mdhs.org/library/baltarch/Page11.html; *Matchett's Baltimore Director for 1835*, vol. 493, preface 2, Advertisements, Maryland State Archives, www.mdarchives. state.md.us/megafile/msa/speccol/sc2900/sc2908/000001/000493/html/am493p--2.html.

26. Russwurm is here referring to incidents involving the colonist Eden Parker in 1838. In an escalating series of disputes with Greboes, Parker shot and wounded an African in a dispute over a sheep. Parker's home was subsequently raided by armed Africans who killed him and set fire to his home. Russwurm was disappointed that Parker had not drawn on the resources of the authorities to resolve the disputes he had with his Greboe neighbors.

27. Russwurm is referring to the system in which a person accused of witchcraft would be required to drink the poisonous extract from the saswood (or sassy or sassa wood) tree. According to the system, if the person was innocent he or she would survive the poison, if guilty, he or she would die from the poison. The Marylanders had unsuccessfully fought against it since the colony's establishment in 1834. Outlawed in 1839, the practice never ended until the 1850s. See John H. B. Latrobe, "Cape Palmas, Liberia," *African Repository and Colonial Journal* 61 (January 1885): 6–7; Latrobe, *Maryland in Liberia*, pp. 49–53; Jane Jackson Martin, "The Dual Legacy: Government Authority and Mission Influence among the Glebo of Eastern Liberia, 1834–1910" (PhD diss., Boston University, 1968), pp. 111–13.

28. Dr. Samuel F. McGill succeeded Dr. Robert McDowell as the colonial physician for Maryland in Liberia in 1839.

Index

ABCFM. *See* American Board of Commissioners for Foreign Missions

Abolitionists, 151, 154–56; for colonization, 113–14, 209; colonization *vs.*, 115–16, 121, 123–24, 209, 236, 287n30; Liberia *vs.*, 113; pacifist, 123; pessimistic, 123

Abolition Societies, 196

Abyssinia, 219

Accommodations, Russwurm, J. B., on boat, 159

ACS. *See* American Colonization Society (ACS)

Adams, John Quincy, 155–56, 198

"Address Delivered before the General Colored Association," 30–31, 122

An Address to the Free People of Color in the State of Maryland (Hall), 119, 120

"Address to the People of Maryland in Liberia," 106

"Advice to the Young," 63

AES. *See* African Education Society

Africa: civilizationism of, 59, 271n2; descent of, 219; emigration to, 44–45, 47, 59, 230; in *Freedom's Journal*, 263n8; Russwurm, J. B., arrival in, 213–14; Russwurm, J. B., longing for, 104, 238–39; Russwurm, J. B., on, 113. *See also* Africans; Cape Palmas; Liberia; Monrovia

African American(s): Boston population of, 175; Bowdoin College graduates, 16, 18; college graduates, 16, 18, 260n52; colonization *vs.*, 31, 161, 202–3; emigration reluctance, 67; farming, Cornish, S., on, 267n44; fear of, 53; free, 124, 138; Haiti, emigration to, 11–12, 15, 263n17; idea of inferiority of, 172, 194, 204; life in U.S., 45–46; Philadelphia population of, 192–93; response to suffering of, 140; responsibility of, 140; Russwurm, J. B. on, 67–68; Russwurm, J. B., *vs.* Philadelphia's free, 46, 49–50, 65–66; unity of, 28; U.S. citizenship, 201; U.S. population *vs.* colonization of, 40–41

African Education Society (AES), 269n26

"African Eloquence," 24

African Grand Lodge of Boston, 174

African Improvement Society of New Haven, 161–62

African Masonic Lodge, 12

African Meeting House, 12, 163

African Repository and Colonial Journal, 34, 44, 54, 65, 68, 70, 117, 121; on Walker, D., influence of, 122

Africans: colonists attitude toward educated, 70; colonists trading with, 215–16; colonists *vs.*, 97, 98, 101, 281n42, 282n53, 292n26; education of, 61–63, 163, 229–30; Egyptian appearances *vs.* present race of, 144; Hall's address to, 119; rights of, 34, 87, 278n2; Russwurm, J. B., on, 99, 215; on Russwurm, J. B., 97–98; Russwurm's, J. B., diplomacy with, 97; Russwurm's, J. B., treatment of, 98, 281n39

African School, 12, 16

Agriculture, 229; of Cape Palmas, 89, 93, 244, 246–47, 251–52, 279n16; Cornish on, 267n44; of Liberia, 204–5; of Monrovia, 224; trade *vs.*, 89

Alexander, Archibald, 37, 41–42, 181, 265n31

Allen, Richard, on colonization, 42–43

Allen, William, 93

Althorpe, Lord, 152–53

American Asylum for the Deaf and Dumb, 64, 167–68

American Baptist Magazine, 272n8

American Board of Commissioners for Foreign Missions (ABCFM), 100

American Colonization Society (ACS), 24–25, 51, 52, 265n31; African Americans *vs.*, 124; Bancroft on, 117–18; emigration to Africa *vs.* Haiti, 288n36; false perceptions of, 116–17; *Freedom's Journal*, advocacy of, 200–212; *Freedom's Journal vs.*, 31, 38–39, 186, 187–88; Garrison *vs.*, 117; governing of Liberia, 70–72, 74; Hodgkin on, 123;

Gross, Thomas, on freedom, 124–25
Gurley, Ralph, 262n3; AES formation and, 269n26; Andrews' letter to, 268n14; democratizing measures of, 73, 275n47; eulogy for Russwurm, J. B., 106–7; letters to, 46, 52, 66, 68, 72–73, 274n27; recruitment of Russwurm, J. B., 53, 270n33; Russwurm, J. B., meeting with, 199; Russwurm, J. B., on, 274n28; Skinner's letter to, 76

Haiti, 3, 65; ACS celebration of Africa vs. emigration to, 288n36; Boyer's reunification of, 14; development of, 13; diplomatic recognition of, 13; emigration to, 11–12, 15, 263n7; emigration to Liberia vs., 45, 201–2; *Freedom's Journal*, agent in, 30, 264n15; *Freedom's Journal* on, 29, 263n7; government of, 133, 142; interest in, 19, 21; McGill, G., earlier emigration to, 77; McGill, S., on, 77; Paul, T., on, 15–16; people of, 23; Russwurm, J. B., commencement speech on, 132–34; Saunders and, 12–14, 16, 77
Haitian Revolution, 21–23, 64, 77, 131, 132
Hall, James, 18, 20, 240–42, 252, 257n12, 261n61, 287n33; address to African-Americans, 119; *An Address to the Free People of Color in the State of Maryland*, 119, 120; bad tobacco trade of, 98, 281n40; Blyden on, 120; on equality, 119; health problems of, 101, 118; Latrobe on, 120; letters to, 238–39; on McGill, G., family, 79; on Monrovia's elite, 70; on Neh ("Yellow Will"), 119–20; progressive nature of, 118–19; Russwurm, J. B., on, 262n2; on Russwurm, J. B., 18–19, 92; Russwurm, Sarah, on, 120; treatment of African Fever, 88
Hall, Primus, 11
Hall, Prince, 11
Ham, 144, 145
Hannon, Henry, on freedom, 124
Harman, Margaret, 250
Hartford, 166–69; arrival in, 166; education in, 169; New Haven vs., 167; schools of, 169
Hawes, Susan, 82, 232, 291n13; Russwurm, J. B., visit with, 104, 238
Hawes, William, 232, 258n26, 291n13
Hawthorne, Nathaniel, 17, 18, 260n59
Haytian Papers (Saunders), 13, 259n40, 259n43
"Haytien Revolution," 141–43

Health: of colonists, 249; problems of Hall, 101, 118; problems of Russwurm, J. B., 101–3, 105, 233. *See also* Medical care
Hebron Academy, 10–11, 258n30
The History of Jamaica (Long), 256n5
The History of the Island of St. Domingo, from Its First Discovery by Columbus to the Present (Barskett), 21, 77, 261n64; McGill, S., and, 77
Hodgkin, Thomas, on ACS, 123
"How to Teach a Child to Read," 64
Hubbard, Jeremiah, 114, 285n18
Hull, Agrippa, 273n19
Hull, J. T., 82

Ibrahima, Abd al-Rahman, 60, 199–200, 267n5, 290n17
Ignorance, 158, 209, 227, 235; of colonization, 222–23
"Important Testimony from Liberia," 68
India, 152
Industry, 193
Infant School for Coloured children, 192
Infant School Society, 192
Inferiority, 172, 194, 204. *See also* Racism
Inheritance, 7–8, 257nn15–16
Intellectual power, complexion vs., 146–47
Ivory trade, 232

Jamaica: dissatisfaction with, 9; interest in, 8, 258n22; Russwurm, J. B., return to, 3, 8–9, 258n26; slavery in, 153, 256n5
Jamestown, 205
Jefferson, Thomas, 273n19
Jennings, Thomas, 55
Jocelyn, Simeon, 102
Johnston, Harry, on death of Russwurm, J. B., 105–6
Jones, Edward, 66–67, 274nn27–28; letter to, 216–17
Journal of Negro History, 109, 110, 111

Kentucky, emigration from Ohio vs., 66, 274n24
Keynes, John Maynard, 115
Kidnapping, 177, 180
Knowledge, 137, 139, 149; dissemination of, 218; evolution of, 228; Russwurm, J. B., on, 164, 210; youth vs. senior, 227
Kosciuszko, Tadeusz, 64, 273n19

Maryland County, 101

Maryland State Colonization Society (MSCS), 20, 69, 70, 77, 78; ACS *vs.*, 85–89, 118; Board of, 87, 90–92; on death of Russwurm, J. B., 106; dinner in honor of Russwurm, J. B., 103–4, 241–42; doubts about colonization, 241; finances of, 283n61; Fish Town purchase of, 96–97, 98; Latrobe on, 85, 87; legislature for state funding of, 86–87; purchases of land by, *84*; Russwurm, J. B., governor appointment of, 88–92, 234, 241, 279n6; Russwurm, J. B., meeting with, 103; Russwurm, J. B., *vs.*, 100–101; on slavery, 85

Masters, slaves *vs.*, 142, 152, 156, 178

"Maxims for Parents," 63

McDowell, R., 99

McGill, George, 76; celebration of Haitian Revolution, 77; earlier emigration to Haiti, 77; emigration of, 77–78, 277nn65–66; Hall on family of, 79; Latrobe on family of, 78–79; trading business of, 78; wife, death of, 78

McGill, Samuel, 77–79, 82, 95, 97–98, 249, 280n19, 292n24; on death of Russwurm, J. B., 105; on Haiti, 77; on Russwurm, J. B., 94, 98

McGill, Sarah. *See* Russwurm, Sarah McGill

McGill, Urias Africanus, 78–80, *80*

Mechlin, Joseph, 70, 73, 213, 214; Dailey on, 74; resignation of, 74, 276n52

Medical care: of colonists, 70–72; Monrovia *vs.* Maryland, 88; for Russwurm, J. B., 103, 105, 238

Middleton, George, 11

Miller, Samuel, 41, 52; condemnation of *Freedom's Journal*, 36–37; on emancipation, 188; letters to *Freedom's Journal*, 35–36; letters to *New York Observer*, 34–35, 41–42, 188–89; Russwurm, J. B., *vs.*, 34–36; subscription cancellation to *Freedom's Journal*, 35–36, 187, 188–89, 265n31; on "Wilberforce," 189; "Wilberforce's" connection with, 34–37, 181, 185–86, 187, 265n31

Missionaries, 98, 169; British *vs.* American, 281n40; German, 214; racism of, 281n41. *See also* Christians

Monrovia: agriculture of, 224; arrival in, 59, 239; democracy of, 73, 275n47; educational needs of, 60, 214–15, 229–30; Hall on elite of, 70; improvements of, 224–25; laws of, 72–73, 76, 217; medical care in, 70–72; religion of, 214; schools of, 214–15, 229–30; teachers of, 214–15

Montreal, 6

Mother, 5, 256nn3–4, 256n6

Mount Tubman, 244–45, 247

Mount Vaughan, 245, 247

MSCS. *See* Maryland State Colonization Society

"The Mutability of Human Affairs," 29–30, 143–50, 263n8

Name, 7, 257n7; spelling of, 260n58

National Philanthropist, 24

Negro Convention Movement, 125

Neh, Peroh ("Yellow Will"), 119–20

New Castle, 194

New Demeter Street Presbyterian Church, 26

New England, 167, 171; colonization of, 205–6; pilgrim fathers of, 219; racism of, 9. *See also* "A Trip through New England"

New Georgia, 62, 215

New Haven, 157–61, 166; ACS friends in, 163–64, 182; burying ground of, 165; Hartford *vs.*, 167; schools of, 162–63

New York: emigrants from, 69; Philadelphia *vs.*, 191

New York African Free School, 43, 54; evening classes at, 55, 271n42

New York Journal of Commerce, 68

New York Observer, 32, 39–40; *Freedom's Journal*, letters to, 187–88; Miller's, S., letter to, 34–35, 41–42, 188–89; Russwurm, J. B., letter to, 35–36

Nicholson, Joseph: on Liberia, 89; racism of, 89–90

North American Review, 171

North Carolina, colonization in, 114

North Yarmouth Academy, 81, 277n74, 290n14

Norwich Courier, 24

Notes on Haiti, Made during a Residence in That Republic (Mackenzie), 64

Nubia, 219

Oberon, emigrants of, 248

Ohio, 109; "Black Laws" of, 65–66, 273n20; emigration form Kentucky *vs.*, 66, 274n24; laws of, 65–66, 230, 273n20

Onderdonk, Benjamin, 266n37
Oppression, 150, 152; Emigration vs. fighting, 111–12; religion vs., 112–13; Russell, A. F., on emigration vs., 112
Otis, John, 258n30
"Our Vindication," 110, 204–6

Packard, Alpheus, 17
Padmore, George, 3
Page's Hotel, 292n25; racism at, 103–4, 242, 283n64
Palm oil, trade, 239–40
Pan-African movement, 3, 59, 108, 126; dilemma of, 3–4
Paul, Catherine Anne, 16, 260n51
Paul, Susan, 16, 260n51
Paul, Thomas, 11, 12, 14, 16, 24, 43, 260n46; death of, 16, 260n48; on Haiti, 15–16
Payne, John, 277n77
Pennsylvania Gazette, 193
"People of Colour," 150–57
Perry, Commodore Matthew C., 97, 98, 106; on Russwurm, J. B., 106
Pestalozzi, Johann Heinrich, 54
Pétion, Alexandre, 13
Philadelphia: African-American population of, 192–93; education in, 191–92; fashion of, 193; New York vs., 191; property in, 193; publications of, 193–94; Russwurm, J. B., on, 191, 272n9; Russwurm, J. B., vs. free African-Americans of, 46, 49–50, 65–66; schools of, 191–92
Philadelphia Monthly Magazine, 193
Pierce, Franklin, 17
Pilgrims, 206, 219
Pinney, John B., 73, 292n18; appointment of, 74; proclamation of, 74–75; Russwurm, J. B., conflict with, 74–76
Plumley, A. R, 116; letter to, 60, 213–16
Poland, 149, 222
Portland Transcript, 5, 256n4
Prejudice, 29, 140, 147, 159, 207, 208, 228; Christian, 169; geography vs., 173; traveling vs., 190–91
President's house, 198
Princeton Theological Seminary, 42, 181, 185, 265n31; banning of Freedom's Journal, 37
Prison, 252–53; of Cape Palmas, 248
Property: in Baltimore, 195; in Boston, 175; in Philadelphia, 193; in Salem, 175

"Proposals for Publishing the Freedom's Journal: Prospectus," 139
Protecting Society, 177, 180
Protestant Episcopal Church, 27, 262n3
Prout, Jacob, 75
Prout, William, 95, 102–3, 280n26
Public farms, 244

Quakers, slavery vs., 114, 286n18
Quebec, schooling in, 6–7, 257n12
Quincy, John, 172

Racism, 6; in Baltimore, 103–4; at Bowdoin, 18; colonization vs., 53, 115; of missionaries, 281n41; of New England, 9; of Nicholson, 89–90; at Page's Hotel, 103–4, 242, 283n64; Russwurm, J. B., on, 45–46, 48–49, 268n7
Rahahman, Abduhl. See Ibrahima, Abd al-Rahman
"Raising Us in the Scale of Being," 140–41
Raleigh, Walter, 205
Randall, Richard, 214, 291n2
Recaptured slaves. See Slave(s)
Religion, 26–27, 139, 221, 262n3; of Boston, 174; at Monrovia, 214; oppression vs., 112–13
Rensselaer School, 54
Republic of Liberia, 101, 102
Revey, John, 61, 249
Rice, trade, 239–40, 246
Richmond Colonization Society, 286n20
Rights: of Africans, 34, 87, 278n2; civil, 136, 156, 209; of colonists, 249; of man, 193; states', 290n14
Rights of All, 37–38, 39–40, 267n5; debut of, 57; finances of, 56, 271n48; subscriptions to, 271n47. See also "Freedom's Journal and the Rights of All"
Rio de Janeiro, 220
Roberts, Joseph, 97, 106, 279n6
Rome, 148
Ruby, Reuben, 43, 259n32
Ruggles, David, 177
Runaways, 153, 155; arrests of, 177–78, 179–80, 290n11; lists of, 196. See also Slave(s)
Russell, A. F., 285n13; on oppression vs. emigration, 112
Russell, Henry G., 17–18
Russia, 148, 149, 221
Russwurm, Angelina, 81, 82, 83

Russwurm, Francis Edward, 258n19; death of, 104; letters to, 10, 69–70, 76, 231–34
Russwurm, Francis Edward ("Frank"), 81–82
Russwurm, George Stockbridge, 80–82, 233
Russwurm, James Hall, 81–82
Russwurm, John Brown, ii. *See also specific topics*
Russwurm, John R., 5–6, 256n1; death of, 7–8; marriage of, 257n10; slaves of, 256n6
Russwurm, John Sumner, 8, 257n16, 290n16; letters to, 7, 19; papers, 257n7; Russwurm, S. B., letters to, 8
Russwurm, Samuel Ford, 81–83, 239, 277n77, 292n21
Russwurm, Sarah McGill, 76–77, 79–80, *81*, 103, 238
Russwurm, Susan Blanchard, 6–7, 16, 257n10; letters to Russwurm, J. S., 8; marriage to Hawes, W., 9, 258n26. *See also* Hawes, Susan
Russwurm Literary Association, 95

Salary, 282n61; as teacher, 11
Saswood palaver system, 249, 292n27
Saunders (Sanders), Prince, 11, 14, 16, 77, 259n35, 260n46; at American Convention for Promoting the Abolition of Slavery, 14; on Boyer, 14; Christophe and, 12–14; published *Haytian Papers*, 13, 259n40, 259n42
Schomburg, Arturo, on Russwurm, J. B., 108
Schooling, 6, 8; in Quebec, 257n12; Russwurm's, J. B., children, 81–82, 277n74
Schools, 211, 219, 245; in Baltimore, 196; of Boston, 171–72, 176; Cape Palmas high, 95; of Hartford, 169; infant, 60, 192, 273n9; ladies, 245, 250–51; of Monrovia, 214–15, 229–30; of New Haven, 162–63; of Philadelphia, 191–92. *See also* African School
Science, 136, 218
Self-improvement, 64, 225, 229; through education, 62, 211; improvement of other nations *vs.*, 149; Russwurm, J. B., on, 62, 218
"Self-Interest: [Betrayed by Coloured Persons]", 177–79
"Self-Interest: [Shaming and Naming Names]", 179–80
Self-reliance, 225–26
"Sentiments of the Free People of Color," 124
Seys, John, on Russwurm, J. B., 94

Sierra Leone, 67, 87, 205, 206, 279n6
Skinner, Ezekiel, 71, 73, 292n18; campaign of, 75–76, 276n57; Russwurm, J. B., conflict with, 75–76
Slave(s), 150, 230; Boston's view on trading of, 176; emigration of manumitted, 114–15; escape of, 196; Hubbard on freeing of, 114, 285n18; masters *vs.*, 142, 152, 156, 178; psychology of, 151–52, 153; recaptured, 224, 229, 291n6; of Russwurm, John R., 256n6; ships, 291n6; trade, 176, 217, 219–20, 231–32, 291n6; traffic, 220; "Wilberforce" on, 183. *See also* Runaways
Slavery, 4, 6, 23, 64, 136, 151, 179, 278n2; abolition of, 154–56; ACS *vs.*, 115; children born into, 157; Cornish, S., on, 29; crime *vs.*, 217; foreign relations *vs.*, 155; Freedom *vs.*, 143, 153; in Jamaica, 153, 256n5; laws of, 114, 156, 220; in Maryland, 196; in Massachusetts, 257n9; MSCS on, 85; national business of, 155; Quakers *vs.*, 114, 286n18; Russwurm, J. B., on, 33, 194; sold into, 177; Turkish, 151–52; in Washington, 198–99; "Wilberforce" on, 183. *See also* Abolitionists; Fugitive Slave Law
Smith, Abiel, 12, 172
Smith, Gerrit, on Russwurm, J. B., 26–27, 43, 116, 262n2
Snetter, Charles, 97, 99
Solomon, 146
Spain, 148
Steam mill site, 248
Stewart, Joshua, on death of Russwurm, J. B., 105
Stockbridge, Calvin, 9, 24, 43, 81, 258n27, 270n33; death of, 10, 231
Store supplies, 247
Stowe, Calvin, 17
Sugar cane, 247
Superstition, 225–26
"The System of Slavery: Sanctioned or Condemned by Scripture?," 64

Tabou River, 254
"Take Care of Number One," 51
Talbot, Isaac, 259n32
Teachers: compensation of, 230; Liberia's need for, 63; of Monrovia, 214–15
Teaching, 11
Teague, Colin, 75
Teague, Hilary, 75

Tharaca, 145
Theft, 99, 281n42
Thomson, Thomas, 93
Thoughts on African Colonization (Garrison), 117, 124
Todsen, Dr. George P., 70–72
"To Our Patrons," 135–38, 209–12
"To Our Readers," 218–21
"To Our Readers: [Let the Experiment Be Tried on Africa's Soil]," 229–30
"To Our Readers: [Taking Stock-One Year On]," 223–25
"Toussaint L'Overture," 19, 21, 131, 261n63
Trade, 247; agriculture *vs.*, 89; of colonists with Africans, 215–16; ivory, 232; palm oil, 239–40; rice, 239–40; slave, 176, 217, 219–20, 231–32, 291n6; war *vs.*, 239–40
"Travelling Scraps," 190–200, 268nn6–7
Travels, 45, 157–77, 265n23, 268nn6–7; prejudice experienced on, 190–91
"A Trip through New England," 157–77; New Haven, July, 157–77
Troup, George, 190–91, 290n14
Truth, 210, 228
Tubman, Harriet, 113
Turner, Nat, 286n20

Uncle Tom's Cabin (Stowe), 17
Union, 165–66, 281n37
"Union," 221–22
Union Humane Society, 116
United States (U.S.): African American citizenship in, 201; African American life in, 45–46; colonization in, 205–6, 286n20; constitution, 139, 156, 199; freedom in, 112–13; Great Britain *vs.*, 221–22; population *vs.* colonization, 40–41; Russwurm, J. B., on, 49; Russwurm, J. B., trip to, 103, 240–42, 282n61
U.S. African Squadron, 98–99

Vaccination, of emigrants, 87–88
Vermont, 167
Virginia, colony in, 205

Walker, David, 11, 16, 30–31, 43, 113, 122, 264n17, 288n36; "Address Delivered before

the General Colored Association," 30–31, 47, 122; advertises in *Freedom's Journal*, 47; *African Repository and Colonial Journal* influence on, 122; agent of *Freedom's Journal*, 16, 30, 43, 47; *Appeal*, 31, 122–23; on colonizationists, 122–23, 287n41; defense of Russwurm, J. B., 47
War(s), 99, 101, 254, 282n53; civil, 222; of Europe, 221; trade *vs.*, 239–40
Washington: Russwurm, J. B., on, 197–98; slavery in, 198–99
Washington, Augustus, 80, 81
Washington College, 168–69
Webster, Daniel, 117, 152, 290n5
"We Have Found a Haven," 222–23
Wheatley, Phillis, 172–73; Russwurm, J. B., tribute to, 172–73
Wife. *See* Russwurm, Sarah McGill
"Wilberforce," 33, 41–42, 52; on ACS *vs.* Russwurm, J. B., 34, 182–83; identity of, 36–37, 181; letter from, 182–85; Miller, S., on, 189; Miller's, S., connection with, 34–37, 181, 185–86, 187, 265n31; on objectives of ACS, 183; on relativity of complexion, 184; Russwurm, J. B., response to, 185–86; on Russwurm, J. B., 184; on slavery, 183. *See also* Alexander, Archibald
Wilberforce, William, 37, 122
Wilkeson, Samuel, 72; letter to, 73, 236–37
Williams, Peter, 55, 56, 266n37, 268n16; on colonization, 47; on Russwurm, J. B., 47, 269n17
Wilson, John L., 100, 243
Woods, George, 82
Woodson, Carter G., 109, 285n11
Woolfolk, Austin, 190–91; Lundy *vs.*, 190, 195, 290n14
Wright, Theodore, 37, 42, 265–66n31, 266n38; Cornish's, S., relationship with, 42, 266n37; on *Freedom's Journal*, 37

Yale College, 167; Russwurm, J. B., on, 164–65
Yarmouth Institute, 82
Yeo, James, 208
Youth, 28–29; cause of disappointment in, 227; danger of, 228. *See also* Children